SYNGE AND THE MAKING OF MODERN IRISH DRAMA

SYNGE AND THE MAKING OF MODERN IRISH DRAMA

ANTHONY ROCHE

CARYSFORT PRESS

A Carysfort Press Book
Synge and the Making of Modern Irish Drama
by Anthony Roche

First published in Ireland in 2013 as a paperback original by
Carysfort Press, 58 Woodfield, Scholarstown Road
Dublin 16, Ireland

ISBN 978-1-904505-64-8
©2013 Copyright remains with the author

Typeset by Carysfort Press

Cover design by eprint limited
Printed and bound by eprint limited
Unit 35
Coolmine Industrial Estate
Dublin 15
Ireland

This book is published with the financial assistance of
The Arts Council (An Chomhairle Ealaíon) Dublin, Ireland

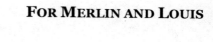
FOR MERLIN AND LOUIS

CONTENTS

ACKNOWLEDGEMENTS

Grateful acknowledgement is made to editors and publishers for permission to reprint material: Edward A. Kopper, Junior, and Greenwood Press for 'J.M. Synge: Christianity versus Paganism' from *A J.M. Synge Literary Companion* (New York, Westport, Ct., London: Greenwood Press, 1988): 106-134; *The Hungarian Journal of English and American Studies* and its editor, Donald E. Morse, for 'Synge, Brecht and the Hiberno-German Connection', *Hungarian Journal of English and American Studies*, 10:1-2 (Spring/Fall 2004): 9-32; James W. Flannery and *Yeats: An Annual of Critical and Textual Studies* for 'Yeats, Synge and an Emerging Irish Drama' from *Yeats: An Annual of Critical and Textual Studies*, editor Richard J. Finneran, X: 1992; *Yeats and the Theater*, guest editor James W. Flannery (Ann Arbor: The University of Michigan Press, 1992): 32-55; editors Donald E. Morse and Csilla Bertha and Greenwood Press for 'Ghosts in Irish Drama' from *More Real Than Reality: The Fantastic in Irish Literature and the Arts* (New York, Westport, Ct., London: Greenwood Press, 1991): 41-66; editor Christopher Murray and the *Irish University Review* for 'Woman on the Threshold' from the *Irish University Review* 25:1 (Spring/Summer 1995), Silver Jubilee Issue: Teresa Deevy and Irish Women Playwrights: 143-162; editor Nicholas Grene and Lilliput Press for 'J.M. Synge and Molly Allgood: The Woman and the Tramp' from *Interpreting Synge: Essays from the Synge Summer School 1991-2000* (Dublin: Lilliput Press, 2000): 163-176; editor Anthony Roche and the *Irish University Review* for 'Friel and Synge: Towards a Theatrical Language' from the *Irish University Review* 29:1 (Spring/Summer 1999), Special Issue: Brian Friel: 145-161.

Three of the essays are published here for the first time: 'Joyce, Synge and the Irish Theatre Movement'; 'Marginal Zones and Liminality: Synge's *The Well of the Saints* and Samuel Beckett's

Waiting for Godot'; and 'Postmodern *Playboy*'. Earlier drafts or portions thereof were tried out at various summer schools and conferences. I would like, therefore, to thank the James Joyce Summer School (Dublin) and its director, Anne Fogarty, for inviting me to lecture on Synge and Joyce in 1997; Irene Gilsenan Nordin and the University of Dalarna, Sweden, for the invitation to give a plenary lecture on Beckett and Synge at a Conference on Liminality and Irish Literature in 2004. I would particularly like to thank the Synge Summer School, Rathdrum, County Wicklow, its former directors, Nicholas Grene and Adrian Frazier, and the School's wonderful organizing committee, for opportunities to talk about Synge for many years. I owe a great debt to three valued friends and great scholars – Nicholas Grene, Declan Kiberd and Richard Pine – for sharing so many ideas over the years on matters Syngean. Eamonn Jordan, Lilian Chambers, and Dan Farrelly of Carysfort Press have been immensely helpful in seeing this book into publication. My greatest debt, as ever, is to my wife, Katy Hayes, and our sons, Merlin and Louis.

I wish to acknowledge and to thank the National University of Ireland for a grant-in-aid towards the publication of this book.

Anthony Roche

ABBREVIATIONS

The following abbreviations are used for the texts of Synge cited throughout the book:

I J.M. Synge, *Collected Works*, Volume I: *Poems*, edited by Robin Skelton (London: Oxford University Press, 1962); reprinted Gerrards Cross: Colin Smythe, 1982).

II J.M. Synge, *Collected Works*, Volume II: *Prose*, edited by Alan Price (London: Oxford University Press, 1966; reprinted Gerrards Cross: Colin Smythe, 1982).

III J.M. Synge, *Collected Works*, Volume III; *Plays* Book I, edited by Ann Saddlemyer (London: Oxford University Press, 1968; reprinted Gerrards Cross: Colin Smythe, 1982)

IV J.M. Synge, *Collected Works*, Volume IV: *Plays* Book II, edited by Ann Saddlemyer (London: Oxford University Press. 1968; reprinted Gerrards Cross: Colin Smythe, 1982).

CL I *The Collected Letters of John Millington Synge*, Volume One: 1871-1907, edited by Ann Saddlemyer (Oxford: Clarendon Press, 1983).

CL II *The Collected Letters of John Millington Synge*, Volume Two: 1907-1909, edited by Ann Saddlemyer (Oxford: Clarendon Press, 1984).

Introduction

At the end of 2009 *Irish Times* theatre critic Peter Crawley surveyed not only the year's theatrical offerings but those of the previous decade, the first of the twenty-first century, and concluded that the 'defining play' of this most theatrically experimental and diverse of decades was first produced in 1907. He backed up his claim by looking at the range of theatrical approaches that had been taken towards John Millington Synge's masterpiece, *The Playboy of the Western World*, by some of the most cutting edge companies.[1] Pan Pan Theatre Company, for example, produced a resolutely contemporary *Playboy* set in a Shanghai dressing salon doubling as a brothel, with Synge's lines spoken in Mandarin; the production played first in China, then in Dublin. The first to note the ability of Synge's play to translate to another culture was Mustafa Matura, who in 1985 produced a *Playboy of the West Indies* which found Caribbean equivalents to Synge's West of Ireland characters, and a local patois version of Synge's Hiberno-English dialect. Something similar was done in 2007 at Dublin's Abbey Theatre, Ireland's National Theatre, where Synge's original had premiered ninety years earlier, when Dubliner Roddy Doyle and Nigerian Bisi Adigun co-authored a version which moved Synge's play to a contemporary West Dublin setting.

But the most important Synge production of the decade was by the Druid Theatre Company from Galway. This was the case for two reasons. Co-founder and director Garry Hynes brought a wealth of experience to her productions of *The Playboy of the Western World* in 2004 and 2005, having first engaged with Synge and his drama in the 1970s, the first decade of the founding of Druid with actors Marie Mullen (who was to briefly play Pegeen Mike and many times the Widow Quin) and Mick Lally (who progressed from Christy to Old

Mahon). In 1975, Druid was the first professional theatre in the Republic of Ireland to open outside Dublin, premiering productions in Galway and undertaking an increasingly ambitious programme of touring, both in Ireland and abroad. From the first, Synge became what Hynes was to describe on more than one occasion as the 'house playwright' of Druid.[2] The association was an important one for a re-visioning of Synge, so often accused of being an interloper from the east coast of Ireland, an urbanite and a Protestant, misrepresenting the people of the West in his writings. Hynes and company staked a claim for the authenticity of Synge and did so by stressing the realism of his writing. This reached some kind of apogée in the 1982 production of *The Playboy* at the company's small, intimate theatre in Garter Lane, Galway. The setting stressed the poverty of the inhabitants with their bare feet and a muddy shebeen. But what Hynes really restored was the violence in the play, which its frequent productions had muted, so the arrival of a bloody-pated Mick Lally as Old Mahon posed a real threat. This realism became the hallmark of Druid productions, with Marie Mullen presenting a young and sexy Widow Quin rather than the traditional playing of the part as an older grotesque.

In 2005, Hynes and Druid realized a long-time ambition when they staged the six canonical plays together as DruidSynge. In the years just before that, they had staged independent productions of individual plays before the culminating cycle of six. What impressed me most about this ambitious and bravura staging of Synge was how Garry Hynes did not set about achieving an ever more perfect reproduction of a certain kind of approach to the plays. Rather, there was sometimes a sharp variation to the same play: Anne-Marie Duff, for example, in the 2004 production, was more of a petit bourgeois Pegeen Mike; whereas Catherine Walsh in 2005 was much more earthy in her portrayal; and the film star fine-boned features of Cillian Murphy as Christy Mahon had given way to the comic quicksilver metamorphoses of Aaron Monaghan. This suggested that Hynes did not set her productions in stone but continued to work on and evolve her approach, keeping them theatrically live. The settings of the individual plays were simplified and stylized for the joint production of all six. Most strikingly, the white boards of a coffin which lay against the wall for the drowned son in *Riders to the Sea* (1903) remained there throughout the next five plays and were still available to help bury the dead lovers at the close of *Deirdre of the Sorrows* (1910). Synge's entire dramatic *oeuvre* was revealed as a coherent and singular body of work, stylistically dizzying in its range but focusing on central concerns of language, identity and issues of power and powerlessness. If it was fascinating to see how Garry Hynes reworked the more familiar plays, the DruidSynge cycle offered a rarer opportunity to view *The Tinker's Wedding* (1971) and *Deirdre of the Sorrows*, the two plays unproduced in Synge's lifetime and receiving only a rare production since. It was moving to hear and see Druid's founding members Mick Lally and Marie Mullen thirty years on as the aged High King Conchubor and Deirdre's nurse Lavarcham; and the violence of the Ulster Sagas now given a contemporary staging in the style of Martin McDonagh, whose work Hynes had brought to the world. *The Tinker's Wedding* was the only one to receive a contemporary staging: to witness Marie Mullen in her outlandish mix of cast-off modern clothing was to behold a member of the travelling community rather than a 'tinker'.[3]

The DruidSynge is placed at the head of this Introduction because of its individual theatrical and historical importance in relation to the playwright but also because the success of Hynes's project underscores the two core beliefs on which this book of inter-connected essays is constructed. The first is that Synge was a deliberate and self-conscious artist rather than a naïf who stumbled into being a great playwright. Accordingly, his career will be assessed *in toto* and not just from the moment he decided to leave Paris and return to Ireland. It will be read as a series of 'moves' in both the sense of artistic strategy and of physical relocation (it is no accident he identified with tramps and wanderers). Synge trained as a musician and, when he made the decision to turn from music to literature, it was not undertaken lightly. That life-altering decision (and its profound consequences for the development of a distinctly Irish drama with strong European associations) was made in Germany, where Synge appears to have attended the theatre for the first time, the place where he read the work of Henrik Ibsen and drafted his first play. On the Continent, Synge first encountered the model of a National Theatre, and he was therefore best equipped and placed to be a national playwright for Ireland when W.B. Yeats and Lady Gregory began to bend their energies in that direction. W.J. McCormack's 2000 biography, *Fool of the Family*, makes clear how important were Synge's first two years in Germany, away from Dublin and home for the first time.[4] But McCormack displays a hankering for Synge to stay on the continent and has no great *grá* for the decision to go to the Aran Islands. This book argues that the famous advice offered by W.B. Yeats – 'Go to the Aran Islands and express there a life which has never found expression' – is not so much in need of demythologizing (of that there has been a good deal) as somewhat beside the point. The writing Yeats intended to inspire in Synge with his advice was a prose volume which eventually emerged in 1902 as *The Aran Islands*. Despite Yeats's active promotion and the volume's considerable merit, Synge's book was not published for a further five years and then only on the back of his plays' success. An arguably more fruitful and necessary conjunction, conducted during the same years as his five annual visits to the Aran Islands, was Synge's active involvement with the three-year experiment of the Irish Literary Theatre initiated by Yeats and Gregory. (This does not merit a single mention in McCormack's biography.) Synge attended the opening productions of Yeats's *The Countess Cathleen* and Edward Martyn's *The Heather Field* in Dublin in 1899 and wrote about them (in French) for *L'Européen* (II, 378-372). The riots which attended the staging of Yeats's play in 1899 are eerily prophetic of those which would greet the staging of *The Playboy of the Western World* eight years later. Synge did not attend the second season of the ILT in 1900 but was present the following year for the full season. He came to it from an important meeting with Yeats and Gregory at Coole, where he had shown them two pieces of original work: the manuscript of *The Aran Islands* and a draft of his first play, *When the Moon Has Set*, situated among his own landlord class in Wicklow. The first was approved, the second rejected. From this charged encounter, Synge went directly to Dublin and a viewing of the Irish Literary Theatre's third and final programme of plays. He was particularly drawn to and (after his Aran immersion) had the knowledge of Irish to follow carefully Douglas Hyde's one-act play, *Casadh an tSúgáin/The Twisting of the Rope* (1901). Synge later wrote that Hyde's play was the only one which 'gave a new direction and impulse to Irish drama'[5]: set in a peasant cottage in the west of Ireland, a marriage is disrupted by the arrival of a romantic outsider, who is finally sent on his way by the community. This 'germ of a new dramatic form', which Nicholas Grene has termed the 'stranger in the house' motif,[6] was to be developed dramatically by Synge, as became evident in the two one-act plays he presented to Yeats and Gregory the following year, *Riders to the Sea* and *The Shadow of the Glen*. Both were immediately accepted and scheduled for production by the new Irish National Theatre.

These plays focused on what Lady Gregory was to term 'the people', peasant characters of a different class and religion from the Abbey's directors. When Synge most fully developed Hyde's 'germ' into the full-blown achievement of *The Playboy of the Western World*, he countered the outrage it provoked by the claims of its linguistic and representational authenticity, writing in his Preface to the published play:

> In writing *The Playboy* [...], as in my other plays, I have used one or two words only that I have not heard among the country people of Ireland [...]. A certain number of the phrases I employ I have heard also from herds and fishermen along the coast from Kerry to Mayo, or from beggar-women and ballad-singers nearer Dublin; and I am glad to acknowledge how much I owe to the folk-imagination of these fine people'. (III, 53)

Similarly, the DruidSynge production of 2005 staked its own primary claim on Synge's authenticity. In the tour of Ireland they undertook after the Galway premiere, the company staged the plays in the various locales named in the play. Druid had been the first to bring Synge's theatre to the Aran Islands and the 2005 tour culminated in the day-long presentation of all six on Inishmaan, the central island on which Synge had stayed. On the one hand, in their sensitive delivery of Synge's complex language and their grounding of his plays in a realistically rendered sense of place, Druid have done a great deal to validate and vindicate the claims Synge (and Yeats) made about the authenticity of his work in relation to the Irish people he represented, their behaviour and manner of speaking. But it could also be said that in doing so they endorsed and deepened the mythologizing which surrounded Synge from the start, particularly the view (first floated by Yeats) that Synge found his artistic identity and became a great artist by going to and writing about the West of Ireland.

The 'authenticity' debate has bedeviled the perception of Synge in Ireland ever since. What it overlooks is that his plays are not an unmediated reflection of social reality but a self-consciously constructed dramatic artifact. Synge himself may be said not only to have contributed to but to have initiated this debate. In an interview he gave to the Dublin *Evening Mail* in January 1907 during the first week of *The Playboy*'s production and a week after he had penned his Preface to the play, he contrarily stated: 'I don't care a rap how the people take it. I never bother whether my plots are typical Irish or not; but my methods are typical. [...] It is a comedy, an extravaganza, made to amuse.' It is worth bearing in mind that, when it came to the genre of drama, there was virtually nothing in the native tradition for the Irish Literary Revival to revive. The closest to such a form, Douglas Hyde argued, lay in the dialogues between Saint Patrick and Oisín, a dialectical development of two radically juxtaposed world views: those of the bringer of Christianity to Ireland and those of the last pagan revenant.[7] I argue in the first chapter that Synge drew on this material for the writing of *The Well of the Saints*. But Synge also verbally claimed that he drew for his play on a pre-Molière French farce, which his notes revealed to be André de la Vigne's medieval morality play, *La Moralité de l'Aveugle et du Boiteux* [*The Morality of the Blind Man and the Lame Man*] (1496). Yeats may have said that he told Synge to give up Paris and Racine and go to the Aran Islands; but as contemporary Irish playwright Frank McGuinness astutely remarked, what if he did so with Racine in his back pocket?[8] The evidence of *Riders to the Sea*, with its profound awareness of ancient Greek and eighteenth century French tragedy, certainly suggests that he did. Those years on the Continent, as Synge criticism has increasingly shown, are not to be so readily dismissed. The Germany period gave Synge his first notion of being a playwright; the French sojourn, and his studies at the Sorbonne, turned him into a deeply read student of comparative literature. His course with Professor Henri d'Arbois de Jubainville was a comparative course aligning Celtic literature with that of Homer. When Synge came across the story of the Lady O'Conor on the Aran Islands he would have recognized the same folk narrative that informed Shakespeare's *Cymbeline*.[9]

   With the development of a nascent Irish national theatre, Synge was uniquely placed and well equipped to lay out a template for its plays, securely Irish in their sources, in their language and their folklore, informed by his acute observation and his musical ear, yet nourished by an awareness of parallels with world culture. As a result, it increasingly seems to me that the charges brought against Synge and his work by Irish nationalists at the time on the score of foreign influence were all true. As a student of comparative literature, Synge would only have been too well aware of the debt the story of the Unfaithful Wife dramatized in *The Shadow of the Glen* owed to the Widow of Ephesus story as well as to that which he heard on Inishmaan from Pat Dirane; but he had to remain silent on that score in the face of Arthur Griffith's charge and refer only to the Aran source. The answer was not either/or but both/and. In productions of his plays, there have been two comparable strains to the authenticity/foreignness debate vying with each other throughout. If the DruidSynge staging epitomizes the 'authenticity' approach (which is not to deny the level of theatrical sophistication on display), the first decade of the twenty-first century also saw a line of Syngean productions of *The Playboy of the Western World* foregrounding the self-consciously theatrical, the meta-dramatic impulse running through all of Synge's plays. This was especially the case in the National Theatre which premiered the play a century earlier.

One of these, Roddy Doyle and Bisi Adigun's version, which moved the play to contemporary Dublin and translated Christy Mahon into a Nigerian immigrant, has already been referred to. But there were two important productions of *Playboy* at the National Theatre earlier in the decade. Ben Barnes' production of 2004 is dismissed as conservative by Peter Crawley,[10] and did not fare well with US critics when it toured there.[11] I think this is unfair to a production which genuinely sought to liberate Synge's play from some of the constraints which could be seen as continuing to confine it. One was that of the internal setting; in the Barnes, the set opened up on key occasions (such as the mule race on the strand). But the production also recognized the extent of the play's self-conscious artifice by introducing a character called the Bellman who formally commenced each scene by handing out the necessary props to a central character. The list of props kept by the Abbey for the play when it toured the United Kingdom in 1907 is extraordinary.[12] At the beginning of Act II, the three girls bring Christy Mahon a brace of gifts and he is only done enumerating the contents of the shebeen when they arrive (as well as holding a mirror to wash himself). The dizzying array of props shows the extent to which Synge's world is a constructed theatrical artifact, something 'made'; and yet for all of the putting in place of a solid world, these are not enough to hold Christy Mahon in place or provide him or Synge with an abiding home. The set is struck each night.

If Crawley is critical of Barnes's production, we are as one in our reaction to Niall Henry's extraordinary production of *Playboy* at the Peacock Theatre in 2001. This production provides the cover of the book and is discussed in detail in the 'Postmodern Synge' chapter. Henry had laid the groundwork for this production by tackling Synge's play several years earlier in a production for his Blue Raincoat Theatre Company in Sligo, where Synge's text had received a 'mumblecore' approach. At the Peacock, the text was restored to pristine audibility; but the other postmodern features of the Blue Raincoat production were still in place. Gifted mime Mikel Murfi played Christy with an unprecedented level of physical expressivity. Curled in a foetus-like position for much of Act One, he increasingly came to life as he told his story; and while the mule race on the strand remained offstage, there was a stunning moment when Murfi traversed the stage in mid-air clad in his jockey's outfit, like the Jack B. Yeats illustration come to life. Where Druid have shown considerable freedom with regard to the age of the actor playing the Widow Quin, Pegeen Mike has consistently been represented in their productions as in her late teens/early twenties. In the Henry, Pegeen was cast older than the Widow, with the forty-something Olwen Fouéré pacing the shebeen like a character out of a Beckett play. The two old bachelors became young punks, something akin to Reservoir Dogs of the Western World. The meta-theatric implications of Christy's self-scrutiny in the mirror were for once realized when the young women did not appear; instead, Christy performed all the parts and improvised the dialogue, replacing the young women with conjurings of his own theatrical imagination.

What the Henry approach has done even more than all of the other approaches of the twenty-first century is to show how theatrically alive and fertile *The Playboy of the Western World* remains. What DruidSynge has done is draw spectacular attention to the whole of Synge's dramatic *oeuvre*, to draw the less produced plays into the spotlight, and to underscore how seminal his dramatic creations are to the century of Irish drama which followed. These two beliefs underwrite the following book. The first, already referred to, is to provide a sustained analysis of Synge's six plays as they try out possibilities for an Irish theatre. This will involve a rereading and contextualization of Yeats's legendary advice to show that Synge became a dramatist despite rather than because of it; but to establish equally that the two writers still had a great deal to offer each other when it came to the creation of a national drama. The context of Joyce will argue that, far from his rude dismissal of *Riders to the Sea* when he was twenty-one, Joyce's subsequent career shows his awareness (however tinged with jealousy) of Synge's prophetic importance and the originality of his writing. The persistence of the past into the present in the country's experience will be seen to demand a different dramatic handling of ghosts in Irish theatre from the example of Ibsen. Synge's positioning of his Nora on the threshold of the peasant cottage is taken up and developed by subsequent Irish women playwrights. Synge cast *The Well of the Saints* in the form of a parable which worked at one remove from its own time and centred on two talkative tramps. Samuel Beckett was to do the same almost a half century later in his first staged play, *En Attendant Godot/Waiting for Godot* (1953). The possibilities for a postmodern *Playboy of the Western World* are raised in relation to various interpretations of the play, not least by reading it in the light of the Martin McDonagh phenomenon. Synge's last unfinished play, *Deirdre of the Sorrows*, though apparently his most remote, is also his most autobiographical and revealing.

The second impulse which underlies this volume is the profound effect which Synge has had on many of the Irish playwrights who followed him. This book may be seen as a two-way Syngean dialogue: synchronically, with the artists and theatrical collaborators of his time; diachronically, with many of those Irish playwrights who have drawn most powerfully on him since: Samuel Beckett, Brian Friel, Stewart Parker, Marina Carr, Martin McDonagh.[13] When his official biographer James Knowlson asked Beckett whose work had most influenced his, the octogenarian playwright murmured only one name in response: 'Synge.'[14] When Brian Friel spoke at the re-opening of the Synge cottage on Inishmaan in 1999, he acknowledged Synge's influence not only on his own formidable body of work but on that of every other Irish dramatist: 'On this occasion, on this island, it is very important to me to acknowledge the great master of Irish theatre, the man who made Irish theatre, the man who reshaped it and refashioned it, and the man before whom we all genuflect.'[15] As Friel openly acknowledged, Synge laid out the template of what an Irish theatre might be. The situations he developed in his scenarios, the language he fashioned for his characters, the issues he raised in his works, have in turn been taken on and responded to by the playwrights who came after him in a century-long dialogue which shows no signs of ending.

---

[1] Peter Crawley, 'A decade framed by playboys,' *The Irish Times*, 12 February 2009. For a more detailed discussion of the various productions of *The Playboy of the Western World* from 2000 to 2010, see Sara Keating, 'Evolving *Playboys* for the Global World,' in *Synge and His Influences: Centenary Essays from the Synge Summer School*, edited by Patrick Lonergan (Dublin: Carysfort Press, 2011), pp. 245-257.

[2] See, for example, my interview with Garry Hynes and with Ann Saddlemyer conducted at the Synge Summer School in 2007 while I was director and available on film in *DruidSynge: The Plays of John Millington Synge* (RTÉ, Wildfire Films and Druid Theatre, 2007).

[3] On this subject, see Mary Burke, *'Tinkers': Synge and the Cultural History of the Irish Traveller* (Oxford: Oxford University Press, 2009).

[4] See W.J. McCormack, *Fool of the Family: A Life of J.M. Synge* (London: Weidenfeld and Nicolson, 2000), pp. 103-122.

[5] J.M. Synge, 'The Dramatic Movement in Ireland,' in *The Abbey Theatre: Interviews and Recollections*, edited by E.H. Mikhail (London: Macmillan, 1988), pp. 54-58. The article was never published, which presumably explains why it is not in Synge's *Collected Prose*.

⁶ Nicholas Grene, *The Politics of Irish Drama: Plays in Context from Boucicault to Friel* (Cambridge: Cambridge University Press, 1999), pp. 51-76.

⁷ Douglas Hyde, *A Literary History of Ireland* (London: Unwin, 1899), p. 511.

⁸ Frank McGuinness, Opening Address, Synge Summer School, Rathdrum, Co. Wicklow, June 2005.

⁹ For Synge's own efforts to make a play out of the same material, see 'Scenarios, Dialogues and Fragments' (III, 208-214).

¹⁰ Peter Crawley, 'A decade framed by playboys'.

¹¹ Lisa Coen writes: 'a round-up of [U.S.] reviews reveals a pattern of dissatisfaction that the play was presented in such an unconventional way.' Lisa Coen, 'Departures: the Abbey Theatre on International Stages 1975-2005', PhD thesis, School of English, Trinity College, Dublin, 2011, p. 279.

¹² The list of props accompanies the copy of Synge's *The Playboy of the Western World* script submitted by the Abbey to the Lord Chamberlain in order for the play to tour the U.K. See the file of submitted scripts for 1907 in the Lord Chamberlain's Collection, Manuscript Division, British Library, London.

¹³ For a consideration of Synge's work in relation to the drama of Tom Murphy, Conor McPherson and other plays by Marina Carr, see Anthony Roche, 'Synge and contemporary Irish drama,' *The Cambridge Companion to J.M. Synge*, edited by P.J. Mathews (Cambridge: Cambridge University Press, 2009), pp.173-184.

¹⁴ James Knowlson, *Damned to Fame: The Life of Samuel Beckett* (London: Bloomsbury, 1996), pp. 56-57.

¹⁵ Brian Friel, in TG4 documentary, *Synge agus an Domhan Thiar* [*Synge and the Western World*, directed by Macdara O Curraidhín, 1999.]

1 | J.M. Synge: Christianity versus Paganism

Of all the creative oppositions to be found in John Millington Synge, none more fully unites the man, the Anglo-Irish culture into which he was born, and the native Irish drama he did so much to bring into being than the opposition between Christianity.and paganism. Synge's diaries and journals reveal a dual strain initially: his inability to accept his family's Christian beliefs and their inability to appreciate or share his interest in artistic expression. More than a decade's worth of sporadic but persistent reading in a number of European literatures, with a particular emphasis on Irish, showed him cultural equivalents for almost all of the strains in his character and life. The Aran Islands completed his growth in personal perception by introducing Synge to a group of people who could mingle the pagan and Christian beliefs that in him were so divided. What he found in the writing of his plays was not an image of himself but a medium in which those conflicting strains of paganism and Christianity could be worked out to their fullest extent and find a resolution through art impossible in life.

The Shadow of the Glen, while it engages the central Syngean theme of a constricting environment and the dream of a fuller life elsewhere, does not do so primarily in terms of Christianity and paganism. Deirdre of the Sorrows, since it is set exclusively in the pagan past, has no opportunity to engage the dialectic. But Riders to the Sea, the one play in which Synge directly dramatized his Aran experience, represents the same mingling of Christian and pagan beliefs he encountered among the islanders. The Tinker's Wedding directly sets a Roman Catholic priest and a trio of Rabelaisian tinkers in opposition on the stage and was for that reason precluded from ever getting there during Synge's lifetime. The Well of the Saints treats a similar conflict in a more subtle and distanced way, bringing a latter-day St. Patrick into dialogue with two unregenerate heathens who in their turn evoke the pre-Christian warrior-poet Oisin. Synge's masterpiece, *The Playboy of the Western World,* although it is concerned with much else, makes mock of Father Reilly and the courts of Rome while hinting at a resemblance between Christy Mahon and Christ the Son of Man, a potential redeemer for the people of Mayo whom they first acclaim and then reject. Christy also serves to reincarnate a mock-epic modern version of ancient Irish heroism and brings something of the mystical land of promise to the starved imagination of Pegeen Mike. The plays carry on the debate between Christianity and paganism on their naturalistic surfaces, where the opposition tends to be more clear-cut, and in their deep structures, where biblical and mythical symbolic patterns form a complex weave.

Raised in a strongly evangelical household, Synge's crisis of faith led him to write later about the experience: 'By the time I was sixteen or seventeen I had renounced Christianity after a good deal of wobbling' (II, 11). The apparent absoluteness of this renunciation was undercut emotionally when he went on to add that although 'this story is easily told, it was a terrible experience. By it I laid a chasm between my present and my past and between myself and my kindred and friends' (II, 11). For the legacy of evangelical Protestantism was not so easily abandoned and left Synge with recognizable traits of mind that marked all of his subsequent pursuits.

But the crisis did propel him away from the self-enclosed world of the Synge family, an evangelical minority within the Anglo-Irish Church of Ireland minority, toward a larger identification: 'Soon after I had relinquished the Kingdom of God I began to take a real interest in the kingdom of Ireland. [...] Everything Irish became sacred' (II, 13). The language of conversion here is striking. Synge's interest in Ireland as a whole and his apostasy from his family religion did not entail a conversion to the Catholicism of the majority; that was no more an option for him than the reverse would later be for a disaffected Stephen Dedalus or James Joyce. In the manuscript version of the autobiography, Synge is more explicit about what constituted for him the kingdom of Ireland: 'the Irish country, rains, mists, full insular skies, the old churches, MSS. [manuscripts], jewels – everything in fact that was Irish became sacred in my eyes.'[1] The Irish imaginative legacy was made up, on the one hand, of the palpable yet shifting qualities of the Irish countryside he would explore in forays through his native Wicklow, West Kerry, and the Aran Islands. From his earliest days, Synge declared himself to be 'passionately fond of nature'[2] and, through his youth, evolved a pantheistic mysticism that significantly increased as his Christianity waned. But in his Wordsworthian progress, Synge's purely instinctual communion with nature soon craved an intellectual dimension and, after an intermediary progress through music, found it in a sustained scholarly application to learning the Irish language,[3] studying the ancient manuscripts, and acquiring a solid cultural foundation for his subsequent writing career.

That foundation, first attempted in his studies in Irish at Trinity College, Dublin, in 1892, was securely laid in 1898 when Synge took a series of courses 'sur la civilization irlandaise comparée avec celle d'Homère'[4] with Professor H. d'Arbois de Jubainville at the Sorbonne. Several months later, the first of his five annual visits to the Aran Islands not only brought the texts he had been studying to embodied life but placed him at the furthest geographic and cultural remove within an Irish context from his Anglo-Irish background on the eastern seaboard. While on Aran, Synge's imagination was stirred not by the Catholicism of the islanders, in which he showed scant interest, but in their retention of many of the pagan beliefs predating the arrival of Christianity in Ireland. These beliefs primarily manifested themselves in talk of the fairies, a real presence in the lives of the islanders; of the appearance and intervention of these supernatural beings at moments of crisis; and of the afterlife to which they summoned the island's young. The locus for such beliefs was the storytelling, whose preservation in the Irish language and method of oral transmission account for the survival into the twentieth century of such archaic beliefs. This imaginative legacy had a profound impact on Synge, helping to transform him from a mediocre man of letters to a playwright of genius.

The earliest biography of Synge paid scant attention to his religious background. Maurice Bourgeois described Synge's view of life as 'nonreligious' and attributed as cause 'the desire to return to the relentless savagery of ancient paganism.'[5] As a result, Bourgeois's life downplayed the matrix of evangelical beliefs in which Synge was raised. The David Greene and Edward Stephens biography, however, establishes how strong the Protestant legacy was on both sides of the family: 'The Irish branch of the [Synge] family produced five bishops, beginning with the first Synge who came to Ireland in the seventeenth century.'[6] Vivian Mercier has drawn attention to the wide role of Victorian evangelicalism in unwittingly fostering the Anglo-Irish literary revival and has noted that 'John Synge, the dramatist's grandfather, made Glanmore Castle available for clerical meetings at a time when these were a rallying point for the evangelically inclined'.[7]

But the dominant force in Synge's religious formation came not from his father's but from his mother's side of the family; this might still have been the case had his father not died just a year after his son's birth. His mother, Kathleen Traill, was the daughter of Robert Traill, the Protestant rector of Schull, County Cork, whose staunch evangelical zeal 'apparently stood in the way of his ecclesiastical advancement'.[8] Synge's religious upbringing lay firmly in the hands of Robert Traill's wife and daughter, whose influence was all the greater since his recurrent bouts of illness meant that the young John had little formal education and received most of his schooling in the atmosphere of the home.

In the biography of his uncle, Edward Stephens encouraged the idea that Synge did not so absolutely reject the religious ideas he had been taught as his bold declaration of 'renouncing Christianity' might suggest, but rather that he went on to use those ideas in a more independent, less orthodox fashion than his family could accept: 'His mother's teaching, like a running commentary on all that happened, emphasized the importance of searching out and utilizing every opportunity that life might afford. John applied her wisdom in a way that she could not understand.'[9] Of all Synge's critics, Weldon Thornton in *J.M. Synge and the Western Mind* most followed the direction indicated by Stephens to argue in general for the dramatist's profound religious sensibility. In particular, Thornton emphasized that, 'while [Synge] could not accept his family's dogmas, he was in temperament and attitude quite close to them, and in his own thinking he transmuted rather than rejected their religion.'[10] Above all, he stressed Synge's 'passionate concern for the truth and for the integrity of his own mind and thought.'[11]

The rock on which Synge's earlier unquestioning faith foundered was the Christian concept of Hell and the terrorizing hold it acquired on his youthful imagination:

> I was painfully timid and while still very young the idea of Hell took a fearful hold upon me. One night particularly I thought I was irretrievably damned and cried myself to sleep in vain yet fearful/terrible efforts to form a conception of eternal pain. In the morning I renewed my lamentation and my mother was sent for. She comforted me with the assurance that my fears were caused by the Holy Ghost who was now convicting me of sin and thus preparing me in reality for ultimate salvation. [...] [My mother] was always judicious – except perhaps in her portrayal of Hell. From this time religion remained a difficulty and occasioned terror to me for many years, though I do not think the brand I was brought up in was peculiarly Calvinistic. The well-meant but extraordinary cruelty of thrusting/throwing the idea of Hell into the imagination of a nervous

child has probably caused more misery [than] many customs that the
same people send missionaries to eradicate.[12]

Already implicit here is Synge's sense that any religion that might
subsequently win his allegiance would do away with the notion of Hell
and promote instead the many pagan customs that other immediate
members of his family, his uncle Alec or brother Samuel, took as their
missionary goal to eradicate at home or abroad.

Synge returns to this idea years later, in 1898, during his studies on
Irish civilization with d'Arbois de Jubainville, when his by-now
extensive reading gave him the scholarly authority to make the
following observation on the 'progress' of Irish literature over the
centuries: 'Observe that idea of *Hell* absent from most primitive texts.
Gradually assumes such prominence that it at last completely
overshadows idea of heaven. In Irish and non-Christian texts no hell.'[13]
Here was objective testimony of his earlier experience, a cultural
parallel of a personal dilemma that both confirmed it and showed him a
way imaginatively to escape its constraints. In his autobiography, he
had written of his crisis of faith:

> Till I was twenty-three I never met or at least knew a man or woman
> who shared my opinions. Compared with the people about me,
> compared with the Fellows of Trinity, I seemed a presumptuous boy
> yet I felt that the views which I had arrived at after sincere efforts to
> find what was true represented, in spite of my immediate
> surroundings, the real opinion of the world. (II, 11)

Synge's account of his 'sincere efforts to find what was true' testify to
Stephens's and Thornton's view of his enduring debt to Evangelicalism
and its urgings to devote one's life to a quest for spiritual truth. But the
gulf or chasm that he described separating him from his brethren was
opened up by the idea of hell; it separated him emotionally from
'kindred and friends' and no longer made the attainment of his family's
form of salvation possible. Synge's reading of the ancient Irish texts at
the age of twenty-seven cemented the association in his mind between
the evangelizing zeal of the Christian missionary, the totalizing
promotion of the concept of hell, and the consequent extinction of any
heavenly intimations.

Six years later, in 1904, the idea of hell made its appearance in *The
Well of the Saints* at the close of Act Two. The blind couple have been
cured by the wandering Saint, and as one result, Martin Doul is now
forced to labour in Timmy the Smith's forge. He shows the effects of his
conversion by a perverse prayer of revenge in which the idea of hell,

earlier absent from his imaginings, has now assumed such prominence that it completely overshadows the idea of heaven:

> Oh, God, pity a poor blind fellow the way I am this day with no strength in me to do hurt to them at all. [...] Yet if I've no strength in me I've a voice left for my prayers, and may God blight them this day, and my own soul the same hour with them, the way I'll see them after, Molly Byrne and Timmy the smith, the two of them on a high bed, and they screeching in hell ... It'll be a grand thing that time to look on the two of them; and they twisting and roaring out, and twisting and roaring again. [...] it won't be hell to me I'm thinking, but the like of Heaven itself. (III, 123)

But if the idea of hell made acceptance of evangelical dogma impossible to the youthful Synge, another crisis was precipitated by his reading of Charles Darwin's *On The Origin of Species* (1859). What it introduced into his mind was the question and possibility of doubt:

> Till then I had never doubted and never conceived that a sane and wise man or boy could doubt. I had of course heard of atheists but as vague monsters I was unable to realize. It seemed that I was become in a moment the playfellow of Judas. (II, 10-11)

Although the reading of Darwin was destructive in its immediate effects, most critics see the longer-term impact of the experience as crucial in Synge's evolution as a playwright. ·Weldon Thornton argues that it would be wrong to conclude that the event turned Synge into a rationalist; he was 'too aware of the mystery behind all things to regard reason as definitive.'[14] Thornton analyzed the experience to show that, given Synge's detailed interest in natural history, what he acquired from reading Darwin was not new facts but a new perspective on the facts he already possessed. Henceforth, he was to regard no single perspective, Darwin's or his mother's, as adequate. Mary C. King views the effect of reading Darwin as equally liberating on Synge's attitude to language, since it not only 'undermined the naive historicism of Mrs. Synge's interpretation of the rest of sacred scripture, [...] its undeviating literalism.'[15] It also prepared the way for Synge's subsequent discovery of the symbolic nature of words, first as a student of foreign languages in France and Germany and then through his exposure to the Hiberno-English speech of the Aran Islands.

But there is a third crisis in the youthful Synge's life to which scarcely any critical attention has been paid. In addition to the ideas of the Christian hell and of Darwinian evolution, a third sundering force in the area of belief occurred with the onset of puberty, which had the equivalent negative effect on his earlier beliefs that the other two did on his Christianity. I am here referring to the current of pantheistic nature worship that runs through all of Synge's writings and constitutes arguably his greatest religious belief. His earliest childhood imaginings are of this paradisal or Edenic interaction with the natural world:

> Even at this time I was a worshipper of nature. I remember that I would not allow my nurses to sit down on the seats by the [River] Dodder because they were 'made'. If they wished to sit down they had to find a low branch of a tree or a bit of rock or bank. (II, 5)[16]

He shared this heightened otherworld of nature with his cousin Florence Ross:

> We were always primitive. We both understood all the facts of life and spoke of them without much hesitation [...] [talking] of sexual matters with an indifferent and sometimes amused frankness that was identical with the attitude of folk-tales. (II, 7)

Synge was writing with a later awareness of the cultural equivalents to his own development and the suggestion that, through his avid interest in folktales and the 'primitive' life of the Aran Islands, he was seeking at some level to reconstruct and recover this paradise lost. What effected the loss was the onset of puberty, the removal of his cousin from his presence, and the casting of his passionate sensuality into the category of 'sin'. He wrote of this period of trauma:

> Sometimes I was obsessed by the ideas that beset man at this period and thought myself a low miscreant because I had a tendency which was quite natural and healthy. [...] Vulgar sensuality did not attract me but I was haunted by pagan dreams of a time when there was yet no fear of love.'[17]

An alternate version of this passage, which breaks off in Synge and is edited out by Alan Price in the second volume of the *Collected Works,* reads: 'I was torn with passions.'[18]

What remains to be considered is the kind of heaven to which Synge was converted, or rather the concept of heaven that his imaginative beliefs and practices presupposed. His readings in early Irish literature first afforded a glimpse of this by showing the pagan vision and version of the afterlife that the arrival of Christianity displaced (but did not destroy). Weldon Thornton and Declan Kiberd, as late as 1979, were the first critics to take account of Synge's scholarly interest in the Celtic otherworld. In *Synge and the Irish Language,* Kiberd wrote:

> In 1898 [Synge] had read an old Irish tale from the Mythological Cycle, *The Voyage of Bran,* edited and translated by Kuno Meyer. [...] Meyer's volume contained an essay by Alfred Nutt entitled 'The Irish Vision of the Happy Otherworld and the Celtic Doctrine of Rebirth.' Synge cited this essay and Meyer's text in an essay written in French in

1902 to support his thesis that Old Irish and Greek literature shared a position of major importance in the Indo-European scheme.[19]

The relevant portion of Synge's article 'La Vieille littérature irlandaise' for *L'Européen* of March 15, 1902, reads:

I have spoken above of the European importance of this Irish literature and this claim is not exaggerated. [...] Nothing, for instance, is as primitive as that belief common to Greeks and Irish, a belief in an other world where the dead continue to enjoy a life like that of earthly existence without hope of being rewarded for their virtues or fear of being punished for their misdeeds. (II, 354, translation mine)

As Synge put it six years earlier in his extensive notes on Alfred Nutt's essay, the Celtic otherworld is an 'Elysium dissociated from eschatological belief (i.e., framed without reference to man's future life)'.[20] It inclines more to the Christian concept of heaven in its promise of endless delight and its exclusion of strife or rancour and has least to do with the unrelenting physical punishment of hell. But the pagan otherworld differs from the Christian heaven, as Synge noted, in being more 'like that of earthly existence' and offering a vision of a world in which natural pleasures were extolled; sensuality heightened into artistic patterns of music, poetry, and dance; and the curse of mortality kept at a distance. If his Continental studies in Celtic literature first introduced these concepts to Synge, it would take his voyages to the Aran Islands to bring him into direct living contact with what remained of these ancient beliefs.

A final irony, and a final connection with his family background, is that Synge was not the first of his family to visit the islands. When he landed at Aranmore, he was spotted by an older man who told him that evening:

I was standing under the pier-wall mending nets [...] when you came off the steamer, and I said to myself in that moment, if there is a man of the name of Synge left walking the world, it is that man yonder will be he. (II, 53

John had been preceded there in 1851 by his uncle, the Reverend Alexander Synge, the first Protestant missionary to the Aran Islands, who wrote: 'I get on with the people so far very well, but how will it be when we begin to attack their bad ways, religion, etc., I don't know.'[21] Whereas the Reverend Alexander Synge came to the Aran Islands to convert, his nephew John travelled there fifty years later to be converted.

What Synge's prose work *The Aran Islands* records is his imaginative interaction with the oral folktales of which he had so far read only the literary equivalent. Elsewhere in the French essay already cited, he had specifically located the value of the Irish legends and cycles in their 'mythology which forms [...] a kernel of the most primitive beliefs of the Indo-European peoples' (II, 354, my translation) before going on to cite a belief in the pagan otherworld as the most primitive of all. The key terms in this assessment, the *mythology* comprised of *primitive beliefs,* recur in Synge's evaluation of the Aran Islands. Aranmore, Inishmaan, and Inishere are ranked by him according to the 'primitive' qualities preserved in their environment: 'Aranmore has been so much changed by the fishing industry [...] that it has now very little to distinguish it from any fishing village on the west coast of Ireland. The other islands are more primitive' (II, 47).[22] Synge is correspondingly eager to leave Aranmore and sail to Inishmaan, where 'Gaelic is more generally used, and the life is perhaps the most primitive that is left in Europe' (II, 53). These remarks make clear the importance of Irish for Synge as a linguistic means of preserving and transmitting this 'primitive' culture.[23] (They also help to explain his hostility to the modernizing techniques of the Gaelic League.) For over and over again in his encounters with the islanders it is the body of imaginative beliefs dating from pre-Christian times, 'the wild mythology that is accepted on the islands' (II, 54), that draws his interest.

This discernible bias has led to charges that Synge wilfully ignored the deeply held Catholicism of the islanders, downplaying its central role in their lives in favour of exaggerating the remnants of a few prior superstitions. Daniel Corkery is chief among Catholic Irish critics to make the accusation, contending that Synge 'did not frequent the really authoritative people on the islands who could have told him everything about everything' but rather 'spent most of his days lying alone in the sun or, equally alone, moping around under the stars!'[24] But the criticism of Synge's anti-Catholicism has also been made by his international commentators, first and formidably by Maurice Bourgeois:

> Synge's archaic quest of the older Gaelic civilization made him blind to the profounder spirit of modern Ireland. [...] At bottom [the Irish peasant] is an ardently religious being, whose whole life is coloured by faith and belief – especially Catholic faith. This aspect of [the] Irish mind is ignored by Synge; it has no place in his works; and on this score his fellow-countrymen are justified in finding fault with his plays.[25]

The incident in *The Aran Islands* on which this controversy focuses is Synge's description in Part I of a funeral he attended on Inishmaan. The account is notable for the passionate grief with which the normally reticent islanders are seized and in particular for the wild cry of the keen (from the Irish *caoineadh,* lament) through which it is expressed:

> This grief of the keen is no personal complaint for the death of one woman over eighty years, but seems to contain the whole passionate rage that lurks somewhere in every native of the island. In this cry of pain the inner consciousness of the people seems to lay itself bare for an instant, and to reveal the mood of beings who feel their isolation in the face of a universe that wars on them with winds and seas. [...]
> Before they covered the coffin an old man knelled down by the grave and repeated a simple prayer for the dead.

> There was an irony in these words of atonement and Catholic belief spoken by voices that were still hoarse with the cries of pagan desperation (II, 75).

Many of his plays will dramatize the great gap in that irony, between words of Catholic belief and the passionate rage of the pagan.[26]

Synge held that the islanders' Christianity was only the merest veneer or layer covering over the earlier pagan beliefs and that, under the pressure of the lives they led on the westernmost edge of the Atlantic Ocean, the islanders' conventional pieties rapidly gave way before sympathies closer to nature mysticism than Christian orthodoxy. His concern was not with the uppermost layer, the Catholicism to which as a Protestant he was antipathetic, but with the underlying strata of primitive beliefs that he thought constituted the islanders' more profound allegiances and to which he could give his own imaginative assent.

There is objective support for such a view. In *Christianity and Paganism,* J.N. Hillgarth pointed out:

> Since Ireland was never politically or culturally subject to Rome, Christianity was forced to evolve there in ways distinct from those it had naturally assumed. [...] Ireland – unlike Western Europe – possessed a living culture of its own, expressed in a vernacular literature that had not been obliterated by a Roman overlay.[27]

Christianity in Ireland adapted itself to the indigenous (and pagan) culture to a much greater extent than anywhere else, so that

> if one turns to the literature produced in Irish – much of it probably in monasteries – one finds that the heroes of the pagan past continued to

be revered in a way which would be hard to parallel elsewhere in Western Christendom. [28]

This was particularly the case in the remotest areas of the west of Ireland, where the oral tradition in Irish continued unbroken into this century and carried with it, as Synge noted, many archaic features that had vanished from the written literature.

Accordingly, the people he sought out on the Aran Islands were not the priests (though when he met any the exchange was cordial enough) but the storytellers, latter-day descendants of the bardic class. Michael, Pat Dirane, and Old Mourteen are the preeminent storytellers of their respective locales and central to the narrative design in *The Aran Islands*. Synge's first encounter with Mourteen climaxes the account of his arrival on the islands: 'one old half-blind man spoke to me in Gaelic. [...] [He] had great confidence in his own powers and talent, and in the superiority of his stories over all other stories in the world' and proceeded to relate how 'one of his children had been taken by the fairies' (II, 50-51).

The topic of Mourteen's discourse raises the question of the presence and purpose of the fairy lore in Synge's book. Unlike Yeats and Lady Gregory, Synge never recorded such material purely for its own sake, never detached it from the occasion and context of its telling or from the personality of its narrator:

> As we talked he sat huddled together over the fire, shaking and blind, yet his face was indescribably pliant, lighting up with an ecstasy of humour when he told me of anything that had a point of wit or malice, and growing sombre and desolate again when he spoke of religion or the fairies. (II, 50)

Synge responded to these old men as inheritors of a number of traditions – of the Irish language, of oral storytelling, of beliefs that originally formed part of a pre-Christian religion. But the people retain the emphasis since, in the words of Walter Benjamin, it is only in the 'full corporeality' of the 'experience which is passed on from mouth to mouth' that these traditions can be restored to full living currency. [29]

Synge not only situated the stories in the personalities of the tellers; he in turn situated those tellers and their stories in the communal life of the islands. His technique can be best illustrated through a consideration of Part IV. Mary C. King, who has provided the fullest account of Synge's narrative technique in this apparently artless book, noted how in the last part 'references to dying and to death [...] accumulate until mortality itself becomes the dominant theme'. Juxtaposed with the deaths are 'the folktale element', which King does not discuss, and three long poems, 'political allegories about Ireland's struggle for freedom, [which] act as a counterpoint to the funereal *cantus firmus* of the prose.'[30] But the three poems only account for the second half. What the first half counterpoints with the stark realism of the death by drowning of one of the island's young men is the presence and function of storytelling in the lives of the islanders. Storytelling abounds in Part IV of *The Aran Islands* to such an extent that it displaces the primary account of activities on Aran. But then the primary activity with which IV concerns itself is death, not only of the drowned man but of a young woman stricken with typhus. So Synge gathers with the people in their cottage at night for the rituals of storytelling by which they acknowledge the dead and keep their own terror at bay.

Early in Part IV, a story about the sudden, unexpected killing of two neighbours by each other – having wrought a context in which the most fundamental beliefs surrounding life and death are brought into play – is interrupted by 'a gust of wind [that] came and blew up a bundle of dry seaweed that was near us, right over our heads' (II, 156). This inspired another old man to a story that tentatively suggested the hovering, airy presences of the Shee or fairy host behind such an intrusion. By this point, the current of pagan belief tapped by the storytelling is gathering momentum: 'There was more than that in it,' said another man,

> 'for the night before a woman had a great sight out to the west in this island, and saw all the people that were dead a while back in this island and the south island, and they all talking with each other.' (II, 157)

This particular account of the resurrected dead serves not just as reminiscence but as prophecy, with the next page of Synge's text disgorging 'the body of a young man who was drowned a few weeks ago' (II, 158). In so doing, it establishes a recurrent juxtaposition of story and incident for the rest of the work, oscillating between a verbal land of the fancy where familiar figures enjoy an extended existence and the realm of the real where their decomposing mortal remains are elaborately laid to rest. The only healing refuge in the pages of *The Aran Islands* is found not in the appeal to an avowedly merciful God but in the consolations of storytelling, the communal act by which the islanders' suffering is confronted and assuaged.

Synge drew directly on his experience of the Aran Islands in writing his one-act tragedy *Riders to the Sea*. As almost every critic has pointed out, *Riders* displays the same mixture of pagan and Christian beliefs as

Synge encountered among the islanders. Almost the first words we hear are those of the young priest, offering Maurya and her daughters words of consolation: 'let you not be afraid. Herself does be saying prayers half through the night, and the Almighty God won't leave her destitute,' says he, 'with no son living' (III, 5). That the play is going to run directly counter to this confident assertion is suggested by the immediate juxtaposition of the priest's disembodied words with Nora and Cathleen's fearful apprehension of the sea's presence. The two women's reading of the factors that influence their destiny provides a much more accurate prophecy than that of the young priest, one more in tune with the climate and pervasive environment of *Riders to the Sea*:

> **CATHLEEN**: Is the sea bad by the white rocks, Nora?
> **NORA**: Middling bad, God help us. There's a great roaring in the west, and it's worse it'll be getting when the tide's turned to the wind. (III, 5-7)

The sea is rapidly established as the centre of power and influence in their lives, an association that will continue to develop throughout the drama. But one could expect little else in any naturalistic representation of those who eke out a precarious existence on a small island, even if Synge *has* concentrated all the potential catastrophes on a single, unfortunate house. What is more subtle is the process by which he invests the physical presence of the Atlantic Ocean with metaphysical overtones. The first step has already been noted in the repeated statements by the priest, whose claims about 'the Almighty God' establish the sense of a transcendental power operating invisibly in and through the lives of humans. The priest's invocations are at once countered in the play by the opposing power of the sea. In so doing, Synge implicitly calls into being a countervailing metaphysical realm with its own presiding deities and impact on human affairs.

In an important essay, Denis Donoghue argued that the

> relationship between 'Catholic' and 'Pagan' becomes one of the most significant of the dramatic tensions established within the context of *Riders to the Sea*: the tension between orthodox, institutional religion and the implacable power of the Sea.[31]

But Donoghue did not consider the pagan values or beliefs associated with the sea, merely continuing to insist on that power as 'silent' and 'inhuman'. Rather, it was Robin Skelton who enlarged on how Synge

> incorporated into the play many images with supernatural significance. [...] Thus there are references to Sarnhain (or Hallowe'en) the time when ghosts walk, to holy water, and to the 'black hags' that 'do be flying on the sea'. [...] The sea itself is regarded

> as a godlike power in the play, and the priest is dismissed as being of
> very little significance.[32]

Skelton stopped short, however, of identifying the god associated with
the sea in Celtic mythology as Manannan Mac Lir. The play's very title
invokes the sea god Manannan in its distinctive yoking together of
horseriding and the ocean. Its preposition points Bartley and his horses
not toward the fair on the mainland that he assumes is his destination
or even the boat that will transport them thither but the sea to which
(and on which?) he will ride. In the Old Irish *Voyage of Bran,* the hero
and his comrades encounter Manannan in the midst of their voyage:
'When he had been at sea two days and two nights, [Bran] saw a man in
a chariot coming towards him over the sea [who] [...] said that he was
Manannan son of Lir.' He presented them with a double vision
whereby, although the mariners only see 'a clear sea. [...] There are
many steeds on its surface / Though them thou seest not.'[33] Declan
Kiberd, in his scholarly amassing of the numerous folk beliefs
embedded in *Riders to the Sea,* noted that 'pigs were sacrificed to
Manannan Mac Lir, the god of the sea, in order to ward off evil,
including death by drowning', and argued that 'by neglecting this duty,
the island family has exposed itself to the danger of drowning'.[34]
Manannan's presence is pervasive in Synge's play in the actual form of
the sea and in the number of references to gestures, sayings, and rituals
designed to propitiate him. What Kiberd demonstrated is how all
through the play 'members of the family have violated folk prohibitions'
and so heightened 'our sense of the inevitability of Bartley's death'.[35]

That significance associated with the sea begins to develop more
explicitly with the entrance of the mother Maurya. As the play opens,
she is sleeping but her two daughters know that, once awake, 'herself
will be down looking by the sea' (III, 5). Maurya is repeatedly drawn
there by the fact that her son Michael has been missing for a week,
hence the sustained scrutiny she directs at the ocean, urging some kind
of response to her eloquent unspoken entreaties. Cathleen speculates
that 'maybe when the tide turns she'll be going down to see would he be
floating from the east' (III, 7). Any aural reception of this second line is
bound to be influenced by the first in hovering between 'sea/see' as
actual locale or as source of vision. What Maurya hopes to see there is
not yet made explicit: the body of her son washed ashore at the selfsame
spot from which he cast off? Unlikely, at best, but possible to a grief-
distracted mother. The return of other islanders with the body of her
son? Again, unlikely, since the Aran practice was to bury the body
where it was recovered, as we learn elsewhere in the play. There is

always the possibility of Michael's actual safe return home, but after this length of time Nora and Cathleen have yielded to the unlikelihood of such an outcome. The final possibility is that Michael, having been 'away' – that is, taken to the Celtic otherworld by fairy forces – might yet put in a reappearance, as many others had been reported doing in island lore.

That possibility is confirmed when Maurya returns from pursuing the remaining son Bartley to give him her blessing. What she says indicates that she has had a vision not of this world:

> I'm after seeing [Michael] this day, and he riding and galloping. Bartley came first on the red mare; and I tried to say 'God speed you', but something choked the words in my throat. He went by quickly; and 'the blessing of God on you', says he, and I could say nothing. I looked up then, and I crying, at the grey pony, and there was Michael upon it – with fine clothes on him, and new shoes on his feet. (III, 19)

The colours of the two horses have been taken by more than one critic as a reference to the Four Horsemen of the Apocalypse in the Book of Revelations.[36] But Nicholas Grene, who is generally resistant to a symbolic reading of *Riders,* argued that 'if we are looking for analogues here, we should not be thinking in terms of the apocalyptic image of the four horsemen, but of the folk concept of the conspiracy of the dead'.[37]

The period of the year in which the dead have greatest freedom to return is Samhain, the Celtic feast referred to by Maurya in her long closing lament: 'I'll have no call now to be going down and getting Holy Water in the dark nights after Samhain' (III, 25). Prionsias MacCana wrote:

> The Celts have treated the festival of Samhain [November 1] [...] as a time apart which was charged with a peculiar preternatural energy [when] the barriers between the natural and the supernatural are temporarily removed, the *sidh* [fairy fort] lies open and all divine beings and the spirits of the dead move freely among human beings and interfere, sometimes violently, in their affairs.[38]

As a result, Maurya's wish to see her son again is answered but in a way that brings little satisfaction. Not only does her vision at the well confirm that Michael drowned but also that his spirit has returned to interfere violently in their affairs by drawing the living Bartley after him. Maurya's Christianity fails her at this crucial intersection, and the words of blessing are stopped in her throat by the superior stranglehold exerted at that moment by the old religion. Her vision of Michael sustains a double loss, not only confirming in retrospect the drowning of one son but serving as infallible prophecy of the death of the other. Cathleen's rational side attempts to deny the truth of what her mother has seen by equating Michael with the remains retrieved from the sea. But in Maurya's reply – 'I'm after seeing him this day, and he riding and galloping' – the oppressive facts of death and loss are simultaneously confirmed and counterbalanced by the alternate prospect of his continued active existence in the otherworld, clad not in a few pitiful rags but in the seamless imaginative splendor of 'fine clothes on him, and new shoes on his feet'.

The question that most concerns the critics is the extent to which Maurya regains a Christian perspective at the close of the play. Robin Skelton would have none of it and argued that the references to 'holy water' do not carry the usual Christian connotations: 'It may be that she collects it from a Holy Well, even the Spring Well, mentioned in the play, but it is clear that the only time she does collect it is in the nights after Samhain. [...] Thus the Holy Water is much more the magical water of pre-Christian belief than the water blessed by the priest.'[39] Nicholas Grene used the holy water to argue the opposite point of view – that Maurya, after reaching the depths of pagan nihilism in the face of death, now attains a Christian quietude and resignation.[40] But Declan Kiberd pointed out that despite her blessing on Bartley, 'Maurya's closing speech holds no orthodox Christian promise of a life to come' and goes on to cite instead the Irish faith in another world 'where the dead continue a life similar to their terrestrial existence'.[41] What is clear is that Maurya's final attitude, like the line in which she refers simultaneously to 'Holy Water' and 'Samhain', mixes Christian and pagan beliefs and that the conflict between them which the play has staged now attains at least temporary equilibrium in her soul.

The most direct staging of the confrontation between Christianity and paganism in Synge' s drama occurs in *The Tinker's Wedding*. The work is also the most problematic and least esteemed of his six plays. Is there a connection between the two – the possibility that the explicit foregrounding of the Christian-pagan conflict leads to dramatic breakdown and that Synge is best when treating the theme as an adjunct of the dramatic action? This question needs to be considered, but it is also worth remembering that *The Tinker's Wedding* has a complicated structural evolution, first emerging as a one-act play, one of the three of the miraculous summer of 1902. It can be argued that the flaws of the play are as much the result of that most difficult of dramatic moves, away from the self-imposed limitations of the one-act toward a full-length play. The best way to demonstrate this is to compare the treatment of Christianity and paganism in the two-act *Tinker's Wedding* with the three-act *The Well of the Saints*, where the confrontation of man of God and unregenerate pagan is equally central and more successfully resolved.

In terms of Synge's artistic treatment of Christianity, *The Tinker's Wedding* is most notable in presenting the first (and only) onstage appearance of a Catholic priest. That appearance was necessitated from the start by the priest's dramatic centrality to the folktale on which Synge based the play, in which a pair of tinkers attempts to trick the cleric into marrying them for nothing. In the earliest version of this play, the only one-act draft preserved, the financial transaction has already taken place and is represented indirectly through reported speech, as with the words of the young priest throughout *Riders:* 'You're a thieving lot,' says he 'and I'ld do right to make you give a pound surely but maybe if I left the like of that bit of money with you you'd be drinking it below in the fair' (IV, 273). The climax, however, in which the tinkers fail to present the agreed sum and are sent packing, requires the direct onstage presence and involvement of the priest. In preparation for this, Synge brings him on not in a private capacity (in black) but in full ceremonial costume from the '*chapel door*' (IV, 275), which is a requirement of the stage directions throughout.

The stage settings of both *Wedding* and *Well* require the combination and severe juxtaposition of two contrasting visual motifs: a church doorway on the one side, the symbolic portals across whose threshold the tinkers and beggars are impelled but which they finally refuse to cross or enter, and on the other side a roadside, sign of the unfettered imaginative life they lead, as social itinerants outside the bounds of bourgeois society. They are also living a life in greater contact with the physical world. Both settings are outside, rather than in the peasant cottage of Synge's first two one-act plays, more open to the influence of nature and so provide an implicit contrast to the settled world of domestic interiors represented by the bond of marriage.

The priest emerges in his surplice from the chapel doorway to complete the monetary details before bringing the tinkers in to marry them. His questions are direct and terse, allowing for no more characterization than already contained in the reported narrative, that of a man whose mind is as much on material as spiritual matters, if not more so. When he discovers their imposture, the priest opens up into a full-throated denunciation that while drawing on his full social and spiritual authority as a Catholic cleric also displays an intimate knowledge of the tinkers and their ways: 'If I catch you again in this village you bawdy thief I['ll] tell the peelers who it was stole the grey ass' (IV, 276). Mary Byrne, the oldest of the tinkers and the play's

Rabelaisian earth-mother most in touch with the Romany traditions, defends their way of living, both in defiance of the priest and in rebuke of her daughter-in-law's perverse desire to get married in the first place: 'You and your marriage! Isn't generations and generations we are walking round under the Heavens and what is it we ever wanted with [your like]?' (IV, 276). So the original one-act draft concludes – in a much more innocuous way than the notorious revised ending Synge was later to provide.

The addition of an entire act is the much more substantial alteration Synge made to the play. In so doing, he went back to the night before (rather than the more leisurely three weeks of the prose) and dramatized the making of the match between priest and tinker as an uneasy liaison between the traditions of Christianity and paganism in Ireland. Robin Skelton gave the fullest account of the presence of pre-Christian beliefs and customs in Synge's representation of the tinkers. Many of his examples, however, such as the fertility figure of the 'green man' invoked by two children (IV, 281), are from earlier, suppressed fragments rather than the finished version. Skelton did, however, make the best argument for Sarah Casey, building on the play's original title of *The Movements of May:*

> Disturbed by the 'change of the moon' at the time of the vernal equinox, she is filled with a rising excitement and sense of her own royal beauty, and expresses this in language that conflates folk-tale and ancient belief with the commonplace.[42]

Sarah's pride in her own physical appearance and confidence in her ability to attract another man strike the keynote not only of her personality but of the essentially pagan beliefs of the tinkers. It is in this context that her decision to insist belatedly on a Christian marriage with Michael is viewed by the other two tinkers (and by the play) as at best a temporary aberration, and at worst a betrayal of the values of her itinerant tribe.

Although the priest when stopped by Sarah the night before is initially as brusque as on the following day, the first act builds sympathy for him and shows some unexpected affiliations between the disparate lives of 'his reverence' and the tinkers. Vivian Mercier, in his article on the play, carefully showed how the priest reveals a 'basic kindliness'[43] in the face of Sarah's tears and, when pressed to it by Mary Byrne, finally lets down his guard and agrees to share a drink with them. As he does so, he admits: 'it's well for the like of you that do be drinking when there's drouth on you. [...] What would you do if it was the like of myself you were, saying Mass with your mouth dry?' (IV, 19).

It is presumably this behaviour and admission on the priest's part that led Maurice Bourgeois to his verdict on the play. Having remarked how 'it was Synge's object to contrast [...] the two types of Irish civilization, the Heathen and the Christian-Ireland before and after St. Patrick,' Bourgeois argued that 'this attempt at dramatic synthesis [...] remains on the whole incongruous and unsuccessful; for is not the Priest in the play himself a Pagan?'44 The answer, surely, is no. The priest's confessing to a degree of dissatisfaction with his lot is no more (or less) than human. When Mary proceeds to make fun of his praying in church, he is scandalized by her blasphemy, prepares to leave and criticizes her in the following terms: 'Stop your talking, Mary Byrne; you're an old flagrant heathen' (IV, 21). But before he departs, he renews his promise to Sarah Casey, and for the reduced price they have agreed. The first act of *The Tinker's Wedding* would, I believe, have been readily accepted by Irish country people as a convincing account of relations between tinkers and priests. Denis Johnston, an Irishman and a fellow playwright, made this claim up to a point (that of the ending, which we have yet to consider). He argued that the play depicts, 'not unsympathetically, the rapacity and practicality of the clergy, who are [...] quite prepared to allow their parishioners to remain living in mortal sin indefinitely if they fail to produce the necessary cash to pay for a sacrament'.45 But the first act is also a superior dramatic representation, moving adroitly between the two poles of belief. The priest shows an unexpected measure of sympathy and insight into the ways of the tinkers, going beyond the pale of his social role but not of his religious beliefs. The tinkers, in their turn, address him respectfully as 'your reverence'; Sarah shows a commendable desire for the sacrament of marriage, and it is only with the verbal and physical mischief making of Mary Byrne that matters get out of hand and the boundaries dividing pagan from Christian again reassert themselves.

The second act is far less satisfactory. Too much of it has not been transformed beyond either its folktale or one-act origins. As a result, the character of the priest reverts to being simply a remote authority figure, alternately condemning the tinkers or trying to take their money. Too much of the act centres on the trick whereby Synge, deciding not to have Michael and Sarah directly attempt to cheat the priest, now has Mary Byrne acquire sole blame in making off with the can and selling it for porter. When this is discovered, the full mutually condemnatory exchange, which is retained in all versions, then takes place. But it goes one crucial step further in the final version when the tinkers lay violent hands upon the priest, tie him up in a bag, and threaten to kill him.

The ending has been almost universally condemned by Synge critics and is certainly the reason the play was never staged during his lifetime. In addition to its direct affront to any (especially a Catholic) audience's sensibilities, there are crucial problems of tone here, veering from the farcical (the incident itself) to the serious (when they consider killing him). The tinkers finally, reluctantly, agree to let the priest out of the bag when he gives 'a mighty oath' in the name of his God not to turn them over to the police. He emerges with the following lines in the play's overly hasty denouement:

> **PRIEST** [*lifting up his hand*]. I've sworn not to call the hand of man upon your crimes to-day; but I haven't sworn I wouldn't call the fire of heaven from the hand of the Almighty God. [*He begins saying a Latin malediction in a loud ecclesiastical voice.*]
> **MARY**. There's an old villain.
> **ALL** [*together*]. Run, run. Run for your lives. [*They rush out, leaving the* **PRIEST** *master of the situation.*] (IV, 49)

The crude explicitness here is bad enough. But the ending is affected by a more serious and disabling lack of ambiguity, even a downright contradiction, in terms of our theme. I would focus this by looking at the attitudes in the play toward the two rituals by which its beliefs are formulated, prayers and stories. The former are the exclusive preserve of the priest, from the tinkers' point of view, and Mary urges him to recite one over the fire as his contribution. The oral storytelling by which the Irish pre-Christian legends were preserved and transmitted is associated with the tinkers, their migratory way of life, and their regard for and display of fine speeches. The older Mary Byrne is more conscious of this tradition than the younger couple:

> let you sit down there by the big bough, and I'll be telling you the finest story you'd hear any place from Dundalk to Ballinacree, with great queens in it, making themselves matches from the start to the end, and they with silks on them the length of the day, and white shifts for the night. (IV, 23)

But in her soliloquy that closes Act One, Mary Byrne reveals a crucial ambiguity toward the stories in whose telling she takes such pride: 'What good are the grand stories I have when it's few would listen to an old woman, few but a girl maybe [...] or a little child wouldn't be sleeping with the hunger on a cold night?' (IV, 27). Perhaps her stories are no more than illusory compensations for the undeniable facts of her growing old and her aloneness. The play's attitude toward the storytelling therefore gravitates between admiration and distrust, affirmation and doubt.

In the tinkers' attitude toward Catholic prayer, there is no such ambiguity but rather downright contradiction. In the first half, they display ignorance of the 'queer noise' (IV, 21) people make in church and ask the priest for an example of something they claim never to have heard. At the end, there is a certain justifiable fear at the threat of the peelers. But their awe-struck terror before the priest's Latin maledictions not only comes out of nowhere but contradicts their earlier insouciance toward the metaphysical potency of Roman Catholic prayer. The ending makes them seem like ignorant, superstitious heathens, an appalling stereotype that the rest of the play – and of Synge's dramatic career – has been at pains to counter in its sympathetic, complex, and detailed representation of the figure of the Irish peasant.

In *The Well of the Saints,* staged in the opening months of the Abbey Theatre in early 1905, priests were still causing problems. As Nicholas Grene pointed out in his Introduction to his edition of *The Well of the Saints,* the players balked at performing the line: 'Looking on your face is it? And she after going by with her head turned the way you'd see a priest going where there'd be a drunken man in the side ditch talking with a girl'.[46] Despite writing indignantly to Frank Fay that 'I most emphatically will not change a syllable of it because A. or B. or C. may think they know better than I do'(CL I, 91), Synge altered the offending line in his own copy of the 1905 edition to read: 'And she after going by with her head turned the way you'd see a sainted lady going where there'd be drunken people in the side ditch singing to themselves' (IV, 107). Nicholas Grene pinpointed the change as occurring 'at the dress-rehearsal stage after more complaints' and, in his edition of the play, restored the original line in place of what he termed a 'forced bowdlerization'.[47]

The protest over this line apart, *The Well of the Saints* had a relatively tranquil passage, attracting little criticism (and, hence, attention) when first staged. Although Willie Fay wished 'that the Saint anyway might be made into a goodnatured easy-going man',[48] and Synge wrote to Lady Gregory that 'Padraic Colum finds my play unsatisfactory because the Saint is really a Protestant!' (CL I, 94), the character of the Saint did not arouse the anticipated protest. There are several reasons for this. One is the deliberate distancing and stylization made possible by Synge's decision to set the play not in the present but *one or more centuries ago* (III, 69). This removed the action from the immediate realm of the real to an intermediate zone of fact and fancy where the central miracle would not strain credibility and to an archetypal level of the drama where he could draw more explicitly on mythic forebears. Another reason for the lack of protest is that *The Well* resolves many of the problems attendant upon *The Tinker's Wedding* in terms of satisfactory dramatic development and a balance of sympathies.

The play engages much more fully with the theme that Bourgeois saw as central to the earlier play: 'the two types of Irish civilization, the Heathen and the Christian-Ireland before and after St Patrick.'[49] Although Synge's Saint is never given a name, any critical tendency to associate him with the archetypal Irish saint is corroborated by Synge's placing in his character's mouth words and sentiments taken directly from Patrick. In a letter to Max Meyerfeld, the play's German translator, Synge commented on 'the words of women and smiths' (III, 91) that 'this phrase is almost a quotation from an old hymn of St. Patrick' (CL I, 121) known as 'St. Patrick's Breastplate'. In explicitly evoking St. Patrick, he is removing his Saint from the sectarian divisions of the present to a time when the name of Christian transcended sectarian division. Despite Padraic Colum's protest, St. Patrick could be seen as either Catholic or Protestant, since he was claimed by both traditions. Vivian Mercier wrote that there were 'two patriotic tendencies peculiar to the Irish version of Evangelicalism: its interest, however narrow and utilitarian, in the Irish language, and its determined efforts to link the post-Reformation Church of Ireland with the pre-Norman Celtic Church of St. Patrick and his successors.'[50] The presentation of the Saint therefore allows for greater identification on Synge's part with the 'austere asceticism'[51] of this spokesman for a spiritual way of life than with the well-fed Catholic clergy of the present day – like the priest in *The Tinker's Wedding*.

With this linking of his Saint with Patrick and our awareness of Synge's scholarly grounding in early Irish literature, we are in a much better position to understand the extent to which the conflict in the play between the Christian Saint and the blind couple is a dramatic treatment of the debates between St. Patrick, representing the new forces of Christianity making changes in the land, and Oisin, aged survivor of the Fenian warriors. In these traditional dialogues, Oisin is the spokesman for a world of pagan values of which he is the sole survivor but which he vigorously defends. David Krause developed the Oisin/St. Patrick connection in his important essay '"The Rageous Ossean": Patron-Hero of Synge and O'Casey,' where he established the debate between them as the primary example of the dialectic between Christian and pagan values from the Irish literary past.[52] In these narratives, the Fenian hero has returned after a three hundred-year sojourn in Tír na nÓg, the Land of Youth or Celtic Otherworld, to an Ireland demythologized and Christianized, with Patrick as its spokesman. He is no longer the fine physical specimen preserved in Tír na nÓg; having once more come into contact with the earth, he is old, feeble, and blind. The paradox by which a blind old man like Synge's Martin Doul can be said to inhabit the Land of Youth is resolved through this image of Oisin. Although physically much debilitated, what remains as vital and undiminished as ever is his imaginative apprehension of the natural world, his unabashed celebration of the senses and delight in the peculiarities of existence – a vision like that shared by Martin and Mary Doul in Synge's play.

So I argued in an essay, 'The Two Worlds of Synge' s *The Well of the Saints*,' that Synge was not only identifying Martin Doul with the figure of Oisin but further representing, through the ironic cure by which he and Mary are disillusioned, the 'fall' from the pagan world of the Fianna and the Celtic Otherworld into a Christianized world in which the oppressive vision of Patrick dominates.[53] Vivian Mercier has suggested as a mythic archetype for the action of the play that of the biblical Fall of Man: the blind couple are expelled from a visionary state into a postlapsarian world where they must labour in the sweat of their brow and where they become only too conscious of the burden of mortality.[54] I think this theory does justice to the world into which they fall but less so to that from which they are banished, particularly when a Christian Saint is the agent of their expulsion. A sustained comparison between what they perceive when blind and what they confront when cured will bear this out. When Martin and Mary Doul were blind, they were given gold and silver for their storytelling; when they can see, they must labour. When blind, they appeared to each other as the finest man and the finest woman, Mary in particular with her 'yellow hair', her 'white beautiful skin [...] on your neck and on your brows' (III, 71); when they can see each other, they behold a pair of tattered scarecrows, 'things would make the heavens lonesome above, and they scaring the larks, and the crows' (III, 99). When deprived of physical sight, their mind's eye constructed visions, as their correspondingly heightened other senses brought to them 'the sound of one of them twittering yellow birds do be coming in the spring-time from beyond the sea' (III, 131). The gold and silver, a beautiful fair-haired woman, the singing birds, the opened natural store of the earth's fecundity – all of these things are specific elements of the pagan nature-poetry of the Fianna and of the otherworld, a celebration of physical beauty in a natural morality devoid of Christian overtones.

It is to just such a perspective that Martin and Mary are restored in Act Three. The knowledge of each other's physical decrepitude that accompanied their 'cure' would appear to present too great an obstacle to imaginative conversion now that their sight has failed once more. But as these 'saints' of the eternal imagination gaze into 'a well, or a clear pool, maybe' (III, 129), the abundance of luxuriant white hair verbally reflected by those visionary waters is finer than the actual, since unsullied by it.

A dissonant note is introduced when the *'faint sound of a bell is heard'* (III, 133). This sound of the bell signals the re-entry of the Saint (Patrick) into the play and threatens the destruction of the pagan vision Martin and Mary have only just succeeded in re-establishing. As Krause pointed out, one of 'the countless ways in which the Fenian life is superior to the cleric's austere Christianity' is marked by Oisin's contrasting 'the melodious songs of the blackbirds and thrushes with the gloomy bells of St. Patrick'.55 The prospect of the Saint's return leads to the most heartfelt prayer in *The Well of the Saints:* 'The Lord protect us from the saints of God!' (III, 133). Furthermore, whereas Martin submitted meekly, even eagerly, the first time, he is now in a defiant mood, willing to challenge the authority of a Christian saint in order to defend his hallowed imaginative ground. Forced to kneel and be cured a second time, 'MARTIN DOUL *with a sudden movement strikes the can from SAINT's hand and sends it rocketing across stag'* (III, 147). The stark simplicity of this action stands in marked contrast to the hurried and overdone physical rough stuff at the close of *The Tinker's Wedding.* Here, the Saint's person is physically respected while the symbol of his spiritual power is definitively rejected. In this last heroic stand, and the eloquence it inspires in him, Martin most completely incarnates the spirit of Oisin:

> Go on now, holy father, for if you're a fine saint itself, it's more sense is in a blind man, and more power maybe than you're thinking at all. [...] [If it's] a right some of you have to be fasting and praying and talking holy talk the like of yourself, I'm thinking it's a good right ourselves have to be sitting blind, hearing a soft wind turning round the little leaves of the spring and feeling the sun, and we not tormenting our souls with the sight of the grey days, and the holy men, and the dirty feet is trampling the world. (III, 149)

Despite its claim to be a revival, there was very little the Irish Literary Renaissance could look to in the native tradition by way of precedent and example in the area of drama. Douglas Hyde argued in his *A Literary History of Ireland* of 1899 that 'the Irish never developed a drama. The nearest approach to such a thing is in [the] Ossianic poems'.[56] Declan Kiberd has demonstrated in detail 'Synge's debts to the work of Douglas Hyde, in particular his scholarly use of *A Literary History of Ireland*'.[57] So Hyde's argument with respect to a native Irish drama would have had a particular impact on Synge:

> The dialogue between St. Patrick and Ossian ... is quite dramatic in its form. Even the reciters of the present day appear to feel this, and I have heard the censorious, selfsatisfied tone of Patrick, and the querulous vindictive whine of the half-starved old man, reproduced with considerable humour by a reciter. ... The conception of bringing the spirit of Paganism and of Christianity together in the persons of the last great poet and warrior of the one, and the first great saint of the other, was truly dramatic in its conception, and the spirit and humour ... in the pieces which have come down to us are a strong presumption that under happier circumstances something great would have developed from it.[58]

Five years after Hyde's *Literary History* was published, something 'great' and 'truly dramatic in its conception' emerged with the staging of Synge's elaborately Ossianic *The Well of the Saints* at the new Abbey Theatre.

Synge's apotheosis as a playwright came with *The Playboy of the Western World*, immediately in terms of the first-week riots it engendered and generally as the most complex and achieved of his dramas. In a letter to *The Irish Times* written four days after the famous opening night, Synge made a rare public pronouncement on his work: 'There are, it may be hinted, several sides to "The Playboy"' (CL I, 286). The truth of its creator's statement has been borne out by the apparent inexhaustibility of the play when it comes to interpretation. The principles of ironic qualification and contradiction that Synge has built into the fabric of *The Playboy* ensure that no one line of interpretation can claim to be exhaustive, since any train of imagery or symbolic reference that a critic may start to trace is bound not to complete itself or else be disrupted and brought into conflict by another. One example of this in *The Playboy* is its treatment of the theme of Christianity and paganism.

The lines at first, as we acclimatize ourselves to the Mayo shebeen and its inhabitants on this particular night, seem clearly drawn. The one consistent spokesman for Catholic beliefs as promulgated by the local priest, Father Reilly, is Shawn Keogh, Pegeen's fiancé. What constitutes the traditional comic obstacle to an imminent marriage between the pair, opening up a delaying gap into which a more appropriate suitor will step, is never explicitly indicated. Whatever it may be (an earlier draft suggested they were first cousins), the obstacle requires 'Father Reilly' s dispensation from the bishops or the Court of Rome' (IV, 59). Synge did not bother to specify since he was evidently more concerned to establish the literalism with which the question of the satisfactoriness or unsatisfactoriness of the match is proposed. He and the play suggest other and more convincing grounds for choice: the spineless, endlessly whining Shawn Keogh is no match for the lively, spirited Pegeen Mike. She counters his references to Father Reilly and the pope with a lament for the passing of pugnacious men who would knock 'the eye from a peeler' or would prove 'a great warrant to tell stories' (IV, 59). When she asks him to stay the night as her protector, Shawn's cringing refusal, couched in response to what he imagines Father Reilly would say, carries within it Synge's Protestant critique of the oppressive system of hierarchical authority, proceeding from the local priest via the bishops to the Court of Rome, to which the individual Catholic conscience is subject and which has, if Shawn is anything to go by, an emasculating effect. But the contrast is even more that between the servile Christianity of the present and a more authentic pagan past, which would yield flesh-and-blood heroes willing to stand up and defend themselves. The ground is being prepared for the arrival of Christy Mahon, the locals' acclaim for his father-slaying and the rapid development of his romance with Pegeen.

This opening exchange between Pegeen and Shawn is amplified with the entrance of her father, Michael James, and his drinking companions. They enlarge on the scorn directed at Shawn for his fear of incurring the priest's disapproval by elaborating a scapegoating game and threatening to make him stay:

> MICHAEL [*catching him by the coat-tail*]. You'd be going, is it?
> SHAWN [*screaming*]. Leave me go, Michael James, leave me go, you old Pagan, leave me go or I'll get the curse of the priests on you, and of the scarlet-coated bishops of the courts of Rome. [*With a sudden movement he pulls himself out of his coat and disappears out of the door, leaving his coat in* MICHAEL's *hands.*]
> MICHAEL [*turning round, and holding up coat*]. Well, there's the coat of a Christian man. (IV, 65)

On its verbal and physical surface, this scene clearly represents the conflict of Christianity (Shawn Keogh and, by extension, the Catholic priests, bishops, and pope) versus paganism (Pegeen, her 'old Pagan' father and his cronies). But Synge has no sooner demarcated the lines of conflict than he begins, characteristically, to complicate them. The meanspiritedness of their attack on the hapless Shawn and the disparity in strength of numbers draw a timely rebuke from Pegeen: 'What right

have you to be making game of a poor fellow for minding the priest?'
(IV, 65).

But the play's more consistent and developed approach to
Christianity is to affirm at a more archetypal level what its characters
verbally asperse or disparage. When Shawn has earlier reported that he
passed by 'a kind of fellow above in the furzy ditch, groaning wicked like
a maddening dog' (IV, 61), Pegeen's reply draws on the parable of the
Good Samaritan, as more than one critic has pointed out: 'And you
never went near to see was he hurted or what ailed him at all?' (IV, 61).
This use of the biblical archetype as implicit model for behaviour does
not contradict the disparagement of Christianity if we regard the first as
a Protestant affirmation of the Bible against the legalism, literalism,
and hierarchical decision-making of the Roman Catholic Church. But at
another level it sets up a disturbing tension between the play's
fluctuating affirmation and denial of Christianity.

The most widespread use of biblical archetypes noted by critics has
been the suggestive parallels between Christy, son of Mahon ('a name
pronounced as if almost of one syllable, Maan'[59]) and Christ, son of
Man. Howard D. Pearce's important essay 'Synge's Playboy as Mock-
Christ' examines the process by which the unlikely, impoverished figure
taken in by the Mayo people gradually discloses a messianic identity
that offers a 'kind of salvation' to various of the play's characters.[60] This
is truest where the women are concerned: three 'stranger girls' who
have heard the legend of the father-slayer travel to meet him and bring
a series of gifts that 'effectively parody the gifts of the Magi'.[61] The
Widow Quin may be redeemed if she can persuade Christy to marry her
and save her from the worst fate Synge can imagine, loneliness and
isolation in the face of an approaching death. Pegeen is offered an
escape from the materialistic bargain with the unsatisfactory Shawn
Keogh into the romantic fulfilment of a life with Christy. But Synge's
play also shows Christy's impact on the community as a whole; his
storytelling fires up the rich imaginations of these literally
impoverished people, whose existence is not only on the edge of the
Western world but on the margins of survival itself. Christy's apotheosis
occurs at the climax of the races, when they carry him on their
shoulders in a scene reminiscent of Christ's Palm Sunday acclamation.
There is an equally precipitate fall, whereby the crowd, feeling he has
betrayed their belief, turn on him and come within inches of putting
him to death – by rope and by fire. But Christy rises up in the last of the
play's numerous death-and-resurrection scenes patented by old Mahon

and proclaims the new life they have made possible for him, as he gives his final blessing:

> Ten thousand blessings upon all that's here, for you've turned me a likely gaffer in the end of all, the way I'll go romancing through a romping lifetime from this hour to the dawning of the judgement day. (IV, 173)

This speech also indicates the way Synge uses biblical references to extend the play's sense of time and place from the local to the universal ('from this hour to the dawning of the judgement day'). But even in a relatively straight reading of the Christ/Christy parallel, it is impossible to suppress completely the disturbing ironic disruptions that refuse to confirm and complete the parallel. Mary C. King best described Synge's method of deploying the Bible by remarking how the 'dramatic strategy' draws 'its symbolic strength from the Bible and at the same time stands the sacred text on its head'.[62] It does so through Synge's characteristic use of irony, parody, and inversion, reflecting a modernist tendency to refer selectively to biblical motifs without endorsing a one-on-one identification of meaning or implying an entire value system (cf. Beckett's use of biblical references in *Waiting for Godot* [1953]).

In *The Playboy,* what prevents a thoroughly Christian interpretation are the pagan elements that persistently obtrude at every level – most notoriously, the father-slaying for which Christy is applauded, not condemned, *and* the vision of endless women, 'a drift of chosen females, standing in their shifts itself maybe' (IV, 167), at which the opening night audience broke up in disorder. Anyone who knows Irish literature will find this speech echoing the incident in the Ulster saga whereby the warrior Cuchulain, still in the throes of a battle-rage, was finally calmed (and abashed) by the sight of thirty naked virgins sent from Emain Macha. Declan Kiberd drew on this incident as part of a detailed comparison, first suggested by Michael J. Sidnell, between Christy Mahon, the champion of the Western world, and Cuchulain, the Red Branch hero of the Ulster court.[63] Like Cuchulain, Christy, too, according to Kiberd, 'is filled with the battle-rage of triumph after the sports and his frantic speech recalls the parade of chosen virgins at Emain Macha'.[64]

Other mythic avatars for Christy's pagan heroism have been put forth. Kiberd, in a separate essay, 'The Frenzy of Christy', has suggested a parallel with mad Sweeney, whose poem pivots around a similar pagan/Christian contrast to those of Oisin and St. Patrick.[65] Toni O'Brien Johnson has looked outside the Irish tradition to *Sir Gawain and the Green Knight,* identifying Christy with the 'green man' or fertility figure.[66] The point, surely, is that no single figure from the legends can be unequivocally identified with Christy. In this play, Synge's procedure differs from the unmistakable centrality of the Oisin/St. Patrick myth to *The Well of the Saints*. If Martin Doul draws strength from the identification, here the process is reversed and Christy subsumes his great number of heroic predecessors, drawing on their mythic energies but reshaping them in his own name and image. The technique is best exemplified by one of Synge's poems, 'Queens':

> Seven dog-days we let pass
> Naming Queens in Glenmacnass,
> All the rare and royal names
> Wormy sheepskin yet retains,
> Etain, Helen, Maeve, and Fand,
> Golden Deirdre's tender hand, ...
> Yet these are rotten – I ask their pardon –
> And we've the sun on rock and garden,
> These are rotten, so you're the Queen
> Of all are living, or have been. (I, 34)

The area in which *The Playboy of the Western World* most richly mixes its Christian and pagan elements is in the love talk between Christy and Pegeen. In her presence, he declares himself 'a good Christian' (IV, 149) and appears to demonstrate it by the fervour of his praying, which has the petitioning force of a litany (like the naming in 'Queens') and is irradiated by liturgical imagery: 'Isn't there the light of seven heavens in your heart alone, the way you'll be an angel's lamp to me from this out' (IV, 149). But a subtle process of subversion is underway whereby the traditional imagery of worship shifts, in the manner of courtly love, from the divine to the human, and the love object is invested with the sacramental charisma of prayer. When Martin Doul considered the role of the Saint and acknowledged considerable affinities with the man of God in their mutual quest for a spiritual reality, he finally drew back from the comparison on the grounds that 'if bell-ringing is a fine life, [...] it's better I am wedded with the beautiful dark woman of Ballinatone' (III, 87). Similarly, the true paradise Christy seeks, for all the symbolic energy it draws from the Christian Heaven, is the one that is shared – and created – between a man and a woman. In Christy's and Synge's most audacious inversion, the lovers' otherworld renders the Christian equivalent a place of isolation and confinement, more Hell than Heaven. Christy thus talks of 'squeezing kisses on your puckered lips till I'd feel a kind of pity for the Lord God is all ages sitting lonesome in his golden chair' (IV, 147). Synge expressed almost identical sentiments in his poem 'Dread':

> Beside a chapel I'd a room looked down,
> Where all the women from the farms and town,
> On Holy-days, and Sunday used to pass
> To marriages, and Christenings and to Mass.
> Then I sat lonely watching score and score,
> Till I turned jealous of the Lord next door....
> Now by this window, where there's none can see,
> The Lord God's jealous of yourself and me. (I, 40)

The four periods mark not only a dramatic pause before the poem's triumphant reversal of situation and mood but also the two-year gap before he had met Molly Allgood and added the last two lines.[67]

Synge sensed his own approaching death and wrote several epitaphs marred by excessive self-pity and literary self-consciousness. His question 'Will you go to my funeral?' provoked a response from his fiancée that he turned into one of his finest poems, drawing as in his plays on the speech of others as a means of freeing up his own powers of self-expression. The poem 'A Question' serves as fitting epitaph. Synge, as Yeats remarked, 'was not sure of any world to come'.[68] Yet his end was marked with a Church of Ireland funeral acknowledging the Protestant dimension of his life. But the enduring conflict between those beliefs and the pagan passion he sought to express in his writings is finely caught in the living speech of the woman he loved:

> I asked if I got sick and died, would you
> With my black funeral go walking too,
> If you'd stand close to hear them talk or pray
> While I'm let down in that steep bank of clay.
>
> And, No, you said, for if you saw a crew
> Of living idiots, pressing round that new
> Oak coffin – they alive, I dead beneath
> That board, – you'd rave and rend them with your teeth. (I, 64)

---

[1] Synge Manuscripts, Trinity College, Dublin, MS 4382, ff. 51-2.

[2] Synge Manuscripts, TCD, MS 4382, ff. 51-2.

[3] See Declan Kiberd, *Synge and the Irish Language* (London: Macmillan, 1979), *passim*.

[4] Synge Manuscripts, TCD, MS 4378, Notebook 10, f. 49.

[5] Maurice Bourgeois, *John Millington Synge and the Irish Theatre* (London: Constable, 1913), p. 218.

[6] David H. Greene and Edward M. Stephens, *J.M. Synge 1871-1909* (New York: Macmillan, 1959), p. 16.

[7] Vivian Mercier, 'Victorian Evangelicalism and the Anglo-Irish Literary Revival', *Literature and the Changing Ireland*, edited by Peter Connolly (Gerrards Cross: Colin Smythe; New York: Barnes and Noble, 1982), p. 61.

[8] See David H. Greene and Edward M. Stephens, *J.M. Synge 1871-1909*, p. 16.
[9] *My Uncle John: Edward Stephens's Life of J.M. Synge*, edited by Andrew Carpenter (London: Oxford University Press, 1974), p. 34.
[10] Weldon Thornton, *J.M. Synge and the Western Mind* (Gerrards Cross, Bucks.: Colin Smythe, 1979), p, 34.
[11] Weldon Thornton, *J.M. Synge and the Western Mind*, p. 32.
[12] Synge Manuscripts, TCD, MS 4832, v. 59; II, 4-5.
[13] Synge Manuscripts, TCD, MS 4378, f. 50.
[14] Weldon Thornton, *J.M. Synge and the Western Mind*, p. 40.
[15] Mary C. King, *The Drama of J.M. Synge* (Syracuse: Syracuse University Press, 1985), p. 6.
[16] The editor of the Prose volume, Alan Price, has replaced 'made' with '[man-]made'. I have gone back to the original.
[17] Synge Manuscripts, TCD, MS 4382, f. 53.
[18] Synge Manuscripts, TCD, MS 4382, v. 52.
[19] Declan Kiberd, *Synge and the Irish Language*, p. 168.
[20] Synge Manuscripts, TCD, MS4378, notebook 10, f. 49.
[21] Cited Vivian Mercier, 'Victorian Evangelicanism and the Anglo-Irish Literary Revival', p. 62.
[22] As cartographer Tim Robinson has observed in his edition of *The Aran Islands*, 'nowadays the name Aranmore is reserved for the island off Co. Donegal,' while the biggest of the three Aran Islands is now habitually referred to as Inishmore, 'a name first introduced by the Ordnance Survey in 1839'. For consistency, I will use Synge's designation of the island as 'Aranmor' throughout. See J.M. Synge, *The Aran Islands*, edited and with an introduction by Tim Robinson (London: Penguin, 1992), p. vii.
[23] On how 'primitivism' was in transition from a romantic to a scientific discipline, and how this change impacted on Synge, see Sinéad Garrigan Mattar, *Primitivism, Science and the Irish Revival* (Oxford and New York: Clarendon Press, 2004). For a related study of Revivalist ethnography in relation to Synge's *The Aran Islands*, see Gregory Castle, *Modernism and the Celtic Revival* (Cambridge: Cambridge University Press, 2001).
[24] Daniel Corkery, *Synge and Anglo-Irish Literature: A Study* (Dublin and Cork: Cork University Press; London: Longmans, Green, 1931), pp. 111-112.
[25] Maurice Bourgeois, *John Millington Synge and the Irish Theatre* (London: Constable, 1913), pp. 218-219.
[26] Cf. Nicholas Grene, *The Politics of Irish Drama: Plays in Context from Boucicault to Friel* (Cambridge: Cambridge University Press, 1999), p. 104: 'Synge wrote as the unbeliever he was, and gave to his characters a colourful language of the sacred emptied out of belief.'

27 J.N. Hillgarth (editor), *Christianity and Paganism. 350-750: The Conversion of Western Europe* (Philadelphia: University of Pennsylvania Press, 1969), p. 117.

28 J.N. Hillgarth, *Christianity and Paganism*, p. 120.

29 Walter Benjamin, 'The Storyteller', *Illuminations*, translated by Harry Zohn, edited by Hannah Arendt (New York: Schocken, 1969), pp. 83-109.

30 Mary C. King, *The Drama of J.M. Synge*, p. 24.

31 Denis Donoghue, 'Synge: *Riders to the Sea*: A Study', *University Review* 1 (1955), p. 46. Reprinted in David R. Clark (editor*), John Millington Synge: Riders to the Sea*, The Merrill Literary Casebook Series (Columbus: Charles E. Merrill, 1970), pp. 46-53.

32 Robin Skelton, *J.M. Synge*, The Irish Writers Series (Lewisburg, Pa.: Bucknell University Press, 1972), p. 32.

33 Kuno Meyer (editor and translator), *The Voyage of Bran Son of Febal*, 2 volumes (London: David Nutt, 1895) pp. 16, 18-20.

34 Declan Kiberd, *Synge and the Irish Language*, p. 165.

35 Declan Kiberd, *Synge and the Irish Language*, p. 167.

36 See, for example, David R. Clark. 'Synge's "Perpetual Last Day": Remarks on *Riders to the Sea*', in S.B. Bushrui (editor), *A Centenary Tribute to John Millington Synge, 1871-1909: Sunshine and the Moon's Delight* (Gerrards Cross: Colin Smythe: New York: Barnes and Noble, 1972), p. 43.

37 Nicholas Grene, *Synge: A Critical Study of the Plays* (London: Macmillan, 1975), p. 54.

38 Prionsias MacCana, *Celtic Mythology* (London: Newnes, 1983), pp. 127-128.

39 Robin Skelton, *The Writings of J.M. Synge* (Indianapolis and New York: Bobbs-Merrill, 1971), p. 51.

40 Nicholas Grene, *Synge: A Study of the Plays*, p. 56.

41 Declan Kiberd, *Synge and the Irish Language*, pp. 167-168.

42 Robin Skelton, *The Writings of J.M. Synge*, p. 51.

43 Vivian Mercier, '*The Tinker's Wedding*', in *A Centenary Tribute to John Millington Synge, 1871-1909*, p. 79.

44 Maurice Bourgeois, *John Millington Synge and the Irish Theatre*, p. 182.

45 Denis Johnston, *John Millington Synge* (New York and London: Columbia University Press, 1965), p. 27.

46 See Nicholas Grene (editor), *The Well of the Saints by J.M. Synge*, Irish Dramatic Texts (Washington,D.C.: The Catholic University of America Press; Gerrards Cross, Bucks.: Colin Smythe, 1982), p. 57.

47 Nicholas Grene, *The Well of the Saints by J.M. Synge*, p. 28.

[48] William G. Fay and Catherine Carswell, *The Fays of the Abbey Theatre: An Autobiographical Record* (New York: Harcourt Brace; London: Rich and Cowan, 1935), p. 31.

[49] Maurice Bourgeois, *John Millington Synge and the Irish Theatre*, p. 182.

[50] Vivian Mercier, 'Victorian Evangelicanism and the Anglo-Irish Literary Revival', p, 88.

[51] Nicholas Grene, '*The Well of the Saints by J.M. Synge*', p.13.

[52] David Krause, '"The Rageous Ossean": Patron-Hero of Synge and O'Casey', *Modern Drama* 4:3 (1961), pp. 268-291.

[53] Anthony Roche, 'The Two Worlds of Synge's *The Well of the Saints*', *Genre* 12 (1979), pp. 439-450. Reprinted in book form as Ronald Schliefer (editor), *The Genres of the Irish Literary Revival* (Norman, Ok., Pilgrim Books; Dublin: Wolfhound Press, 1980).

[54] Vivian Mercier, '*The Tinker's Wedding*', p.82.

[55] David Krause, '"The Rageous Ossean": Patron-Hero of Synge and O'Casey,' p. 275.

[56] Douglas Hyde, *A Literary History of Ireland* (London: Unwin, 1899), p. 511.

[57] Declan Kiberd, *Synge and the Irish Language*, p. 149.

[58] Douglas Hyde, *A Literar History of Ireland*, p. 511.

[59] Denis Johnston, *John Millington Synge*, p. 34.

[60] Harold D. Pearce, 'Synge's Playboy as Mock-Christ', *Modern Drama* 8:3 (1965), p. 90. Reprinted in Thomas R. Whitaker (editor), *The Playboy of the Western World: A Collection of Critical Essays*, Twentieth Century Interpretations (Englewood Cliffs, N.J.: Prentice-Hall, 1969), pp. 88-97.

[61] Harold D. Pearce, 'Synge's Playboy as Mock-Christ', p. 91.

[62] Mary C. King, *The Drama of J.M. Synge*, p. 80.

[63] Declan Kiberd, *Synge and the Irish Language*, p. 118.

[64] Declan Kiberd, *Synge and the Irish Language*, pp. 118-119.

[65] Declan Kiberd, 'The Frenzy of Christy: Synge and *Buile Shuibhne*', *Éire-Ireland* 14:2 (1979), pp. 68-79.

[66] Toni O'Brien Johnson, *Synge: The Medieval and the Grotesque* (Gerrards Cross, Bucks.: Colin Smythe; Totowa, N.J.: Barnes and Noble, 1982), p. 66.

[67] David H. Greene and Edward M. Stephens, *J.M. Synge, 1871-1909*, p. 204.

[68] W.B. Yeats, *Mythologies* (New York: Macmillan, 1959), p. 328.

2 | Synge and Germany: Drama as Translation

Many of the Irish writers who created a national literature at the turn of the previous century forged links with the Continent. In doing so, they were aware of how in earlier centuries Irish monks and missionaries had gone out from the small island to the European mainland, both to receive education and to disseminate a little known culture. James Joyce, in a lecture delivered in Trieste in April 1907, developed this theme, by referring to the 'very ancient times, when the island was a true centre of intellectualism and sanctity, that spread its culture and stimulating energy throughout the continent'.[1] His comments make clear that Joyce, however unlikely a prospect this may appear, saw himself as a latter-day representative in that tradition. He noted that 'the Irish nation's desire to create its own civilization is not so much the desire of a young nation wishing to link itself to Europe's concert, but the desire by an ancient nation to renew in a modern form the glories of a past civilization'.[2] In this remark, Joyce identifies the Irish impetus towards the continent as a conscious step in the decolonizing process and seems to claim it as something held in common by Irish writers striving to create a new civilization. This sense of a shared aim among Revival authors, one in which Joyce is proud to claim kinship, needs to be set against the overly familiar remarks in the 1901 broadside, 'The Day of the Rabblement', where Joyce is rude at their expense. Douglas Hyde's 1892 lecture, 'On the Necessity for DeAnglicizing Ireland', which has been read by Declan Kiberd as a 'declaration of cultural independence',[3] assumed that the best way to deanglicize and so to decolonize was to speak Irish and to emulate all things Irish. The Irish Literary Revival may have seemed to follow this route, by writing a literature in English but one which adhered closely to Irish linguistic and cultural models, where Joyce by contrast was determined to reject the Celtic Twilight and embrace an Ibsenian modernity. But Joyce's work may be said to have done both, since it Europeanizes even while it remains distinctively Irish. The Irish National Theatre inaugurated by the opening of the Abbey Theatre in Dublin in 1904 was to do no less, especially through the work of John Millington Synge.

Of the three writers associated with the theatre movement, Yeats adhered most to the Anglo-Irish axis. For one thing he resolutely refused to speak any language other than English. George Yeats surmised in 1949 to Canadian scholar Donald Pearce: 'W.B. liked to be decisive and impressive when he spoke. He couldn't bear stumbling about in a language as a beginner. And that, I would think, would make it impossible for him to get started in a foreign language [...] even to speak commonplaces.'4 Nevertheless, Yeats throughout his life and career manifested an insatiable curiosity about foreign languages, one which always reveals a curiously gendered configuration, whereby a woman translator mediates between Yeats and the foreign other by translating it into words he can understand, by acting as a linguistic medium. Thus, in 1894, at the Paris production of Villiers de l'Isle Adam's symbolist play, *Axël* (which ran for five hours) Yeats was accompanied by Maud Gonne, who supplied a simultaneous translation.5 George Yeats was the source of Yeats's firsthand knowledge of the plays of Pirandello, and also (as Seamus Deane has remarked) of the only foreign language in which Yeats became adept, the occult. Lady Gregory not only supplied Yeats with translations from the Irish but also read and translated Goethe for him. Gregory's own translations into Kiltartan English of Molière's French and Goldoni's Italian are a clear indication of the European dimension of the Abbey's early years.

Of the three Abbey Theatre directors, it is John Millington Synge who proved the most practised and fluent in continental languages and literature. In Synge's *Collected Letters*, the first eight letters are in German, the next fifteen in French, and several more in Italian before the opening section concludes. Only when writing to Maud Gonne (in Paris) on 6 April 1897 is Synge forced to use English. The first letter in his *Collected Letters* has been dated February 1894, when Synge was already twenty-two, since his earlier letters have not survived; and this makes the fact of his working through various languages all the more striking. As an undergraduate student at Trinity College, Dublin, Synge's degree subjects were Hebrew and Irish; and he had also taken private lessons in German from 1891 on as an accompaniment to his study of music at Dublin's Royal Irish Academy of Music. By the time of the first extant published correspondence, Synge had graduated from Trinity and had moved to Germany to pursue a career as a musician.

The various languages in the *Collected Letters* mirror those of the countries in which he was staying – Germany, France, Italy – and show his determination to write in the language of the culture in which he was residing rather than remaining a determined linguistic Anglophile. This practice is more familiar from Synge's later and more famous visits to the Irish-speaking Aran Islands and West Kerry, but was clearly a long-established practice with him.

Synge's correspondence in German is written from his residence in Wurzburg to the von Eicken family in Oberwerth, with whom he had stayed when he first arrived in the country. He appears to have carried on a semi-flirtation with Valeska, the youngest of the six von Eicken sisters and the one who taught him German. Synge goes to great lengths to explain why his letters to her in German may have appeared more intimate and confidential than he intended:

> I think that the other letter which I wrote to you was a thoroughly silly, absurd, tasteless epistle, but I have been terribly sentimental for a few weeks. Further you must understand that I have to write such well-behaved, sensible letters to Ireland I find it very pleasant just as I am doing now to be able to talk straight out of my head (or rather heart) about all kinds of silly and foolish things without caution and quite informally (CL I, 11; trans. Paul Botheroyd).

The irony here is considerable – only in a foreign language (German) can Synge write what he truly feels, 'from the heart'; in his 'native' English only the most formal of sentiments can be expressed. Mary King has written of 'the introverted and censoring character of Anglo-Irish evangelicalism'[6] and quoted Synge's nephew and biographer Edward Stephens on the household run by the dramatist's mother: 'So strict was her rule that it almost paralysed language as an expression of feeling.'[7] King surmises that Synge's initial attraction to music was as a means of escape but one that he came to fear would provide 'too nearly a physical intoxication'.[8] His profound decision to change from the study and practice of music to literature was made in Germany and while the official reason given was that he suffered too much from nerves ever to sustain a full-time career as a performer, there may well have been a decision on his part to re-engage with the matter of language, this time from a multilingual perspective.

Synge's period in Germany during the years 1893 and 1894 has been given insufficient attention, at least until the 2000 biography by W. J. McCormack. It has conventionally been seen as the merest of interludes, and the main European focus in Synge studies has been his time in Paris, where he spent much of the following eight years. In terms of his lengthy sojourn on the Continent, where are the seeds of Synge's own interest in the drama to be located?

Again, the year in Germany proves crucial. For when Synge went there in July of 1893, at the age of twenty-two, he does not appear ever to have stepped inside a theatre. In this, he was at one with the other members of his evangelical family and their friends, who continued this cultural boycott even after Synge began to have his own plays produced at the Abbey Theatre. W.J. McCormack's chapter entitled 'Escaping Home Rule in Germany' (1893-1894) indicates how much of Synge's year there furnished his first encounter with drama and the theatre.[9] On 30 October 1894 he attended a performance of Goethe's verse-play, *Iphigenie auf Tauris*, a translation of Greek tragedy – his *Riders to the Sea* was to owe a considerable debt to Greek tragedy. The following month he saw another German Romantic verse-drama, Schiller's *Die Jungfrau von Orleans*, about a persecuted visionary, like so many of the characters in Synge's plays.

As well as repeated exposure to live theatre and to the classics and themes of the past in translation, it was in Germany that Synge first read the plays of the most acclaimed and notorious dramatist of the age, Henrik Ibsen. His notebooks record that in Oberwerth he read *The Pillars of Society*, *A Doll's House*, *Peer Gynt*, and *Rosmersholm*. McCormack writes:

> His diary names the plays in German. As he was saturating himself in the language and had little access to books in English, we can conclude that he used German translations. Or, to be precise, if he had been reading Ibsen in English [presumably, McCormack means in the period before Synge came to Germany, back in Ireland] then he postponed any record of the fact until he got away from home for the first time.[10]

Synge's attitude to Ibsen is a complex, ambiguous one and has frequently been misconstrued as entirely or mainly negative. The main reason is Synge's statement in the preface to *The Playboy of the Western World* that Ibsen (who is paired in this respect with Zola) dealt 'with the reality of life in joyless and pallid words', whereas for Synge 'in a good play every speech should be as fully flavoured as a nut or apple' (IV, 53-54). What Synge is anxious to do in this rare public pronouncement, written in the immediate aftermath of *The Playboy* riots, is to make a claim for the authenticity of his dramatic speech in terms of its Irishness and to keep at arm's length any possible suggestion of foreign influence. But early and late the figure of Ibsen haunts Synge's drama, not least because he performs what Synge regards as the most valuable artistic imperative: he 'deal[s] with the reality of life' (IV, 53). As Synge remarked in a letter to Stephen McKenna:

> On [the] French stage you get sex without its balancing elements: on [the] Irish stage you [get] the other elements without sex. I restored sex and the people were so surprised they saw the sex only. [...] no drama can grow out of anything other than the fundamental realities of life. (CL I, 76)

The objection against which Synge is defending his drama is the same one levelled against Ibsen's plays throughout Europe. He is referring in the letter to McKenna to his own *The Shadow of the Glen*, which had been staged in Dublin the previous year to the accompaniment of walkouts and resignations because in it a wife called Nora had stood up to criticize her own marriage, and by extension the entire bourgeois institution, and at the close of the play had walked out the door on her husband, accompanied by a tramp. How much has Synge's objection to the language of Ibsen's plays as 'joyless and pallid words' to do with the fact that he read them not in the Norwegian original (as the eighteen-year-old James Joyce was to do) but in German translation? The supposition is that in Ibsen's original the language was richer and that much of its local idiom was flattened out in translation; something that Synge himself had to deal with when his own plays were translated into German. Ibsen's plays dealt with the reality of life, an artistic aim of which Synge approved and which he sought to emulate when he undertook the writing of plays for an Irish theatre. But if his and Ibsen's language were the same, then where would the difference be? This is the reason, I think, why Synge stressed the absolute difference between Ibsen's use of language and his own, to create the ground of difference between them. And not every speech in a Synge play is 'as fully flavoured as a nut or an apple', though many of his detractors and parodists would have it so. The dramatic language which Synge was to fashion for his plays covers a variety of linguistic registers and moves ceaselessly between a high and a low style. Synge was introduced to Ibsen via translation. But, as has already been suggested, translation is crucial to Synge's own artistic endeavour (and would become even more so when he founded so much of his own syntactic construction and linguistic usage in English on direct translation from the Irish). So Synge would be a translator of Ibsen, not into a German but into an Irish linguistic context.

It was during this first year in Germany that – no doubt stimulated by the experience of live theatre and by his reading of Ibsen – Synge attempted writing his first play. A diary entry for 25 April 1894 reads, in

German, 'Plan for a play', and that for 12 May of the same year, 'Began writing a play' (III, 181). All that survives is the plan or prose outline, which was translated from German into English by Edward Stephens during his work on the biography of his uncle. It has become known as 'the Wurzburg fragment' and stands as the first of the 'Scenarios, Dialogues and Fragments' scrupulously assembled by editor Ann Saddlemyer and dated 1894-1908, the last full working year of Synge's life (III, 181-2). Of the fifteen items contained in this section of the *Collected Plays*, all but the first two are dated 1902 and later. In other words, for almost a decade after Synge turned from music to literature and declared his vocation as a writer, there survive only two pieces of evidence that drama would become the means by which he would make his reputation. In the main, during this period he produced the poems and prose impressions to which Yeats referred when criticizing Synge's literary production up to the time of their meeting in 1896.

Although Synge's draft for his play amounts to little more than two pages, there is much in it that is prophetic and revealing. For one thing, even though written in German, it is not set in Germany. Unlike the prose pieces in French, which take place in Paris, the Würzburg fragment has an Irish setting and begins with the introduction of a 'young clever man who is fed up with London life and wishes to enjoy nature and art on a farm in Ireland' (III, 181). The repudiation of a shallow cosmopolitan existence in a foreign country in favour of a return from exile to an authentic existence in one's own native country: these are precisely the terms in which Yeats claimed he was to advise Synge some nineteen months later. The familiar London/Ireland axis when cast into a drama also makes one reflect on the Anglo-Irish playwrights who had so far won favour by moving from Ireland to England and leading a 'London life', as Wilde and Shaw (and, to a considerable extent, Yeats) were doing during this decade. Synge's relocation from Ireland to Germany and thence to France, gave him an opportunity to look from an alternative Continental perspective at the usual colonial fate of the Anglo-Irish playwrights in becoming (as both Stephen Dedalus and Joyce put it) 'a jester at the court of his master'.[11] The proposed play would suggest that a return to Ireland – and the embrace of an authentically Irish subject matter – was on the cards for Synge, long before he met Yeats. The fragment has most in common with Synge's first completed play, *When the Moon Has Set*, in that it dramatizes directly, in the form of transposed autobiography, many of the features of Synge's class, religious, and family background.

The 'clever young man' is identified as a property owner when 'his agent comes to him and tells him he has rented a farm to a widow and her daughter' back in Ireland. The Synges had been landowners in Wicklow throughout the nineteenth century but by its close were themselves renting property on land they had previously owned. They still had holdings in the west of Ireland, and McCormack's biography frequently juxtaposes Synge's admiring and idealizing visits to the Aran Islands with the contrasting behaviour of his brother Edward on the Galway mainland. As agent and landowner, Edward Synge presided over evictions in both Wicklow and the west of Ireland – the sites of two of the three of Synge's prose sequences. The issues of landowning and of inheritance are also central features of *When the Moon Has Set*. After Synge turned to writing peasant drama in 1902, no member of his own class is represented in his plays. But in the Wurzburg Fragment and in *When the Moon Has Set*, the central romantic conflict directly addresses issues of class and religion in ways more relevant to Synge's own later autobiography than the plays on which his reputation is founded. For the clever young man, fairly predictably and extremely rapidly, falls in love with the young woman whose mother has rented the property. She responds to his overtures without realizing that her admirer and 'the son of the house' are one and the same. The romantic complications are twofold: not only have the hero and heroine to overcome internal differences before they can marry, but there is also the shocked reaction of his family to the courtship, as when 'his sister appears in the background, [and] looks at the pair in amazement' (III, 181).

Synge's meeting with and courtship of the young Abbey actress Molly Allgood lay almost a decade in the future. During the 1890s, the woman he became romantically drawn to (and to whom he proposed marriage) was Cherrie Matheson, daughter in a family of Plymouth Brethren believers who lived near the Synge family. Synge's offer of marriage was rejected by Cherrie Matheson because of his lapsed religious beliefs. The 'clever young man' and the young woman hold their romantic trysts in the woods, but even that idyllic spot is not impervious to social barriers. In Act III a letter is received from 'the sister announcing her forgiveness' (III, 182). Synge's own letters to Molly Allgood, as Chapter Nine will examine in detail, painfully and rather patronizingly describe how he brings various family members, in particular his formidable but loving mother, around to the notion of his relationship with her. The internal obstacles the couple face are never entirely overcome and as Synge's health worsens the plans for a wedding are repeatedly postponed. In the Wurzburg Fragment, the hero and heroine are married, not at the play's close but at the end of Act II. Act III scene I is set in the hero's room: 'He is there alone in a sad mood. He is joined by his wife' [only this description indicates that they have married] 'who thinks he is not pleased with her but he really is dissatisfied with himself.' The romantic union, far from bringing fulfilment, has opened up a gulf of intellectual incompatibility between the pair; this the hero seeks to surmount through his companionship with two brothers, a poet and a ne'er-do-well (a version of the tramp figure familiar from Synge's later plays). The poet is to wed the hero's sister and the play climaxes when 'the hero and his wife join them and rejoice in their union'. In what amounts to a *ménage a quatre*, the hero finally declares 'that what he had missed had been a broader view of mankind and that he had learnt much from the two brothers and that from now on he would be able to live aiming at higher things' (III, 182). The poet in Synge's life would emerge in the figure of Yeats. Both of them clearly had a great deal to teach each other, as the next chapter will discuss. The relationship with Molly Allgood drew equal hostility from Yeats and Lady Gregory, horrified that their fellow director should be fraternizing with the actors, almost all of whom were Catholic. What is so striking about the Würzburg Fragment is that it anticipates and even dramatizes so many of the conflicts in Synge's own later life: the decision to return to Ireland; the effort to marry into the class that would take over from and replace his own; the struggle to break out of inherited narrow creeds into a broader vision of humanity. Its main prophecy is that the writer would become a dramatist, an ambition that was to lie dormant for much of the rest of the decade, but which finds its first and most revealing expression during his year in Germany.

If German was the linguistic medium through which Synge first explored the possibility of writing drama, then it is singularly appropriate that in 1905, in the months after the opening of the new National Theatre in Ireland, the first approach to translating the plays of the movement into a foreign language and thereby reaching a wider audience should come from a German translator. The thirty-year-old theatre critic for the *Neue Zürcher Zeitung*, Max Meyerfeld, approached the (by now established) playwright J. M. Synge and asked to translate *The Well of the Saints* into German. The play did little to impress a Dublin audience, and both houses and response were moderate. But it caught the attention of a visiting French writer Henri Lebeau who promptly wrote and published an appreciative critical notice for *Revue de l'Art Dramatique* in Paris, which was reprinted in the April 1905 issue of *Dana*, still in the original French.

Dana, 'An Irish Magazine of Independent Thought', is mentioned in relation to Synge by one of its editors, John Eglinton, in the National Library chapter of Joyce's *Ulysses*, where the growing importance of the national literary movement is under discussion: '--Synge has promised me an article for *Dana* too. Are we going to be read? I feel we are.'[12] Here, Eglinton means *read* in an international (primarily European) context, of which Synge is the relevant case. More will be said about the relationship between Synge and Joyce in Chapter Four. Cherrie Matheson recalls that Synge thought well of *Dana*: 'He said it was too good to get a paying circulation in Ireland, that Ireland was too remote from the world of thought.'[13] Nothing by Synge ever appeared during *Dana*'s short run of twelve issues during 1904 and 1905. There is some evidence that a piece by Synge on Anatole France was submitted and rejected by Eglinton as 'incorrect'; but since the source is the malicious George Moore, one cannot be sure.[14] Moore was the one who recommended Lebeau's review of *The Well of the Saints* to Max Meyerfeld, who had translated Moore's novels into German. After reading it the translator wrote to Synge requesting permission to translate the play and subsequently talked it up to Max Reinhardt at the Deutsches Theater with the hope of a securing a production in Berlin. Synge responded positively. What his letter to Meyerfeld immediately makes clear is that Synge was proficient in the language and knowledgeable about German culture:

> I should be very glad to have it translated into German but – as you will see – it will not be easy to render adequately a great part of the dialogue which depends for its effect on the peculiar colour-quality of the dialect I have used. I imagine in the German 'Volkslieder' one would get a language that would be pretty nearly what is needed, but when you have read the play you will see for yourself. [...] I know German pretty well – I spent some 13 months in Germany some years ago – and I would be glad to help you in your version in any way I could. (CL I, 111)

Lebeau had described Synge's language in the play as a 'tour de force' and instanced some of the deviations from Standard English that were such a marked feature of the dialect employed: 'Mr. Synge has created a tour de force in drawing a literary work out of such a bizarre language, full of idiomatic phrases and of unusual words, as spoken by peasants in the west of Ireland. [...] Such a transformation into artistic language of a local dialect is probably only possible in Ireland.'[15] Synge's comment on the 'Volkslieder' shows how, rather than completely throwing over one artistic profession for another while in Germany, he carried the idea of music with him into his study and practice of literature. The reference also provides further evidence of the extent to which his visit to Germany provided him with a European model for the possible development of a national drama in Ireland. In most cases, when writers have their work translated from English into a foreign language, they are almost entirely dependent on the literary and linguistic skills of the translator. But English is and is not an Irish writer's native language; rather, it is in Joyce's famous words both 'familiar and foreign'.[16] And if Irish is the original source of the country's linguistic dividedness, it drives a wedge in the imperium of English, which other languages can also fill, towards an ideal of hybridity. As necessary Europeanizing contexts to Synge's studies in Irish should be set his reading in German, French, and Italian; he was later to rework Petrarch's sonnets into his Hiberno-English dialect. When this exchange with Meyerfeld is put alongside the fact that Synge's first attempt at writing a play was undertaken in German, we have a powerful precedent for the peculiar case of Samuel Beckett some forty-odd years later, when that other Trinity-educated Dublin writer turned from prose to the medium of drama and chose to write *En Attendant Godot* in French, before translating it into English. As comments by Beckett attest, and as Chapter Seven will explore, his favourite Synge play was *The Well of the Saints*, with its two marginalized beggars awaiting a miracle and passing the time until then in verbal banter. Synge knew the language into which he was being translated and this led Meyerfeld at the end of the process to remark ruefully: 'You really must know a good deal of German being able to find out where I have made blunders', thanking him for 'reading and correcting my translation. Your suggestions are really excellent and I have used them nearly all.'[17]

No copy is extant of Synge's markings on Meyerfeld's translation. But his letter of 23 September 1905, while showing he clearly respected Meyerfeld as the translator, makes fourteen comments directly addressing the German words and phrases used in the translation. Some are concerned with precise literal meaning: 'Mary Doul's first speech. Would it be better (clearer) to say "Am Loch in der Mauer vorbei." I mean does Loch give the sense of "gap", as definitely an opening in the wall?' (CL I, 132-133). Some have to do with the overall dramatic and aesthetic effect: 'I would be inclined to strike out "*wahrhaftig*," it seems to weaken the speech.' And others give illuminating insight into the substructure of ideas and imagery informing the play: '"Hier in der östlichen Welt." He does not mean here in the east of Ireland, but away in the "eastern world", a sort of wonder-land very often spoken of in Irish folk-tales.' This exchange of letters makes clear that Meyerfeld's translation of *The Well of the Saints* is in striking measure a collaboration with the play's original author.

Despite Synge's own warnings in the letter already quoted and the details in Lebeau's review, neither seems to have prepared Max Meyerfeld for the sheer linguistic and syntactic oddity of *The Well of the Saints*. His letter of 27 May 1905 responds to the script Synge sent him: 'I have read your play with the greatest interest, but I frankly admit the language seemed rather strange to me, and I think it will be extremely difficult to find a German equivalent of it. You could make the translation much easier for me if you would send me an English transcript of the play.' In other words, before Meyerfeld can translate Synge's play into German, he feels Synge should first translate it into English! This is a perverse tribute to the extent to which Synge had fashioned a distinctive dramatic speech of his own, but one whose sheer originality resisted translation. Synge counterclaimed to Meyerfeld that 'I do not think you will find the general language hard to follow when you have done a few pages, as the same idioms are often repeated, and the purely local words are not very numerous' (CL I, 115). He nevertheless concedes that 'it will be a difficult language to translate' and says he will do what he can to help. In the end, Synge provided an English 'translation' for the first four or five pages of the play (the opening exchanges between the blind couple Martin and Mary Doul) and the scene from Act II between Martin and the beautiful young Molly Byrne. Lebeau had declared the latter to be the passage in which the dramatist most revealed himself, as Martin strives but fails to persuade Molly to share his vision. A comparison of the two versions of the Synge play is fascinating, as Synge struggles to rework his stage dialect into standard English. The result is more cumbrous and wordy, with the terseness of Synge's idiom sacrificed to a profusion of *thats*. For example, Molly Byrne's tart remark, 'I've heard the priests say it isn't looking on a young girl would teach many to be saying their prayers' (III, 111) becomes 'I have heard the priests say that it isn't by looking at young girls that most men learn to say their prayers' (III, 272). The part of speech most affected is the verb, particularly Synge's characteristic use of the Irish habitual present, rendered in English as 'I do be thinking'. For example, 'If I didn't talk I'd be destroyed in a short while listening to the clack you do be making' (III, 71) becomes 'the chatter you are always making' (III, 269). Synge's use of the habitual present replaces the straightforward linearity of subject-active verb-object with the habitual deployment of recurrence and repetition as key elements in his drama. In the questions he directs to Synge, Meyerfeld does best with individual phrases; but he persistently misreads those speeches which reflect on the tramps' talking – as, for example, Martin's 'There's talking for a cute woman! There's talking surely!' (III, 131). Instead of identifying this as the talking which Martin and Mary themselves generate and which keeps their loneliness at bay, he persistently asks whether the phrases refer to the talking done by others about the couple.

What Max Meyerfeld manages to do as a service for all students of Synge is to make this most reticent of authors declare himself. Asked for a biographical sketch 'since I don't know whether you are a young man or an old man', Synge provides one in which the first sentence tackles the correct pronunciation of his surname (CL I, 129). For a dramatist who rarely discussed his work, Synge's answers to Meyerfeld's questions shed light on many of the sources that feed into the language and ideas in his plays. One key source is the Bible. For 'The image of the Lord thrown upon men', Synge provides the gloss 'the image of God reflected by men, he is thinking of [the] text, "God created man in his own image"' (CL I, 124). When the translator queries the phrase 'a slough of wet', Synge points him in the direction of moral allegory: 'a slough of wet = a wet quagmire or bog. Do you remember the "Slough of Despond" in *Pilgrim's Progress* of Bunyan? The word is used in same sense in Ireland now' (CL I, 125). As will be examined in Chapter Seven, Synge based *The Well of the Saints* on a medieval morality play, with character types like the Saint and much invocation of the Day of Judgement. But this is an ironic, inverted, modernist fable, and, not surprisingly, the translator had some trouble with the play's heterodox theology: 'In the very last line of the second act, Martin says "and it's fine care I'll be taking the Lord Almighty does not know…" What does he mean by it? Does he think he can deceive God? But then he is in Hell and has nothing to do with the Almighty.' To which query Synge replied: 'You are right in supposing that Martin wishes to deceive God, his theology – folk-theology – is always vague and he fears that even in Hell God might plague him in some new way if he knew what an unholy joy Martin had found for himself' (CL I, 126).

Notwithstanding these minor problems, the production of the translation went rapidly. Meyerfeld ended by declaring the importance of the play and his confidence that it would do well with the German public. He wrote of his eagerness to translate Synge's two one-act plays but as the opening date of 12 January 1906 approached he began to hedge his bets by raising for the first time the 'Irishness' of Synge's writing: 'I shall like very much [...] to translate both of your one-act plays. But we'll wait and see whether the German public is able to appreciate a thoroughly Irish play or wait until one of your new plays has had a broader success with our public.' If troubling intimations concerning a failure of cultural translation had reached Meyerfeld from the Deutsches Theater rehearsal room, they were confirmed by the brief letter he sent Synge after the opening night: 'Just a line to let you know that *Well* was not a great success, but some of the papers are full of compliments for you.' None of the cuttings Meyerfeld sent have survived. His next letter was even gloomier, saying that no published translation of a play that had done badly could succeed: 'People only buy the book if a drama was very successful on the stage.' The Deutsches Theater took off the production of *The Well of the Saints* after six performances. In the run up to its performance, Synge had offered Meyerfeld his two-act play, *The Tinker's Wedding*, for translation, describing it as a comedy which 'we have never played here as they say it is too immoral for Dublin!' (CL I, 148). Initially, Meyerfeld responded positively to the suggestion: 'I am very anxious to read *The Tinker's Wedding*. A comedy, especially if it is immoral, will always interest the German public.' But Synge did not have the play ready for him until April 1906 and Meyerfeld's response, coming in the wake of the poor reception of *The Well*, was negative: 'I need hardly tell you that there is no chance whatever for this comedy in Germany. It is too undramatic and too Irish – in fact, no one in this country would understand it. [...] I should like to ask you why you stick to Ireland.' [The implicit contrast here was clearly with Wilde and Shaw, who were invoked by Meyerfeld as fellow Irish writers who had enjoyed great success in Germany.] 'Ireland is not the world, and it seems very doubtful to me whether you will ever be able to conquer the world by dealing exclusively with Irish peasants' (quoted in CL I, 167). Synge's reply was polite, restrained, and demurring: 'I am glad to hear your opinion about my "peasant" plays, though naturally I do not share it' (CL I, 167). The two men remained on cordial terms, with Meyerfeld repeatedly requesting to see the script of Synge's new play, *The Playboy of the Western World*, even claiming at one point that the Deutsches Theater had got back in touch and were interested. Meyerfeld had been in London in the meantime and had noted to the author: 'Everyone is speaking here [in London] of you and your work with the greatest esteem. How about your new play? [...] please keep in mind that you are not only writing for the Irish National Theatre, but the German stage also expects very much of you.' No written record of their exchange about *The Playboy* exists. But the subject was obviously discussed between them when Synge and Meyerfeld met for the first time at a London performance of the Abbey production of the play in June 1907. Meyerfeld appears to have decided against translating *The Playboy* and to have done so on the basis of his objections to the earlier play – that it was 'too Irish'. In their final epistolary exchange, on August 17th 1908, Synge apologizes for his long silence on the grounds of serious health problems and records his pleasure at hearing 'that my "Well of the Saints" has been produced in Munich' (CL II, 183) – evidence that the play was not such a dead duck on the German stage as his translator had first feared. Synge tries to interest Meyerfeld in a revised version of *The Tinker's Wedding* and mentions 'a prose play on the story of Deirdre – I hope to finish it for our next season at the Abbey' (CL II, 183-84). Death had other plans and though Synge wrote many drafts of *Deirdre of the Sorrows* the play remained uncompleted when he died of Hodgkins Disease on 24 March 1909. The only play of Synge's translated into German by Max Meyerfeld, therefore, was to remain *The Well of the Saints*. With Synge's growing posthumous fame, translations of his other plays into German were naturally forthcoming. Johannes Kleinstuck gives a valuable survey of them in his article 'Synge in Germany' and discusses the particular 'difficulty, if not the impossibility, of translating him'.[18]

In terms of theatre as 'translation' in a more than literal sense, of the drama as a medium which constantly recreates and recycles itself through 'versions, adaptations, reflections [and] meditations',[19] it is important to consider what the greatest German playwright of the twentieth century, Bertolt Brecht, made of Synge. It has frequently been noted, but rarely commented on in any depth, that a play of Brecht's from 1937 entitled *Die Gewehre der Frau Carrar*, translated as *Senora Carrar's Rifles*, has the epigraph 'Partly based on an idea of J. M. Synge'.[20] His source was a 1935 translation of *Riders to the Sea* into German by Werner Wolff. With Brecht, the idea of translating the play into German goes well beyond the usual attempt to produce a strictly faithful literal rendering of Synge's words, phrases, and syntax into their German equivalents. The truer term for Brecht's theatrical process might be 'adaptation', since he treats the original sources with a great deal of creativity and freedom, some might say license. Certainly, the claim that *Frau Carrar* has any great affinity with Synge has been vehemently denied, by Johannes Kleinstuck for one. He does so mainly on the basis that Brecht has revised Synge's ending away from Maurya the mother's stoic resignation in the face of her last son's death towards an overtly revolutionary gesture. Frau Carrar is moved by her son's death to put aside her pacifism in favour of taking up and supplying rifles to the rebels. Kleinstuck puts the argument as follows: 'Brecht writes in order to change and influence the march of contemporary events; Synge shows a situation where no change is possible.'[21] He considers the works by Synge and Brecht as having only the most superficial of links: 'The mere fact that the scene is set near the sea, and that Juan's body is carried in by two fishermen, surrounded by a group of wailing and praying women, does not prove that there are any significant links between the two works.'[22]

Brecht manifested a lifelong interest in Synge's work, beyond this one adaptation, an interest which has been insufficiently noted or assessed. As early as 1920, when Brecht was only twenty-two, a remark in his diary indicates a deep reading of Synge and already reveals a debt to him in Brecht's own development as a writer and playwright: 'Verbs have long been my weak point. I've started working on them (since reading Lorimer and Synge). Have gained a tremendous lot from this.'[23] G.H. Lorimer was the editor of the American *Saturday Evening Post* and Brecht particularly liked his 1902 publication, *Letters from a Self-Made Merchant to his Son*. The conjunction with Synge is fascinating. It shows that Brecht was reading both Lorimer and Synge in English, and that he was interested not in a Standard English but one which would be enriched by American argot and Irish dialect. As we have already seen, it was in the area of the verb that Synge showed the greatest deviation from normative English practice. Brecht's attention to the matter indicates that he is more interested in a subtlety and range of verbal action in his dramatic practice than he is often credited with. And if the German verb comes at the end and therefore creates a sense of suspension for much of the German sentence, the same can operate in Synge's English, given the freedom and flexibility which the underlying use of Irish gave to his dramatic language: 'It should have been a young man from his words speaking' (IV, 61). A statement can rarely be said to be definitively concluded in Synge, because another appositional phrase with a present participle can always be added: 'it's a queer father'd be leaving me lonesome [...], and I piling the turf with the dogs barking, and the calves mooing, and my own teeth rattling with the fear' (IV, 63).

So Brecht was steeped in Synge's language and drama a full fifteen years before he undertook his adaptation of *Riders to the Sea*. The first great debt owed by *Die Gewehre der Frau Carrar* to Synge's original is visual, both in relation to the physical setting and the placing of the actors on the stage. *Frau Carrar* is also set in 'a fisherman's cottage'[24] and at the start one of the characters is baking bread, a daughter in Synge, the mother in Brecht. The nurturing role of the woman and the traditional nature of the activities in the two peasant cottages are immediately established. Both houses depend on the livelihood of fishing and in both cases one son remains alive in the cottage while the other is feared lost or in danger at sea. In both plays, there is a sustained watch under way. Maurya has been going down to the sea in order to see if there is any sign of her missing son Michael; and throughout *Riders to the Sea* the conditions at sea are always looked for outside the window. For much of *Frau Carrar*, the son Jose is posted looking out the window in order to confirm sight of his brother Juan's boat. The physical and social environment of Brecht's play, therefore, very much takes its cue from Synge's. This is particularly the case when the dead son's body is brought on stage in a formal and consciously ritualistic manner:

> *Murmuring is heard outside the door, then the door opens and three women come in, hands folded over their breasts, murmuring an Ave Maria. They line up along the wall. Through the open door two fishermen carry the dead body of Juan Carrar on a blood-soaked oilcloth. Jose, deadly pale, walks behind. [...] The fishermen set the body on the floor. [...] While the mother sits there petrified and the women pray louder, the fishermen explain with subdued voices what happened.*[25]

This closely parallels the sequence and actions which accompany the Aran Islanders carrying Bartley's dead body onstage in *Riders to the Sea*. In each case, the ritual unfolding of the action visually parallels the verbal account we have already been given of the earlier death of a male member of the family. And each play contains a key sequence when the mother is persuaded to go outside the cottage so that those remaining can examine something they do not wish her to see: the stored rifles in the Brecht, the few remnants of clothing from a drowned man in the Synge.

There are also specific verbal traces of Synge's play in *Frau Carrar*, most notably in another old woman's account of the deaths of the various members of her family. In both cases, comment is made on how unnatural it is for the old to be presiding at the burial of the young. Wolfgang Sauerlander, in his translation of Brecht's text into English, underscores the debt to Synge by translating 'Siehst du denn nicht, dass du ihm nichts Schlimmeres antun kannst, als ihn jetzt vom Kampfen zuruckzuhalten?'[26] as 'Can't you see there's nothing worse you can do to him now than hold him back from fighting?'.[27] This significantly echoes even as it revises the opening of Maurya's concluding monologue from Synge's play: 'They're all gone now, and there isn't anything more the sea can do to me ...' (III, 23).

But Brecht's play supplies two things which have outraged purists: a specific historic location and timescale and a deliberately revolutionary ending. The first context is added to the fisherman locale from the start: 'A fisherman's cottage in Andalusia on a night in April 1937.'[28] The time and setting are explicitly those of the Spanish Civil War, with proFranco broadcasts over the radio and members of the local community involved in the insurgency. No such context is explicitly supplied in the Synge. But an Irish play staged a few months prior to Synge's writing of *Riders to the Sea* in 1902 did supply such an overtly politicized context to the peasant cottage setting which was such a feature of Irish Revival plays. Yeats and Lady Gregory's *Cathleen ní Houlihan* caused a sensation when it was first staged in Dublin with the revolutionary Maud Gonne in the title role of the Poor Old Woman allegorically representing Ireland. *Cathleen ní Houlihan* is set in Killala, County Mayo, in the revolutionary year of 1798 and concludes with the landing of the French forces in the bay, to be joined by the young man of the house, who forsakes his upcoming marriage at the behest of the old woman to take up arms in a revolutionary cause. Such was the reaction to the play that Yeats was to write decades later: 'Did that play of mine send out / Certain men the English shot?'[29] For years, critics followed Yeats's line on Synge, that he was a man unfitted to think a political thought; but recent criticism has detected a strong political subtext in the plays. *Riders to the Sea* contains a conscious verbal paralleling of *Cathleen ní Houlihan*, as the next chapter will demonstrate in its study of the intertextual relations between the plays of Synge and those of Yeats; and its Poor Old Woman cannot but be read as Mother Ireland in the immediate aftermath of that play's reception. But Synge's play is a subversion of the revolutionary promise of the Yeats/Gregory play. Cathleen ní Houlihan promises that, though the young men who decide to enlist in her service will die young, their recompense is that they will be remembered forever. In contrast, what Synge's Poor Old Woman Maurya believes is that 'No man at all can be living forever and we must be satisfied' (III, 27).

A problem is still posed by the ending of *Frau Carrar* where the mother Teresa, having deliberately held her sons back from joining the revolution and kept them to the traditional practice of fishing, has to confront the dead body of her son. Juan has not drowned at sea, as all of the auspices seemed to predict, but has been gunned down by a passing government boat. In the face of this, the mother rejects her Catholic quietism and urges revolution: 'They're not human. They're a canker and they've got to be burned out like a canker.'[30] Much of the conflict in Synge's *Riders to the Sea* derives from the clash between the Catholicism of the islanders and their adherence to certain pagan beliefs and practices, as the previous chapter has argued. In Brecht's play, the conflict is between a no less sincerely held Catholicism and the disruptive effect of Marxist revolution. In his original version of *Frau Carrar*, Brecht had represented the mother as passively accepting and acquiescing in her fate. When the Republicans were defeated in the Spanish Civil War he altered the ending in favour of a more overtly revolutionary protest on Frau Carrar's part. The ending of the play caused actress Helene Weigel particular problems for her interpretation of the part in the Berliner Ensemble production. Weigel's initial interpretation was that the mother gave way further with each loss she sustains in the play, and that finally she crumbles in the face of her son's death. But to switch from this collapse to the firm decision to support the revolution was simply too contradictory and hence was 'nicht glaubhaft' ('not plausible'). Weigel decided to change her interpretation into one much closer to that followed in the Syngean version, whereby Teresa became increasingly more stoic in the face of each successive blow, with the son's death providing the catalyst for her breaking down and undergoing a change of heart. Brecht's response was to laugh and say 'Curious [...] how a fresh effort is needed every time if the laws of the dialectic are to be respected.'[31]

The full meaning of *Frau Carrar* does not rest on the printed page. With Brecht's emphasis on process over product, the contribution of the actor to the interpretation of the role is clearly crucial. His remark also suggests a dialectical relationship between Synge's *Riders to the Sea* and his *Frau Carrar*, with the ending of one as deliberately antithetical to the other. The need and desire for synthesis may well have prompted the very next play Brecht wrote (in 1939, two years later), *Mutter Courage und ihre Kinder*, a much more famous work. But *Mutter Courage*, no less than its predecessor, should have appended to it 'from an idea by J. M. Synge'. The continuity between the two Brecht plays is highlighted by the identification of Helene Weigel with the title character of each, playing an archetypal Mother figure. In both plays, the mother devotes a good deal of her energies to struggling (and failing) to prevent her two sons being swept away by some overwhelming force with which they are surrounded: the physical sea which gives the household its livelihood, the rising tide of revolution or the sea of economic necessity which dominates the drama of *Mutter Courage*. Synge is much more explicit in his prose work *The Aran Islands* than in the somewhat idealized representation of *Riders to the Sea* about the determining effect of economic forces on the lives of the islanders. To take but one example: he remarks that 'in general the men sit together and talk with endless iteration of the tides and fish, and of the price of kelp in Connemara' and that they 'do not care to undertake the task of manufacture without a certainty of profit' (II, 74,77). The economic motive is more muted in *Riders to the Sea*. But it is still present and marked in everything Bartley discusses before he leaves: for example, the kelp that will need to be gathered as one of the few native products they can sell. And Bartley adds that 'if the jobber comes you can sell the pig with the black feet if there is a good price going' (III, 9). Bartley is on his way to the market on the mainland to sell a horse, but as Maurya protests: 'what is the price of a thousand horses against a son where there is one son only?' One of her daughters tellingly answers, in the play's most lethal pun: 'It's the life of a young man to be going on the sea' (III, 11). Much of Mutter Courage's energy in Brecht's play involves trying to keep her family from being caught up in and being directly harmed by the Thirty Years War. Her two sons Eilif and Swiss Cheese both get recruited, when their mother's vigilance is relaxed as she is drawn into haggling over a financial transaction. In a scene reminiscent of Synge, the body of one of her dead sons is brought before Mutter Courage and she looks on him unmoved, without the recognition that would cause all of them to be properly identified and to suffer the consequence. But is not this a kind of stoicism, of fortitude? Where Mutter Courage differs from Frau Carrar is that she retains the same outlook on life throughout the harrowing experiences of the play, including the deaths of son and daughter. There is no change in her outlook, no greater insight into the central contradiction of her life: that she thinks she can trade in the war while keeping immune from it. Brecht maintained that she was a stupid character, someone who failed to learn from her mistakes. In defiance of the dramatist's stated intentions, Brecht's audiences have more often seen Mutter Courage as a tragic heroine of indomitable will, as someone who keeps going and demonstrates an ability to survive, as a figure in the end both tragic and moving. There is more in her of Synge's Maurya than Brecht realized or would consciously have condoned.

Brecht's interest in Synge remained lifelong. *Frau Carrar* was revived in Berlin in 1952. And the last full Berliner Ensemble production supervised by Brecht before his untimely death (at the age of fifty-eight) on 14 August 1956 was an adaptation from a translation by Peter Hacks of Synge's *The Playboy of the Western World*, with Brecht's daughter Barbara in the role of Pegeen Mike. Brecht worked on the adaptation with Peter Palitzsch and Manfred Wekwerth, with whom he also co-directed the play. He chose Synge's play as one of four classics from the world repertoire deliberately to strengthen the Berliner Ensemble in the area of what he called strong or serious comedy – an area in which he thought German actors weak: '[Our] task is to entertain the children of the scientific age, and to do so with sensuousness and humour. This is something that we Germans cannot tell ourselves too often, for with us everything easily slips into the insubstantial and the unapproachable.'[32] We can see much in Synge's *Playboy of the Western World* that would have appealed to Brecht. There is the mixture of high and low, where the description of the heroine with 'the love-light of the star of knowledge shining from her brow' is ironically undercut by another character remarking 'There's poetry talk for a girl you'd see itching and scratching, and she with a stale stink of poteen on her from selling in the shop' (IV, 125-127). Brecht's objections to dramatic character as something fixed and immutable would be satisfied by the extent to which Christy Mahon's character is constructed for him by those with whom he comes into contact; and if Christy finally becomes that character he does so by embracing it in a deliberate act of will rather than by any organic evolution. Synge's play more than anything probes and dissects the need for a hero in the inhabitants of the west of Ireland and anticipates a discussion on the subject in Brecht's *Life of Galileo*. A follower says to Brecht's scientist: 'Unhappy the land that has no heroes!' Galileo replies: 'No. Unhappy the land where heroes are needed.'[33]

In October of 1908, with less than six months to live, Synge returned to Germany, to Wurzburg and the von Eickens, for the first time in fourteen years. He left a dying mother whose death he could not face and who passed away a week after his arrival in Germany. The reasons for the visit were not economic or professional, but personal and psychic. Synge's letters to his fiancée are full of references to a hoped-for renewal, a restoration of his manhood and his strength: 'I hope this will set me up'; 'I hope this will make a man of me again' (CL II, 206-207). He read the poets Walter von der Vogelweide and Hans Sachs in the hope of doing some translations from the German as he had already done from the Italian of Petrarch and the French of Villon. More than anything else it was a last-ditch return by Synge to the country which had done so much to nurture his own creativity, the place and culture which had decided him in favour of becoming, not a talented musician-composer, but a great Irish playwright, one of the most considerable of the western world.

----

[1] James Joyce, *Occasional, Political and Critical Writing*, edited by Kevin Barry (Oxford: Oxford University Press, 2000), p. 108.

[2] James Joyce, *Occasional, Critical and Political Writing*, p. 111.

[3] Declan Kiberd, *Inventing Ireland* (London: Jonathan Cape, 1995), p. 138.

[4] Quoted in Donald Pearce, 'Hours with the Domestic Sibyl: Remembering George Yeats,' *The Southern Review* 28:3 (Summer 1992), p. 490.

[5] R.F. Foster, *W.B. Yeats, A Life, 1, The Apprentice Mage* (Oxford: Oxford University Press, 1997), p. 139.

[6] Mary C. King, *The Drama of J.M. Synge* (London: Fourth Estate, 1985), p. 5.

[7] Edward M. Stephens, quoted in Mary C. King, *The Drama of J.M. Synge*, p. 3.

[8] J.M. Synge, quoted in Mary C. King, *The Drama of J.M. Synge*, p. 7.

[9] See W.J. McCormack, *Fool of the Family: A Life of J.M. Synge* (London: Weidenfeld and Nicolson, 2000), pp. 103-120.

[10] W.J. McCormack, *Fool of the Family*, pp. 160-161.

[11] James Joyce, *Ulysses*, introduced by Declan Kiberd (London: Penguin, 1992), p. 29.

[12] James Joyce, *Ulysses*, p. 247.

[13] Quoted in W.J. McCornmack, *Fool of the Family*, p. 284.

[14] W.J. McCormack, *Fool of the Family*, pp. 284-285.

[15] Henri LeBeau [writing under the pseudonym 'A Lover of the West'], 'The Well of the Saints,' *Dana* 12 (April 1905), p. 367. The translation is mine.

[16] James Joyce, *A Portrait of the Artist as a Young Man* (Harmondsworth: Penguin, 1976), p. 150.

[17] Max Meyerfeld's correspondence with J.M. Synge is contained in the Synge Manuscript Collection held at Trinity College, Dublin. The relevant reference is MSS 4424-4426. Those extracts from Meyerfeld reproduced by editor Ann Saddlemyer in the *Collected Letters* will be individually cited.

[18] Johannes Kleinstück, 'Synge in Germany,' in *A Centenary Tribute to J.M. Synge: 'Sunshine and the Moon's Delight*, edited by S.B. Bushrui (Gerrards Cross: Colin Smythe, 1972), p. 272.

[19] The words are those of contemporary Irish playwright Thomas Kilroy, in an interview with the author. See Anthony Roche, 'An Interview with Thomas Kilroy,' *Irish University Review* 32:1 (Spring/Summer, 2002), p. 155.

[20] Bertolt Brecht, *Senora Carrar's Rifles*, translated by Wolfgang Sauerlander, in Bertolt Brecht, *Collected Plays* 4, edited by Tom Kuhn and John Willett (London: Methuen, 2001), p. 207.

[21] Johannes Kleinstück, 'Synge in Germany,' p. 276.

[22] Johannes Kleinstück, 'Synge in Germany,' p. 276.

[23] Bertolt Brecht, *Diaries 1920-1922*, edited by Herta Rumthun, translated by John Willett (London: Eyre Methuen, 1979), pp. 49-50.

[24] Bertolt Brecht, *Collected Plays* 4, p. 209.

[25] Bertolt Brecht, *Collected Plays* 4, p.234.

[26] Bertolt Brecht, *Stücke* 4, edited by Werner Hecht, Jan Knopf, Werner Mittenzwei, Klaus-Detlef Müller (Frankfurt am Main: Surhkamp Verlag, 1988), p. 337.

[27] Bertolt Brecht, *Collected Plays* 4, p. 233.

[28] Bertolt Brecht, *Collected Plays* 4, p. 209.

[29] W.B. Yeats, 'The Man and the Echo,' *The Variorum Edition of the Poems of W.B. Yeats*, edited by Peter Allt and Russell K. Alspach (New York: Macmillan, 1957), p.632.

[30] Bertolt Brecht, *Collected Plays* 4, p. 235.

[31] Bertolt Brecht, *Collected Plays* 4, p. 363.

[32] Bertolt Brecht, *Brecht on Theatre*, translated by John Willett (New York: Hill and Wang; London: Methuen, 1964), p. 204.

[33] Bertolt Brecht, *Life of Galileo*, translated by John Willett, in Bertolt Brecht, *Collected Plays* 5, edited by John Willett and Ralph Manheim (London: Methuen, 1995), p. 91.

3 | Yeats, Synge and an Emerging Irish Drama

The purpose of this chapter is to consider what William Butler Yeats and John Millington Synge made of each other, not primarily as people but as writers. The complex mutual influence that both writers exerted upon each other had much to do not only with their own development but with the emergence of an Irish National Theatre and especially the vexed question of what form and direction it should take. The blend of likeness and difference that existed between Yeats and Synge can best be studied textually and will involve a certain amount of demythologizing. At almost every stage of their joint career, one text is privileged while another is concealed. My critical approach will be to juxtapose one text with another and to supply a series of contexts by which the nature and extent of the Yeats and Synge relationship can be reformulated. That effect can be summarized as follows: behind or in the shadow of Synge's prose work, *The Aran Islands*, lies Yeats's aborted novel, *The Speckled Bird*; preceding Synge's first two official plays – *Riders to the Sea* and *The Shadow of the Glen* – is the rejected, non-canonical *When the Moon Has Set*; only at the end of Synge's life, with his version of Deirdre following hard upon Yeats's, are the two texts equally visible. But with the death of Synge the axis of relationship shifts, and his ghostly and textual example lies behind Yeats's fashioning of a new form of drama based on the Japanese Noh.

The first matter to address is the standard view on Synge's attitude towards Yeats's work, which promotes his realism at the expense of his fellow writer's otherworldliness. According to this view, Yeats wrote of fairies and of other supernatural manifestations in dreamy, unreal poems and plays. Synge reacted against this by wanting to express an artistic vision that was real and rooted, earthy and violent.[1] A closer examination will reveal that, instead of this stark opposition, there is a more complementary relationship between the two bodies of work. The text usually advanced to support Synge's hostility to Yeats and the Celtic Twilight is a poem of his entitled 'The Passing of the Shee'. One meaning of the title refers to the passing by of the fairy folk, as in Yeats's '*Horseman, pass by!*'[2] But the poem has also been interpreted as Synge's effort to write the epitaph and declare the obsolescence of the fairy folk as poetic currency, where 'passing' may be read as their extinction. But the occasion of the poem, as revealed in its little noted sub-title, is important in considering this argument. The full title reads 'The Passing of the Shee – *After looking at one of AE's pictures*':

> Adieu, sweet Angus, Maeve and Fand,
> Ye plumed yet skinny Shee,
> That poets played with hand in hand
> To learn their ecstasy.
> We'll stretch in Red Dan Sally's ditch,
> And drink in Tubber Fair,
> Or poach with Red Dan Philly's bitch
> The badger and the hare. (I, 38)[3]

Against this, I would set one of the very few occasions when Synge made explicit reference to his view of Yeats's work, praising it at the expense of AE's. Yeats once commented, somewhat ruefully in view of his extravagant praise of Synge, that he never really knew what the younger writer thought of his work: 'I never knew if he cared for work of mine, and do not remember that I had from him even a conventional compliment.'[4] Yet from Synge's unpublished manuscripts we can tell that he deeply admired the broad range of Yeats's dialectical aesthetic, especially in contrast with the narrow perspective of AE In a notebook entry in 1908, Synge declares his distaste for theory in the arts unless it has some personal application to one's own life. He then articulates the following theory: 'For a long time I have felt that Poetry roughly is of two kinds, the poetry of real life [...] and the poetry of a land of the fancy.' (II, 347). For Synge, the greatest writers are not confined to one sphere or the other but rather reach out to embrace the opposite. He illustrates his argument with international writers such as Dante, Chaucer and Goethe before proceeding to the Irish context:

> In Ireland Mr. Yeats, one of the poets of the fancy land, has interests in the world and for this reason his poetry has had a lifetime in itself, but AE, on the other hand, who is of the fancy land only, ended his career in poetry in his first volume. (II, 348)

This passage shows Synge's severe discrimination between the narrowness of AE and the range of Yeats. What it leaves open and unnamed in an Irish context is the writer of real life who is forever reaching out to the land of the fancy, someone who is 'supremely engrossed with life, and yet with the wildness of [his] fancy [is] always passing out of what is simple and plain.' (II, 347). By 1908, when his theory was formulated, this best described the space clearly occupied by Synge himself, especially in the language and characterization of his drama. Its formulation suggests Synge's perception of the kind of complementary rather than oppositional relationship that existed between his writing and that of Yeats. Each of them fulfils possibilities in the emerging cultural situation which the other cannot manage by coming at them from a different angle or perspective and (frequently) in a different medium. One interesting feature of the Irish Literary Revival in its early stages is that none of the major writers was sure what form their genius was going to take, whether it would best express itself in drama or poetry or prose. Thus, they began by trying virtually everything. Essentially, the question younger Irish writers of high ambition like Synge and Joyce addressed to themselves was: what has Yeats left for me to do? The programmatic nature of the inquiry was increased by the fact that Yeats was consciously setting up a national literary movement and not only trying to sign up writers but to assign them their places in it. Synge, unlike Joyce, did not decline the invitation. However, in doing so, he engaged in a creative struggle with Yeats in which he put his own distinctive stamp on everything he produced.

Let us consider the famous meeting between Yeats and Synge in Paris in December 1896. What one discovers in combing through the various textual accounts is that Yeats tells a great deal, but always leaves something crucial out, while Synge tells virtually nothing. All the latter has left is a characteristically terse entry for his diary of 21 December 1896: 'Fait la connaissance de W.B. Yeates.'[5] Yeats, in contrast, wrote at least three extensive prose accounts of their meeting: in his Preface to the First Edition of *The Well of the Saints* (1905); in the original draft of his *Autobiography/Memoirs* (1906); and in Section XIX of 'The Tragic Generation' in *The Trembling of the Veil* (1922). In considering the first of these with reference to the later accounts, I want to ask the question: what did Yeats think he was doing in advising Synge? And what did Synge do with Yeats's expectations? Yeats's January 1905 account begins: 'Six years ago I was staying in a students' hotel in the Latin Quarter.'[6] Immediately it's wrong. The meeting did not take place six years earlier, which would make it 1899. Even allowing for Yeats's notorious inexactitude with details and dates, especially when he was in the process of mythologizing a friend or colleague, there is something curious in this error. Does he supply a later meeting-time in order to diminish the delay and imply a greater cause-and-effect between his giving the advice and Synge's acting upon it?[7] Later Yeats writes: 'I am certain of one date, for I have gone to much trouble to get it right. I met John Synge for the first time in the autumn of 1896, when I was one-and-thirty and he four-and-twenty.'[8] Was Yeats's trouble over accuracy due to the fact that somebody (Synge himself, the realist?) had obviously pointed out to him that he was three years out in his date?

A further question emerges at this point: why was Yeats in Paris? The *Memoirs* reveals he was there to see Maud Gonne, 'the old lure'.[9] The actual introduction to Synge was casual: 'and somebody [...] introduced me to an Irishman, who, even poorer than myself, had taken a room at the top of the house.'[10] In fact, according to Roy Foster, Synge at this time had a small private annuity and was relatively better off; but Yeats may not have known this or preferred to believe otherwise.[11] The narrative continues: 'it was J.M. Synge, and I, who thought I knew the name of every Irishman who was working at literature, had never heard of him.' This serves to expose the self-conscious extent to which Yeats was the architect of a literary revolution, tracking the emergence of potential collaborators and assigning them positions in his artistic agenda. But there is also a genuine concern on Yeats's part because it seems undeniable that Synge was in a bad way both artistically and economically. Nothing much was emerging from his years of literary labours on the Continent and so the intervention on the older Irishman's part was benevolent and well-meaning, however patriarchal in the telling. Yeats goes on: 'He was a graduate of Trinity College, Dublin, too, and Trinity College does not, as a rule, produce artistic minds.' This consideration did not appear to prevent Yeats from applying for the Professorship of English Literature at Trinity many years later when his father's friend Edward Dowden died. And if, in Yeats's view, Trinity College, Dublin, does not produce artistic minds, then what does one say about the extraordinary number of major Anglo-Irish writers, especially dramatists, who have passed through its portals? The line extends from Oliver Goldsmith in the eighteenth century through Oscar Wilde in the nineteenth to J.M. Synge and (subsequently) Samuel Beckett in the twentieth.

Initially, Yeats perceived Synge as a scholar-critic of and for the Irish Literary Revival. As Yeats expressed it: 'he told me that he had been living in France and Germany reading French and German literature, and that he wished to become a writer. He had, however, nothing to show but one or two poems and impressionistic essays'. Yeats then proceeded to criticize Synge's essays by saying that they contained 'too much brooding over methods of expression, [...] not out of life but out of literature. [...] Life had cast no life into his writings.' This description uncannily echoes some of the criticisms that had been made of Yeats's own writings, especially the 'Celtic Twilight' poetry of the 1890s, that a volume like *The Wind Among the Reeds* (1899) had been written too much out of literature, not enough out of life.

In this 1905 narrative, Yeats then introduces a biographical detail of considerable linguistic and cultural significance: 'He had learned Irish years ago, but had begun to forget it, for the only language that interested him was the conventional language of modern poetry which has begun to make us all weary.' Yeats explains this comment – and in the process the deeper reasons for his initial interest in Synge – by making reference to an impasse he had come to in his own development as a writer. As he put it, the ornately wrought prose of his *Secret Rose* and *Red Hanrahan* stories was making him 'weary' too because the style he had chosen 'had separated [his] imagination from life'. He notes that 'since writing this, I have with Lady Gregory's help put *Red Hanrahan* into the common speech'.[12] Thus, acting out what he had determined for himself was a literary dead-end, Yeats claims that he advised Synge as follows:

> Give up Paris. You will never create anything by reading Racine, and Arthur Symons will always be a better critic of French literature. Go to the Aran Islands. Live there as if you were one of the people themselves; express a life that has never found expression.

In this initial account of their meeting Yeats just mentions in passing that Synge had studied Irish at Trinity and was in the process of losing the language. In the next version, however, he makes a crucial, causal link between Synge's Irish and the famous piece of advice quoted above: 'He told me that he had learned Irish at Trinity College, so I urged him to go to the Aran Islands.' In the *Autobiographies* account of 1922, Yeats goes so far as to concede that he would probably have given 'the same advice to any young Irish writer who had Irish'. In a final demythologizing stroke, he adds: 'I did not divine his [Synge's] genius.'[13]

Throughout all of the accounts, Yeats discloses that he had just come from the Aran Islands. However, he gives no reason for that visit except to remark that 'my imagination was full of those grey islands where men must reap with knives because of the stones'.[14] This line is a wonderful, brief anticipation of the later, hard-edged style Yeats was to adopt, a verbally minimalist style which was to replace the earlier lushness and which is found, for example, in the opening lines of his play *At the Hawk's Well*: 'A man climbing up to a place/The salt sea wind has swept bare.'[15] The reason for Yeats's journey earlier in 1896 to the Aran Islands (with the aforementioned Arthur Symons), which he does not reveal or touch on in any of the published accounts, was that he was pursuing research for a book he was engaged in writing, a novel. This fact only emerges in his letters, specifically a letter of August 1896, where he writes: 'I have just returned from the Aran Islands where I had gone on a fishing boat, and where I go again at the end of this week. I am studying on the islands for the opening chapter of a story I am about to set out upon.'[16] The 'story' was a projected prose novel by Yeats, the never-completed *Speckled Bird*. One might describe *The Speckled Bird* as the antithetical side of the prose volume Synge was to write, the suppressed complementary volume or pre-text of *The Aran Islands*. Significantly, Yeats never alludes to his own Aran book in connection with Synge. But it clearly lies behind and has a textual affinity with his encouragement to Synge to go to the Aran Islands and to write a book about the experience in English, to 'express there a life that has never found expression.' Furthermore, although he was aware of Synge's knowledge of Irish, Yeats also would have known that Synge was not an ardent Gaelgeoir or active supporter of the Gaelic League. Thus he must have assumed (rightly, as it turned out) that Synge would not write up his experience of the Aran Islands in Irish but would rather choose to express his account in English, a Hiberno-English modeled on the syntax and idiom of the Irish spoken on the islands. The question is initially one of language and ultimately one of style. It is much on Yeats's mind when he moves from discussing Synge to critically evaluating his own poetry and prose of the 1890s. The language issue involved the decision to write an Irish national literature in English and the question of what stylistic form or forms that English should take if it were to retain a national character. It was a crucial question in the development of both Irish writers and of the entire Irish dramatic movement.

In moving from the medium of the oral to written expression, it is natural to ask: what literary form would such writing in English about the Aran Islands take? Since at the time Yeats went there his own interests had not yet turned to drama, the answer was likely to be a prose narrative of some kind. *The Speckled Bird* is a rarity in Yeats's entire *oeuvre*, a quasi-autobiographical prose narrative, in which the leading character Michael Hearne is a thinly disguised version of the poet himself. As he writes in a letter of January 1897, his proposed novel 'moves between the Islands of Aran and Paris'.[17] The setting of the prose narrative Synge produced, *The Aran Islands*, is obviously the same as Yeats's *The Speckled Bird*. Moreover, in each of the book's four sections covering four separate annual visits, Synge has just moved there from Paris. For Synge, Paris functions as a kind of sub-text or counterpoint to his main subject, only occasionally becoming explicit:

> The women of this island are before conventionality, and share some of the liberal features that are thought peculiar to the women of Paris and New York.[...] The greatest merit they see in a woman is that she should be fruitful and bring them many children. As no money can be earned by children on the island this one attitude shows the immense difference between these people and the people of Paris. (II, 143-4)

Whereas Synge's narrative foregrounds life on the islands as a natural alternative to urban sophistication, Yeats's narrative moves back and forth between various locales without favouring any of them. In Synge there is a filtering and interweaving of his own views with those of the islanders. In Yeats's volume, by contrast, the transcribed oral narratives so central to Synge's narrative merely serve as prelude to the leading character's mystical visions and are soon swept aside by them. The narrative of *The Speckled Bird* spends most of its first Irish section on the mainland, in the Burren and County Galway, coming tantalizingly in sight of but never landing on the Aran Islands: 'They could see Aran away to the westward [...] and here and there a fishing boat out beyond Aran.'[18] In his autobiographical memoir of Synge, Yeats records that on his visit to the islands he had been told the story of how a man on the run would be safely hidden from the authorities by the islanders. Yeats was unable to make anything of the story, probably because of his ignorance of Irish, but he was storyteller enough to know there was material there for development, even if he and no one else at that stage could envisage a *Playboy of the Western World*. He never finished *The Speckled Bird*: it reached the beginning of the fourth book and then petered out. But Yeats kept working at it for several years, right through the time Synge was struggling to compose *The Aran Islands*, up until the latter's completion in 1902.

If *The Speckled Bird* is the textual complement to *The Aran Islands*, then the period of Synge's annual visits to Aran from 1898 to 1902 is paralleled by another event involving Yeats that helped to turn both of them into playwrights in a National Theatre Movement. That important event was the annual series of productions from 1899 to 1901 of the Irish Literary Theatre in Dublin. Although the performances were few, they were well attended and provided a seminal chapter in the development of modern Irish drama. Synge, despite his continued residence in Paris, managed to be in the audience for two of the three Irish Literary Theatre annual seasons and wrote about that experience in an article entitled 'The Irish Intellectual Movement,' published in *L'Européen* of 31 May 1902. Unfortunately, perhaps because the original article is in French and is printed untranslated in Synge's *Collected Works II: Prose*, it has not had the attention it merits. But it provides an invaluable documentation of Synge's own response to the first plays of the movement, not as read but as performed.

Early in the article, Synge poses the question: 'If we wish to survey the progress made since the death of Parnell, what do we find?' (II, 378; translation mine) He then supplies an answer by observing that 'in Ireland nothing gets done without the influence of a dominant personality.' In terms of their differing personalities and their future collaboration, Synge was always willing to concede this dominant position to Yeats in recognition of the force of personality that it takes to mobilize disparate energies towards a common cultural goal. Synge attended the 1899 programme of the Irish Literary Theatre, the performances of Yeats's *The Countess Cathleen* and Martyn's *The Heather Field* on separate nights. He was also present at the 1901 series and was particularly interested in Douglas Hyde's one-act *Casadh an tSúgáin/The Twisting of the Rope*, a play in Irish. Synge's description of the contents of Yeats's play, whose selling of souls led to clerical disapproval and sections of the audience hissing their opposition (as Joyce recorded), culminates in the ironic understatement: 'That seems innocent enough' (II, 380). Synge always thought the plays he was to write were 'innocent enough' until the responses of Dublin audiences proved otherwise. What is intriguing about Synge's attitude towards the audience who protested against *The Countess Cathleen* is that it is identical to the feelings he expressed about those who rioted over *The Playboy of the Western World* eight years later. On both occasions, Synge was scathing in his denunciation of the hypocrisy he witnessed, contrasting the sentiments of the critics with their actual behaviour. Of *The Countess Cathleen* audience, he remarks on 'scandalized drunkards who from the height of the gallery delivered moral observations in the direction of Mr. Yeats and his colleagues' (II, 380). In his discussion of Martyn's *The Heather Field*, Synge favourably contrasts the sensitivity of the Dublin audience to the predicament of the central character, 'this dreamer who consoles himself with grand visionary hopes,' rather than siding with the viewpoint of 'his brutally realistic wife,' (II, 380) as the London audience was to do.

Of all the Irish Literary Theatre presentations, by far the one that made the most meaningful impression on Synge was Douglas Hyde's one-act play in Irish, *Casadh an tSúgáin*, in 1901. He concentrates his discussion on how, during the interval, the linguistically and politically divided audience was momentarily united and transformed through the spontaneous singing of old popular songs in Irish. The impact on Synge of the play itself is addressed in a prose article, in English rather than in French, 'The Dramatic Movement in Ireland,' which was not published until 1988 and is not in the *Collected Prose*. Written in 1906 during the composition of *The Playboy of the Western World*, Synge claims that in Hyde's play he discerned 'the germ of a new dramatic form' and that *The Twisting of the Rope* 'gave a new direction and impetus to Irish drama'.[19] He then extends the observation to include the plays of Yeats, Lady Gregory and (by implication) himself:

> [It was] a direction towards which, it should be added, the thoughts of Mr. W.B. Yeats, Lady Gregory and others were already tending. The result has been a series of little plays with Irish peasant life as their subject which are unlike, it is believed, anything that has preceded them.

That new form, which might be dubbed the peasant cottage play, will be examined in this chapter, in particular to show how Synge built on suggestions from Yeats's and Gregory's early plays as well as on Hyde's to develop 'the germ of [this] new dramatic form'. Informing the writing of his two breakthrough plays, *Riders to the Sea* and *The Shadow of the Glen*, it reached its fullest development in the three acts of *The Playboy of the Western World* four years later.

Synge attended the performance of Hyde's play in Dublin in October 1901 shortly after a first visit to Coole Park to meet with Yeats and Lady Gregory. That visit had two literary purposes and very different outcomes. Synge showed them the manuscripts both of his prose work, *The Aran Islands*, and of his first play, *When the Moon Has Set*. The first received praise and encouragement from Yeats and Gregory; the second was rejected outright. Clearly, at this point, Yeats did not consider Synge as the great national playwright-in-waiting, even though the candidates he had been promoting for that position had all proved disappointing in one way or another: Edward Martyn, who lacked the ability to construct plays; George Moore, who wished to adhere to an excessively literary conception of drama; and Douglas Hyde, who refused (or was unable) to develop his folklore material in a more individualist manner and style. In giving Synge the advice to go from Paris to the Aran Islands, Yeats clearly had in mind that a prose narrative would be the result, whether a quasi-anthropological travel book or a fictional novel along the lines of his own *The Speckled Bird*. He perceived that someone like Synge would have a greater grasp of the islanders' language than a non-Irish speaker like Yeats could manage and so would actually succeed in writing the book-length Aran narrative with which Yeats was struggling and which he ultimately abandoned. And up until its belated appearance in 1907 Yeats keeps pushing Synge's *The Aran Islands* on publishers, offering to write a preface if that will help, acting throughout in a generous manner. As he writes to Lady Gregory on 14 February 1899: 'He [Synge] is really a most excellent man. [...] He will be a very useful scholar.'[20] So the role in which Yeats cast Synge from the time of their original meeting in 1896 for at least the next six years is as a scholar and/or prose writer for the Irish Literary Revival he was founding.

Synge's visit to Coole Park from 14 to 20 September 1901 is particularly significant in the context of other of Synge's activities at this time. First there was his first visit to Coole Park, Lady Gregory and Yeats, at the peak of the ongoing Irish Literary Theatre experiment, an experiment which, as we have seen, he was following closely. Second, Synge was about to pay a fourth visit to the Aran Islands, which would result in his writing a final section (Book IV) for his prose volume on the islanders' life. And third, Synge went straight to the theatre in Dublin. Two days after leaving Inishere, on 21 October, he attended the Irish Literary Theatre's third and final annual productions, Yeats and Moore's *Diarmuid and Gráinne* and Hyde's *Casadh an tSúgáin*. But in the midst of this theatrical activity, what is most surprising is that the correspondence between Synge, Yeats and Lady Gregory only discusses *The Aran Islands*. The first three sections of his book (covering his visits there in 1898, 1899 and 1900) have been written. When submitted by him to Yeats and Lady Gregory during the Coole visit, they read the manuscript and approve: 'We both like it very much and think very highly of it. It is extraordinarily vivid and gives an imaginative and at the same time convincing impression of the people and of their life, and it ought, we think, to be very successful.'[21] This is only part of the story, however. The same letter contains two very revealing suggestions that Yeats and Gregory wish to make. The first is that he leave out 'the actual names of the islands [...] which [would give] a curious dreaminess to the work.' The fact that Synge stubbornly retains the names of Aranmor, Inishmaan and Inishere throughout the book has too often been read simply as his outright rejection of Yeats and the Celtic Twilight. But this argument is controverted by the fact that Synge adopted the second piece of advice, a suggestion that the 'book would be greatly improved by the addition of some more fairy belief'. If one examines Book IV of *The Aran Islands*, it turns out to be absolutely crammed with fairy lore, a virtual compendium of translated oral narratives, ballads and poems, to the extent that this lore displaces the primary account of the activities of the islanders themselves. What is evident from this is that Synge was not averse to taking Yeats's advice if it suited his artistic purposes. The seemingly contradictory response to the two sets of advice can be reconciled if we recall how Synge situated the work of Yeats in his own theory of artistic practice. By adhering to the specific names of the three Aran Islands, Synge was establishing his primary contact and contract with the real. However, in his evident willingness to place a strong emphasis on the fairy lore derived from the islanders' oral tradition, and to admit it on its own terms to a central position in his own text, Synge was equally willing to reach out and embrace the land of the fancy. Working from opposite ends of the reality/fantasy spectrum, Synge and Yeats are meeting at the halfway mark, two intersecting arcs at a crucial point of contact.

It is striking that Book IV of *The Aran Islands* succeeds in combining an examination of the folklore with the lives of the islanders, one of the points on which Yeats's *Speckled Bird* foundered. Knowing this, it is all the more interesting that Yeats urged Synge to complete *The Aran Islands* just at the time when he abandoned his own project. Synge makes very interesting use of the folklore material he reproduces so extensively in Book IV by organizing it through the narrative technique of juxtaposition rather than by means of overt commentary. Accordingly, Book IV is open to all kinds of allegorical and political readings, as Mary C. King has demonstrated.[22] For example, Synge records the story of a man going around Ireland looking for a possession he has lost until he comes upon a Poor Old Woman and she has sold it. That same night Synge and a young island man talk about the stock exchange. As this demonstrates, the economic conditions of the lives of the islanders are much more implicated in the material than Yeats would ever have allowed in his own practice, at least at this stage of his career.

In the following summer of 1902, Synge was to write both *Riders to the Sea* and *The Shadow of the Glen*, two one-act plays which made his reputation. The talk at Coole Park in September 1901 is all of Synge's prose work, however. There is no mention of drama or the theatre except for a brief closing remark: 'We shall, I hope, meet at the Theatre, and talk more fully over these things.'[23] What is not mentioned at any time in their correspondence is that Synge had already written a play, which he had shown to Yeats and Lady Gregory at that fateful meeting. The play was *When the Moon Has Set*, and it was the only one of Synge's dramatic works to draw on his own background as a member of the Protestant Anglo-Irish Ascendancy. The setting of the play is a Big House located in County Wicklow, a locale very much like Glanmore Castle, the ancestral family home of the Synge family. The leading character, Colm Sweeney, is a thinly disguised version of Synge himself (as Michael Hearne was of Yeats in *The Speckled Bird*). There are even quotations in Colm's speeches which are identical to those in Synge's autobiographical manuscripts and fragments – his views on music and creation, for example. The play also features the first appearance of the famous Synge dialect, spoken by the servants in the Sweeney household. One of them says, in a line that is retained throughout all of the drafts: 'we were thinking it's destroyed you'd be driving alone in the night and the great rain, and you not used to anything but the big towns of the world.' (III, 157).

Synge, therefore, was already making partial dramatic use of dialect when he wrote this very disjointed play, in which he was trying (and failing) to reconcile all kinds of contradictions, cultural and personal. *When the Moon Has Set* involves a fraught love affair between Colm Sweeney of the Protestant Big House and his distant cousin, Sister Eileen, a Catholic nun. Sister Eileen can be seen as a kind of Catholicized Cathleen ní Houlihan, particularly when she exchanges her nun's habit for a dress of nationalist green at the end of the play. The action of the play, therefore, is symbolic on the nationalist level. But the green dress is also a relic, a family heirloom. It was intended to be used as a bridal dress by the crazy uncle of the house who once seduced a serving girl and promised to marry her but never did. She too has run mad and puts in an appearance in one of the versions of the play. This *mèsalliance* between social classes in Ireland is covered up in the play, but remains disturbingly present nonetheless. It is also strangely prophetic of Synge's own difficult relationship with the Abbey actress, Molly Allgood/Maire O'Neill, which will be discussed in Chapter Eight.

Synge showed and offered a two-act version of his *When the Moon Has Set* to Lady Gregory and Yeats during their meeting of September 1901. Though no reference occurs to this important event in the correspondence of the time, there are two crucial later references to it that are worth noting. One is in a letter Synge wrote late in his playwriting career to an Australian journalist Leon Brodzky on 12 December 1907, where he states: 'I wrote one play – which I have never published – in Paris, dealing with Ireland of course, but not a peasant play, before I wrote *Riders to the Sea*' (CL II, 103). What this denies is the deployment in *When the Moon Has Set* of a considerable amount of peasant dialect, spoken by the servant Bride, as we have seen. By this rhetorical means, Synge is retroactively suggesting a cleaner break between the dramatic practice of this early work and that of his official plays than actually existed. The other reference to *When the Moon Has Set* occurs in a memorandum that Yeats, acting as literary executor, prepared in 1909 for the Synge estate, when he had gone through all of Synge's writing after his death and decreed what could and could not be published in the proposed four-volume *Collected Works*. Yeats declares that he is absolutely opposed to *When the Moon Has Set* and to the idea of publishing it: 'It was Synge's first play, he read it to Lady Gregory and myself in either two or three acts. [...] *It was after its rejection by us he took to peasant work*' (III, 155, note 1, emphasis mine). Yeats proceeds to complain about the 'morbid' nature of the play. But everything else written by Synge, from the unpublished prose essay 'Étude Morbide' in 1899 through to his final play, *Deirdre of the Sorrows*, ten years later, is open to the same accusation of morbidity, as his Dublin critics never tired of pointing out. So Yeats's explanation of his opposition to the work is insufficient. Clearly, something else is going on here. I would argue that Yeats is acting in such a way as to move Synge away from writing about his own background, the stratified Ascendancy milieu of the Big House. But Synge, for a time at least, was attracted to Ascndancy subject matter, as evidenced by the suppressed *When the Moon Has Set* and the following observation in his essay, 'A Landlord's Garden in County Wicklow': 'if a playwright chose to go through the Irish country houses he would find material, it is likely, for many gloomy plays that would turn on the dying away of these old families' (II, 231). There is matter in this for an Irish playwright, in the Chekhovian mode, one poignant textual reflection of what might have been. But whether Yeats and Lady Gregory explicitly advised Synge to play up the dialect because they preferred that area of *When the Moon Has Set*, or whether because of their cultural emphasis on 'the people,' Synge realized that if he were to succeed in having plays of his accepted and produced in the forthcoming national theatre, he would have to concentrate exclusively on representing 'the people' and privileging their mode of speech, by writing peasant and folk drama. Therefore, he turns in the next plays he attempts to writing *Riders to the Sea* and *The Shadow of the Glen*. As Yeats acutely put it, 'it was after its rejection by us [that] he took to peasant work.'

Forced or encouraged to look in another direction, Synge immediately went from Coole Park in the west of Ireland via the Aran Islands to the premiere of Douglas Hyde's *The Twisting of the Rope* in Dublin. As a result, he perceives 'the germ of a new dramatic form' which as an Irish playwright in the new national theatrical movement he now fully intends to develop. The central situation of Hyde's play involves a young woman in a small rural community who, on the eve of her wedding, is attracted by a stranger from another province. He captures her attention and attempts to woo her with poetry talk. He is well on his way to succeeding, when, alarmed at this prospect, the rest of the small community band together to oust the stranger and see him hanged or sent packing. In *The Playboy of the Western World*, Synge is to undertake a much more complex and elaborate version of essentially the same scenario, but with the onus of sympathy now shifted from the community to the outsider. Indeed, three of Synge's six 'official' plays are a development of that peasant cottage form. It begins in *Riders to the Sea*, develops through *The Shadow of the Glen* and reaches its apotheosis in *The Playboy*. The same basic dramatic situation is to be found in Yeats's early plays, as Synge himself was the first to suggest when, in praising Hyde's play, he took care to remark as we have seen that 'the thoughts of Mr. W.B. Yeats [...] were already tending' in the same direction.[24] Denis Johnston, an Irish playwright from the 1920s on, made a more explicit and elaborate comparison when he noted that the tramp in Synge's plays took the place of the fairies in Yeats's, that they both occupied the same structural and thematic space.[25]

It could be argued that in *The Shadow of the Glen*, where the iconic figure of the tramp makes his first appearance in a Synge play and a crucial intervention in the life of the peasant cottage, Synge is writing his own version of *The Land of Heart's Desire* (1894). In this, the first play of Yeats's to be produced, a fairy child comes to take away the dissatisfied new wife Mary Bruin from the stultifying confinement of a remote rural cottage. In both cases, the emphasis is on a peasant cottage setting in which a way of life is being dramatically represented and brought under scrutiny. In each case too, that way of life is not idealized, but rather characterized as materialistic. The action of the plays written in this genre usually involves some kind of bargaining, a bartering to do with human relationships. Usually, a marriage is in question: money is placed on the table at some point in each of the plays and somebody, usually a young woman, is being sold into bourgeois bondage. Invariably, Synge's sympathy – and Yeats's before him – is with the situation of the woman who may be financially dependent but whose spirit remains free. In *The Shadow of the Glen*, while her young lover is counting out the money left by her supposedly dead husband, Nora is reckoning her losses in existential rather than material terms. In *The Land of Heart's Desire*, Mary, who has recently married into the Bruin family, is pictured standing at an open door, looking out. For all the differences that Yeats and Synge had with Ibsen, a heroine called Nora cannot help but link up with Nora in *A Doll's House*. At the centre of all three plays by Ibsen, Yeats and Synge is a young woman placed in a claustrophobic domestic environment, offered no alternative but a marriage based on pure material necessity, and looking with increasing desperation for an escape.

The peasant cottage form developed by Hyde, Gregory, Yeats and Synge differs from Ibsen in its presentation and foregrounding of a figure who comes into the cottage. This is inevitably a stranger from outside the region and unknown to the inhabitants, representing some kind of alternative reality to the life portrayed in that environment. (The closest parallel in Ibsen would be Hilde Wangel in *The Master Builder* [1892] but she remains consistently subordinated to Solness.) In *The Land of Heart's Desire* it is the fairy child who crosses the threshold and calls on Mary Bruin to 'come away'. What Denis Johnston highlights in identifying Yeats's fairies with Synge's tramps is that the appeal is to come away to a place where nobody grows old, or where the consciousness of growing old will not weigh a person down. Nora in *The Shadow of the Glen* talks about looking out, on the mist rolling up and down, and being aware of old age coming upon her. The tramp here emerges as a figure who offers her an open-ended imaginative possibility, first through encouraging Nora to talk about her life and finally through stepping into the space abandoned by her husband and lover.

In the original folk tale on which Synge based his play, the same set-up is apparently adhered to. Both oral folk narrative and play feature an old man lying dead on a table with a young woman moving around the body. In the first the narrator comes in, the wife goes out, the man sits up and reveals that he has an unfaithful wife whom he is determined to expose. He takes two sticks, one for himself and the other for the unnamed narrator, goes into the bedroom and kills the young male lover, and him only; after all, a man does not destroy his own goods and chattels, only the one who seeks to steal them from him. Synge rewrites that ending, away from the act of violence, and towards an assertion of the wife's independence and freedom. When neither the old man nor the young lover in Synge's play can tolerate this new condition they combine forces to throw the wife out of her home. The tramp rises to meet and counter that male hostility and invites the wife to come away with him. His verbal promise is that they will live in the natural world and because of that find some kind of transcendence of old age or at least of remaining conscious of its burdens: 'You'll not be getting your death with myself, lady of the house [...] [or] making yourself old with looking on each day, and it passing you by' (III, 57). One is immediately struck by the parallels between the deathless appeal of Synge's tramp and that of the fairy child in Yeats's *The Land of Heart's Desire*:

> You shall go with me, newly-married bride,
> And gaze upon a merrier multitude
> [...]
> Where beauty has no ebb, decay no flood.[26]

In contrast to Yeats's heroine, however, Synge's Nora does not die or succumb to romantic ecstasy. Instead, regarding her two alternatives with a cool eye, she responds with the low-key, realistic argument: 'I'm thinking it's myself will be wheezing that time with lying down under the Heavens when the night is cold, but you've a fine bit of talk, stranger, and it's with yourself I'll go' (III, 57). Throughout their brief encounter the talk between Nora and the Tramp has worked to open up a space of alternative possibilities running counter to the actual 'plot' of the play. Indeed, this strategy of Synge's functions as a corrective to what may at first appear to be a failing of the play, namely the melodramatic situation of the Victorian husband who points out the door to the 'fallen woman'. The escape is as much from a worn-out late nineteenth century dramatic form and has as many dramaturgic as thematic implications. No matter how uncertain, the life Nora Burke is going to is far better than the one she has left behind in the cottage. The nature of that life is summed up by the final image of the play: the two men sit down and pour each other drinks, consummating a male hegemony won, as it were, by the exclusion of the woman in and on whom they have traded.

If *The Shadow of the Glen* can be related in these and other ways to *The Land of Heart's Desire*, then *Riders to the Sea*, through the centrality it affords the figure of an old woman, can be seen as a variation on and response to Yeats and Gregory's *Cathleen Ní Houlihan*. In modern Irish drama, it would seem that every time an old woman comes on stage, the audience has to consider the possibility that she may be a version of Mother Ireland. In these two plays, we find two archetypal poor old women trying to move their sons in a particular direction. Each of them employs an incantatory, repetitive, heightened mode of speech to win her young male listener – and indirectly the audience – to her own particular perspective.

On closer examination, however, one realizes that the perspective of Synge is the opposite from that of Yeats and Gregory and that he has worked to undercut and reverse the direction of the appeal in *Cathleen Ni Houlihan*. His old woman, Maurya, is the biological mother of Bartley and Michael as well as 'Sheamus and Patch, and Stephen and Shawn' (III, 27) rather than the metaphorical mother of 'sons' out of Irish history: 'There was a red man of the O'Donnells from the north, and a man of the O'Sullivans from the south, and there was one Brian that lost his life at Clontarf by the sea.'[27] The threatening metaphysical presence that intrudes in Synge's play is the sea rather than the force of nationalist history one feels so strongly in *Cathleen Ní Houlihan*. Maurya's efforts are directed at keeping her sons *there*, in the peasant cottage, rather than having them go out and be killed, as in Yeats and Gregory's play. The promise in the latter for such a sacrifice is that 'they shall be remembered forever, / They shall be alive forever'.[28] Blood sacrifice is mingled with the glory of dying for a worthy ideal. But what is so terrible in the tragedy of Synge's play is the obliteration of life itself. The two young sisters in *Riders to the Sea* look at their brother's clothes and say: 'Isn't it a pitiful thing when there is nothing left of a man who was a great rower and fisher, but a bit of an old shirt and a plain stocking?' (III, 17). Yeats and Gregory's play stresses the life of physical hardship and deprivation those who follow Cathleen's service will endure; but it does so only by way of affirming the immortal life they will earn in the minds of 'the people'. Synge's play also offers a vision, when Maurya sees her son Bartley riding ahead of her missing son Michael on a red mare. But this scene is not a consoling one, since it confirms the earlier death of one son and the imminent drowning of another. And yet the two magnificent formal speeches with which each play concludes do match up in a way that reaffirms their complementary relationship: Yeats and Gregory's allegorical figure becomes real through the historical actuality she represents while the actual mother in Synge becomes symbolic as she refers beyond her own life-span to generations of dead fathers and sons.

The 'germ of a new dramatic form' is developed most completely by Synge in *The Playboy of the Western World*. Once again, there is a cottage setting, in a lonely spot, with a way of life inside it that is oppressive for a young woman. Following the model of *Casadh an tSúgáin*, a marriage is imminent. But Pegeen Mike is in a dilemma. The reality is that she is trapped in a rural society where there is a dearth of eligible young men because, presumably, they have almost all emigrated. It is a demoralized, impoverished place, deriving its authority from elsewhere (whether it is approval to marry from the courts of Rome or selling judgements of the English law). Whatever comes through the door would look good by comparison with Pegeen's fiancé, the craven Shawn Keogh. This is precisely the point at which Synge draws on what had been a central feature of Yeats's plays but which he had so far resisted in his own: the possibility of transformation. With Yeats the metaphysical strangers who enter his peasant cottages present a dual aspect. The fairy forces in *The Land of Heart's Desire* assume the most innocent and pleasing incarnation they can, by taking the form of a child. Cathleen ní Houlihan appears at the door as a poor old beggar woman but departs with 'the walk of a queen'.[29] Synge's earlier characters, though they all make crucial choices, fundamentally do not alter in the course of the drama. *The Playboy of the Western World* marks a major departure for Synge because of his treatment of Christy Mahon. Throughout the play it is increasingly stressed that there is not one but two Christy Mahons, the stuttering, squinting lout described by his father and the utterly transformed 'playboy of the western world'. Throughout much of the play, as audience members, we register that transformation as potential and fluctuating. We also come to realize how much of that potential derives not from Christy Mahon but from the desire of Pegeen Mike and the other Mayo inhabitants, because they want and need him to be that way. Had Synge kept Christy's character objectively untransformed, as he originally intended, the play would have been a farce in the Lady Gregory manner. But as Christy reflects on what the others are making of him, he begins to realize his own hitherto undisclosed possibilities. This is best expressed as he gazes into the mirror at the start of Act II: 'Didn't I know rightly I was handsome, though it was the divil's own mirror we had beyond, would twist a squint across an angel's brow, and I'll be growing fine from this day' (IV, 95).

In contrast to Yeats, Synge's perspective is ironic. Because Christy's transformation chiefly occurs in the perception of other people, both he and Pegeen remain trapped. Repeatedly, Pegeen Mike's apprehensions about seizing the initiative and acting upon her own desires comes from imagining how people will perceive her. Indeed, she is even fearful of her own judgment on her imaginings, saying at one point: 'And to think it's me is talking sweetly, Christy Mahon, and I the fright of seven townlands for my biting tongue' (IV, 151). Jimmy, Philly, her father and the others have built Pegeen up into the image of a shrew, and this is the image she is forced to live up to. What Synge accomplishes is to make the possibility of transformation genuinely two-way and reciprocal, so that Christy and Pegeen present to one another the possibility of transcending a restricted life. That transcendence actually occurs in Christy's case, when he walks out the door with the step of a playboy. Pegeen, on the other hand, is left only with the tragic recognition of the possibilities she has forfeited. By focusing at the beginning and the ending of the play on Pegeen Mike, Synge suggests where the revolutionary potential is located. Through her refusal to follow Christy to a romantic otherworld, Synge implies that it is in the real world where the revolutionary struggle needs to take place.

The Playboy of the Western World is Synge's fullest exploration of the peasant cottage play that Yeats had earlier begun to develop. Synge ended his life and career by writing a version of the Deirdre legend, another subject previously explored by Yeats. Before either of them, AE's version of Deirdre had provided the first Irish play to be staged by the Fay brothers. Yeats's *Deirdre* shows a considerable advance in his dramatic power from many of his earlier plays, so from Synge's point of view there was less for him to develop. Moreover, because he died before *Deirdre of the Sorrows* was complete, Synge did not fully have the opportunity to experiment with the new ideas he was in the process of exploring. *Deirdre of the Sorrows*, even in its incomplete form, may be seen as a point of departure from Synge's previous writing, particularly in relation to the work of Yeats. With his Deirdre play Synge for the first time began to move over from a primary grounding in the real world to that of the fancy land – i.e. the position occupied by Yeats. The result is a parallel rather than an antithetical or complementary relationship with Yeats; and in the case of a dramatization of the Deirdre legend the result is too close for comfort. When Synge introduces the dialect to bring the play down to earth, it frequently results in such bathetic lines as 'Conchubor'll be in a blue stew this night' (IV, 185) in an effort to avoid being 'poetic' in the Yeatsian manner. *Deirdre of the Sorrows* as a whole, for all of its many individual virtues, has nowhere to go. Up to this, there is a wonderful freedom in Synge's development of the elements of his various plays; and when he draws on something that Yeats has in a sense suggested to him, he builds on it in his own way. But in this instance the dramatic representation of Deirdre was something that Yeats had put his mark on; and it proved much harder for Synge to wrest something distinctive from it.

Many critics have tried to find in *Deirdre of the Sorrows* some hints as to the future directions Synge might have taken had he lived. In my view, the work of Synge that offers the most possibilities for development is not *Deirdre* but the underestimated *The Well of the Saints*. I make the claim despite the fact that in its first production *The Well of the Saints* played to poor houses and failed to provoke any riots or walkouts. Moreover, it has never been popular with general audiences. On the other hand, it has found a following among other Irish playwrights. For Samuel Beckett, it was the play by Synge that most informed his own practice as a dramatist. And contemporary playwright Thomas Murphy directed a production of the play at the Abbey Theatre in 1979. But the first Irish playwright to be impressed by *The Well of the Saints* was W.B. Yeats. Towards the end of his life, Yeats recalled the first night of the play at the Abbey Theatre in 1905 as the night he became 'Synge's convert' as he witnessed a compelling drama being created from the most minimal of means, a scenario in which 'the two chief persons [sat] side by side' conversing for the entire first act.[30] But Yeats was not yet sufficiently advanced in his own theatrical evolution to the point where he could respond creatively to Synge's *The Well of the Saints* as Synge had responded to Yeats's earliest plays. The peasant cottage form proved a more confining environment for Yeats's theatre than it did for Synge's. He chafed at its naturalistic constraints and needed a more flexible, open-ended form wherein his poetry could be related to music, physical gesture and stylized visual imagery. He worked throughout his playwriting career to develop a theatrical form whose conventions enabled readier and more equal interchange between the natural and the supernatural. Throughout the early years of the Abbey Theatre Yeats was in search of such a form; and the form was not that of peasant drama.

When Synge was dying in 1909, Yeats quoted him as having said that 'style comes from the shock of new material'.[31] For five years following the death of Synge, Yeats gave up writing new plays even though he continued to experiment with stagecraft and revised several of his earlier plays. It was the shock of the new material of the Japanese Noh drama, as introduced to him by Ezra Pound in 1914, that stimulated Yeats to commence a whole new phase in his playwriting career. That phase saw him returning to the dramatic lessons learned from Synge. Once Yeats discovered the Japanese Noh, whose absence of conventional setting abolished the outside/inside distinction of the peasant cottage, he proceeded to write his own Noh-influenced versions of several of Synge's plays. One of these plays contains the line: 'We're but two women struggling with the sea.'[32] If that were quoted out of context, it would seem almost inevitably to be from Synge's *Riders to the Sea*. Instead it figures in Yeats's *The Only Jealousy of Emer*, the second of his 'Plays for Dancers'. The setting of the play is described by the First Musician as being a poor fisherman's house with oars and nets – in effect, an Aran fisherman's cottage – where Cuchulain lies dying. The chief difference from Synge is that, because of the conventions of the Noh drama, Yeats can dramatically follow the departing spirit of the drowned man into the otherworld. Synge, because of the limitations of the realistic dramaturgy of *Riders to the Sea*, keeps us always within the cottage setting. We can only gain access to Maurya's vision of her dead son at one remove, that is when she comes back inside the cottage and tells her daughters about it. One of Yeats's primary intentions was to stage the transactions between the living and the dead directly. I will go into this dramaturgic process more fully in Chapter Five.

It is Yeats's metaphysical comedy *The Cat and the Moon* that most directly builds upon a Synge play, *The Well of the Saints*. In the latter Synge for once eschewed the peasant cottage form and set his play in the open, at a crossroads. There, his liminal characters sit and talk, as Yeats observed, at one remove from the settled community. The two characters in Yeats's play have been directed to the holy well of St. Colman by 'the beggar of the crossroads'.[33] More than any other of Synge's plays, as I suggested earlier, *The Well of the Saints* points to the future of modern Irish drama, not only to Yeats's *The Cat and the Moon*, but beyond it to Samuel Beckett's *Waiting For Godot*. In all three plays we encounter two tramp-like figures who appear and are waiting for a Saint or a Godot to show up and cure them of a physical or psychic infirmity. In place of a traditional plot the characters simply wait and, while they wait, they talk or, to use the more appropriate Irish term Beckett employs, they 'blather'. It is the physical activity of waiting and the vocal activity of blathering that together form the shape of the play. In each of the three works the fulfilment of the characters' expectations, the 'miracle' they long for, is baulked and ironized in varying degrees. In the Synge play the Saint actually appears and cures Martin and Mary Doul's blindness; but they are disillusioned at what they see and, after a period of death-like separation, find their way back to each other in Act III. When they once more go blind and are again threatened with a cure, Martin strikes the can of holy water out of the Saint's hands and defends their imaginative right to 'see' in their own way. In the Beckett play, notoriously, Godot never arrives in either of the two Acts, unless it be in the travestied form of Pozzo and Lucky.

Indeed, the audience comes to suspect that, if Godot *had* shown up, there would have been vast disappointment all around. In the Yeats play the Saint is not represented directly on stage; his lines are spoken by the First Musician and he is seen by one of the characters but not the other. Yeats opts for a blind man and a lame man, both beggars, and they come on as one, with the blind man on the lame man's shoulders, masked, walking to the rhythmic beat of a drum. The stage directions call for them to '*wear grotesque masks*'[34] and together they seem to represent two halves of the same personality. I think Yeats is drawing a great deal of the physical and verbal grotesquerie in *The Cat and the Moon* from his reading of Synge. The same symbiotic relationship exists between Martin and Mary Doul in *The Well of the Saints* and between Vladimir and Estragon in *Waiting For Godot*.

In the Yeats play, the Blind Beggar's cure confirms all of his worst suspicions that the Lame Beggar has been cheating him all along; and they split up. But the Lame Beggar chooses to be blessed and finally the Saint climbs up (invisibly) on his shoulders and tells him that, being blessed, he must dance: 'Then dance, and that'll be a miracle.'[35] The play climaxes and concludes with the Lame Beggar throwing away his crutch and, to his own astonishment, dancing. Towards its close, *The Cat and the Moon* switches from resembling Synge and becomes more like Shaw's visionary Peter Keegan talking to the grasshopper in *John Bull's Other Island* (1904). The paradox is that Yeats's most Syngean play needed the conventions of the Japanese Noh, in this case the particular form of the *kyogen* or farce, in order to achieve its full theatricalization.

In the moving final stanza of his late poem 'The Muncipal Gallery Re-visited', Yeats brings on 'John Synge himself' and concludes by bidding the future 'say my glory was I had such friends'.[36] And yet the relationship between W.B. Yeats and J.M. Synge hardly comes under the category one would usually ascribe to friendship. The close Yeatsian companion for Synge was Jack B. Yeats, with whom he travelled around Connemara in 1906. It is worth noting that, when Yeats made the above claim, he did not have the living Synge before him but was in a gallery looking at images of the dead. What really developed between Yeats and Synge, I believe, was the profound kind of relationship between writers that is ultimately textual. Synge was the 'dying' man who 'chose the living world for text'.[37] Whatever Yeats made of him when he was alive, it was only when Synge died and became a ghost and there were only the ghostly writings and only ghostly memories that he could fully textualize and invoke his playwriting and theatrical colleague.

Throughout their joint careers, as I have endeavoured to show, one was reacting *against* the other. If Synge developed as a writer by reacting against and interacting with Yeats, then Yeats himself also developed through his relationship with Synge. What they ultimately mapped out between them were the possibilities for an emerging and distinctive Irish drama for the twentieth century.

---

[1] See, for example, Jon Stallworthy, 'The Poetry of Yeats and Synge,' in *J.M. Synge Centenary Papers 1971*, edited by Maurice Harmon (Dublin: Dolmen Press, 1972), p. 156: 'In 1898 he exchanged dreams for realities, city for country, the Gallic twilight for bright mornings in the West of Ireland.'

[2] W.B. Yeats, 'Under Ben Bulben,' *The Variorum Edition of the Poems of W.B. Yeats*, edited by Peter Allt and Russell K. Alspach (New York: Macmillan, 1957), p. 640.

[3] Professor Andrew Carpenter of University College Dublin, editor of Edward Stephen's biography of J.M. Synge, *My Uncle John* (London: Oxford University Press, 1974), agrees with me that Robin Skelton, the editor of Synge's poems, has misread 'stretch' as 'search' in line five of the poem.

[4] W.B. Yeats, 'J.M. Synge and the Ireland of his Time,' *Essays and Introductions* (London: Macmillan, 1961), p. 329.

[5] Synge Manuscripts, TCD, MS 4417.

[6] W.B. Yeats, 'Preface to the First Edition to *The Well of the Saints*,' *Essays and Introductions*, p. 298.

[7] Another reason for the error may be that it was at a subsequent meeting between the two writers in 1899, a year after Synge had first visited the Aran Islands, that Yeats proffered the famous advice. Nicholas Grene argues that 'two different meetings, both in Paris in the winter but separated by more than two years, are being conflated.' See 'Yeats and the Re-making of Synge,' in *Tradition and Influence in Anglo-Irish Poetry*, edited by Terence Brown and Nicholas Grene (Houndmills: Macmillan, 1989), p. 49.

[8] W.B. Yeats, 'The Tragic Generation', *Autobiographies* (London: Macmillan, 1955), p.343. This section of Yeats's autobiography, 'The Trembling of the Veil', was first published in 1922.

[9] W.B. Yeats, *Memoir: Autobiography: First Draft/Journal*, edited by Denis Donoghue (London: Macmillan, 1972) p. 104.

[10] W.B. Yeats, *Essays and Introductions*, p. 298.

[11] R.F. Foster, 'Good Behaviour: Yeats, Synge and Anglo-Irish Etiquette,' *Paddy and Mr. Punch: Connections in Irish and English History* (London: Allen Lane/The Penguin Press, 1993), p. 198.

[12] The footnote was added in 1918. See W.B. Yeats, *Essays and Introductions*, p. 299.

[13] W.B. Yeats, *Autobiographies*, p. 343.

[14] W.B. Yeats, *Essays and Introductions*, p. 299.

[15] W.B. Yeats, *At the Hawk's* Well, *The Variorum Edition of the Plays of W.B. Yeats*, edited by Russell K. Alspach (London: Macmillan, 1966), p. 399.

[16] *The Letters of W.B. Yeats*, edited by Allan Wade (New York: Macmillan, 1955), p. 266.

[17] *The Letters of W.B. Yeats*, p. 280.

[18] W.B. Yeats, *The Speckled Bird*, Volume 2, edited by William H. O'Donnell (Dublin: The Cuala Press, 1974), p. 68.

[19] J.M. Synge, 'The Dramatic Movement in Ireland,' *The Abbey Theatre: Interviews and Recollections*, edited by E.H. Mikhail (Houndmills: Macmillan, 1988), pp. 54-5.

[20] *The Letters of W.B. Yeats*, p. 314.

[21] *Theatre Business: The Correspondence of the first Abbey Theatre Directors: William Butler Yeats, Lady Gregory and J.M. Synge*, edited by Ann Saddlemyer (Colin Smythe: Gerrards Cross, 1982), p. 30.

[22] See Mary C. King, *The Drama of J.M. Synge* (Syracuse: Syracuse University Press, 1985), pp. 18-47.

[23] *Theatre Business*, p. 30.

[24] One strong reason may well have been that Douglas Hyde's dramatic scenario was based on one of Yeats's prose narratives about Red Hanrahan.

[25] See Denis Johnston, *John Millington Synge* (New York: Columbia University Press, 1965), p. 14.

[26] W.B.Yeats, *The Land of Heart's Desire, The Variorum Edition of the Plays of W.B. Yeats,* p. 205.

[27] W.B.Yeats, *Cathleen ní Houlihan, The Variorum Edition of the Plays of W.B. Yeats*, p. 225. It is now commonly accepted that the play was co-authored by Yeats and Lady Gregory. For the confirmatory detail on this, see James Pethica, 'Patronage and Creative Exchange: Yeats, Lady Gregory and the Economy of Indebtedness,' *Yeats and Women*, edited by Deirdre Toomey (London: Macmillan, 1992), pp. 60-94.

[28] W.B. Yeats, *Cathleen ní Houlihan*, p. 229.

[29] W.B. Yeats, *Cathleen ní Houlihan*, p. 231.

[30] W.B. Yeats, 'An Introduction for my Plays,' *Essays and Introductions*, p. 529.

[31] W.B. Yeats, *Memoirs*, p. 105.

[32] W.B. Yeats, *The Only Jealousy of Emer, The Variorum Edition of the Plays of W.B. Yeats*, p. 541.

33 W.B. Yeats, *The Cat and the Moon, The Variorum Edition of the Plays of W.B. Yeats*, p. 793. The phrase may well be a coded acknowledgement of the direction Synge provided to Yeats in the latter's development as a dramatist.

34 W.B. Yeats, *The Cat and the Moon*, p. 793.

35 W.B. Yeats, *The Cat and the Moon*, p. 801.

36 W.B. Yeats, 'The Municipal Gallery Revisited', *The Variorum Edition of the Poems of W.B. Yeats*, pp. 603-4.

37 W.B. Yeats, 'In Memory of Major Robert Gregory,' *The Variorum Edition of the Poems of W.B. Yeats*, p. 325.

4 | Joyce, Synge and the Irish Theatre Movement

Although he wrote a play which has not survived, and a translation of a German drama by Gerhart Hauptmann, Joyce's claims as a dramatist come to rest on his one surviving play, *Exiles* (1918). The play was submitted to Yeats after the latter had responded enthusiastically to *A Portrait of the Artist as a Young Man* (1916) and subsequently rejected. It would make for a neat case of the great artist done down if it could be confidently asserted that *Exiles* is a dramatic masterpiece. But whatever the daring of its themes, the play seems to many people stilted in its dialogue and conservative in its dramatic treatment, too much in the shadow of Ibsen. A celebrated London production of the play in 1970 by Harold Pinter raised the possibility that, in its deliberate uncertainty regarding a key sexual encounter and its strategic and structural use of silence, Joyce's play might be more modernist than had at first been realized. The uncertainty of *Exiles*' reputation and level of achievement is well captured in editor J.C.C. Mays's remark: 'The success of the enterprise is not generally agreed upon because there is no agreement over Joyce's purpose.'[1]

My primary purpose in this chapter is therefore not to consider Joyce as a playwright, potential or actual, failed Ibsenite or Pinteresque precursor. Rather, it is to offer a reading of the key role certain dramatists played in Joyce's artistic development. One must begin, inevitably and naturally, with Ibsen and the high claims made on the Norwegian playwright's behalf by a young James Joyce at the outset of his own career. I also wish to consider Joyce's views on Ibsen in line with his fluctuating, even contradictory, views of the three-year experiment of the Irish Literary Theatre and its successor, Ireland's national theatre at the Abbey. The context might generally be described as Ibsen in Ireland. The dramatist I most wish to consider in relation to

Joyce is Synge, the greatest that native movement produced; and work out some of the literary complexities surrounding their relationship. In W.J. McCormack's view: 'As contributors to the Irish Literary Revival (loosely defined), Joyce and Synge complement each other, stressing the same hemiplegia, a paralysis of the half-body, the half-state.'[2]

Some of Joyce's earliest critical pronouncements attest to the high regard in which he held drama. In a paper addressed to UCD's Literary and Historical Society on 20 January 1900, entitled 'Drama and Life', Joyce proceeds through the Greeks and Shakespeare but as he does so he shows scant reverence to the classic past, declaring that 'Greek drama is played out. For good or for bad it has done its work'.[3] Higher and more enduring claims are made for Shakespeare. But it is with the present that Joyce is primarily concerned. His argument is directed against those who wax nostalgic about the drama of the past and claim the present scientific age provides little of the materials for great drama: 'Still I think out of the dreary sameness of existence, a measure of dramatic life may be drawn. Even the most commonplace, the deadest among the living, may play a part in a great drama'(28). Ibsen is emerging to the forefront of Joyce's argument and 'Drama and Life' concludes with direct quotation from the Norwegian dramatist's *The Pillars of Society* (1877): '"... what will you do in our Society, Miss Hessel?" asked Rorlund – "I will let in fresh air, Pastor." – answered Lona' (29). In his closing peroration on Ibsen's importance for literature, Joyce appropriates the Ibsenian mask to make a statement which will have profound artistic consequences for his own career: 'Life we must accept as we see it before our eyes, men and women as we meet them in the real world, not as we apprehend them in the world of faery' (28). These lines anticipate Joyce's later self-defence in the face of the criticisms levelled at the low mimetic realism of the short stories in *Dubliners* (1914) and the explicit treatment of the body and its functions in *Ulysses* (1922).

But this defence of Ibsen has already shifted the argument to the contemporary Irish cultural context. Joyce's dismissive closing gibe about 'the world of faery' is clearly aimed at the writings of Yeats and Lady Gregory. It would be tempting to array Joyce the Ibsenian realist against the Celtic Twilight mythologizing of Yeats – clearly, that is in part what Joyce himself is doing here. The actual situation of Joyce's relation to the work of those who were self-consciously founding an Irish Literary Revival is much more complicated than that. With regard to Yeats's poetry, Joyce found room to praise *The Wind Among the Reeds* (1899) as 'poetry of the highest order'[4] and an early love letter of his to Nora Barnacle consisted exclusively of the written out lines of Yeats's 'Down by the Salley Gardens'. What Joyce criticized in Yeats, in his scorching pamphlet 'The Day of the Rabblement'(1901), was what seems more a failing of character, the aesthete's 'floating will' and 'treacherous instinct of adaptability'.5 Joyce's argument with Yeats would come to centre on drama, not poetry, and the direction being taken by the Irish theatre movement.

In May 1899 Joyce (like Synge) was present at the opening night of Yeats's play, *The Countess Cathleen*, in Dublin's Antient Concert Rooms. On the following night, he also attended Edward Martyn's *The Heather Field*, a play consciously written in the style of Ibsen. The Irish Literary Theatre was founded by Yeats, Martyn, Gregory and the novelist George Moore as a conscious three-year experiment 'to bring upon the stage the deeper thoughts and emotions of Ireland' and to pursue 'that freedom to experiment which is not found in theatres of England, and without which no new movement in art or literature can succeed'.6 So far, so good, as far as Joyce was concerned. But Yeats and Gregory's stated desire to show that Ireland 'was the home of an ancient idealism'7 and an implied valorization of the past was the issue over which Joyce would break with them. Yeats's play, which had already been published and therefore could be read before it was staged, caused considerable controversy. Its depiction of Irish peasants during a time of famine who sell their souls to the devil and are redeemed by the woman of the Big House, the Countess Cathleen, was bad enough; but even worse from an orthodox Catholic point of view was the play's ending, in which an angel appears on stage to reverse the Countess's damnation, because 'The Light of Lights/ Looks always on the motive, not the deed'.8 This heterodox theology and the sensitivity about the manner in which Irish peasants were represented stirred public controversy and eventually led to the police being called. A valuable first-hand account of the staging of Yeats's *The Countess Cathleen* is given in Joyce's *A Portrait of the Artist as a Young Man*. In Section V, Stephen Dedalus remembers the scene of

> the hall on the night of the opening of the national theatre. He was alone at the side of the balcony, looking out of jaded eyes at the culture of Dublin in the stalls and at the tawdry scenecloths and human dolls framed by the garish lamps of the stage. A burly policeman sweated behind him and seemed at every moment about to act. The catcalls and hisses and mocking cries ran in rude gusts round the hall from his scattered fellowstudents:
> - A libel on Ireland!
> - Made in Germany!
> - Blasphemy!

- We never sold our faith!
- No Irish woman ever did it!
- We want no amateur atheists!
- We want no budding buddhists![9]

One suspects the hand of Joyce in supplementing the catcalls of the night by adding that final rhyming couplet, however organized the opposition to the play by his fellow students at UCD may have been – an opposition from which he is consciously standing aloof. And however much his irony may also seem to be directed at the puny onstage efforts at representation, it is the potency of key lines from the play, 'crooned in the ear of his memory', which has brought the scene back to life before his eyes: 'Bend down your faces, Oona and Aleel,/ I gaze upon them as the swallow gazes/ Upon the nest under the eaves before/He wander the loud waters'.[10] The appeal of the 'soft long vowels' lapping over his memory may suggest that Joyce's response is more to the poetry of *The Countess Cathleen* than to the drama. But there are elements of Yeats's play that recall Ibsen, albeit the Ibsen of *Peer Gynt* more than that of the realistic plays. The male poetic figure Aleel, invoked in these lines and played by a woman Florence Farr, has an androgynous power and appeal which matches up with Joyce's praise of that quality in Ibsen, as discussed in his article 'Ibsen's New Drama', printed in the 1 April 1900 edition of *The Fortnightly*:

> Ibsen's knowledge of humanity is nowhere more obvious than in his portrayal of women. [...] Indeed, if one may say so of an eminently virile man, there is a curious admixture of the woman in his nature. His marvellous accuracy, his faint traces of femininity, his delicacy of swift touch, are perhaps attributable to this admixture.[11]

Clearly, Joyce found Yeats's *The Countess Cathleen* a complex and valuable work. One would have expected him to have adverted more to the play of the following night, Edward Martyn's *The Heather Field*, as a conscious effort to introduce Ibsen, one might even say translate him, into a contemporary Irish context. But the Martyn play was not lost on Joyce, and years later, in March 1919, he proposed its production in Zurich as part of the programme for the English Players that he was helping to organize. Joyce the producer also contributed a programme note on the play, presenting Edward Martyn in the following terms: 'As a dramatist he follows the school of Ibsen and therefore occupies a unique position in Ireland, as the dramatists writing for the National Theatre have chiefly devoted their energies to peasant drama.'[12] He then proceeds to a lengthy account of the plot and its unhappy marriage, sympathetic to the play's unstable idealist Carden Tyrrell and his efforts to cultivate 'a vast tract of heather land'. These events end in failure when 'the old wild nature' breaks out again in both the heather field and the husband his wife has sought unsuccessfully to domesticate.[13] Joyce's positive remarks here are in marked contrast to the dismissive tones in which Martyn is represented in 'The Day of the Rabblement', where his writing is characterized as 'disabled [...] by an incorrigible style, [which] has none of the fierce, hysterical power of Strindberg, whom he suggests at times'.[14] Curiously, there is no mention of Ibsen here; rather, Martyn is rebuked for failing to be more like Strindberg. We know Joyce thought well of *The Heather Field*. The diatribe of 'The Day of the Rabblement' was provoked when Joyce learned that the announced programme of the third year of the Irish Literary Theatre experiment was to see a turning away from the dramatic treatment of contemporary Ireland towards plays in the Irish language and plays of heroic legend. Joyce could see that Martyn was missing from the third year's lineup and could have been presumed to use this as part of his grounds for castigation of Yeats and Gregory. Instead, Martyn must be misrepresented in order first to incorporate him and hence to see him off as part of Joyce's wholesale dismissal of the nascent national theatre movement.

What has already been apparent in Joyce's representation of Ibsen becomes even clearer in his exchanges with W.B. Yeats. Joyce is consciously casting himself in an Ibsenian role in his own life drama: the prophetic figure bringing the gospel of the Norwegian messiah to the unenlightened Irish (the 'rabblement'); the idealist doomed to isolation and misunderstanding among the uncomprehending bourgeoisie and philistines (the 'trolls'). Yeats first comes across to Joyce as a possible fellow bringer of light to darkness. But there is ambivalence from the start, and Joyce's criticism comes to focus on Yeats's relationship with Irish society and is cast in terms which equal the later Yeats for their arrogance and snobbery. This self-conscious casting of the protagonists in this struggle for the soul of an emergent nation as figures from an Ibsen drama appears to have been contagious. After his first meeting with Joyce, Yeats wrote to AE (George Russell) to say how he had got on with the arrogant, brash young man Russell had recommended to him. Yeats concluded his account by consciously echoing lines from Ibsen's *The Master Builder*: 'Presently he [Joyce] got up to go, and, as he was going out, he said, "I am twenty. How old are you?" I told him, but I am afraid I said I was a year younger than I am. He said with a sigh: "I thought as much. I have met you too late. You are too old." [...] The younger generation is knocking at my door.'[15]

When Joyce came to write his own play over ten years later, the shadow of Ibsen was inescapable, as has been widely recognized. *Exiles* concentrates on a couple, Richard and Bertha Rowan, who have just returned to Ireland after nine years in Rome, along with their young Italianate son, Archie. They meet up with two figures from their past, Protestant first cousins Robert Hand a journalist and Beatrice Justice a music-teacher. For all of their apparent equanimity there is a dissatisfaction in or between the couple which manifests itself in their relations with the other two characters. Details about the past reveal that it was by no means clear whether Richard would depart for the Continent with Bertha or Beatrice; and while the former has physically spent all this time with Richard and borne him a son, the latter has continued to haunt his thoughts and provide inspiration, subject matter and theme for his writing. The parallel with Ibsen's *Hedda Gabler* (1890) is clear, with the frustrated Hedda – bored with her husband – rekindling her passion for Eilert Lovborg through his renewed act of writing. The destruction of Lovborg's manuscript is explicitly likened to the killing of their baby. But the differences, especially pertaining to gender, are no less telling. For one thing, Richard and Bertha have never undergone any form of marriage, institutional or religious, but have united and remained together voluntarily, as James Joyce and Nora Barnacle were to do. For another, Bertha is not the restless one in the 'marriage'; rather, it is her husband. Her flirtation with his best friend, Robert, has been reported to him in detail; and the desire that they should consummate their relationship appears to proceed more from him than from her.

When Joyce submitted the manuscript of *Exiles* to Yeats early in 1917 for a possible Abbey production, he did so via Ezra Pound, who had come to play an increasingly important role in the two Irish writers' careers. Yeats approached the prospect of *Exiles* with great anticipation, whetted by his first reading of Joyce's novel: 'My dear Ezra, I have almost finished *A Portrait of the Artist*. I think it a very great book – I am absorbed in it. If you have the play [*Exiles*] bring it tomorrow night. If it is at all possible the Abbey should face a riot for it.'[16] Yeats would have to wait almost another ten years for his Abbey riot with Sean O'Casey's *The Plough and the Stars* and the opportunity to denounce a Dublin audience's philistinism from the stage for once more (after Synge) 'rock[ing] the cradle of genius'. Yeats's appreciation of the prose of Joyce's *A Portrait of the Artist* seems genuine, but must have been aided by reading how the verses from his *Countess Cathleen* crooned in the ear of Stephen Dedalus's memory. Yeats would also have been uniquely placed to recognize how the more burnished prose of *A Portrait* (after the 'scrupulous meanness' of *Dubliners*) bore out the young Joyce's professed admiration when they first met for Yeats's two prose stories, 'The Tables of the Law' and 'The Adoration of the Magi'. But whatever Yeats may have been expecting from *Exiles*, all Joyce got in return was a lengthy silence, finally broken after repeated solicitations by the following:

> I do not recommend your play to the Irish Theatre because it is a type of work we have never played well. It is too far from the folk drama; and just at present we do not even play the folk drama very well.[...] It is some time since I read your play and my memory is not very clear – I thought it sincere and interesting but I cannot give you the only criticism worth anything, detailed criticism of construction. I could at the time I read it, I have no doubt. I do not think it at all so good as *A Portrait of the Artist* which I read with great excitement.[17]

'The type of work we [the Abbey Theatre] have never played well' might refer to the drama of Henrik Ibsen, or even more specifically to those plays by Irish writers taking Ibsen as their example. Where Lady Gregory ensured that plays by Bernard Shaw featured in the Abbey repertoire, Oscar Wilde's drawing room comedies found no place on the Abbey stage. And Yeats had seen off the Ibsenite Edward Martyn during the three-year experiment of the Irish Literary Theatre. Joyce was never to write another play. His energies increasingly went into the elaboration of *Ulysses* and its more successful and arguably more dramatic treatment of a husband who half wills his wife into being unfaithful with a mutual acquaintance. These developments may well account above all for Joyce's failure to write another play; but no doubt Yeats's rejection played its part.

   If another Irish writer had reacted in the same way to such rejection by Yeats of an Irish Ibsenite play, then the direction of the entire national theatre movement might well have been very different. For John Millington Synge also had to deal with the rejection of his first play, the little known, non-canonical *When the Moon Has Set*, by Yeats and Lady Gregory on a visit to Coole Park in October 1901; the details of this rejection were examined in Chapter Three. The following summer saw him write and submit (successfully) to Yeats his two one-act plays, *Riders to the Sea* and *The Shadow of the Glen*. But renewed attention to the rejection of his first play the previous year casts a somewhat different (and less ineluctably predestined) light on Synge's development as an Irish playwright. Synge and Joyce were to have a series of intense meetings in Paris in March 1903, when he showed his fellow Irishman the manuscript of *Riders to the Sea*; and there is much worth comparing in their two bodies of work. But I propose to start with a comparison of their two Irish Ibsenite plays.[18]

Frank McGuinness has likened Synge's *When the Moon has Set* to Ibsen's *Rosmersholm*.[19] Certainly, the burden of the past lies heavy on Synge's play, set on a Big House estate in County Wicklow, which the young man of the house Colm Sweeney has come back from Paris to inherit. His uncle has died under mysterious circumstances and the interrrelated questions of legacy and inheritance are troubled by repeated suggestions that the uncle has been guilty of an act of *mésalliance* with one of the servants. Having gone insane as a result of her trauma, the betrayed woman makes several Ophelia-like entrances in the course of the play. Colm has returned from Paris full of aesthetic notions, anxious to pursue a career as a writer and to break with the conservative Protestant beliefs in which he was raised. His most intense relationship is with a Catholic nun, Sister Eileen, whom he eventually persuades to convert to his aesthetic creed. There is also a political or nationalist dimension to this Irish woman, particularly evident at the end of the play when she symbolically changes from her nun's black garb to a dress of nationalist green. Colm and Eileen wed each other in the pantheist terms of sun, moon and stars, in lines which would be repeated in the overtly mythological context of Synge's last play, *Deirdre of the Sorrows*.

When the Moon Has Set cannot be reckoned a success. But the grounds on which Yeats condemned it – 'morbidity' – can be and were applied with no less force to most of Synge's other dramatic productions. What resonates most strikingly with Joyce's *Exiles*, along with the Ibsenite setting, character and themes common to both, is the explicit address and denomination of characters as Catholic or Protestant. This is a notable feature of both plays in and of itself but all the more so because that dimension was to be so thoroughly erased from the Irish drama of the Abbey Theatre. Protestant playwrights like Synge, Lady Gregory and O'Casey were to concentrate exclusively on Catholic characters in the present (as did Shaw in his Abbey play of 1904, *John Bull's Other Island*) or to retreat into mythology. A key element of potential transgression in *Exiles* resides in the fact that two of the four main characters are Catholic, Richard and Bertha, while two are Protestant, Robert and Beatrice. For all that Beatrice has been named after Dante's beloved, her ivory tower unapproachability is presented by Richard in terms of her Protestantism:

RICHARD. (*gently*) Does nothing then in life give you peace? Surely
it exists for you somewhere.
BEATRICE. If there were convents in our religion perhaps
there. At least I think so at times.[20]

It suits Robert to reenforce this portrayal of his cousin as puritanical,
since he can then claim that he derives from a more full-blooded
version of Protestantism than she does:

> I know what is in Beatty's ears at the moment [...] the buzz of
> the harmonium in her father's parlour [...] The asthmatic voice
> of protestantism. [...] She goes there [to her family in Cork] on
> retreat, when the protestant strain in her prevails – gloom,
> seriousness, righteousness. [...] But she comes back here to
> my mother, you see. The piano influence is from our side
> of the house.[21]

The erotic and the religious are no less entwined in the crucial
exchanges between Synge's Colm Sweeney and Sister Eileen:

> **COLM.** A day will come when you will mourn over your
> barrenness.[...] I do not blame you, I only blame the creed that has
> distorted the nature God made for you in the beginning.
> **SISTER EILEEN.** [... *picks up an old book*] May I take Saint Theresa
> with me as a remembrance? You are not likely to read her.
> **COLM.** [...] Why will you worship the mania of Saint Theresa?
> Your own beauty, your own expression of the divinity
> of woman, is holier than she is.[22]

In eroticized exchanges like these, the language of romance is infused,
not with imagery from the natural world, nor even with a subliminal
biblical cadence, but with an explicitly denominational bias.This is
virtually without precedent in the classical canon of Irish drama. There,
on the rare occasion when a Protestant character does appear, as in
O'Casey's plays, they are relegated to the margins while the dramatic
emphasis – even if it is critical – remains on the Catholics.

The characters in the Synge play speak in formal, occasionally stilted
terms, as do those in *Exiles*. Nor is it a case of bad English translations
of Ibsen. If Synge was to read him in German, Joyce – notoriously –
learnt Norwegian so as to read the master's plays in the original. It is
not that formal prose cannot answer; more that there is something
pallid and restricted in its dramatic use in these two plays. The
exception in the Synge play emerges in the servants of the Big House,
Mrs. Byrne, a family servant, and Bride, a young country girl. The latter
addresses Colum as follows: 'My uncle is a bit queer too, one time and
another. I'm thinking it was him your honour seen this night upon the
roads, for he does be always walking around like your self, God bless
you, a fine handsome man'.[23] Here, in an instant, we come across the

dramatic speech that is so familiar from Synge's canonical plays, closely modelled on Irish syntax and with a looselimbed expressiveness. When Bride declares that 'we must be satisfied, and what man at all can be living forever'[24], we realize with a start that we are hearing a near double of one of the most famous lines in Synge's drama, the closing lines to Maurya's stoical response to the death by drowning of her last son in *Riders to the Sea*. This is its first appearance in Synge's writing a full year earlier than the two one-act peasant plays and in a very different social and dramatic context.

When the Moon has Set, as we have seen, was rejected by Yeats, where he writes in the memorandum he drew up for the family executors after Synge's death in 1909: 'It was after its rejection by us he took to peasant work' (III, 155). A question this study has sought to address is the extent to which Synge moved away from writing plays about his own Anglo-Irish Protestant Ascendancy background in favour of the peasant plays which Yeats and Lady Gregory were already writing entirely of his own volition or as a canny response to the kinds of plays more likely to win acceptance in an emerging Irish national theatre. With the two one-act plays he produced the following summer, one promotes the myth of the west of Ireland through its setting on the Aran Islands. The other, though set like *When the Moon has Set* in Wicklow, has erased the class distinctions of the area along with the religious. Instead, it has chosen to focus on the dramatic contrast between a restrictive bourgeois household and a romantic outdoors, something which was to become a leitmotif of Synge's canonical plays.

At Coole Park in October 1901, where his play was rejected, Synge's just-completed prose volume *The Aran Islands* was conversely praised by both Yeats and Lady Gregory: 'We like it very much and think very highly of it. It is extraordinarily vivid and gives an imaginative and at the same time convincing impression of the people and of their life, and it ought, we think, to be very successful.'[25] Notwithstanding Yeats and Gregory's confidence in the work's ultimate success and indeed their letter-writing support, Synge was to undergo six years of fruitless effort with London publishers before getting *The Aran Islands* into print, exactly half the twelve Joyce was to experience in his efforts to have *Dubliners* published. These two experimental Irish prose works encountered much the same incomprehension both as to their genre and as to how they should be read. The direction Synge's other plays were to take would emerge from what he was about to see at the Irish Literary Theatre in 1901: not Yeats's and Moore's *Diarmuid and Gráinne,* whose influence would not register until his last play where he would decide to take on 'the mythology people' [as he called them], but Douglas Hyde's one-act play *Casadh an tSúgáin.* Joyce's hostile response to the 1901 programme of the Irish Literary Theatre led him to denounce it in 'The Day of the Rabblement', and to do so in specifically Ibsenian terms:

> the Irish Literary Theatre by its surrender to the trolls has cut itself adrift from the line of advancement. [...] Elsewhere there are men who are worthy to carry on the tradition of the old master who is dying in Christiania.[26]

Joyce concludes with the strong implication that he is one of them. Synge, by contrast, was to write positively of the third year of the Irish Literary Theatre, and specifically of *The Twisting of the Rope,* as an important breakthrough, since Hyde's play 'gave a new direction and impulse to Irish drama',[27] an 'impulse' which he was to develop so decidedly in his own manner, as the previous chapter examined.

But the matter should not be allowed to rest there (as it so often has), with Joyce electing to go off 'elsewhere' than Ireland with Ibsen in 1901 and Synge signing up with Yeats and Lady Gregory to treat dramatically of 'the people' in plays of peasant life at the Abbey Theatre. For one thing, Ibsen was not as comprehensively banished from the Irish stage as this binary opposition makes it appear. For another, there was the complicated reaction of James Joyce to the emergence of a near contemporary like John Millington Synge, which the rest of this chapter wishes to explore. In Joyce's subsequent life and writing career, Synge refuses to stay confined in and by the satiric couplets of Joyce's 1904 poem *The Holy Office*: 'Or him who sober all the day/ Mixes a naggin in his play.'[28]

In March 1903, in Paris, a memorable series of encounters between Synge and Joyce took place. These two major Irish modernist writers offer interesting and intersecting trajectories at this point in their respective careers. Synge is about to return permanently to Ireland after a decade in exile on the Continent to play a crucial role in the founding and development of Ireland's National Theatre; Joyce is arriving on the Continent for the first time, taking the initial step in what would prove (after 1912) permanent exile from Ireland 'to forge', as the last page of *A Portrait of the Artist* puts it, 'in the smithy of my soul the uncreated conscience of my race'.[29] Synge had gone to Paris for the last time to give up his room at 13, rue d'Assas. Richard Ellmann writes that he did so because he had 'failed to get on in Paris';[30] but this is to conflate 1903 with the period over six years earlier when Yeats had advised the drifting Synge to 'give up Paris'. The situation in 1903 was quite different. The period in-between had seen Synge move back and forth between Ireland and France, engaged in the concentrated writing across four years of *The Aran Islands* and taking an increasingly vested interest in the emergence of an Irish National Theatre. Ellmann writes that Synge 'had shown *Riders to the Sea* to Yeats late in 1902';[31] but as Ann Saddlemyer's Chronology in the *Collected Letters* records, and as the previous chapter examined, he had shown not one but two plays, *Shadow of the Glen* as well as *Riders to the Sea*, and not just to Yeats but to Lady Gregory, since they were at Coole Park. (Ellmann frequently erases Gregory's presence in this way.) Within a year of the meeting with Joyce in March 1903 both of Synge's plays would be produced, by Willie Fay's Irish National Theatre Society at the Molesworth Hall and the plans for the opening of the Abbey Theatre advanced. For Synge it was now imperative to return full time to Ireland and to Dublin in particular, where he would become the one of the Yeats-Gregory-Synge directorate to spend most time in the Abbey Theatre, overseeing the production of his (and others') plays.

Nor did he and Joyce meet just on the one occasion but, according to Herbert Gorman 'seven or eight times' in the course of the week 6-13 March 1903.[32] Stanislaus Joyce reveals that Synge and his brother had 'many quarrelsome discussions',[33] always with literature as their focus, both proving equally voluble and argumentative. The portrait of Synge which emerges from the encounter, as Ellmann notes, is very different from the reticent and enigmatic side he presented when in the company of Yeats. In a January 1903 meeting, as Joyce recalls in a letter to Stanislaus, Yeats had praised Synge's *Riders to the Sea* to Joyce as 'quite Greek'. Joyce went on to prophesy accurately: 'I suppose Synge will be boomed now by the Irish Theatre.'[34] Insufficient attention has been given to this detail in interpreting the apparent animus Joyce displayed when Synge showed him a manuscript copy of *Riders to the Sea* and asked for his opinion. As Joyce wrote gleefully to Stanislaus: 'I am glad to say that ever since I read it I have been riddling it mentally till it has [not] a sound spot. It is tragic about all the men that are drowned in the islands; but thanks be to God Synge isn't an Aristotelian' (35). Joyce objected to the play's one-act form, its brevity; Aristotle had argued in *The Poetics* that the action of a tragedy must have 'a proper magnitude' to attain 'beauty' and to encompass a credible change of fortune.[35] Joyce's particular objection was to 'the manner in which the catastrophe [in Synge's play] was brought about' (35). Presumably he objected because the young son Bartley dies by being thrown from his horse into the Atlantic Ocean rather than being drowned outright in the 'inexorable sea which claims all her [Maurya's] sons', as he later phrased it.[36] During the week he was debating with Synge, Joyce was working on the aesthetic theory which Stephen Dedalus propounds in *A Portrait of the Artist*. This places drama at the apex of literary achievement and, rather than advocating strict fidelity to Aristotle's concise dicta in *The Poetics*, claims the right to elaborate and a certain independence in the following proud claim: 'Aristotle has not defined pity and terror. I have.'[37] This is not the case. In Section 13 of *The Poetics*, Aristotle offers the following definitions of pity and terror/fear: 'pity is aroused by the plight of the man who does not deserve his misfortune, and fear by the predicaments of men like ourselves.'[38] Stephen memorably defines them as follows:

> Pity is the feeling which arrests the mind in the presence of whatsoever is grave and constant in human sufferings and unites it with the human sufferer. Terror is the feeling which arrests the mind in the presence of whatsoever is grave and constant in human sufferings and unites it with the secret cause.[39]

The Paris notebook in which Joyce elaborated his aesthetic theory has an entry on pity and terror dated 13 February 1903, less than a month before his meetings with Synge. The passage defining pity and terror is virtually identical with the passage in *A Portrait*, except that the two terms are defined in reverse order. Nowhere in his definition has Aristotle anything to say about what might be the source of the suffering visited upon humans; his concern is exclusively with the kind of people to whom these awful events occur. Joyce is the one to introduce the issue of a 'secret cause' and identify it with the feeling of terror. (He writes elsewhere in the Notebook that a work which evidences 'some manifest cause of human suffering' is not art, tragic or otherwise.)[40] Joyce identifies the 'inexorable sea' as that 'secret cause' in Synge's *Riders to the Sea*, the metaphysical as much as merely physical force which influences the lives and fates of the islanders. He then proceeds to object to Synge's denouement (as non-Aristotelian) because the catastrophe comes about not because of the sea but because of an animal. There seems to me a double animus operating here: against Synge's dramatization of folk beliefs concerning the return of the dead on the Aran Islands, which is where the horses become central, as was explored in Chapter One. But Joyce is also reacting to Yeats's praise of *Riders to the Sea* as 'quite Greek', which suggests reasons for his hostility and line of attack. By demonstrating that Synge's play is not Aristotelian, and hence not 'quite Greek', he can refute Yeats as being less than knowledgeable in such matters. But the imputing of a 'secret cause' betrays Joyce into a definition of Aristotelianism which is itself not accurate and to which Joyce himself did not adhere in his and Stephen Dedalus' definitions of pity and terror.

Although his 'riddling' of *Riders to the Sea* may suggest a desire to dismiss it, Joyce's interest in and continued engagement with Synge's one-act tragedy may be said to begin rather than end in March 1903. Even at this (early) stage where he is apparently pointing out its deficiencies as a tragedy, Joyce has already (as Stanislaus's letter about the seven or eight meetings with Synge reveals) begun committing the play to memory: 'Synge [...] listened and countered my brother's arguments calmly. Perhaps he was mollified by the fact that the rhythm of certain phrases had stuck in my brother's memory – he already knew Maurya's final speeches almost by heart – and he repeated them with such a keen sense of their beauty that it must have tempered his strictures.'[41] This reveals something of the same contradictory disjunction of Joyce's attitude towards Yeats: castigating the floating aesthete's 'treacherous adaptability' while memorizing many of the early poems. The lines from Synge's play must have continued to stick in Joyce's memory because, almost exactly five years later, on 6 March 1908, Ellmann recounts how Joyce decided to translate *Riders to the Sea* into Italian. He enlisted the translating cooperation of his friend and pupil, the lawyer Nicolo Vidacovich, interested the Italian Grand Guignol Company in producing it and, shortly after Synge died in March 1909, approached the Synge estate seeking permission to stage it. Ellmann briefly and bluntly states that 'the Synge heirs refused consent', without further comment or any citation of a source.[42]

W.J. McCormack's Synge biography is rather more forthcoming on what might have motivated the refusal:

> When Ned [Edward Stephens, Synge's nephew and literary executor] required from Joyce a specific indication 'how often and at what fee' his Italian friends proposed to stage the translation of *Riders to the Sea*, he was only doing his duty by the financial beneficiaries of the will he was charged to execute.[43]

As so often with Joyce, therefore, the reason behind the Synge's estate's 'refusal' of his request was financial squabbling. One could see how far he could go in these matters when, in 1918 and living in Zurich, Joyce engaged in a furious row with the young British embassy official, Henry Carr, who had been signed up by him to play Algernon Moncrieff in a production of Wilde's *The Importance of Being Earnest*. The incident is well-known and formed the basis for Tom Stoppard's 1974 play, *Travesties*. Joyce and a British actor, Claud Sykes, had the previous year founded a theatrical troupe known as the English Players to stage plays in Zurich in English (with one eye on the financial support of the British Embassy there): Sykes was to be producer and director, Joyce business manager. Their first production was Wilde's play. Henry Carr, whom Joyce had met in the British Embassy in Zurich, agreed to take the part of Algernon based on a complex (if low-level) financial arrangement in which he claimed he had bought his own suit for the part and Joyce counter-claimed Carr had agreed to sell a certain number of tickets. In June 1918, even while the court case he had launched against Carr proceeded, Joyce and Sykes staged the English Players' second season, a series of three one-act plays. One of them was Synge's *Riders to the Sea*. According to Ellmann, Joyce had throughout 1909 'pursued his efforts to secure acting rights for the translation of *Riders to the Sea* into Italian, but made no headway with the Synge estate'.44 The translation was no longer an issue, since Synge's play would now be presented in its original (Hiberno-)English rather than Italian. Four of the five plays eventually staged by the English Players in Zurich were Irish. They opened with Oscar Wilde, a suggestion by Claud Sykes which Joyce readily endorsed; during the applause at the end of the opening night, he called out: 'Hurrah for Ireland! Poor Wilde was Irish and so am I.'45 The second programme featured Synge's *Riders to the Sea* and Shaw's *The Dark Lady of the Sonnets* (the third was by J.M. Barrie); the third and final production in 1919 was to be a double bill of Martyn's *The Heather Field* and Yeats's *The Land of Heart's Desire*; but Sykes could not find a cast for the Yeats, and the Martyn was presented as a stand-alone. The second and third year bills of the English Players made crystal clear whose was now the determining hand in these artistic choices.

Joyce's investment in the Synge play was markedly higher than in any of the others. His wife Nora was cast in the role of Cathleen, the elder of Maurya's two daughters. She had never acted before; but a major incentive to cast her would have been that Nora was not only from Ireland (all of the others actors, Claud Sykes and his wife Daisy Race, who was to play Maurya, the embassy officials like Henry Carr, etc., were English) but she came originally from the city of Galway, fronting on the Aran Islands in which Synge's play was set. The association of Nora with the Aran Islands and with Synge's writing would have been consolidated by the visit she and James paid to Inishmore in late August 1912, on Joyce's last visit to Ireland (seeking to have *Dubliners* published in Dublin by George Roberts of Maunsel and Co.). As a contribution to the cost of the visit, Joyce had secured agreement with the Triestine newspaper *Il Piccolo della Sera* to write a number of articles on Irish subjects of cultural interest. One of these was entitled 'The Mirage of the Fisherman of Aran', a piece of prose which immediately places Joyce not only in the company of Synge and his prose account, *The Aran Islands*, but in the extensive company of those writers who throughout the nineteenth and into the twentieth century had visited the islands as cultural tourists and/or as those wishing to learn the Irish language. Not knowing any Irish, Joyce in this respect resembles Yeats on his 1896 visit to the islands, which was discussed in Chapter Three. Like Synge, Joyce encounters islanders who speak not only Irish but English; it is, however, as Joyce remarks of one of the islanders, 'an English all [their] own'.[46] In this and subsequent conversations with the Aran Islanders recorded in Joyce's Aran article, it is clear that the conversational lead is taken, not by him, but by the person consistently referred to in the article as 'my companion' (201, 204): Nora Barnacle. Throughout the visit, Nora acts as an interpreter of island speech for her husband. When Joyce quotes a sample of that Syngean speech – 'it has been a horrible summer, thanks be to God' – he initially proposes that this remark 'seems to be one of the usual Irish blunders' (204). But this blundering interpretation is then revised (one imagines under the guidance of his 'companion's' local knowledge and intuitions) towards a more accurate perception that the island man's statement 'comes, rather, from the inmost heart of human resignation.' Synge's *The Aran Islands* would also have been a guide to interpreting local Aran speech, with its insight into 'the mood of beings who feel their isolation in the face of a universe that wars on them with winds and seas' (II, 75). When it comes to Joyce's description of how the islanders dress, his prose mirrors that of Synge in its detailed mimetic precision: 'The fisherman of Aran is sure-footed. He wears a rough, flat sandal of oxhide, open at the shank, without heels and tied with laces of rawhide' (204). The one element omitted from this account of the unusual footwear worn by the Aran Islanders is its name: pampooties. That honour is given to Buck Mulligan in *Ulysses* when he reports to Stephen: ' – The tramper Synge is looking for you, he said, to murder you. [...] He's out in pampooties to murder you.'[47]

The English Players presented Synge's *Riders to the Sea* on 17 June, 1918. Nora was thirty-eight at the time, and could have been considered for the lead, if made up to look older; but her age made her rather a mature choice for Cathleen, who is described in Synge's stage directions as '*a girl of about twenty*' (III, 5). Her not being cast as Maurya makes sense given her theatrical lack of experience; as Ellmann recounts, 'she had never acted before and was timid at first, but her rich contralto voice, with its strong Galway accent, gradually acquired confidence.'[48] But Nora's influence on the production proved pervasive. In a situation uncannily reminiscent of J.M. Synge taking over from Willie Fay to guide the National Theatre players through the pronunciation of the unusual words and complex rhythms of his language, James Joyce stepped in ahead of the credited producer [*recte* director] of the play in Zurich, Claud W. Sykes, to train the other (English) actors 'to imitate [Nora's] speech and the Aran speech rhythms'.[49] Ellmann describes Cathleen in the play as 'a minor role', an example of how inaccurate he can be in his accounts of Synge's writing and career. Cathleen is not a minor role but one of the three major characters, all women, who dominate *Riders to the Sea*. Maurya is offstage for the lengthy opening scene in which Cathleen and her younger sister (who also bears the name Nora) discuss the possibility that a drowned man's clothes may be their brother's. Brenda Maddox in her biography more readily recognizes that Nora 'set the pace for the rest to follow' but is equally inaccurate when she has her speak 'the opening line of the play', "'She's lying down, God help her, and maybe sleeping, if she's able."' (III, 5)[50] The first line of *Riders to the Sea* is in fact spoken by her sister Nora: 'Where is she?', a question to which Cathleen's line is the reply. Cathleen remains onstage throughout the play and is the more dominant of the two sisters in engaging either with her mother or the other islanders. Her part consists of over a hundred lines; Maurya's numerically is barely a few lines longer, though she gets the major monologues with which the play concludes. Maddox does add some valuable detail about the degree and kind of the entire Joyce family's involvement in the production: 'Giorgio [who was thirteen] and Lucia [about to turn twelve] played children in the crowd, and Joyce himself contributed an off-stage tenor.'[51] This final detail provides another resonance with Synge. Both men came close to a career in music (one as a singer, one as a musician) before opting decisively for literature, but not without bringing musical principles to the fore in their writing.

From their first meeting in 1903 to the Zurich production of *Riders to the Sea* in 1918, Joyce moved from a position of extreme ambivalence towards Synge to the degree of identification conveyed by this collaborative family production. The decisive change to a more unequivocally positive view would appear to have occurred in 1907 when Joyce in Trieste intensely and minutely tracked the tumultuous response back in Dublin to the Abbey Theatre's production of *The Playboy of the Western World*. Ellmann records that on 5 May 1907, four months after the play's premiere, Joyce confided that 'he thought highly now of Synge and even said, with unwonted modesty, [...] that "Synge's art is more original than my own"'. [52] Reacting to the furore over Synge's masterpiece when it premiered, Joyce wrote in Jaunary 1907 to Stanislaus in words that, as Emer Nolan puts it, 'confess his disappointment at missing the excitement of the riots'[53]: 'I feel like a man in a house who hears a row in the street and voices he knows shouting but can't get out to see what the hell is going on' (212). Joyce's first recourse to find out more was to read the *Daily Mail* in Rome and send on an account of what he discovered there to Stanislaus, who remained in Trieste. The English newspaper, under the heading 'Riot in a Dublin Theatre', was covering the trial in the Police Courts of several playgoers for 'disorderly conduct'. Joyce mistakenly assumes that the Padraic Colum who has been arrested is the playwright and poet whose own works had been staged at the Abbey Theatre rather than his father and is hence puzzled over the description of Colum as a 'clerk'. His first encounter with Synge's play, therefore, is the newspaper's description: 'The story, I believe, is of a self-accused parricide with whom all the girls of a district FALL IN LOVE' [capitals Joyce's own] (208). There is a dig at Yeats as a phrase-maker for describing the play as 'an example of the exaggeration of art' by way of supporting his claim that 'it was Synge's masterpiece'. Joyce was used to Yeats's extravagant claims on Synge's behalf but on this occasion the statement is let stand and Joyce goes on to make the cautious and jealous observation: 'I suspect Synge's naggin is on the increase'. This glances at the satiric couplet assigned to Synge in 1904's *The Holy Office*: 'Or him who sober all the day/Mixes a naggin in his play'.[54] There, Synge is only one of the many figures associated with Yeats, Gregory and the Literary Revival who is accorded a dismissive couplet. But Synge is now breaking out of that subsidiary role and assuming an importance of his own. Joyce admits a degree of self-identification when he speaks without irony of the travails Synge will undergo in Ireland. As a man of conscience, Synge is a writer who like Ibsen risks condemnation from the pulpit for daring to speak the truth about a repressive and hypocritical society, particularly in matters sexual: 'Synge will probably be condemned from the pulpit, as heretic: which would be dreadful'. (208-209) Joyce hopes that John Eglinton and Frederick Ryan, the editors of the short-lived *Dana* in 1904, will 'start another paper in defence of free thought, just for a week or so.' The irony is that Joyce had submitted his first (and briefest) fictional self-exploration, 'A Portrait of the Artist', to *Dana* in that year, and had had it rejected. The editors admired Joyce's style but rejected it because, as Ellmann recounts, 'Eglinton told Joyce "I can't print what I can't understand," and objected to the hero's sexual exploits.'[55] From this first brief journalistic account of Synge's *Playboy of the Western World* in the *Daily Mail*, Joyce may not have realized yet how much of the opposition to the play was generated by the hero's sexual exploits, and how unlikely it was that Eglinton and Ryan would come to the defence of such an Irish writer. But matters sexual were on Joyce's mind with regard to Synge, for he closes this account by speculating that '*Sinn Fein* and *The Leader* will find out *all* about Synge's life in Paris: which will be nice for Lady G[regory] and Miss H. [Annie Horniman, benefactress of the Abbey]' (209). This, one of Joyce's several innuendoes about the life Synge led in Paris being sexually promiscuous, is not borne out by any the biographical accounts; but it exhibits the classic Dublin prurience towards that Continental capital exhibited by Little Chandler and Ignatius Gallagher in the *Dubliners* short story, 'A Little Cloud', when they discuss Paris as an 'immoral' city.[56] In relation to 'The Holy Office', this representation of Synge now resembles not the sober man depicting drunkards but a man of sexual daring like Joyce's own self-portrait elsewhere in the same poem.

Joyce is not long in acquiring copies of the Dublin-published *The Freeman's Journal* which, as he puts it himself, provide 'fuller accounts of the Abbey riots' (211). They also cover not only or primarily the legal trials for disorderly conduct but the debate held within the Abbey Theatre itself. Joyce is provoked to mirth, finding the debate 'very funny', as the play is condemned by 'our old friends', his college companions Francis Sheehy-Skeffington and Richard Sheehy, the latter holding that 'the play was rightly condemned as a slander on Irishmen and Irishwomen'. But he makes a serious exception to his scorching irony in the case of Richard T. Sheehan, whom he had also known at University College Dublin, who defended the play and whose contribution Joyce read 'with pleasure and surprise'. Sheehan's position was unusual, since he spoke not as an urban upper-middle-class Dubliner but as a rural 'peasant', one of those represented in Synge's play. He did so to praise the play's social accuracy and authenticity in representing 'a particular form of marriage law which [...] was very common in Ireland' and which presented 'a fine woman like Pegeen Mike [with] a tubercule Koch's disease man like Shaun Keogh'.[57] Sheehan took this to be the play's main point rather than the murder. Joyce would have been particularly struck by Sheehan's larger and more general claim that 'when the artist appears in Ireland who was not afraid of life and nature, the women of Ireland would receive him.' This statement of Sheehan's is going to provide the foundation stone and basis on which Joyce will develop a close kinship with Synge in his subsequent prose writings. Synge is acclaimed on the same lines as Joyce's self-presentation in *The Holy Office*, the artist as unhypocritical apostle of sexual liberation, shaming his fellow writers for their timidity and performing 'a similar kind service [...] for each maiden, shy and nervous'.[58] When Sheehan uttered his remark about 'the women of Ireland', the newspaper reports that 'at this stage in the speech many ladies, whose countenances plainly indicated intense feelings of astonishment and pain, rose and left the place.' Joyce's response is keen, his interest clearly piqued in a play he has not yet read or seen: 'I would like [...] to hear the phrases which drove out the ladies with expressions of pain on their faces.' He is glad to record with admiration the 'great phrase' which was reported in the newspaper account of the debate: '"if all the girls in Mayo were standing before me in their shifts", wonderful vision.' Although Joyce remarks later in the same letter 'about Synge himself I cannot speak', he goes so far to venture to Stanislaus a revealing remark: 'One writer speaks of Synge and his master Zola (!) so I suppose when *Dubliners* appears they will speak of me and my master Synge.' Synge was six years younger than Yeats, and nine years older than Joyce. Accordingly, he oscillates between being an older blocking figure whose influence must be got around and a contemporary writer with whom Joyce can identify.[59] The process was complicated by the delays surrounding the publication of *Dubliners*, which were to continue a full seven years beyond 1907.

When Joyce makes the comparison of the reaction in Dublin over Synge's *Playboy* to a row in the street, he further adds: 'It has put me off the story I was going to write' (212) – to wit, 'The Dead'. As is well known, 'The Dead' was a late addition to the volume of short stories Joyce thought he had already completed. It is also the volume's masterpiece. In it, Joyce was consciously moving away from the style of 'scrupulous meanness' and unrelenting irony in which all of the other stories are composed. He was aiming instead for something less 'harsh' and narrow, more accommodating of the country's 'ingenuous insularity and its hospitality'.[60] Part of that newfound accommodation was to find room in the story for Synge, rather than continuing to reiterate the harsh dismissal of *Riders to the Sea*. Ellmann notes how the presence of Synge can be detected in 'The Dead' through the figure of the nationalistic Miss Ivors, who 'tries to persuade Gabriel to go to Aran (where Synge's *Riders* is set) and when he refuses twits him for his lack of patriotic feeling'.[61] The reference is even more to Synge's prose work, *The Aran Islands*, than it is to his play, as Miss Ivors' opening remark makes clear: '- O, Mr. Conroy, will you come for an excursion to the Aran Isles this summer? We're going to stay there a whole month. It will be splendid out in the Atlantic. You ought to come.'[62] Annual sojourns of approximately a month on the Aran Islands were exactly what Synge had undertaken in the course of his five years' composition of his prose work. Although not published until the year of Synge's *Playboy*, 1907, *The Aran Islands* was already complete when the two writers met in Paris in March 1903 and individual portions from it had already been published in 1898 and 1901. Ellmann finds 'small echoes' of Synge in Gabriel's exchange with Miss Ivors and the debate between them as to whether Irish or English is the native language.[63] But these echoes go considerably further than Ellmann allows, resonating and building as the movement of the story turns westwards. For what he omits is the association forged in 'The Dead' between the Miss Ivors who makes a brief but charged contribution before rapidly exiting and the figure of Gabriel's wife, Gretta, who comes to the fore as the story progresses. Miss Ivors herself makes the connection when recommending a month on the Aran Islands to Gabriel: 'It would be splendid for Gretta too if she'd come. She's from Connacht, isn't she?' Gabriel's reply is brusque and dismissive: 'Her people are' (189). But the call of the west will not be so readily silenced by Gabriel's determination to look singly and determinedly towards the Continent. The heated exchange between her husband and Miss Ivors has not escaped Gretta's attention. When she inquires as to its cause and is told 'she wanted me to go for a trip to the west of Ireland and I said I wouldn't', Gretta's response is enthusiastically to endorse the suggestion: 'O, do go, Gabriel, she cried. I'd love to see Galway again.' Gabriel's reply is even more dismissive and rude: 'You can go if you like' (191). But as the rest of the story movingly and compellingly depicts, Gabriel is going to come to a symbolic place and position where, as the last paragraph puts it, 'the time had come for him to set out on his journey westward' (225).

A narrative from Gretta's formative years there, buried beneath the bourgeois married life she and Gabriel have lived for many years in Dublin, surfaces when a traditional song is sung at the party earlier that night. Later, in their bedroom, she gives Gabriel an account of Michael Furey, the young man from the west who died for her. Syngean phrases accumulate as the story reaches its close. Rebuked by 'this figure from the dead', Gabriel now sees himself as cutting, not the impressive figure he had projected in his after-dinner speech, but a 'ludicrous figure, acting as a pennyboy for his aunts' (221). Gabriel's phrase is a variant of the 'penny pot-boy' Pegeen asks her father to provide (II, 65). Feeling an increasing chill, Gabriel 'stretched himself cautiously along under the sheets and lay down beside his wife. One by one they were all becoming shades' (224). This invocation of death with a married couple lying down under the sheets comes close to Nora and Dan Burke in *The Shadow of the Glen*, especially Nora's closing access of sympathy for the husband from whom she is sundered: 'let you be getting up into your bed, and not be taking your death with the wind blowing on you' (I, 55). In the darkness, Gabriel imagines he beholds 'the form of a young man', the ghost of Michael Furey: 'Other forms were near. His soul had approached that region where dwell the vast hosts of the dead' (224). This is no Christian vision but of a piece with the folklore beliefs Synge encountered on the Aran Islands, where (as Chapter One examined) an island woman could report 'a great sight out to the west in this island, and saw all the people that were dead a while back in this island and the south island, and they all talking with each other' (II,157).[64] Harold Bloom writes in *The Anxiety of Influence* that post-Enlightenment poetry 'takes as its obsessive theme the power of the mind over the universe of death' and argues that this knowledge first comes to the young poet through their 'experience of another poet'.[65] Joyce's profound engagement with Synge in his prose fiction has only just begun in 'The Dead'; it will continue through *A Portrait of the Artist as a Young Man* (1916) and *Ulysses* (1922).

In the closing pages of *A Portrait* the formal third person narrative in which the novel has been conducted (albeit with considerable stylistic variation) is replaced by a series of diary entries covering the last six weeks prior to Stephen Dedalus's taking the emigrant boat. Many of the entries record exchanges with members of his family and the close friends he has made during his time at University College Dublin, the period covered by this fifth and final section of the novel. The fourth section has concluded with Stephen's decision not to follow a religious vocation and become a priest of the Holy Roman and Catholic Church. Instead, he will become an artist, a 'priest of eternal imagination'.[66] Accordingly, many of the dialogues with Stephen's college friends are taken up with aesthetics and politics, with crucial issues that dedicating himself to a life as a writer involve. So the diary entries at the end also touch on issues of culture; but they are as much private as public, as much public as private, the two repeatedly intersecting. The entry for 13 April picks up and refers back to his conversation with the English Dean of Studies at the university which has led this precocious young Irish undergraduate to observe, in a famous and much-cited passage: 'The language in which we are speaking is his before it is mine. [...] His language, so familiar and so foreign, will always be for me an acquired speech. I have not made or accepted its words' (189). The debate has hinged on Stephen's use of the word 'tundish' to describe a funnel, a word the Dean of Studies claims never to have heard. The dairy entry records how Stephen has looked up the word in a dictionary: 'I looked it up and find it English and good old blunt English too. Damn the dean of studies and his funnel! What did he come here for to teach us his own language or to learn it from us? Damn him one way or the other!' (251). The penultimate sentence in the diary can be spoken in two ways, one of them placing the pause after the 'for' as standard English practice would require; the second would stumble over the 'for' and be drawn to affix it to the verb to create the Hiberno-English oral verbal construction, 'for to teach us'. On the very next day, the diary records an entry in which John Millington Synge makes an unexpected appearance, under the transparent disguise of 'John Alphonsus Mulrennan':

> 14 April: John Alphonsus Mulrennan has just returned from the west of Ireland. (European and Asiatic papers please copy.) He told us he met an old man there in a mountain cabin. Old man had red eyes and short pipe. Old man spoke Irish. Mulrennan spoke Irish. Then old man and Mulrennan spoke English. Mulrennan spoke to him about universe and stars. Old man sat, listened, spoke, spat. Then said: Ah, there must be terrible queer creatures at the latter end of the world. I fear him. I fear his redrimmed horny eyes. It is with him I must struggle all through this night till day come, till he or I lie dead, gripping him by the sinewy throat till... Till what? Till he yield to me? No. I mean him no harm. (252)

This passage is of a stylistic piece with those recorded in *The Aran Islands* and the term 'queer' one of Synge's most distinctive linguistic features (e.g. 'the seeing is a queer lot and you'd never know the things they'd do' in *The Well of the Saints*). In that sense, it is a full textual quote transposed from Synge's prose work in a way the diary form facilitates. But it has also undergone a degree of assimilation as an oral prose narrative passed on to Stephen Dedalus (and James Joyce) by John Alphonsus Mulrennan ('told us'), who in turn heard its contents from the old man in the west. The act of listening is being foregrounded and a complex act of cultural transmission being enacted. Both processes resonate off the key scene in 'The Dead' when Gabriel comes across Gretta caught in the act of listening to 'The Lass of Aughrim' being sung upstairs; and he in turn both listens to the song and watches her listening. Beside this can be positioned and aligned the passage in

Synge's Preface to *The Playboy of the Western World* where he writes of the considerable aid he received in the composition of *The Shadow of the Glen* through the act of listening, 'from a chink in the floor of the old Wicklow house where I was staying, that let me hear what was being said by the servant girls in the kitchen' (IV, 53). The two diary passages – that with the Dean of Studies and that with John Alphonsus Mulrennan – hover between English and Irish: the different meanings which words like 'home, Christ, ale, master' accrue when spoken by an English or an Irish person; the complex linguistic exchange between Mulrennan and the old man which moves from Irish to English in the same conversation. Joyce was among the first to note that when Synge went to the Aran Islands he was not met by islanders who simply spoke Irish which he subsequently translated into English but by islanders who were bi-lingual and already employing the forms of Hiberno-English he was to develop in his plays. These two dairy entries are themselves a dialogue, in counterpoint, between Joyce and Synge about the complex issues surrounding and consequences attendant upon an Irish writer who wishes to write in English rather than Irish but also to remain open and sensitive to what such a decision necessarily involves.

Joyce did not have to travel to the west of Ireland to find his artistic identity, as Synge had done; but like his fellow writer from within the Pale, he did have to travel and in the opposite direction. The irony in the diary entry, which seeks to deny kinship and distance affinity both racial and authorial, is scorched away by the primal life-or-death struggle in which Stephen Dedalus finds himself engaged. Its ostensible object is the old Irish story-teller whose archaic tongue, peasant ways and limited ideas are scorned by the sophisticated, European-leaning Dubliner but whose imaginative inheritance he is still anxious to secure. This same conflict has been dramatized in 'The Dead', where Miss Ivors and Gabriel argue over the Irish language as a writer's 'own' and which progressively exhumes Gretta Conroy's earlier life in the west of Ireland to expose the shortcomings of Gabriel's Continental ways. The old man speculates about the kind of existence sustained 'at the latter end of the world'; Stephen has been earlier described in *A Portrait* as 'burn[ing] to set out for the ends of the earth' (170). They are both pointed in the same imaginative direction, to the margins of the known where this world shades off into the other, though their means of getting there will differ.

But the old man from the west of Ireland scarcely seems a sufficient object for the depth and intensity of the violent emotional reaction provoked in Stephen: 'I fear his redrimmed horny eyes. It is with him I must struggle all through this night till day come, till he or I lie dead, gripping him by the sinewy throat till...'. The maculine singular object, the pronominal 'him', against whom this psychic violence is directed, is ambiguous, slippery, and may equally refer to John Alphonsus Mulrennan as to the old man, since both feature in the previous passage. What Joyce is expressing here, towards both Synge and his textual production, is what Harold Bloom diagnosed and described in Freudian terms as the 'anxiety of influence'. In writing of poetic influence, Bloom argues that the 'strong' poet 'is condemned to learn his profoundest yearnings through an awareness of other selves. The poem is within him, yet he experiences the shame and splendour of being found by poems – great poems – outside him. Bloom then quotes Malraux on the '"few mighty, often antagonistic ghosts" who haunt the heart of the young poet'.[67] For Joyce, Synge is such a ghost. In order to distance the closeness, the poet resorts to such strategies as parody (such as Joyce will deploy on Synge in the 'Scylla and Charybdis' chapter of *Ulysses* through the mockery of Buck Mulligan). The defining characteristic of such influence is what Bloom terms 'misprision', a swerve away from the precursor's poem through an act of poetic misreading. This process exactly describes Joyce's reaction to Synge's *Riders to the Sea*, which he insistently misreads as not being an Aristotelean tragedy; he's still at it in the generally favourable *Playboy* letters of 1907 to an extent that suggests compulsion repetition: 'Synge asked me to read [*Riders*] in Paris and when I told him what I thought of it and expounded a long critical attack on the catastrophe as he used it he did not pay the least attention to what I said. So perhaps his later work has merit' (212). This statement stubbornly adheres to Joyce's misprision of *Riders to the Sea* while cautiously entering a new note of praise. Throughout *The Anxiety of Influence*, Bloom repeatedly refers to the complex and psychically overdetermined engagement with an influential poetic predecessor in such graphic physical terms as 'wrestling'. The account in Stephen's diary is no less aggressive in his account of the psychic struggle, until the rational mind breaks free of the dream-like compulsion to make the literally true claim: 'I mean him no harm.' In Chapter Seven of *Ulysses*, Stephen vividly recalls the face of John Millington Synge from their Paris meeting in the following terms: 'Harsh gargoyle face that warred against me over our mess of hash of lights in rue Saint-Andre-des-Arts' (256). This harsh portrait of Synge is of a piece with the 'redrimmed horny eyes' and 'sinewy throat' of the passage about John Alphonsus Mulrennan in *A Portrait*. The metaphor used to describe their verbal encounter is in both cases extremely aggressive and violent.

Although the diary entry suddenly introduces a scenic shift to the west of Ireland in the last pages of *A Portrait*, Synge's presence has been signalled earlier in the novel through two major 'quotations' from his writings. The first occurs towards the close of Section Four in which Stephen, as he walks along the beach, works through his decision to be an artist. This process culminates and is crystallized in an epiphany where he sees a beautiful young woman wading in the water:

> A girl stood before him in midstream, alone and still, gazing out to sea. She seemed like one whom magic had changed into the likeness of a strange and beautiful seabird. Her long slender bare legs were delicate as a crane's and pure save where an emerald trail of seaweed had fashioned itself as a sign upon the flesh. Her thighs, fuller and softhued as ivory, were bared almost to the hips where the white fringes of her drawers were like featherings of soft white down. Her slateblue skirts were kilted boldly about her waist and dovetailed behind her. (171)

Some readers may need reminding of just how unlikely such a display of womanly flesh would have been in the petit-bourgeois precincts of a Dublin beach at the turn of the nineteenth century; the briefest glance at one of the photographic collections of the period shows how sartorially encumbered any young woman had to remain when venturing seaward. The same social and psychological restrictions did not apply in the more 'primitive' west of Ireland, as Synge remarked in a passage in *The Aran Islands* where he compared the greater freedom the women of the west enjoyed in such matters in comparison to their Dublin counterparts. This freedom, in Synge's eyes, brought them closer to the women of Paris than to those of Dublin. The passage is strikingly similar to that in *A Portrait*, even down to the sea-bird comparison, and argues that *The Aran Islands* served as a crucial exemplar in an emerging tradition of modern Irish prose on which Joyce felt he could draw:

> And as I walk round the edges of the sea, I often come on a girl with her petticoats tucked up round her, standing in a pool left by the tide and washing her flannels among the sea-anemones and crabs. Their red bodices and white tapering legs make them as beautiful as tropical seabirds, as they stand in a frame of seaweeds against the brink of the Atlantic. (II, 76)

The Joyce passage is interwoven with images from Celtic mythology, as I have argued elsewhere.[68] Stephen may not be physically alone on the beach, but he is isolated in his perception of the visionary possibilities of the scene. This effect is in part achieved by the transposition of an iconographic visual image of a beautiful young Irish woman from the west to the east of Ireland and from Synge's text of *The Aran Islands* to that of Joyce's *A Portrait of the Artist as a Young Man*. The heightened liminal qualities of the bird-girl passage are of a piece with the ghost of Michael Furey in the closing passages of 'The Dead'.

It is worth recalling that, of Synge's six canonical plays, only one is set on the Aran Islands. Although he heard the folktale of the unfaithful wife from a storyteller there, the narrative is set on the Irish mainland, somewhere between Galway and Dublin. The play's notoriety had made it well known, especially through Arthur Griffith's remark about the unlikelihood that the woman would leave with the tramp. Section Five of *A Portrait* records extensive cultural conversations between Stephen Dedalus and several of his closest college companions – on his aesthetic theory regarding pity and fear in tragedy, for example. Stephen's friend Davin is introduced as 'the peasant student' (180), in this regard akin to the Richard T. Sheehan who defended *The Playboy of the Western World* (though not based on him). Davin is an ardent cultural nationalist, dedicated to the GAA, the Gaelic League and 'the sorrowful legend of Ireland' (181). Joyce's text devotes two full pages to a story told by Davin to Stephen which has remained in the latter's consciousness and is described by him as 'a strange vision'. Davin's speech is markedly Hiberno-English in its syntax, repetitions and locutions: 'A thing happened to myself, Stevie, last autumn coming on winter, and I never told it to a living soul and you are the first person now I ever told it to.' His story adheres closely and recognizably to Synge's *The Shadow of the Glen*, as it tells of Davin's long walk through the dark, his stopping at a lonesome cottage and his heightened exchange with the young wife who comes to the door. If Synge has reworked the story of the unfaithful wife to his own ends, as will be explored in detail in Chapter Six, Joyce both models Davin's story on Synge's scenario while working significant changes on it in turn. Some of the alterations are minor: Synge's tramp asks for milk and is given whiskey; Joyce's peasant asks for water and is given milk. Where Joyce most follows Synge is in the emphasis on the young wife and her sexual frustration rather than on the husband and his self-righteous quest for revenge on his wife's adultery. In both cases, the young woman who answers and opens the door to a male stranger is alone: Synge's Nora, because her husband is ostensibly dead and laid out on the table; Joyce's young wife, because she assures Davin 'she was all alone in the house [because] her husband had gone that morning to Queenstown with his sister to see her off' (183). The Tramp accepts the invitation to cross the threshold and spend some time resting by the fire; Davin and the young woman linger on the threshold in undisclosed 'talk' at the door until 'she asked me was I tired and would I like to stop the night there'. Essentially, Davin is being offered the role of the young male lover, the adulterous other in the love triangle, of both the Aran story and the Synge play. Both young women are frank in their declaration of female desire. Synge's Nora describes how her husband was 'always cold, every day since I knew him – and every night, stranger' (III, 35) and how her loneliness and unhappiness were relieved by Patch Darcy, who would 'always look in here and he passing up or passing down' (III, 39). The young woman in Davin's story is pregnant; and the sexually explicit invitation for him to stay the night is confirmed by the fact that 'her breast and her shoulders were bare': 'she took my hand to draw me in over the threshold and said: *Come in and stay the night here. You've no call to be frightened. There's no one in it but ourselves...*' The sexually intimidated Davin balks at and refuses the invitation, though he admits to being 'in a fever' as he heads down the road; nor can he refrain from looking back to see the figure of the pregnant young woman still 'standing at the door'. In the Aran story the woman fetches her young man and makes love to him in the bedroom; he is punished for his presumption and sinfulness when the husband kills him (something of what Davin psychologically fears). The lover in Synge's play is timid, neither making love to Nora nor facing up to either the revivified husband or the aggressive Tramp. The sexual invitation is now from the Tramp to the wife but couched in nature imagery, a verbal transaction rather than any explicit act of love-making. In his reflections on the 'vision' Davin has held before him, Stephen interprets the young woman 'as a type of her race and his own [...] and through the eyes and voice and gesture of a woman without guile, calling the stranger to her bed.' Later, he questions how as a writer he can understand and communicate with 'the thoughts and desires of the race to which he belonged' (238) and presses into parabolic service the story of

> a woman [who] had waited in the doorway as Davin had passed by at night and, offering him a cup of milk, had all but wooed him to her bed; for Davin had the mild eyes of one who could be secret. But him no woman's eyes had wooed.

The type of the Irish race has traditionally and iconographically been a woman. But for Joyce as for Synge 'Mother Ireland' is a fertile, sexually active woman in her prime, not the Poor Old Woman of Yeats and Gregory's *Cathleen ní Houlihan*. Joyce's *Ulysses* is bookended by these considerations. In its opening chapter, Stephen, Mulligan and Haines are visited in the tower by an old woman who delivers the milk. The text explicitly mythologizes her as 'silk of the kine and poor old woman, names given her in old times'.[69] Cathleen ní Houlihan is in service to the Literary Revival, fashioned by Yeats and Gregory, servile to Buck Mulligan/Oliver St. John Gogarty and the Anglophonic interest in translated Gaelic literature: 'A wandering crone, lowly form of an immortal serving her conqueror and her gay betrayer' (15), Cathleen ní Houlihan enters and exits Joyce's novel in the first chapter and is effectively dismissed. If she is under the sign of Yeats and Gregory, the Molly Bloom who gets the novel's final chapter and word is under the sign of Synge.

During the 1990s several Joyce critics argued that, although *Ulysses* is famously set on 16 June 1904, a no less relevant series of dates is inscribed at its close, after Molly's final 'Yes' (933). These are 1914 to 1921, the years of the novel's composition; and the dates are preceded by the three Continental locales in which the writing was undertaken: Trieste-Zurich-Paris. From these closing dates, Enda Duffy argued that events which occurred in Ireland during the years of the novel's composition cast a discernible shadow on the narrative of Joyce's three central characters earlier in the twentieth century: '*Ulysses*, written during the same seven years, encodes successive reactions to the events occurring in Ireland.'[70] While I think Duffy eloquently proves his case, I have never understood why he excludes the nine years between the day on which *Ulysses* is set and the year in which Joyce began its composition, 1904 to 1913, from his analysis. It may have to do with the fact that the events with which he is concerned are all overtly political: the Easter rebellion of 1916, the guerilla War of Independence of 1919-1921, and so forth. The political events which more immediately follow the novel's 1904 historical setting, or at least the two I want to draw attention to and address in this chapter, are theatrical. One is the opening of Ireland's National Theatre at the Abbey a mere six months later, in December 1904. The other, and the one I wish to concentrate on, is the opening of Synge's *The Playboy of the Western World* at the Abbey in January 1907. In Chapter Seven, Buck Mulligan warns Stephen: 'The tramper Synge is looking for you, he said, to murder you' (256), a clear allusion to both the father-slaying of *The Playboy* and in particular to the father's murderous pursuit of his son to avenge the deed. But the key sign of the presence of a play that was not to be staged for two and a half years after the events depicted in Joyce's *Ulysses* is the word 'shift' and it occurs, or rather it recurs, (as one would expect) through the most sexually challenging chapter of the book, Molly Bloom's soliloquy.

As discussed earlier, Joyce's attention was drawn by what he took to be the key word and line of the play, the one that he hoped had driven the offended young women at the Abbey debate to the exits: 'what'd I care if you brought me a drift of chosen females, standing in their shifts itself, maybe' (IV, 167). Lady Gregory's famous telegram to Yeats confirmed this reading: 'Audience broke up in disorder at the word shift.'71 In his connecting Christy Mahon to the Ulster warrior-poet Cuchulain in the sagas, Declan Kiberd notes how Cuchulain when in his notorious 'battle-rage' was as likely to turn on his Ulster companions as his enemies and was only deflected from his assault on Emhain Macha when 'thirty of the province's chosen women were sent naked from the fort to meet the hero.'72 Kiberd surmises that 'Synge had clad his maidens demurely in "shifts" to appease the prudish members of the Abbey audience' and then wonders at their inflamed reaction, finding it ironic.73 Nicholas Grene, who notes that 'up until [Synge's] final typescript version he had them fully "stripped"', finds the use of the term 'shift' for a Dublin audience as deliberately 'indelicate, vulgar', all the more so as having been 'fetishized by intimate contact with the [female] body.'74 The word 'shift' occurs three times in Molly's monologue (the same number of times as in the play). Each time Joyce plays with and exploits the sexual ambiguity of which is the most erotic, a female nude as in a classical painting or a woman wearing a shift, as in the late Victorian softcore pornography which both of the Blooms read. Molly has only the vaguest idea of time and so has been surprised by the distinctive knocking on the door by Mulligan, since she thinks that he may have chosen not to come to the rendezvous: 'I hadnt even put on my clean shift or powdered myself or a thing' (884). The phantasmagoric 'Circe' has staged a full-blown emergence of a naked Molly from the bath, assuring Boylan: 'I'm in my pelt' (670). In lower middle-class Dublin, in social reality, Molly wants to greet her lover attired in a 'clean shift'. She goes on to employ the more decorous and less vulgar term 'chemise' later in the monologue, only to reflect that in the Gibraltar where she was raised, with its Mediterranean mores, 'half the girls never wore them either naked as God made them' (888). Even in the extreme heat of a Gibraltar summer, however, Molly is keen to stress that she still wore underclothes. But the line is doubly provocative, both because she reverts from 'chemise' to 'shift' and because the extreme heat only makes the garment adhere to the contours of the female body: 'I used to be weltering then in the heat my shift drenched with the sweat stuck in the cheeks of my bottom' (896). Towards the end of her soliloquy, Molly resolves to improve relations with Bloom and so to 'go about rather gay' and to 'put on my best shift and drawers' (929). She knows that this will sexually excite him. But with Joyce's characteristic irony Molly also wants to acknowledge her adulterous liaison with Blazes Boylan and to use the event to shame Bloom into being a better husband. This is equally achieved in the same performative gesture of wearing the shift, which will 'let him know if that's what he wanted that his wife is fucked yes and damn well fucked too up to my neck nearly not by him'.

In terms of sexual candour, the woman in Synge's *Playboy* who comes closest to Molly Bloom is not the virginal twenty-year-old Pegeen Mike but the Widow Quin, who has been married and borne several children, as Molly has. Traditionally, the Widow has been played as in her fifties or even sixties, which renders her a grotesque. In recent productions, however, particularly those by Galway's Druid Company, the Widow has been played by an actor in her late thirties, so that she becomes a viable sexual alternative to Pegeen. The extent to which the Widow's sexually frank expressions of desire challenged the norms of Edwardian theatre is best measured, not by the Abbey Theatre audience's reaction, but by the comments of the Lord Chamberlain's reader when a copy of Synge's script (since the play was not yet published) was submitted by the Abbey in 1907 in order for their production to tour England.[75] The reader's ire was roused by the reference to the 'loosed khaki cut throats' but his greatest and most frequent excisions were reserved for such lines of the Widow's as the following with its reference to 'hairy fellows' as well as to 'shifts':

> I'm above many's the day [...] darning a stocking or stitching a shift, and odd times looking out on the schooners, hookers, trawlers is sailing the sea, and I thinking on the gallant hairy fellows are drifting beyond, and I long years living alone. (IV, 127)

Synge's 'wonderful vision' has clearly worked a profound influence on Joyce in terms of sexual candour. But it also enables him to express the longing and in particular the loneliness behind Molly's vehemence. The Widow Quin is left 'living alone' after the death of her husband and two children. But Molly has lost a son, Rudy, her daughter Milly is away in Mulligar for the summer and above all her husband departs in the morning, is gone all day and only returns late at night. Bloom may deliberately have stayed away to facilitate Molly's rendezvous with Boylan; but one senses in the following lines that the pattern of many of Molly's days and nights (except when she is on a rare concert tour) is one of just such isolation and loneliness: 'I don't like being alone in this big barracks of a place at night [...] I couldn't rest easy till I bolted all the doors and windows to make sure but its worse again being locked up like in a prison or a madhouse' (909). The fate of being locked up in a madhouse is one that is articulated more than once throughout Synge's play and Pegeen complains frequently about her father going off overnight to a wake and 'leaving me lonesome on the scruff of the hill. [...] Isn't it long the nights are now, Shawn Keogh, to be leaving a poor girl with her own self counting the hours to the dawn of day' (IV, 59). Molly goes so far as to imagine an urban but very Syngean tramp trying to make his way into the house: 'then leaving us here all day you'd never know what old beggar at the door for a crust with his long story might be a tramp and put his foot in the way to prevent me shutting it' (910). Pegeen gives more of a welcome to a tramp 'with his long story' than Molly; but any alleviation of her loneliness Christy might seem to offer is threatened by his confession that he is 'a lonesome fellow' (IV, 85), someone shut out from life's feast. The profound and desolating note of loneliness can be heard in Synge's play and Joyce's novel behind all the sexual bravado; one informs the other.

Molly Bloom's soliloquy does not engage just with Synge's *The Playboy of the Western World* but with all of his plays, its stream of consciousness a textual conduit through which Synge's lines and situations are channelled. Her language and lines are more markedly Hiberno-English than anything Joyce has written up to this point, with a line like 'if it was a thing I was sick' (872) surfacing on the first page and followed by many another. The most uninhibitedly free-living women in Synge's drama are found in *The Tinker's Wedding*, with Sarah Casey frequently alluding to and threatening to run off with a character called Jaunting Jim: 'It'd be a fine life to be driving with young Jaunting Jim' (IV, 11). When Molly imagines going to Belfast in a train the following week with Boylan, she declares: 'O I love jaunting in a train or a car with lovely soft cushions [...] he might want to do it in the train' (885). Sarah and her man have lived happily for years together and have raised a family; her sudden desire to get married is seen by the older woman as a result of her period, a notion that will pass. But the tinkers in Synge's play offer one of the few representations in Irish literature (other than *Exiles*) of the life James, Nora, Giorgio and Lucia were to live for many years on the continent. And there is a specific reference in the soliloquy to tinkers (as distinct from tramps) when Molly recalls 'one of those wildlooking gypsies in Rathfarnam had their camp pitched near the Bloomfield laundry to try and steal our things if they could' (925). The sexual allure of Christy's violence for the women of Mayo is also recalled in Molly's explicit sexual fantasy relating to one gypsy in particular, 'that blackguardlooking fellow with the fine eyes peeling a switch attack me in the dark and ride me up against the wall without a word or a murderer' (925). Her refusal to blame a woman for murdering her husband (a hanging crime) and the belief that 'if that was her nature what could she do' (880) are of a piece with the Aran Islanders' belief noted by Synge that 'a man will not do wrong unless he is under the influence of a passion which is as irresponsible as a storm on the sea' (II, 95). The close of the soliloquy finds a positive note of resolution in remembering the loving exchange between Bloom and Molly on Howth Head. The synaesthetic imagery signals as much a resumption of their relationship – 'all sorts and shapes and smells and colours springing up even out of the ditches' (931) – as it does for the two tramps Martin and Mary Doul in *The Well of the Saints*: 'there'll be a fine warmth now in the sun, and a sweetness in the air, the way it'll be a grand thing to be sitting here quiet and easy, smelling the things growing up and budding from the earth' (III, 131). Leopold and Molly's sensual exchange of seed cake and kisses is of a piece with Christy's love talk to Pegeen:

> When the airs is warming in four months or five, [...] you'll feel my two hands stretched around you, and I squeezing kisses on your puckered lips, [...] drinking a sup from a well, and making mighty kisses with our wetted mouths [...]. (IV, 147-9)

The heightened sensuality of both is conveyed in and through the language. It has to be verbally evoked because this blissful union is in the past in Molly's soliloquy, and is a far cry from her present relations with the man who has just made his way into her bed, mumbled a request for breakfast and fallen asleep. Christy projects his vision of their sexual union into the future rather than the past, but when the four or five months come to pass he and Pegeen will have long been separated.

Synge's greatest prominence in Joyce's *Ulysses* is in Chapter 9, 'Scylla and Charybdis', set in the National Library of Ireland. He is not literally present; on 16 June 1904, Synge was in Dublin, at home in Crosthwaite Park, Kingstown (Dun Laoghaire), bringing a period of sustained writing to a close as he finished *The Well of the Saints*. On Friday 17 June, the play 'was read to the company [...] and goes into rehearsal at once' (CL I, 88). If a ghost is 'one who has faded into impalpability through death, [or] through absence' (240), as the text defines it, then Synge is the ghost who haunts the library scene through absence: although not present, he is repeatedly named in the text and lines from his plays inform the writing. The chapter has two concerns: Stephen's artful intertwining of Shakespeare's life and plays and a discussion of the nascent Irish Literary Revival by the writers and scholars present. At one level, it represents Stephen's social exclusion from the cliques of the Literary Revival and Joyce's Ibsenite resolve to stand apart and alone. But this is undercut by the figure of Synge with whom he is associated all the way through. The character who brings Synge most to the fore in the public discussion is Buck Mulligan, who makes his entrance halfway through the chapter and responds to questions by 'keen[ing] in a querulous brogue' and speaking lines closely and recognizably modelled on Synge's Hiberno-English: 'It's what I'm telling you, mister honey, it's queer and sick we were, Haines and myself [...]. 'Twas murmur we did for a gallus potion would rouse a friar' (255-256). These lines would not, however, have been recognized in June 1904 as explicitly quoting from and referencing Synge's *The Playboy of the Western World*, a play which had not yet been written and which would not premiere for another thirty months: the phrase 'mister honey' is used when Christy Mahon first tells the Mayo villagers of his deed – 'That was a hanging crime, mister honey,' Pegeen's father says '*with great respect*' (IV, 73) – and 'gallous' is the unusual term of approbation used by Pegeen in one of the play's most famous lines: 'There's a great gap between a gallous story and a dirty deed' (IV, 169).

Buck Mulligan enters the librarian's office when Stephen's theory is well advanced and responds to the Bard of Avon's name as follows:

> Shakespeare? he said. I seem to know the name.
> A flying sunny smile rayed in his loose features.
> To be sure, he said, remembering brightly. The chap that writes like Synge. (254)

In his memoir, *As I Was Going Down Sackville Street* (1937), Oliver St. John Gogarty, the real-life original on which Joyce based the character of Buck Mulligan, finally puts into print the oral story he had been circulating since 1902, when Synge, Maud Gonne, Padraic Colum and himself were present at Yeats's first reading of *Riders to the Sea*:

> Suddenly Yeats exclaimed in admiration of a scene he was reading: 'Aeschylus!'
> Who does he mean?' [Padraic] Colum whispered, amazed.
> 'Synge, who is like Aeschylus.'
> 'But who is Aeschylus?'
> The man who is like Synge!'[76]

Yeats's initial promotion of Synge's writing by referencing the classic Greek tragedians goaded Joyce, as we have seen, into 'riddling' *Riders to the Sea* to prove it non-Aristotelian. By the time of writing *Ulysses*, Joyce had moved well beyond this initial position, or at least had placed it firmly to one side, to admit with the staging of *Playboy* at the Abbey in 1907 that Synge's 'naggin was on the increase'. In the *Ulysses* version of Synge's paradoxical relationship to his great dramatic precursors, Shakespeare has replaced Aeschylus and Yeats has been erased. The remark is not reported by Gogarty but made by Mulligan. What it does is posit a parallel between and intricately intertwine Stephen's discussion of Shakespeare and the chapter's more general and immediate concern with the founding of a national Irish theatre.

Hugh Kenner was the first to point out the key meta-textual episode in the chapter: 'Our national epic has yet to be written, Dr. Sigerson says. Moore is the man for it' (246).[77] The chapter foresees that George Moore will undertake just such an ambition in his three-volume autobiography, *Hail and Farewell*. But Sigerson's comment is embedded in the book that when published in 1922 made the most sustaining claim to be Ireland's national epic, James Joyce's *Ulysses* itself. In the same chapter, Joyce also appropriates Yeats's claim on behalf of Lady Gregory's translated collection of the Irish sagas, *Cuchulain of Muirhemne* (1902), and applies it instead to the book we are reading, 'The most beautiful book that has come out of our country in my time. One thinks of Homer' (278). This is the (late) point in 'Scylla and Charybdis' where Buck Mulligan is explicitly quoting from and parodying what he calls 'the Yeats touch'. But in a chapter which circles around William Shakespeare and his plays, the question is not just who will write Ireland's national epic (to which Joyce's *Ulysses* has supplied the answer eighteen years later) but who will write Ireland's national play: 'Our young Irish bards, John Eglinton censured, have yet to create a figure which the world will set beside Saxon Shakespeare's Hamlet' (236). What the use of 'bards' here obscures is whether Eglinton is talking about poets or playwrights, with the term strongly suggesting the former. His remark draws a reply from AE (George Russell), who 'oracle(s) out of his shadow', whose poems are quoted in the text and who, we are told, 'is gathering together a sheaf of our younger poets' verses' (245-246), the volume *New Songs* which appeared later in 1904. Joyce's text also quotes a line and a half from AE's *Deirdre*, the first play to be staged by the Fay brothers, and the first and last to be written by the poet, who had to be persuaded by the Fays into writing a second act. The discussion in the Library, while concentrating on Shakespeare's plays, overtly focuses in relation to the Revival on Irish 'bards' and their verses. In terms of the movement becoming better known, Synge's name is mentioned for the first time. But the work it refers to is a prose article he has promised to *Dana* rather than the two one-act plays which had successfully been staged by this time; the choice of a critical prose essay to represent Synge is perhaps not surprising given that John Eglinton was himself a cultural commentator on the Literary Revival.

There is, therefore, very little overt discussion of the plays that the Irish National Theatre Society had been staging, at least until the arrival of Buck Mulligan. But the title of Synge's second play, *The Shadow of the Glen*, has been explicitly sounded at the beginning of the chapter, not in the public discourse but in the private text, the chapter's subconscious, as it were:

> Cranly's eleven true Wicklowmen to free their sireland. Gaptoothed Kathleen, her four beautiful green fields, the stranger in her house. And one more to hail him: *ave, rabbi*; the Tinahely twelve. In the shadow of the glen he cooees for them. (236)

The overt political reference is to Charles Stewart Parnell and his (as Joyce would see it) inevitable betrayal. But the passage is equally explicit in its referencing of Yeats and Gregory's *Cathleen ní Houlihan* (already invoked in the opening chapter of *Ulysses* in relation to the old milk woman who comes to the tower) and of Synge's *The Shadow of the Glen* as part of the political and cultural revolution in which Ireland was engaged. When Joyce reviewed the staging of Shaw's *The Shewing Up of Blanco Posnet* in September 1909, he referred to the Abbey as a 'small revolutionary theatre'.[78] This revolutionary dramatic sub-text, so much more unruly and charged than the polite discussion of bardic verses, continues throughout the chapter and does so primarily by creating a parallel between England in the late fifteenth and early sixteenth centuries and Ireland at the close of the nineteenth and opening of the twentieth. The very first page cites Goethe's characterization of Shakespeare as the 'beautiful ineffectual dreamer who comes to grief against hard facts'. But this passage has also been chosen by Joyce to echo Matthew Arnold's late nineteenth century construction of the Celt. The parallel works both ways in the sentence 'Elizabethan London lay as far from Stratford as corrupt Paris lies from virgin Dublin' (240) and serves as a reminder of how much Paris served as a necessary other to Dublin in the creation of the Irish literary revival: where Yeats and Synge first met; where Synge and Joyce had their intense week of meetings, recalled as it is by Stephen in the close-up of Synge's 'harsh gargoyle face' (256) as they argued in a café in rue St André des Arts.

The Library chapter also serves to locate the encounter between Joyce and Synge not just in Paris, where they are two relatively déclassé Irish writers in exile, but in Dublin, where the class divide is greater, more marked. When Buck Mulligan, prophesying *Playboy* (as we saw), warns Stephen that the 'tramper Synge is looking for you, he said, to murder you' (256), the word 'murder' is spoken twice more, just as Old Mahon comes back twice to be killed after the original parricide: 'Are you coming to be killed a third time, or what ails you now?' as his son puts it (IV, 171). Buck goes on to supply the motive: 'He heard you pissed on his halldoor in Glasthule.' Stephen protests that Mulligan was the culprit; but in the chapter all of the direct access to J.M. Synge, the reported conversations and accounts of his dress and behaviour ('Synge has left off wearing black to be like nature'), derive from Mulligan; Stephen Dedalus is placed outside that intimidating (and shut) hall door in Glasthule, against which he urinates. Mulligan also reminds Stephen of 'the night in the Camden Hall when the daughters of Erin had to lift their skirts to step over you as you lay in your mulberrycoloured, multicoloured, multitudinous vomit!' (279). The specific night was 20 June 1904 and the rehearsal in the Camden Street Hall of Synge's *The Well of the Saints* by the Fay brothers. Joyce moved the episode to before rather than (just) after 16 June.[79]

During that summer the site of Ireland's National Theatre is under construction. The discussion of a national drama in the National Library of Ireland takes place in the shadow of that fact, which finally surfaces at the close when Mulligan remarks: 'We went over to their playbox, Haines and I [the Mechanics' Institute, site of the new theatre], the plumbers' hall. Our players are creating a new art for Europe like the Greeks or M. Maeterlinck. Abbey Theatre!' (276-277)[80] A mere three years away was the play that was to make the Abbey Theatre's reputation worldwide, Synge's *Playboy of the Western World*, and its lines are prominent throughout the Library chapter. We have already seen how they feature in Mulligan's parody. But they are also to be found in Stephen's account of Shakespeare, especially after Mulligan has inserted Synge's lines into the Library discourse. When Stephen talks of 'Lady Penelope Rich, a clean quality woman is suited for a player, and the punks of the bankside, a penny a time' (258), he does so in Synge's idiom and without embarrassment or exaggeration, echoing Pegeen's written request for a 'hat is suited for a wedding day' (IV, 57) and her wish for a penny pot-boy. If Ireland's national epic in prose is

going to be written by Joyce in *Ulysses*, Synge as national playwright
will in Christy Mahon 'create a figure which the world will set beside
Saxon Shakespeare's Hamlet.' Synge's play contains a loaded reference
to *Hamlet* at the beginning of Act III, when Jimmy Farrell and Philly
Cullen discuss the possible unearthing of Old Mahon's halved skull:
'They'd say it was an old Dane, maybe, was drowned in the flood' (V,
133). Along with the Danish allusion to Shakespeare's *Hamlet*, the
context brings the gravedigger scene and Yorick's skull from the
beginning of Act V to mind. Philly counters with how he used as a
young man to go to the graveyard containing 'the remnants of a man
who had thighs as long as your arm' and how he'd play with the
remains, 'put[ting] him together for fun.' Synge is here making
modernist play with the literary ghost of Shakespeare's *Hamlet*, as
Stephen is doing in Chapter 9 of Joyce's *Ulysses*.[81] If Stephen makes
much of Shakespeare playing the part of the ghost in *Hamlet*, the Irish
ghost is J.M. Synge, the national playwright whose coming is foretold,
not by the speakers in the National Library, but by Joyce's text. W.J.
McCormack has suggested in his biography that Synge needs to be
moved away from the over-familiar association as the disciple of Yeats
into a more fruitful alignment as a near-contemporary of the younger
Joyce.[82] The first person to suggest and work to realise that realignment
was Joyce himself.

---

[1] James Joyce, *Poems and Exiles*, edited by J.C.C. Mays
    (Harmondsworth: Penguin, 1992), p. xxxvii.
[2] W. J. McCormack, *Fool of the Family: A Life of J.M. Synge* (London:
    Weidenfeld and Nicolson, 2000), p. 21.
[3] James Joyce, 'Drama and Life', *Occasional, Critical, and Political
    Writing*, edited by Kevin Barry (Oxford: Oxford University Press,
    2000), p. 23.
[4] James Joyce, 'The Day of the Rabblement', *Occasional, Critical and
    Political Writing*, p. 51.
[5] James Joyce, 'The Day of the Rabblement', p. 51.
[6] Lady Gregory, *Our Irish Theatre: A Chapter of Autobiography*
    (Gerrards Cross: Colin Smythe, 1972), p. 20.
[7] Lady Gregory, *Our Irish Theatre*, p. 20.
[8] W.B. Yeats, *The Countess Cathleen*, *The Variorum Edition of the
    Plays of W.B. Yeats*, edited by Russell K. Alspach (London:
    Macmillan, 1966), p. 167.
[9] James Joyce, *A Portrait of the Artist as a Young Man*
    (Harmondsworth: Penguin, 1976), p. 226.
[10] James Joyce, *A Portrait of the Artist as a Young Man*, pp. 225-226.

[11] James Joyce, 'Ibsen's New Drama', *Occasional, Critical, and Political Writing*, pp,. 45-46.

[12] James Joyce, 'Programme Notes for the English Players', *Occasional, Critical and Political Writing*, p. 210.

[13] James Joyce, 'Programme Notes for the English Players', p. 211.

[14] James Joyce, 'The Day of the Rabblement', p. 51.

[15] For Yeats's account of his first meeting with Joyce, see Richard Ellmann, *James Joyce*, new and revised edition (New York: Oxford University Press, 1982), pp. 100-104.

[16] Yeats's letter to Pound is quoted in Richard Ellmann, *James Joyce*, p. 401.

[17] Richard Ellmann, *James Joyce*, p. 401.

[18] Anne Fogarty also compares Joyce's *Exiles* to Synge's *Deirdre of the Sorrows* as dramas of exile. See Anne Fogarty, 'Ghostly Intertexts: James Joyce and the Legacy of Synge', in *Synge and Edwardian Ireland*, edited by Brian Cliff and Nicholas Grene (Oxford and New York: Oxford University Press, 2012), p. 236.

[19] Frank McGuinness, 'Synge and the King of Norway', in *Interpreting Synge: Essays from the Synge Summer School 1991-2000*, edited by Nicholas Grene (Dublin: The Lilliput Press, 2000), p. 60.

[20] James Joyce, *Exiles*, *Poems and Exiles*, p. 125.

[21] James Joyce, *Exiles*, p. 137.

[22] I am using the two-act version of *When the Moon has Set* rather than the one-act version published in Synge's *Collected Works*. It was published in *The Long Room* 24 and 25 (Spring-Autumn 1982), with an introduction by Mary C. King, published by the Friends of the Library, Trinity College, Dublin, pp. 9-40.

[23] J.M. Synge, *When the Moon has Set*, p. 19.

[24] J.M. Synge, *When the Moon has Set*, p. 36.

[25] *Theatre Business: The Correspondence of the First Abbey Theatre Directors William Butler Yeats, Lady Gregory and J.M. Synge*, selected and edited by Ann Saddlemyer (Gerrards Cross: Colin Smythe, 1982), p,. 30.

[26] James Joyce, 'The Day of the Rabblement', p. 52.

[27] J.M. Synge, 'The Dramatic Movement in Ireland', *The Abbey Theatre: Interviews and Recollections*, edited by E.H. Mikhail (Houndmills: Macmillan, 1988), p. 54.

[28] James Joyce, *The Holy Office, Poems and Exiles*, p. 104.

[29] James Joyce, *A Portrait of the Artist as a Young Man*, p. 253.

[30] Richard Ellmann, *James Joyce*, p. 124.

[31] Richard Ellmann, *James Joyce*, p. 124.

[32] Herbert Gorman, *James Joyce: a definitive biography* (London: John Lane, The Bodley Head, 1941), p. 101.

33 Stanislaus Joyce, *My Brother's Keeper*, edited by Richard Ellmann (London: Faber and Faber, 1958), p. 213.

34 *The Letters of James Joyce* Volume II, edited by Richard Ellmann (New York: The Viking Press, 1966), p. 35. All future Joyce letters quoted are from this edition and will be incorporated in the text.

35 *The Poetics of Aristotle*, translated by Preston H. Epps (Chapel Hill: The University of North Carolina Press, 1970), p. 16.

36 James Joyce, 'Programme Notes for the English Players', p. 209.

37 James Joyce, *A Portrait of the Artist as a Young Man*, p. 204.

38 *The Poetics of Aristotle*, p. 24.

39 James Joyce, *A Portrait of the Artist as a Young Man*, p. 204.

40 James Joyce, 'The Paris Notebooks', *The Critical Writings of James Joyce*, edited by Ellsworth Mason and Richard Ellmann (New York: The Viking Press, 1959), p. 144.

41 Stanislaus Joyce, *My Brother's Keeper*, p. 214.

42 Richard Ellmann, *James Joyce*, p. 267.

43 W.J. McCormack, *Fool of the Family: A Life of J.M. Synge*, p. 396.

44 Richard Ellmann, *James Joyce*, p. 283.

45 Richard Ellmann, *James Joyce*, p. 426.

46 James Joyce, 'The Mirage of the Fisherman of Aran: England's Safety Valve in Case of War', *Occasional, Critical, and Political Writing*, p. 204. All future references are to this edition and will be incorporated in the text.

47 James Joyce, *Ulysses* (Harmondsworth: Penguin, 1992), p. 256.

48 Richard Ellmann, *James Joyce*, p. 440.

49 Richard Ellmann, *James Joyce*, p. 440. The next quotation is from the same page.

50 Brenda Maddox, *Nora: A Biography of Nora Joyce* (London: Hamish Hamilton, 1988), pp. 211-212.

51 Brenda Maddox, *Nora*, p. 211.

52 Richard Ellmann, *James Joyce*, p. 267.

53 Emer Nolan, *James Joyce and Nationalism* (London and New York: Routledge, 1995), p. 43.

54 James Joyce, *The Holy Office, Poems and Exiles*, p. 104.

55 Richard Ellmann, *James Joyce*, p. 147.

56 James Joyce, *Dubliners*, edited by Terence Brown (Harmondsworth: Penguin, 1992), p. 72.

57 The valuable record of Sheehan's contribution to the debate recorded in *The Freeman's Journal* of 5 February 1907 is given by editor Richard Ellmann in his extensive notes to Joyce's letter of 11 February 1907. See *The Letters of James Joyce* Volume II, p. 211.

58 James Joyce, *The Holy Office, Poems and Exiles*, p. 105.

59 These terms are drawn from Harold Bloom, *The Anxiety of Influence: A Theory of Poetry*, Second Edition (New York and Oxford: Oxford

University Press, 1997; 1973), which I will discuss in more detail later in the chapter.

60 Joyce makes these comments in a letter to Stanislaus of 25 September 1906. See *The Letters of James Joyce* Volume II, p. 166.

61 Richard Ellmann, *James Joyce*, p. 245.

62 James Joyce, 'The Dead', *Dubliners*, p. 189. All future references are to this edition and will be incorporated in the text.

63 Richard Ellmann, *James Joyce*, p. 245.

64 Anne Fogarty shows how the closing passage of 'The Dead' also draws on Maurya's 'chilling threnody' in Synge's *Riders to the Sea* to achieve the same 'universalization of perspective'. See Anne Fogarty, 'Ghostly Intertexts: James Joyce and the Legacy of Synge', pp. 231-232.

65 Harold Bloom, *The Anxiety of Influence*, p. 35.

66 James Joyce, *A Portrait of the Artist as a Young Man*, p. 221. All future references are to this edition and will be incorporated in the text.

67 Harold Bloom, *The Anxiety of Influence*, p. 26.

68 Anthony Roche, '"The Strange Light of Some New World": Stephen's Vision in *A Portrait*', *James Joyce Quarterly*, 25.3 (Spring 1988), pp. 323-332.

69 James Joyce, *Ulysses*, p. 15. All future references are to this edition and will be incorporated in the text.

70 Enda Duffy, *The Subaltern Ulysses* (Minneapolis and London: University of Minnesota Press, 1994), p. 2.

71 Lady Gregory, *Our Irish Theatre*, p. 67.

72 Declan Kiberd, *Synge and the Irish Language*, Second Edition (Dublin: Gill and Macmillan, 1993; 1979), p. 118.

73 Declan Kiberd, *Synge and the Irish Language*, p. 119.

74 Nicholas Grene, *The Politics of Irish Drama: Plays in Context from Boucicault to Friel* (Cambridge: Cambridge University Press, 1999), pp. 81-82.

75 Since the play was not yet published, the Abbey submitted a typed copy (by Synge) of *The Playboy of the Western World* to the Lord Chamberlain's Office in London. It is in the file for 1907 in the Lord Chamberlain's Collection, Manuscript Division, British Library, London.

76 Oliver St. John Gogarty, *As I Was Going Down Sackville Street* (New York: Reynall and Hitchcock, 1937; reprinted Dublin: The O'Brien Press, 1994), p. 289. The Gogarty passage is cited and discussed in Anne Fogarty, 'Ghostly Intertexts; James Joyce and the Legacy of Synge', p. 239.

77 Hugh Kenner, *A Colder Eye: The Modern Irish Writers* (New York: Alfred A. Knopf, 1983), p.198.

78 James Joyce, 'The Battle between Bernard Shaw and the Censor: "The Shewing Up of Blanco Posnet"', *Occasional, Critical, and Political Writing*, p. 153.

79 See Richard Ellmann, *James Joyce*, p. 161, for a full account of the episode.

80 Despite his initial disdain, Oliver St. John Gogarty was to stage three plays at the Abbey Theatre years later, one in 1917, two in 1919. Though they were pseudonymous, literary Dublin knew their authorship; *Blight*, set in the Dublin tenements, at least had the distinction of inspiring Sean O'Casey to write his first plays, vowing he could do a better job.

81 P.J. Mathews argues that Synge and Joyce 'both fashioned different but, in many ways, analogous experimental modernist literatures which are solidly anchored in the Irish locale'. See 'Re-thinking Synge', in *The Cambridge Companion to J.M. Synge*, edited by P.J. Mathews (Cambridge: Cambridge University Press, 2009), pp. 12-13.

82 W.J. McCormack, *Fool of the Family: A Life of J.M. Synge*, p. 21, where he describes Synge and Joyce as 'counterparts'.

5 | Ghosts in Irish Drama: Synge's *Riders to the Sea*, Yeats's *The Only Jealousy of Emer* and Parker's *Pentecost*

In February 1998, the Royal Shakespeare Company presented at Stratford a triple bill of one-act plays from the early decades of the Abbey Theatre: Synge's *Riders to the Sea* and *Shadow of the Glen* and Yeats's *Purgatory* (1938). Their Irish director, John Crowley, pointed out in his note to the published text that the three plays are unified by 'the refusal of the dead to leave the living alone'.[1] Michael Billington, in his review for *The Guardian*, elaborated on how the three plays are concentrated on the return of the dead to haunt the living: 'In Irish drama the dead are ever-present: their voices continue to haunt one from beyond the grave.'[2] He noted how persistently this concern runs throughout Irish drama: beyond the period of the Revival, through such mid twentieth-century plays as Brendan Behan's *The Hostage* (1958) and Samuel Beckett's entire dramatic *oeuvre* up to such resolutely contemporary playwrights as Conor McPherson and Martin McDonagh.

This chapter will consider the phenomenon of the return of the dead to haunt the living in three plays: one of the two Synge plays staged at Stratford, *Riders to the Sea*; Yeats's *The Only Jealousy of Emer* (1919), which goes much further dramaturgically than *Purgatory* in staging the encounter between the living and the dead; and from the contemporary canon, Stewart Parker's *Pentecost*. First staged by the Field Day Theatre Company co-founded by playwright Brian Friel and actor Stephen Rea in Derry as their annual offering of 1988, at the height of the Northern Ireland 'Troubles', *Pentecost* proved Parker's most successful play.[3] Tragically, he was to die less than a year afterwards, on 8 November 1988, at the age of forty-seven. This chapter has to do, then, not with two dead and one living dramatist but with a trio of ghosts.

Before proceeding to discuss Synge's *Riders to the Sea* in some detail, where the ghostly presence is most extensive, I would like briefly to consider *The Playboy of the Western World* and *The Shadow of the Glen,* the two other Synge plays where the dead return to challenge the living and where the supernatural character of the event is apparently explained away. It is the repeated capacity of Christy Mahon's father to keep returning from the dead that is the most remarkable aspect of the play. Old Mahon's first reappearance, while unexpected, can be accounted for in comic/realistic terms: Christy overestimated the lethal effects of 'the tap of a loy' (IV, 161) and left before he had ascertained his father's death. Synge decided in his extensive revisions of *The Playboy* not to leave it at that, as the farcical comeuppance of a young boaster by the return of an all-too-real authority figure, but to keep pushing the material in the latter stages of Act Three in an increasingly unreal direction and into an area of increasingly explicit theatricalization. Specifically, there is the physical enactment of the second attempted murder and not only Christy's but also the entire community's certainty that he has effected it, with Old Mahon crawling in to be asked: 'Are you coming to be killed a third time or what ails you?' (IV, 171). The line establishes that Christy is dealing with the ghost of his father, seeking to overcome and subdue the patriarchal tyranny under which he has suffered. The audience simultaneously registers the ghostliness along with the corporeality of a father figure who refuses to remain either symbolic or conveniently off-stage but forces his way into full bodily presence and in so doing transforms the stage into a space where the living and the dead interact on equal terms.

If Synge drew on the Bible for his own characteristic handling of the death-and-resurrection motif, his other great source of ghostly narratives was the oral folklore of the west of Ireland. As Mary King has pointed out, the stories in *The Aran Islands* are not detached from the living contexts which generated them but are interrelated with the activities of the people on the islands to form a complex weave of their mundane and imaginative lives, their waking and dream worlds.[4] As Chapter One explored, much of the folklore Synge recorded on Aran had to do with living people who are taken 'away' by the fairies or, to put it another way, people who die but are imagined living an alternate existence elsewhere; they do so in opulent conditions the exact reverse of the deprivation they have left behind, enjoying an abundance of all good things. The belief in this Otherworld manages to conflate and respond to two central factors in the Aran Islanders' existence: death by drowning and emigration. Unlike those who have departed for England or the United States, however, the dead retain the power to return and intervene in the lives of the island community. They do so under special conditions around which a body of practices has evolved.

In *The Shadow of the Glen*, Synge drew on these folk materials to provide the play's plot, characters, and such details as the Tramp asking Nora Burke for a needle by saying 'there's great safety in a needle, lady of the house,' and proceeding to stitch 'one of the tags in his coat, saying the *De Profundis* under his breath' (III, 41). Since the Tramp is about to be left on his own with what he has every reason to believe is a recently deceased corpse, he is looking for safety and protection from any possibility of the dead man's return. While on Inishmaan, Synge had been drawn aside by the old story teller Pat Dirane and advised: 'Take a sharp needle [...] and stick it in under the collar of your coat, and not one of them [the fairy forces] will be able to have power on you' (II, 80). Later, in Part Four of *The Aran Islands*, another old man tells of his encounter with the uncanny and the danger he was in: 'I remembered that I had heard them saying none of those creatures can stand before you and you saying the *De Profundis*, so I began saying it, and the thing ran off over the sand and I got home' (II, 180). In joining the muttered words of the *De Profundis* to the talisman of the needle, the Tramp in *The Shadow of the Glen* is making assurance double sure by drawing on and fusing Christian and pagan beliefs in the way Synge regarded as characteristic of the islanders, as Chapter One examined. As we and he learn very shortly after, Dan Burke is only feigning death in order to catch his wife in the act of adultery. But the audience has not been allowed in on this 'trick' from the start and has, along with the Tramp and Nora Burke, believed the corpse to be a true one. In terms of the stage, playing at and being dead are representationally one and the same. So Dan Burke's protestations do not entirely convince us to the contrary that he is fully alive and allow for dramatic weight to be given to Nora's suggestion that her husband was 'always cold' (III, 35). In realizing that what she has shared with him in their marriage has been a kind of living death or entombment, Synge's Nora thus comes closely to resemble Ibsen's Nora in *A Doll's House*. But the method of staging her dilemma is very different, even allowing for the shift in setting from comfortable bourgeois household to a very basic peasant cottage. Synge has placed a corpse at centre stage and gone on to enact a full-blown (albeit mock) death-and-resurrection scene, with many of the details appropriate to a wake ritual and the propitiation of the dead not to return.

In his dramatic treatment of Dan Burke as of Old Mahon, then, Synge breaks down the barriers normally separating the living from the dead and makes it increasingly difficult to say which is which. In *Riders to the Sea,* the playwright does not go so far as to bring the dead son Michael on stage; but he does bring Michael's ghostly presence to bear on the women in the cottage and with it the increasing pressure of the accumulated folk beliefs surrounding the dead. The most graphic account of a burial in *The Aran Islands* is that of a young man drowned at sea. As he talks to the men working on the grave, Synge remarks that he 'could not help feeling that I was talking with men who were under a judgment of death. I knew that every one of them would be drowned in the sea in a few years and battered naked on the rocks, or would die in his own cottage and be buried with another fearful scene in the graveyard I had come from' (II, 162). The morbidity already apparent in an early work like *Étude Morbide,* and which long precedes Synge's awareness that he was dying from Hodgkins disease, finds dramatic outlet and objectification through the Aran Islands, where life is lived under the visible shadow of death – the men of their own deaths, and the women a living death, deprived of their menfolk. Rather than concentrating exclusively on the stark facts of disappearance or physical decay, what *The Aran Islands* increasingly records is an oscillation between the realm of the living, where the decaying mortal remains are laid to rest, and the realm of the dead, where paradoxically the remains enjoy an extended imaginative existence. It is primarily through storytelling that reality is extended to encompass two worlds, what Synge in his theory calls 'real life' and 'a land of the fancy' (II, 347), which these figures traverse and which he as a playwright similarly wants to traffic between.

Riders to the Sea presents an audience with two alternative views of what has happened to the missing Michael, one from his sisters, one from his mother. Maurya has broken her vigil for Michael to plead with Bartley, the sole remaining son, not to put out to sea; and when he refuses, she has hastened after him with the bread and blessing she has earlier neglected to bestow. Nora and Cathleen have contrived their mother's absence so that they can examine 'a shirt and a plain stocking were got off a drowned man in Donegal' (III, 5) to determine whether they are their brother's. The sisters finally identify Michael by counting the stitches in the cloth and equating him with his personal effects: 'And isn't it a pitiful thing when there is nothing left of a man who was a great rower and fisher, but a bit of an old shirt and a plain stocking?' (III, 17) Maurya re-enters and begins the slow, inarticulate wail of the keen, the cry of pagan desperation that Synge described in *The Aran Islands* as lurking beneath the islanders' quietude:

> This grief of the keen is no personal complaint [...] but seems to contain the whole passionate rage that lurks somewhere in every native of the island. In this cry of pain the inner consciousness of the people seems to lay itself bare for an instant, and to reveal the mood of beings who feel their isolation in the face of a universe that wars on them with wind and seas. (II, 75)

When her daughters ask if she saw Bartley, Maurya will only reply 'I seen the fearfullest thing' (III, 19) and goes on to invoke the whole realm of supernatural apparitions when she specifies what she has seen as a vision: 'I've seen the fearfullest thing any person has seen, since the day Bride Dara seen the dead man with the child in his arms.' When their mother insists that she has seen not only her living son Bartley but also her dead son Michael accompanying him on the grey pony, Nora and Cathleen immediately deny her claim by pointing to the empirical evidence that Michael has been drowned in far-off Donegal. But their first instinctive reaction to hearing of Bride Dara's vision of the dead man has been a joint and inarticulate response, 'Uah,' which signifies not denial but anguished assent and belief. There is, therefore, a dual recognition scene, one in response to the few tattered fragments of Michael's clothing after a week's immersion in the sea, the other Maurya's epiphanic vision of her dead son, fully clothed and also in a fashion well beyond their meagre means: 'I looked up then, and I crying, at the grey pony, and there was Michael upon it – with fine clothes on him, and new shoes on his feet.' Maurya has been rewarded by the sight of her son who she has been entreating to reappear throughout the play; but that vision is a mockery, since it is insubstantial and fleeting. Michael has returned from the dead only to drag the final living son after him, to confirm a double loss for her.

Synge has prepared the dramatic ground for the audience to give at least provisional credence to Maurya's supernatural vision by carefully and consistently doubling the living Bartley with the dead Michael through the early stages of *Riders to the Sea*. When he enters belatedly, Bartley steps into a zone already charged with the three women's collective act of attention on the absent figure of Michael. Bartley takes the rope which is to be used for his brother's coffin as a halter, and steps not into the dead man's shoes but into his shirt, as the sisters later realize when they search for the identifying flannel of Michael's shirt: 'I'm thinking Bartley put it on him in the morning, for his own shirt was heavy with the salt in it' (III, 15). The rope serves to bind together the figures and fates of the two brothers, blurring the absolute distinction between their two identities and their separate status, one living and the other dead. Nothing is as inevitable as that Bartley will be drowned, and soon, as the pressure from the other side of the grave intensifies.

With her last son gone, Maurya lists the family line of her dead. The brothers Michael and Bartley serve as the first in a ritual naming of the eight 'fine men' of the family and their separate fates. The number of dead begins to outweigh the living, as a succession of off-stage presences comes to surround the three women:

> 'There were Stephen, and Shawn, were lost in the great wind. [...] There was Sheamus and his father, and his own father again, were lost in a dark night, and not a stick or sign was seen of them when the sun went up. There was Patch after was drowned out of a curagh that turned over.' (III, 21)

A story Synge recorded in *The Aran Islands* tells of the gathered hosts of the dead and numbers them in the hundreds, providing a numerically stark and poignant contrast with the bare handful of survivors eking out a living on these barren, windswept islands. The returned ghost of a dead woman 'told them they [the dead] would all be leaving that part of the country on the Oidhche Shamhna [the night of the Celtic feast Samhain, November 1], and that there would be four or five hundred of them riding on horses, and herself would be on a grey horse, riding behind a young man' (II, 159). These are the riders to the sea evoked in the play's title and, while there may be passing reference to the Four Horsemen of the Apocalypse, those four biblical riders are subsumed by the hundreds of horseback riders who make up the pagan hosts of the dead.[5] Bartley may assert that he is riding to the Galway fair and that he will not be drowned; but other forces in the play assert that he will and that his ultimate destination is the sea which wields the presiding influence on the islanders' lives. As the play puts it in its most lethally ambivalent pun: 'It's the life of a young man to be going on the sea' (III, 11).

The doubling of living and dead brothers not only breaks down the notion of individual identity but also undercuts the sense of chronological time. Both events (the drowning of Michael and the feared drowning of Bartley) seem to be occurring simultaneously during the play's brief duration, since they are repeatedly referred to and interrelated as the dominating object of the characters' verbal energies. But in strictly temporal terms one drowning is being reconstructed from the immediate past, the other projected into the immediate future. The stage effect of timelessness and cyclic recurrence is increased when, as Maurya recalls the death by drowning of a previous son Patch, what she evokes verbally is enacted before her and the audience as the door opens, the women enter, followed by the men bearing a body, and the former begin keening:

> I was sitting here with Bartley, and he a baby lying on my two knees, and I seen two women, and three women, and four women coming in, and they crossing themselves and not saying a word. I looked out then, and there were men coming after them, and they holding a thing in the half of a red sail, and water dripping out of it – it was a dry day, Nora – and leaving a track to the door.
> [*She pauses again with her hand stretched out towards the door. It opens softly and old women begin to come in, crossing themselves on the threshold and kneeling down in front of the stage. [...] Two younger women come in and pull out the table. Three men carry in the body of* BARTLEY, *laid on a plank, with a bit of a sail over it, and lay it on the table. [...] The women are keening softly and swaying themselves with a slow movement.*] [III, 21-23]

This acting out on stage of Maurya's description of the past is akin to the single most uncanny moment in Ibsen's *Ghosts* (1881) when Mrs. Alving's account to the pastor of the flirtation between her husband and the maid is simultaneously enacted, in the play's present, by her son and the maid's daughter. At that point, she responds hoarsely with the play's title: 'Ghosts!'[6] But Synge pushes such a ghostly incident further into a fully fledged re-enactment of all eight men dying in one simultaneous moment, abolishing chronological succession and presenting one archetypal scene which can be repeated an endless number of times. We are in the region of ghosts, as Mrs. Alving correctly intuited, where the invocations, incantations, and repetitions of Maurya's heightened speech have replaced realistic dialogue: 'It isn't that I haven't prayed for you, Bartley, to the Almighty God. It isn't that I haven't said prayers in the dark night till you wouldn't know what I'd be saying; but it's a great rest I'll have now, and it's time surely. It's a great rest I'll have now, and great sleeping in the long nights after Samhain' (III, 25). The drama has moved into a place where the measured, hieratic movements of this ritual of worship for the dead have taken over from the more mundane activities of island life and the forward propulsion of plot.

In the ending of *Riders to the Sea*. Maurya, for all of the undoubted authority of her powerful and moving monologues, is not given the absolute final say, nor does her vision of things prevail. Nora and Cathleen are equally allowed to give voice to their scepticism, to the feeling that the strain of loss has been too much for their mother: 'It's getting old she is, and broken' (III, 25). But I have emphasized the non-realistic elements of the close of *Riders* as a gloss on Synge's assertion that on 'the stage one must have reality, and one must have joy' (IV, 53-54), and to pave the way for a consideration of W. B. Yeats's *The Only Jealousy of Emer*.

Where Synge always preserves a realistic base in his drama, Yeats in *The Only Jealousy of Emer* works through an avowedly poetic theatre and dramatic conventions derived from the Japanese Noh to go one crucial transformative step further. Yeats stages directly the encounter between the living and the dead which Synge had kept (just) off-stage and had conveyed primarily through oral storytelling. The line, 'We're but two women struggling with the sea'7, establishes the extent to which Yeats's play has Synge's *Riders to the Sea* as one of its frames of reference, as mediated by the dramatic techniques of the Noh. *The Only Jealousy of Emer* similarly focuses on a drowning, and the setting evoked by the chorus is detailed, naturalistic, and in all respects closer to the fishermen's humble cottages described by Synge in *The Aran Islands* than to any dwelling out of elaborate legend:

> **FIRST MUSICIAN.** [*speaking*]. I call before the eyes a roof
> With cross-beams darkened by smoke;
> A fisher's net hangs from a beam,
> A long oar lies against the wall.
> I call up a poor fisher's house;
> A man lies dead or swooning [...]. (531-533)

The corpse is male and has perished by drowning; those who watch over it are women, though their roles are sexual (wife and mistress) rather than familial (mother and sisters). Yeats's Emer and Synge's Maurya are the still, suffering centres of their respective plays and emerge as tragic figures through the loss of the same thing: hope of a future reunion with the man or men they have lost. Both are mocked by an image of wish fulfilment without any corporeal substance. Maurya sees her son Michael restored and refurbished, but only as an image she cannot contact or release from death. Emer only wins her husband Cuchulain's return from the dead by bartering away 'the hope that some day somewhere/ We'll sit together at the hearth again' (537). But Emer differs from Maurya in being a less passive figure, and this difference has implications for the kind of ghost drama Yeats is writing. Where Maurya is struck dumb by the supernatural manifestation and rendered powerless to intervene, Emer stands her ground in the grotesque face of the changeling Bricriu, resolute in her determination to press through to the other side, to make contact and negotiate with it. This was no less true of Yeats in his lifelong efforts to win wisdom from the dead, to appropriate a measure of the knowledge he believed lay beyond the grave. This aim binds together his early interest in Irish folklore, his occult researches and the later automatic writing of Mrs. George Yeats. Posited in terms of theatricality, it helps to explain Yeats's frustration with conventional realistic dramaturgy, his sense that it represented only one half of reality, and that the less essential.

The Only Jealousy of Emer deals almost diagrammatically with Yeats's desire to bring the natural and the supernatural within the same frame of the stage by dividing the space in half: '*The folding of the cloth shows on one side of the stage the curtained bed or litter on which lies a man in his grave-clothes. [...] Emer is sitting beside the bed*' (531). The bed on which Cuchulain lies is the only property on an otherwise empty stage. It is not placed in a dominant central position but pointedly confined to the '*one side*' while the other so far remains unoccupied, empty, open, charged with possibility. The drama that is centred on the bed, with the younger mistress Eithne Inguba insisting that Cuchulain is dead while the older wife Emer replies repeatedly that despite all appearances he 'is not dead' (535), has its textual antecedents in Synge's *Riders to the Sea*. But Yeats's expanding from the familial to the sexual, from the ideologically endorsed bond (in Irish nationalism) between mother and sons to the institution of marriage and explicitly adulterous liaisons, moves closer to the dramatic terrain of Ibsen and Strindberg. The exchange between Emer and Eithne Inguba that takes place around Cuchulain's bed brings to the surface a clearly psychological drama as the wife urges the mistress to confess her intimacies with Cuchulain. At the realistic level, on that side of the stage, we witness the triangular relationship of wife, husband and other woman. But that side is only one half of the story in Yeatsian dramatic terms; it is what occupies the other zone, and the final synthesis he manages between the two, that take Yeats beyond Synge or Ibsen.

This development was made possible by Yeats's discovery via Ezra Pound of the materials of the Japanese Noh drama and by the form he fashioned from them. Most of the scenarios hinged on an encounter between a travelling priest and the ghost or god haunting some local site. What the Noh drama therefore offered Yeats was an elaborate series of dramatic conventions explicitly designed to stage an interaction between the worlds of the living and the dead, that encounter which is central to so much of the folklore Yeats, Lady Gregory and Synge recorded. Of the many ways in which it did so, space will only permit a focus on one of the most relevant, the use of the mask and its central role in *The Only Jealousy of Emer*. Yeats's first direct experience of the mask as a theatrical device had come through Edward Gordon Craig. Craig had designed a mask for the Fool in Yeats's *The*

Hour-Glass (1914) (though the design was never executed) and, in a note accompanying the design, listed the four qualities he intended it to convey: 'hint of clown / a hint of Death / and of sphinx / and of boy.'[8] Yeats took the hints from Craig but was unable to develop them until through the Noh he found a dramatic form into which the mask could be integrated.[9]

The first 'hint' of clown is not only appropriate to the character but also increases the degree to which the Fool is both an individualized creation and a readily recognizable role with a lengthy popular tradition. Whatever the role, the mask will enhance this suggestion, suppressing the individual player by highlighting the archetypal nature of what is being represented. Yeats's writing in the Noh technique openly acknowledges the properties of drama as a medium: we are shown, not 'people', but players wearing and changing masks; not an actual but an imagined setting called 'to the eye of the mind'[10]; not casual circumstances but a fundamental life-and-death struggle of the entire being. The 'hint of Death' reminds us of death masks, the living person's features permanently embodied in clay but at the expense of animation. Yeats could admit the possibility that 'being is only possessed completely by the dead'.[11] The death mask captures the paradox embodied by Keats's urn, that the figures represented on it purchase immortality at the expense of breathing, just as *The Only Jealousy of Emer* makes it clear that Cuchulain will only acquire immortality at the cost of his humanity. But the figures on the Grecian urn remain eternally youthful, like the Woman of the Sidhe; and Craig's fourth hint, of boyhood, suggests how the mask can represent an inhabitant of the Land of the Ever-Young (Tír na nÓg) by eliminating the process of aging. The Sphinx is another stone embodiment, a traditional symbol and sign of the wisdom which Yeats believed the dead to possess. The mask in his drama gives concrete expression to the meeting of the natural and the supernatural on which so many of his plays are centred. More precisely, since the mask is an imposition of one material upon another, it images the constraining of the natural by the forms of the permanent and increases Yeats's awareness that the relation between the two worlds is not an easy one. For the mask externalizes the idea of contending personalities within a single human frame and signifies that one of them is supernatural or dead. So, at a key moment in the play, the heroic mask of Cuchulain is switched in favour of its antithesis, the grotesque distorted mask of the 'god' Bricriu. The mask indicates that the area on stage is located in a liminal area between the borders of the living and the dead, and that all the major figures inhabit more than one dimension.

Yeats had for many years brooded over the possibility of writing a stage version of *The Only Jealousy of Emer*.[12] But what had effectively stalled him until his discovery of the Japanese Noh was the central problem posed by the episode out of Irish legend: how to dramatize the condition of Cuchulain 'away'? What were the means by which Cuchulain's dual existence, lingering on a sickbed watched over by his wife while simultaneously encountering the Woman of the Sidhe in an otherworldly setting, could be represented on stage? Any approximately naturalistic staging would tip the balance in favour of the deathbed scenario and reduce the other ghostly dimension to a purely verbal, after-the-fact account by a reawakened Cuchulain of what he had experienced there. A more simultaneous trancelike communication would risk the kind of incoherence, through a failure to keep the two realms sufficiently distinct, that finally sabotaged Yeats's earlier play *The Shadowy Waters* (1911).There is also something perilously undramatic in a scenario which threatens its audience with the prospect of a completely immobilized protagonist for most of its duration. Of all the various elements of the Noh, the mask most enabled Yeats to overcome this disabling fixity and to maintain a consistently dual dramatic perspective in *The Only Jealousy of Emer*.

The opening stage directions show not only a man in a heroic mask on his deathbed but also another '*man with exactly similar clothes and mask [who] crouches near the front*' (531). As this opening makes clear, the mask has freed the playwright from the strict realistic necessity of confining the multiple aspects of his hero's personality to a single incarnation. By duplicating Cuchulain's image, the superimposition of the mask makes possible a more exact doubling than even the traditional disguise of costume. There is no reason why this need be restricted to two. Yeats's rewriting of the play in prose eleven years later as *Fighting the Waves* adds another Cuchulain to the sum, and the number is potentially as endless as the supply of masks and the number of phases into which the single personality can be divided. The two Cuchulains are differentiated in the cast list as 'The Ghost of Cuchulain' and 'The Figure of Cuchulain', broadly speaking the departing spirit and the physical shell or husk it has vacated. The doubling clarifies one essential point: neither of these images represents the whole man but rather different aspects of the self. The doubling also makes it possible to view the entirety of what is happening on the stage as a psychic drama emanating from the prone Cuchulain.

With the arrival of Bricriu, signified by the changing of masks, the possibilities for a dramatic interchange between the two zones are enlarged. This exchange is posited in the familiar Yeatsian terms of a bargain: Emer is asked to renounce the hope of ever being loved by Cuchulain again in order to secure his return from the dead. In return she demands, quite understandably, that she be given a greater degree of insight into the place and situation that currently claim her man before she can decide. To so demonstrate, Bricriu gives Emer (and by extension the audience) access to the inner drama unfolding in the otherworld between the Ghost of Cuchulain and the Woman of the Sidhe: 'Come closer to the bed / That I may touch your eyes and give them sight' (547). What Emer now sees for the first time is what we have seen all along, the continuing presence on stage of the Ghost of Cuchulain as evidence that the play admits of spiritual life after apparent physical death, and as confirmation of Emer's negative to the repeated question: 'And is he dead?' But until her eyes are opened to his presence, the Ghost of Cuchulain has been prone, crouching, awaiting release.

Emer is now called upon to perform the role of witness/ audience/spectator by Bricriu in his role as playwright/director/stage manager. His urging her to come 'closer to the bed' stresses the sexual intimacy of this particular play and the more general wish Yeats had to abolish distance and establish intimacy as the foundation of his new drama.[13] Emer has been mounting a watch and, as a result of her concentrated scrutiny, is granted a vision, specifically the ability to view other areas of the stage which have so far been screened from her sight: 'My husband is there.' But the mirror is only one-way so far as Emer is concerned, since it soon becomes clear that Cuchulain can neither see her image in return nor hear her entreaties. The most the Ghost of Cuchulain has been able to discern is the fact that there is an audience urging his presence: 'The longing and the cries have drawn him hither' (549), as Bricriu reveals, and kept him literally in suspense until Emer is explicitly informed of and set up in her role as active spectator. Her darkness is lightened by Bricriu's touch and her gaze is directed toward the so-far vacant other side of the stage, which now reveals a figure ready to be reanimated.

When the Woman of the Sidhe enters and is identified, Emer reacts by drawing a knife and attempting to strike at the image of the 'other woman'. Apart from making the point that such an action is futile under the supernatural circumstances, Bricriu also makes the larger point that violent actions have no place or efficacy in this kind of drama. Emer's effort to express her jealousy by drawing a knife is forestalled by the admonition that her passion can achieve greater and more effective expression by being channeled into the role of a privileged spectator:

> **FIGURE OF CUCHULAIN.** No knife
> Can wound that body of air. Be silent; listen;
> I have not given you eyes and ears for nothing. (551)

What has already become clear is that the absolute separation between the two areas or sides of the stage, the distinction between the 'real' world of Emer's bedside vigil and the avowedly theatrical realm of Cuchulain's ghostly sojourn, is more apparent than real. For one thing, the crouching Ghost is identified by Emer with and as her 'husband' whereas the physical creature by her side with the withered arm is a ghostly impostor. And what is about to ensue between Cuchulain and the Woman of the Sidhe now takes precedence over any other onstage situation and will have permanent consequences back in the waking world. The effect increasingly is to break down any clear-cut distinction between the two worlds and to produce the dramatically uncanny effect that Yeats recorded with pleasure at the first staging of *At the Hawk's Well:* 'Nobody seemed to know who was masked and who was not on Tuesday. Those who were not masked were made up to look as if they were. It was all very strange.'[14] Initially, to judge from the dramatis personae, it would appear that masks are worn by those who are of exclusively supernatural provenance, the Woman of the Sidhe or Bricriu, or those of semi-human, semi-divine origin, like Cuchulain; whereas the women, Emer and Eithne Inguba, are made up to appear as if they were wearing masks, the physical stress and coloration falling on their human character. But as Yeats notes, this distinction breaks down in practice. Similarly, Bricriu's injunction is as much to each member of the audience as it is to Emer, urging them to be silent, listen, and so help to create the drama about to be witnessed which, if successful, will finally bring together the two sides of the stage and the third side, the audience, into a comprehensive unity of atmosphere. What follows is an inner drama in the sense of a psychological exploration of the self and of a play within the play, something implicit since the opening with its double masked incarnations of the hero. The two Cuchulains have also resembled each other in their paralysis. The freeing of the physical, Cuchulain's return to life, is going to depend upon the prior freeing of the soul and a necessary working out of his situation in a consciously dramatic form.

The form chosen by Yeats for this psychic drama is what he called in *A Vision* the 'dreaming back', one of the four stages he believed the soul passes through in its progress toward reincarnation. 'Dreaming back' is his variation on the familiar conceit of the events of a drowning man's life passing rapidly before his eyes. Here, the review of Cuchulain's life follows immediately after rather than preceding the drowning. Instead of reliving the events of his life in their original chronological order, the dead man reverses the sequence and takes his end as his beginning, dreaming 'the events of his life backward through time'.[15] Cuchulain is dreaming throughout *The Only Jealousy of Emer* in his truncated sleep of death, but it is a waking dream, one that has 'place and weight and measure'.[16] This dramatized dream or phantasmagoria brings before him a succession of figures – his wife, his mistress, his otherworldly muse/daimon – and articulates their various relationships with him. It has been argued that Cuchulain appears to have little to do with, or indeed in, the play.[17] But everything we see on stage proceeds from him and returns to him as the centre of the drama, literally and symbolically.

The following exchange with the Woman of the Sidhe confirms that the Ghost of Cuchulain is undergoing the 'dreaming back':

WOMAN OF THE SIDHE. [...]
What pulled your hands about your feet,
Pulled down your head upon your knees,
And hid your face?
GHOST OF CUCHULAIN. Old memories:
A woman in her happy youth
Before her man had broken troth,
Dead men and women. Memories
Have pulled my head upon my knees. (551-553)

Of the troop of figures in his life that pass before Cuchulain's inner eye, his wife Emer is foremost, especially in the moments of greatest shared intensity: 'O Emer, Emer, there we stand; / Side by side and hand in hand / Tread the threshold of the house / As when our parents married us' (556-557). This is a complex dramatic moment. Cuchulain is addressing a figure that we see standing before him on stage. But he cannot see her and his remarks are directed, not to Emer as she is in the play's present, but to an image of her as they were in the past, at the moment of their greatest happiness. And this past union serves only to heighten by contrast their estrangement and isolation in the present, since 'as each but dreams again without change what happened when they were alive, each dreamer is alone'.[18]

The 'dreaming back' is no simple reverse screening of the dominant experiences of a lifetime. For, as the above exchange makes clear, the protagonist of the dream scenario can no longer retain or plead the innocence that may have accompanied such events first time around; rather, he is forced to relive them with full knowledge of their consequences: 'The man must dream the event to its consequence as far as his intensity permit; not that consequence only which occurred while he lived, and was known to him, but those that were unknown, or have occurred after his death.' The events are a working through in both a psychological and a dramatic sense, a full exploration of the consequences of an event. Thus it is that Cuchulain in his 'dreaming back' concentrates on Emer, the woman he married but repeatedly passed over in his drive for new amorous conquests. The consequences of his actions for Emer are what Cuchulain now takes on in his own person, directly experiencing the painful emotions caused by his heedlessness. This is the closest Yeats comes to a concept of hell. It is closer indeed to the state termed purgatory (compare his play of the same name), which also promises an end to suffering when the dead person has worked out his or her guilt in an act of expiation. For Yeats, 'there is no punishment [in the afterlife] but the prolongation of the *Dreaming back*'. In place of a predetermined and irrevocable Christian guilt and virtue, a hell or heaven, in imagining what happens after death, he opts for a process much closer to the Freudian working-through, a more conscious and consciously dramatic re-enactment of all the events, impulses, thoughts, and emotions of a single life.

The Ghost of Cuchulain cries for a way out of the self-created labyrinth of that life at the moment of greatest suffering. He is offered oblivion by the Woman of the Sidhe, whose kiss promises to remove him from the burden of his past to the freedom and ease of the otherworld. She in her turn, who lacks completion by only an 'hour or so' (553), can find it only through direct physical contact with Cuchulain. For 'the dead,' Yeats writes, 'cannot originate except through the living,' for all of their perfection, just as the Sidhe must replenish themselves by drawing 'away' children and newlyweds. In the play, it becomes apparent that Cuchulain has not attained the expiation of his human life with Emer that the otherworldly seductress has urged him towards. Where union with Cuchulain will bring the Woman of the Sidhe to Unity of Being, Phase Fifteen at which no human life is possible, there is a disturbing disjunction in his own case, a sense of emotional division. His cries alternate between 'Your mouth', as they are about to kiss, and 'O Emer, Emer', as he turns away (555-557). And if we bear in mind the staging, what is taking place between the Ghost of Cuchulain and the Woman of the Sidhe cannot be viewed as the whole emotional or dramatic truth. For Yeats has placed this ghostly drama in the framing context of Emer as impassioned witness, and in so doing has matched Cuchulain's continuing memory of her with Emer's embodiment of their lives in a complementary dream which the very shape of the play mirrors. The grit of memory which continues to trouble Cuchulain's vision is referred to disparagingly by the Woman of the Sidhe as the 'wind-blown dirt of their memories' (557); but it is polished by the friction of the play into the pearl of great price which neither can relinquish. The cost to Cuchulain is the promise of immortality. For Emer, it is to continue as knowing, conscious witness to a drama from which she is excluded as her act of renunciation delivers her husband from a deathlike trance into the arms of his living mistress. The final and abiding image is of Emer's isolation on stage, the marginalized other woman, as Cuchulain passes directly from one mistress to another.

In *The Only Jealousy of Emer* Yeats undertook his fullest dramatic exploration of the interaction between the living and the dead. But the subject continued to preoccupy his drama through such late works as *The Words Upon the Window-Pane* (1934), where a seance in contemporary Dublin is invaded by the ghostly triangle of Dean Swift, Stella, and Vanessa; and *Purgatory*, where the Old Man sees the ghosts of his parents and tries to abort the 'dead night' of his conception.[19] As the members of his Anglo-Irish Ascendency class followed a loss of political power with a decline in living numbers, Yeats drew increasingly on the spirits of the departed, both for company and as the chosen ones of his pantheon; the threat of the extinction of his caste was at least one motive behind a late play like *Purgatory*. Synge's own morbidity, aggravated by this inherited cultural experience of loss, was to seek an objective correlative in the fates of the Aran Islanders.

The contemporary equivalent of such social and cultural pressures on an individual playwright was the situation in the North of Ireland over more than thirty years from the late 1960s on. There, the threat of imminent extinction afflicted both sides in the conflict not only on an individual basis but also in a larger context of sectarian conflict; so it is Northern drama which placed a persistent pressure on the subject of ghosts, and with no less an emphasis on their direct onstage manifestation. The dead figure in Stewart Parker's *Pentecost* who returns to haunt the living is not a victim of sectarian assassination, as one might reasonably imagine from the play's setting of Belfast in 1974.

Rather, Lily Matthews, respectable widow of Alfred George Matthews, has died of natural causes at the respectable age of seventy-four, making her as old as the century and in many ways a representative of the history of the Northern Protestant community over that period. It is the lives of the living characters in the play which are under threat at one of the numerous crisis points in the ongoing turbulence of Northern Ireland's decades of violence. Or as Lenny the trombone player ruefully remarks: 'Sure, every bloody day in the week's historic, in this place.'[20]

But even so a particularly historic turning point was the Ulster Workers' Strike of 1974 – the period during which *Pentecost* takes place – given its determination to force the hand of the British government in bringing down the recently established power-sharing Executive, Northern Ireland's first concerted effort at something resembling democratic government. With the army and police standing idly by and the streets full of gun-toting civilians, nobody out there is safe, as we discover when Lenny's estranged wife Marian returns from searching out her car: she is revealed *'in the light of the torch, mud-spattered with her coat ripped, and scratch marks on her face'* (222). Given the life-threatening reality of what is just on the other side of a/the door, the onstage space functions as it does in so many Northern Irish plays as a kind of stay or refuge, an asylum or temporary holding ground, one step removed from the (war) zone of historical circumstance. Marian identifies the house in which she has chosen to live and which provides the play's setting in just these terms – as a refuge – when she complains to Lenny: 'You've been living with me again, here in this house, the very place I chose as a refuge' (225). But the larger point Marian misses is that her estranged husband, and the two friends of theirs who follow in his wake to make up the ill-assorted quartet of the cast, are all equally in need of a refuge, a site for healing in which their psychological, more than their actual, wounds can be tended.

Lenny's relationship with Marian – cannot live together, cannot live apart – has certain features in common with Northern Ireland itself; but both Catholic husband and Protestant wife are reluctant to declare their 'marriage' a failed entity. Ruth, a friend of Marian's from ten years earlier, is on the run from her truncheon-wielding policeman husband not for any crime she has committed beyond that of marriage. And the fourth stray who finds his way to the house Marian has chosen for splendid isolation is not (as we might expect and as someone prophesies) Ruth's pursuing husband but a new, belated character, Peter. An ex-college friend of Lenny's, he has returned to Belfast from years in Birmingham and so brings the perspective of the outside world to bear on the local situation. But *Pentecost* is more crowded than the cast of four would suggest. For the house into which Marian moves at the beginning of the play, '*a respectable working-class "parlour" house, built in the early years of this century*' (171), is a haunted site and not as empty as it strikes the pragmatic Lenny. He has come to inherit it by way of a great-aunt, and when Marian declares a wish to take it over in return for finally granting him a divorce, he protests: 'Marian, you can't possibly live in this gaff, it's the last house on the road left inhabited! – the very road itself is scheduled to vanish off the map' (179). Here, Marian's concern is to preserve the house as an example of the lived culture of a Belfast working-class Protestant community from the early years of the century. But this fossilization of the past, or Ulsterization, is finally resisted by Marian in a change of heart by which she decides that what the house needs is air and light, in order to be lived in.

The agent of this change of heart is the ghost of Lily Matthews, the house's last tenant, who refuses to be evicted even by death. Marian conjures up the ghost of Lily at least partly out of her own loneliness and need; her motives for so doing, like those for moving into the house in the first place, remain initially unclear, even to herself. When she and Lenny first enter the house, it is within hours of Lily vacating it, and the space is still very much suffused with the presence of the dead person. Entering the area where a woman has just died, they are both paradoxically made aware of her presence, evidenced by a half-finished cup of tea, and Marian begins the process of identification which is central to the play by trying to imagine the moment of Lily's death. Since they never knew her and so do not remember her, Marian is consciously working to reconstruct a past, a memory where none had previously existed. Marian cannot do it all by herself; the process is going to require the active presence and participation of the ghost of Lily Matthews.

The process by which the dead person is evoked in Irish drama usually depends on a theatrical, symbolic, and personal prop, like the half-drunk cup of tea, a physical synecdoche by which a more complete reality is summoned onto the stage. In Synge's *Riders to the Sea*, Michael's dead presence is summoned on stage by a few tattered remains of his clothing; as Declan Kiberd remarks, 'on stage, every prop is a symbol', particularly in a charged context like this.[21] In the second scene of *Pentecost*, in ways reminiscent of the discovery scene in Synge's *Riders*, Marian lifts a piece of unfinished knitting out of a basket. In both plays the knitting signifies a severed lifeline and the distinctive fabric of one person's existence which the play is going to draw out. But in Marian's suggestion that 'I might just finish it off for you' (180), there is also the larger point of the overall pattern which is beginning to emerge, the dramatic weave of the ensemble. Here, the two reactions which Synge kept dramatically separate, the sceptical and the visionary, are fused in Marian's response. Her superficially ironic yet emotionally engaged dialogue with the absent figure now calls Lily forth, bringing her on stage dressed as she exited two months earlier:[22]

> **LILY MATTHEWS**, *in Sunday coat and hat and best handbag appears in the shadowy doorway leading from the pantry.*
> **LILY.** I don't want you in my house.
> **MARIAN** *keeps her eyes on the knitting pattern: on guard but not entirely frightened, aware that her mind is playing tricks on her.*
> **MARIAN.** You needn't try to scare me, Lily.
> **LILY.** Don't you 'Lily' me. I don't want you in here, breathing strong drink and profanity. (181)

As in Hugh Leonard's *Da* (1973), where Charlie returns from his father's funeral to find the old man sitting in an armchair, the person is dead but refuses to lie down (or to stop talking). Parker's *Pentecost* is in the Irish dramatic tradition noted by Billington in his *Guardian* review which realizes that, far from keeping to narrowly realistic boundaries, theatre is a means of bringing the dead back to life. And in the objective and ineluctable materialization which is theatre, those ghosts cannot be read entirely in psychological or Ibsenite terms once the playwright has decided to show them on stage. Clearly, as even Marian herself is aware, her own isolation, the strong drink, and her confession that she does not much like herself are all psychologically sufficient to project an imagined alter ego as a way of dramatizing her own divided self.[23] And to the other characters in *Pentecost*, Lily is invisible, nonexistent, a sign merely of Marian's cracking up: 'You've been talking to yourself, you've been counting spoons, you've been babbling in tongues in the middle of the night!' (226). But in theatrical terms once you have assigned an actor to embody an alter ego, a doppelgänger, or a dead person, there is nothing to choose between the real and the ghostly. Yeats makes this clear from the opening of *The Only Jealousy of Emer,* with its precise, masked doubling of the Figure of Cuchulain and the Ghost of Cuchulain.

The same holds true for Lily Matthews's manifestation in Parker's *Pentecost.* Her ghost not only challenges Marian's reality and her grip on it, but also that of the reality the play is representing. The irony is that Lily appears to urge strict segregation into Catholic and Protestant and (we might add) living and dead, while her presence on stage succeeds in crossing all kinds of boundaries and established lines of demarcation. When the ghost invokes her dead husband's absence by saying: 'You'd be singing on the other side of your face if my Alfie was here' (181), Marian, closing her eyes, insists: 'There's nobody here. Nobody.' The audience at this point must register a double take by applying Marian's words reflexively to herself no less than to the ghost of Lily, since who, in theatre, on the stage, is *really* there? Parker has fun with this phenomenon of theatre all the way through the play. He has Lily insist on her greater materiality by way of having more of a right to be in the house, reversing the situation by treating Marian as the interloping ghost who needs to be exorcised; her appearance is usually accompanied by a bout of hymn singing to keep the Antichrist at bay. But Marian plays along with the inverted terms of the identification by stressing the interdependence between living and dead:

> I need you, we have got to make this work, you and me... [...] You think you're haunting me, don't you. But you see it's me that's actually haunting you. I'm not going to go away. There's no curse or hymn that can exorcise me. So you might as well just give me your blessing and make your peace with me, Lily. (210)

What Lily's active questioning presence does with the drama, in ways similar to the Yeats play, is to double it. The urgency with which Marian examines this revenant on the details of her life history, of the intimate hidden life which lies behind the imperturbable respectability of Lily's facade, is the psychic secret which this updated Gothic drama seeks to discover in its haunted house. As she does so, Marian becomes increasingly drawn into the process, in effect taking over and subsuming the role of Lily as she comes to understand and identify with it.

As is usually the case in a ghostly scenario, which Yeats would liken to a phantasmagoria or psychic procession, the appearance of one ghost soon draws others in its train. For example there is Lily's dead husband, Alfie, a ghost in a double sense. He may have died and left her widowed only fifteen years earlier, in 1959, but it turns out that Lily was wed as an eighteen-year-old virgin to this man who, having endured the trenches of World War I and been one of only two men on his street to survive, was already a living corpse:

> Alfie had come back, that's why. Back from Passchendaele. Hellfire Corner. Back from the dead. [...] All in the one week, married and moved in, he couldn't wait ... not after what he'd seen ... this house was his life, same as mine. (181-182)

Marian confronts Lily, however, with incriminating objects, strands of evidence that weave a very different story from the one her house embodies: a rent book signifies the ghost of a third party, Alan Ferris, an English airman; and in a photograph of the three, husband, wife, and lodger, the outlines of a triangular relationship may be discerned. In regard to her and Alfie's childlessness and the sterility the house ultimately represents, Lily is confronted by Marian with a 1930s child's christening gown, which gives the lie to their married relationship. Lily's husband had also been sexually maimed, and her one brief experience of passion had been with the airman. In her most crucial exchange with Marian, Lily evokes a visionary landscape of water and air redolent of her sexual need: 'All we did was stand and look, across the water' (229). This scene, which develops in ways reminiscent of Beckett's *Rockaby,* has Marian sit in the rocking chair and begin speaking Lily's thoughts for her, based on reading her diary: 'That was the moment when it hit you, though [...] the moment you realized that you were going to give yourself' (229). The fruit of Lily's relationship with her airman was the baby she could not bring herself to acknowledge and so abandoned, the sign of her betrayal as she saw it.

There is more than one buried child being exhumed in this interchange. Lenny has let fall to Peter that he and Marian had a baby, which comes as a revelation in the play's second half, a child which is never acknowledged whenever they are together on stage discussing their marriage. The irony is that they only married because Marian was pregnant and then, in having the baby, she and Lenny learned to love each other. Ruth, too, has had more than one miscarriage, not least because her policeman husband repeatedly beats her, and she has been told she can have no more pregnancies. At the close of the first half, the three women are linked across the generations, across the sectarian divide, and across life and death as the revelation of the dead Lily's dead child leads the two living women to acknowledge their own. When Lily completes her suppressed story of the affair with Alan that lay behind the fact of her child, Marian responds with an eloquent gesture, reaching out the hand of the living to that of the dead and holding it against her heart as an act of restoration:

> *MARIAN takes LILY's hand and holds it against her own heart.*
> **MARIAN.** Forgive me, Lily.
> *Lights fade to blackout.* (232)

For Lily's husband Alfie was impotent, neither 'the first nor the last to come back from the dead in that condition', and the house was the sole witness to Lily's labour, birth and what she suffered in giving up her child. This denial of life and her sense of abandonment are the emotional truths which Lily's Unionist cry of 'No surrender' tries to deny and silence.

Lily does not appear again after this. When Marian speaks in the play's closing scene, there is no longer any need to present them as two separate or distinct selves on the stage. This final scene has generally been criticized, in the context of the overall praise *Pentecost* has attracted, as Parker's imposing an overtly religious and didactic conclusion on his play through wholesale quotation from the Bible. There *is* dramatic overkill, with four epiphanies *and* four pentecostal speeches; the biblical speaking in tongues is not sufficiently refashioned in terms of the individual speech of each of the characters. Finally, only Marian's speeches are dramatically convincing. The other three, in offering their solution to how a vision of Christ can be wedded to the reality of street life in contemporary Belfast, speak too exclusively for themselves and in overly rhetorical terms. Marian is the only one who follows the Pentecostal injunction to 'speak with other tongues, as the Spirit gave them utterance' (244). She does so, first, by speaking for and as Lily Matthews in the culmination of a dramatic process we have witnessed throughout the play. She does so by imagining a scene during a Second World War bombing raid on the Belfast house, with Lily alone on the parlour sofa on which she and Alan had made love. In a direct evocation of Ibsen's *Ghosts,* Peter and Ruth had earlier entered that same parlour and made love there, the past repeating itself in the present, and the hidden sexual history of these interconnected lives is being brought to the surface. But with Marian's subsequent storytelling the past is not allowed to dominate and determine the present, as in Ibsen. Rather, it is reshaped in the light of present possibilities.

Marian as actress/playwright takes on and speaks out of her own understanding of Lily Matthew's twilight existence, imagining a unique moment of sexual and spiritual ecstasy in which Lily wishes to die as the bombs rain down from her demon lover. Instead, Lily is suffered to survive, 'condemned to life. A life sentence' (237). Marian realizes that her own making present of that life, her articulation of what lay hidden in Lily's journal, has released the petrified ghost from the bonds of hypocrisy. Marian goes on to speak for and in the tongue of yet another denied ghost, her dead son Christopher. In so doing Marian speaks up effectively for the Christ in each of them that is the tenor of the play's closing: 'I denied [...] the ghost of him that I do still carry, as I carried his little body' (244). There is a ghost trio at this point, since Marian's talk of Christopher is also Lily speaking for the love-child whose existence she has denied. As *Pentecost* ends Lenny touches Marian's hand, as she had earlier touched Lily's, in a reciprocal gesture of support and restoration. [24]

As this chapter has sought to show, ghosts are and always have been a strong and recurrent feature of Irish drama. It is less a case of Ireland being in thrall to its past (though that spectre is raised and confronted in all of the plays discussed) as one in which the past is always living as a potential to be resurrected in the endless present of theatre. The lives of those who have died are keenly felt and registered in Irish drama's insistence on treating ghosts as nothing more (or less) than full corporeal presences. The contemporary canon of Irish drama is replete with examples. In Frank McGuinness's *Observe the Sons of Ulster Marching Towards the Somme* (1985), David Pyper's experiences as a member of the 36th Ulster Division at the Battle of the Somme are not told contemporaneously; rather, the elderly Pyper is pressurized into remembering and reliving the experience by the appearance of his dead comrades around his hospital bed. In Marina Carr's *Portia Coughlan* (1996), the eponymous heroine only leads a half-life in daily consort with her husband, children and friends; her most essential self is communing with the ghost of her dead twin brother, unseen by the other characters but represented on stage, standing by the banks of the Belmont River in which he drowned, singing. Carr does not deploy the folklore terms which the Revival would have; but the phenomenon of the dead haunting the living is no less powerfully present. The next chapter will pursue the connection between Synge's and Carr's drama through the feminist figure of the woman on the threshold which the two playwrights did so much to foreground.

---

[1] John Crowley, 'Director's Note', *Shadows: A Trinity of Plays by J.M. Synge and W.B. Yeats* (London: Oberon Books, 1998), p. 11.

[2] Michael Billington, 'Death Becomes Eire', *The Guardian*, 28 February, 1998.

[3] On the Field Day Theatre Company, see Aidan O'Malley, *Field Day and the Translation of Irish Identities* (Houndmills: Palgrave Macmillan, 2011).

[4] 'The religious, political and aesthetic themes in *The Aran Islands* are carefully contextualized in time and place.' Mary C. King, *The Drama of J.M. Synge* (Syracuse, N.J.: Syracuse University Press, 1985), p. 20. Further, Synge highlights 'the transformation into art of the day-to-day lives, activities and preoccupations of a community.'

5 See Nicholas Grene, *Synge: A Critical Study of the Plays* (Houndmills: Macmillan, 1975), p. 53.

6 Henrik Ibsen, *Ghosts and Other Plays,* translated by Peter Watts (London: Penguin Books, 1964), p. 54.

7 W.B. Yeats, *The Only Jealousy of Emer, The Variorum Edition of the Plays of W.B. Yeats,* edited by Russell K. Alspach (London: Macmillan, 1966), p. 541. All future references to the play are to this edition and will be incorporated in the text.

8 See Liam Miller, *The Noble Drama of W.B. Yeats* (Dublin: The Dolmen Press, 1977), p. 163. Miller's book reproduces the projected Craig designs for *The Hour-Glass,* pp. 163 following.

9 Compare Yeats's letter to Lady Gregory on 26 March 1916: 'I believe I have at last found a dramatic form that suits me.' *The Letters of W.B. Yeats,* edited by Allan Wade (New York: Macmillan, 1955), p. 610.

10 W.B. Yeats, *At the Hawk's Well, The Variorum Edition of the Plays of W.B. Yeats,* p. 399.

11 W.B. Yeats, 'Certain Noble Plays of Japan,' *Essays and Introductions* (London: Macmillan, 1961), p. 226.

12 See Lady Gregory for Yeats's source, her rendering into English of the Irish original as 'The Only Jealousy of Emer'. Lady Gregory, *Cuchulain of Muirhemne* (Gerrards Cross, Bucks: Colin Smythe, 1970), pp. 210-222.

13 W.B. Yeats, 'Certain Noble Plays of Japan', p. 224.

14 *The Letters of W.B. Yeats,* pp. 610-611.

15 See *A Critical Edition of Yeats's 'A Vision',* edited by George Mills Harper and Walter Kelly Hood (London: Macmillan, 1978), p. 226.

16 W.B. Yeats, 'Swedenborg, Mediums, Desolate Places,' *Explorations* (New York: Macmillan, 1962), p. 63.

17 Richard Taylor, *The Drama of W.B. Yeats: Irish Myth and the Japanese Noh* (New Haven: Yale University Press, 1976), p. 140. Taylor holds that the play's 'action' only indirectly focuses upon Cuchulain, that he is 'a mere occasion for the action that takes place around [him].'

18 *A Critical Edition of Yeats's 'A Vision',* pp. 226-227. The remaining references to *A Vision* are all from pages 226-228 and will not be individually cited.

19 W.B. Yeats, *Purgatory, The Variorum Edition of the Plays of W.B. Yeats,* p. 1049.

20 Stewart Parker, *Pentecost, Plays: 2* (London: Methuen Drama, 2000), p. 200. All future references are to this edition and will be incorporated in the text.

21 Declan Kiberd, 'Introduction', *Shadows,* p. 9.

22 As a ghost, Lily initially assumes the form in which she died. In subsequent appearances, which reflect different stages of Lily's life, her dress and appearance are altered accordingly.

23 Brian Friel did no less with his youthful protagonist Gar O'Donnell in *Philadelphia, Here I Come!,* requiring two actors to represent: 'two views of the one man. PUBLIC GAR is the Gar that people see, talk to, talk about. PRIVATE GAR is the unseen man, the man within, the conscience, the *alter ego*, the secret thoughts, the id. PRIVATE GAR, the spirit, is invisible to everybody, always. Nobody except PUBLIC GAR hears him talk.' Brian Friel, *Philadelphia, Here I Come!, Plays: One* (London and Boston: Faber and Faber, 1996), p. 27.

24 This was the conclusion of the 1987 Field Day Theatre Company production of Parker's *Pentecost*, directed by Patrick Mason and featuring Stephen Rea as Lenny and Eileen Pollock as Marian. The gesture, however, is not in the published script.

6 | Woman on the Threshold: Synge's *The Shadow of the Glen*, Teresa Deevy's *Katie Roche* and Marina Carr's *The Mai*

This chapter will examine three Irish plays across the span of the twentieth century which focus on the dilemma of a young woman whose independence is constrained by the circumstances in which she is placed. One of them is by Synge, *The Shadow of the Glen*, two of them by Irish women playwrights, Teresa Deevy's *Katie Roche* (1936) and Marina Carr's *The Mai* (1994). All three focus on the dilemma of a young woman, in each case married to an unsympathetic husband. The plays explore the freedoms the young woman has sacrificed to gain security and find the dramaturgic expression of that tension in the symbol of the door, which operates as a liminal threshold onto a world of possibility rather than a means of keeping outside forces at bay. In each case, there are such forces, a wanderer of the roads who intrudes upon the *status quo* of the household. But the primary disruptive force is the desire of the heroine, operating from within and posing a threat to the male hegemony. Synge's example, as this chapter will argue, has proved an important resource for the dramaturgy of Deevy and Carr.

There have always been woman playwrights in Ireland; Melissa Sihra lists 258.[1] But not many have been accorded prominence. Teresa Deevy is one of the very few to have done so, between Lady Gregory in the Revival and the present moment. Her plays were regularly staged at the Abbey in the 1930s; and are currently being revived by the Mint Theatre Company in New York. Marina Carr broke through with her 1994 play *The Mai* to an unprecedented level of recognition for a woman playwright, and has premiered an important new play approximately every two years since. *The Mai* was awarded the Best New Play of 1994's Irish Life Dublin Theatre Festival and under Brian Brady's direction played to packed houses at the Peacock Theatre. In that same year, Teresa Deevy's *Katie Roche* enjoyed a rare revival, also at the Peacock. Judy Friel's production featured a performance by Derbhle Crotty as Katie Roche which caught the youthful exuberance, contradictoriness and petulance of Deevy's heroine. Crotty also featured significantly in Carr's *The Mai*, as the title character's daughter (in the past) and as the one who assumes responsibility for telling the Mai's story (in the present). The hat trick of Derbhle Crotty's mercurial passage across the National Theatre's stages in 1994 was completed by a performance as Molly Byrne in Synge's *The Well of the Saints*. This play was chosen by the Abbey's then-Artistic Director, Patrick Mason, to honour the theatre's ninetieth anniversary.

But the Synge play which is most relevant to any consideration of Teresa Deevy's *Katie Roche* and Marina Carr's *The Mai* is his *The Shadow of the Glen* of 1903. The controversy generated by *Shadow* accompanied the inauguration of an Irish theatre movement and focused its hostility on the representation of an unsatisfactory marriage between an older man and a younger woman. What drew the strongest protest was the action of the wife at the play's denouement. Rebutting as unjust the charge that he had said there was no such thing as an unhappy marriage in Ireland, Arthur Griffith went on in the pages of *The United Irishman* to indicate where his real objection to Synge's play rested:

> Man and woman in rural Ireland, according to Mr. Synge, marry lacking love, and, as a consequence, the woman proves unfaithful. Mr. Synge never found that in Irish life. Men and women in Ireland marry lacking love, and live mostly in a dull level of amity. Sometimes they do not – sometimes the woman lives in bitterness – sometimes she dies of a broken heart – but she does not go away with the Tramp.[2]

Teresa Deevy follows up on Synge's play in two important ways: by reproducing and extending the dramatic situation of an older man married to a younger woman and by introducing the figure of the Tramp at a key moment in each of *Katie Roche's* three acts. Where both Nora the character and Synge the playwright appear to find satisfactory an ending in which she goes away with the tramp, Deevy has her own reasons – and they are very different ones from Arthur Griffith's – for rejecting the arrival of the Tramp in the Gregg household as a resolution of the new Mrs Gregg's unhappiness.

A crucial element in both plays' dramatic treatment is the heroine's positioning within a peasant cottage setting. The house is what she has married into and her increasing sense of claustrophobia and confinement is counter-balanced by the possibility of freedom beyond the cottage walls. The woman is poised on the threshold between the security of 'in here' and the potential of 'out there'. As these symbolic overtones accrue, crossing over the cottage's front door becomes an increasingly fraught activity for her, a breaching of boundaries which the respectable husbands are anxious to keep in place. I will study these issues as they are represented first in Synge's play, then in Deevy's, and ultimately in Carr's, where they are re-worked in a contemporary context: the unhappily married couple are now the same age, the Tramp has switched gender and the walls of the rural home have become transparently revealing but no less charged with danger for the woman they contain.

As discussed in Chapter Three, Synge's *The Shadow of the Glen* was only one of several important plays in the emerging Irish Dramatic Movement that foregrounded a young woman about to be, or recently, married. Such works as Hyde's *Casadh an tSúgáin/The Twisting of the Rope* and Yeats's *The Land of Heart's Desire* also dramatized the woman's ambivalence through the medium of a peasant cottage setting. Synge's play differs from the Hyde and the Yeats in foregrounding a young woman who is already, rather than on the verge of being, married, and has been for many years. Here the degree of her distress conjures up, not the pre-Raphaelite fairy child of Yeats's play, but the much more sexually dangerous figure of an adult male. In writing a play from the folk narrative, Synge locates the true drama in the plight of Nora Burke rather than in the grotesque charade performed by her husband. The ostensible aim of the trick is to catch his wife in the act of adultery. Many cultures have such a folk-tale in their repertoire. The most famous, the Widow of Ephesus, is the one Synge was accused, by Griffith and others, of importing from abroad, from the classically derived and currently decadent milieu of the outside world, into the pure and chaste regions of Irish culture: 'To take the Widow of Ephesus and rechristen her Mrs. Burke and relabel Ephesus Wicklow is not a brilliant thing.'[3] As Synge was able to rebut, his source for the story could not have been more authentic and indigenous in terms of Irish culture, since he had it orally in Irish from the storyteller Pat Dirane on the Aran Islands. As he records in *The Aran Islands,* 'Pat told me a story of an unfaithful wife' (II, 70). In reproducing the story Synge marks it off from his own narrative, attributes it to its storytelling source and observes: 'In stories of this kind he always speaks in the first person, with minute details to show that he was present at the scenes that are described' (II, 72). Synge has already submitted the story to a degree of translation, by moving from Irish to English, from oral storytelling to a printed prose narrative. But he has preserved the details and sentiments of what he was told. It is in the dramatic version that the sympathies are going to be radically displaced.

In his storytelling, Pat Dirane remains a neutral observer for much of the narrative of the unfaithful wife, a personal witness of the event itself. He is brought in out of the cold by the woman of the house while travelling from Galway to Dublin, given first a cup of tea, then spirits and a pipe. When she leaves, her dead husband sits up and discloses the traditional kernel of the narrative: "'I've got a bad wife, stranger, and I let on to be dead the way I'd catch her goings on." Then he got two fine sticks he had to keep down his wife, and he put them at each side of his body, and he laid himself out again as if he was dead' (II, 72). When the wife returns with a young man, they head for the bedroom and the narrative rushes to its melodramatic and bloody conclusion:

> Then the dead man got up, and he took one stick, and he gave the other to myself. We went in and we saw them lying together with her head on his arm. The dead man hit him a blow with the stick so that the blood out of him leapt up and hit the gallery. That is my story. (II, 72)

The storyteller's sympathies are implicitly aligned with the old man, once he has been told the situation. The producing of the two sticks and his acceptance of one of them signals his adherence to a code of behaviour in which wives who do not submit to being 'kept down' must be made to do so by physical force.

The old man's stick figures prominently in Synge's The Shadow of the Glen; and in Deevy's Katie Roche the play's most shocking action occurs when a man raises a stick 'with surprising vigour [...] [and] hits her across the shoulders. KATIE collapses on to a chair. Groans. Silence ...'4 Synge makes a significant alteration in the received tale when he reduces the number of sticks to one and associates the weapon exclusively with the vengeful husband, Dan Burke. As the Tramp does what he is instructed and furnishes the dead man with the stick, his tone of innocent enquiry prompts the justifying statement: 'it's a long time I'm keeping that stick, for I've a bad wife in the house' (III, 43). The appearance of the black stick suggests to an audience that the play is heading in the bloody direction of the original, with the cheated husband despatching his male usurper and teaching his trespassing wife a lesson. But the Tramp then makes a crucial intervention by directing his sympathy away from the self-righteous husband towards the threatened figure of the wife: 'Is it herself, master of the house, and she a grand woman to talk?' (III, 43). Far from maintaining the alignment between the storyteller and the old man, the play has opened up a gap between them and developed a potentially disruptive alignment of the Tramp with the wife that the old man is quick to detect and warn against. He does so by repeating his original claim, not once but twice, that he has 'a bad wife'; each repetition falls like a verbal blow and each carries less conviction, failing to receive implicit assent from the on-stage audience of one. As he hears his wife and Michael Dara returning, Dan asks the Tramp to put the stick 'here in the bed' with him and to smooth out the sheets so it will not be noticed. When he later rises from the bed to denounce the lovers and shake his stick at them, the physical threat betrays its psychosexual nature: 'you'll see the thing I'll give you will follow you on the back mountains when the wind is high' (III, 53). Dan Burke's marital ambition is giving lumps, not making children, and the stick figures throughout Synge's play as the sign of the old man's impotence rather than the rule by which the sexual regulation of society is administered.

Much of the deviation of the later stages of Synge's *The Shadow of the Glen* from its Aran Islands source derives from the crucial intervention made by the Tramp in the direction the plot is going to take. The ground for that pivotal shift of emphasis, away from the punishing husband towards the threatened wife, has already been prepared earlier in the play. The major addition that Synge makes there, while at one level he is following the direction and action of his source, is to introduce a lengthy and revealing dialogue between Nora Burke and the Tramp. Rather than being presented as a grotesque incident in its own right, the device of the dead man stretched out on the table is pressed into service as a psychological index of the relationship between the married couple. Under the Tramp's gentle prompting, Nora speaks of the life she has led across a span of years and reveals the lack of intimacy afflicting their union: 'Maybe cold would be no sign of death with the like of him, for he was always cold, every day since I knew him, – and every night, stranger' (III, 35). From the beginning of the play, Nora breaks one of the most binding and enduring taboos in Irish society, the lack of discussion of intimate relations between a married couple. She follows this with an implicitly feminist declaration, that she 'never knew what way I'd be afeard of beggar or bishop or any man of you at all' (III, 37). Synge's play, then, rapidly establishes Nora's orality as the potential site and source of her greatest freedom, that zone of language in which she builds up an autonomy and self-deriving authority that is most at odds with her social situation. Characteristically, that talk is reduced and dismissed as 'blathering' (III, 43) by her husband when he revives and chides the Tramp for encouraging and participating in it.

The figure that serves to indicate the greatest level of shared verbal intimacy between the wife and the Tramp is the enigmatic and recently deceased Patch Darcy. The Tramp's mention of his name provokes a jolt of recognition in Nora, who then gives the basis of their relationship: 'God spare Darcy, he'd always look in here and he passing up or passing down, and it's very lonesome I was after him a long while [...], and then I got happy again [...] for I got used to being lonesome' (III, 39). Immediately preceding an enquiry about her young lover Michael Dara, Nora's is a highly ambiguous statement, challenging any audience in its received interpretation of marital fidelity. A sexual implication is unavoidable, but no less so is the portrayal of Nora's loneliness in this travesty of a marriage. Indeed, her remark about Patch Darcy 'passing up and passing down' is later echoed by the most parodied lines in the play, where what Nora beholds when she looks out the door is the omnipresent evidence of the mist, an echo suggesting the extent to which a human face might alleviate the emptiness of her daily existence. The remark about Patch Darcy 'looking in' on Nora is repeated by Michael Dara as an item of gossip in the neighbourhood; here its connotations are exclusively sexual. Nora Burke does not deny the physical aspect of the attraction. Rather she expands it to cover talking and looking, confirming that she has had many suitors and is a woman of exacting standards: 'it's a hard woman I am to please this day, Michael Dara' (III, 49). The central question posed by the play, why such an independent and fiery young woman should have settled for a domineering old man as husband, is answered by Nora as another question, clarifying the stark choices facing women in Irish society at the turn of the century: 'What way would I live, and I an old woman, if I didn't marry a man with a bit of a farm?' (III, 49). If she takes comfort from the men passing on the roads, she recognizes her own lost opportunities, the rights she appears to have forfeited by her match: to have two or three children like her friend Mary Brien, to have the right to wander where she pleases and to talk with whom she pleases.

The ending of Synge's play marks the most significant revision. In this household that may appear rustic and remote, its bourgeois origins are manifested in the punishment which the husband visits upon his wife: showing her the door in the recognizably Victorian pose of the affronted patriarch banishing the fallen woman from the home. With the recognition that the supposedly dead husband is still very much alive and that there is accordingly no inheritance to marry into, Michael reveals his callow and callous nature when he rejects Nora and suggests that she go off to the workhouse. The ground by which the Tramp steps in and is prepared to make his offer, that Nora accompany him to a life of greater freedom on the open roads, has been prepared for earlier, as we have seen, through their discussion of Patch Darcy. And Nora accepts with her well-known line: 'you've a fine bit of talk, stranger, and it's with yourself I'll go' (III, 57). The essentially verbal and fictive nature of the reality the Tramp presents to Nora has long been recognized and is of a piece with the more complex storytelling procedures of Martin Doul in *The Well of the Saints* and Christy Mahon in *The Playboy of the Western World*. When the scene is viewed without the language and its seductions, however, the resolution of the play becomes more troubling. Iconically, the woman is seen to be passed from one male figure who has definitively rejected her to another who now relinquishes his claim until a third steps in and takes her on. Nowhere is Synge's modification of Ibsen's *A Doll's House* more apparent than when he has his Nora shrink from or never appear to consider the possibility of going through the door on her own. Renewed attention to the language of Synge's conclusion shows the extent to which the Tramp's language takes over, telling Nora over and over what she'll be saying and what she'll be hearing. The current of the final scene is a virtual monologue to which she ultimately accedes. Nora's own powerful speech has reasserts itself in one final turn of sympathy for the husband she is leaving. But for the most part she is silenced as, in Synge's later works, Mary Doul and the Widow Quin will be as their plays draw to their denouement.

What Teresa Deevy recognizes in Synge's *The Shadow of the Glen* is the all-pervasiveness of the patriarchy. It extends beyond the alliance in the play's sardonic closing image of the husband and the lover, having banished the woman, sitting down together to occupy the house and to share a drink. At a key moment in each of her play's three acts, Teresa Deevy brings the Syngean figure of the Tramp into *Katie Roche*. The Tramp who appears in the Gregg cottage is looked to by the young wife as a wise man, a Christian ascetic who yet retains his pagan sympathies through continued intimacy with the natural world. Yet *he* is the one who brings the stick crashing down on her back for not observing the strict letter of her marriage with Stanislaus Gregg. The play's most important disclosure, scarcely credible on the level of probability but absolutely accurate in terms of the play's symbolic and social values, is that Reuben the Tramp is the orphan Katie Roche's natural father:

KATIE: A man off the road to talk like that!

REUBEN *(gentle):* Yes, – I'm a man off the road – and your father. (60)

Reuben's gentleness does not last long. Where Katie claims the same licence that her father has asserted in his actions and declares that she will 'make [her] own goodness', he urges her in wrathful Old Testament terms to be 'a good wife' (60). In Act III Katie's father returns to pass on this advice directly to Stanislaus, arguing repeated applications of the stick we have earlier seen him wield with such force:

REUBEN. I'd give her a flogging. [...] She'll make her own goodness. What does that mean? She won't be punished. [...] What she needs is humiliation, – if she was thoroughly humbled she might begin to learn. (105)

The complicity between the Tramp and the husband is briefly acknowledged at this point. When it is revealed that Reuben is Katie's natural father, Stan is obliged to show him a certain deference. His more habitual response to the arrival of the Tramp has been to indicate by a frozen formality that he wants him gone and to express bourgeois disapproval that this wild man of the roads has been let into the house by his wayward wife. He responds with '*Surprise*' to Reuben's suggestion that he should beat his wife. Stan has his own more civilized methods of maintaining control: the weapons of speech and silence have now fully taken over from the big stick.

The other central feature of Synge's play that Deevy develops and explores across three acts is the dramatic situation of marriage between an older man and a younger woman. *Katie Roche* is quite explicit in its details about the gap of age and experience separating Katie from Stan. Stanislaus Gregg is introduced as '*a short stoutish man of about forty-five*' (7). He comes slowly into his sister's cottage as the play opens, moving to stand in the sunlight that is streaming through the window. Katie, who then enters bearing a teatray, is described as '*not yet twenty*' (8) and, in the one additional piece of information that Deevy supplies about her, is distinguished by '*a sort of inward glow, which she continually tries to smother and which breaks out in delight or desperation according to circumstances*'. In the Peacock production, director Judy Friel and actress Derbhle Crotty beautifully conveyed Katie Roche's inward glow of youthful possibility by starting the play with Katie already on, standing at the window in the afternoon sun and basking in its light. As a result of this, Stan's muted entrance was all of a piece, the first inevitable clouding or, to use Deevy's term, smothering.

Any possible equality that might exist between this man and this woman is heavily undercut in the play's clear representation of the givens of the social, economic and symbolic relations between them. This is all the more relevant in that Stan has come expressly to ask her to marry him. The economic conditions are not equal. Katie, as we all too readily see from her entrance, is employed as a domestic in the Gregg household and is always on the watch for the return of her employer, Stan's older sister Amelia. But Stan's relationship to Katie is more exactly that of her employer, since it later emerges that he is the one who provides his sister with a subsistence on which she lives and that Amelia defers to her brother's every wish and opinion. Stan economically controls the lives of both women in the play, and this contributes to the ways in which the Amelia plot is a parodic double of Stan's courtship and marriage of Katie Roche. That a proposal of marriage to her by her ostensible employer's brother alters very little in the power relations governing Katie Roche's existence is borne out in the early months of their married life in Act 2, where Katie reacts to the return of Amelia by rushing to prepare her tea.

The romantic fixation by which Stan has long determined that he will make Katie Roche his wife is not only put in question by our realization that he has had her in mind as a sexual partner since she was a child but by his insistence as employer that his demands must be acceded to. Although Stan has declared more than once that she is free to do as she wishes, and although Katie has at first responded to his proposal in the negative, he withdraws and bides his time. Amelia is deployed as the appropriate medium to convey his wishes:

> **AMELIA.** Katie, Mr. Gregg said to tell you, I mean Stan said to tell you-
> **KATIE.** What? (*Apprehensive.*)
> **AMELIA**. He's in the little room, if you care to go to him.
> **KATIE.** (*Rises, alarmed*): Must I go now?
> **AMELIA.** Do whatever you wish, dear. He said not to try to influence you. Do whatever you wish ... (*Withdraws.*) (42)

In the brief interim she was alone on stage, Derbhle Crotty physically conveyed this most wrenching moment of the play's first act by twisting and turning her body on the rack of indecision – or rather in the constrained space of the lack of any real alternative. The dramatic and social situations directly contradict the reiterated verbal assertion that she is absolutely free to do what she wishes.

Stan steps back into the room to draw Katie into his arms and into the agreement that she will marry him. He compliments her on her decision as 'a good girl' (42). Throughout the remaining two acts, Katie is to grow increasingly irked by her husband's references to her as a little girl. They suggest, of course, that he is not taking her seriously as an equal partner in the marriage, that she is being treated rather like Nora in *A Doll's House*. But the term also brings out the extent to which Stan is old enough to be Katie's father and that as a result there is something profoundly wrong about their entering into marriage. What gives the suggestion strength is the elaborate confession Stan makes during his proposal by which it emerges that he could indeed have been her father, not just symbolically but literally. He reveals that as a young man he was in love with Katie's natural mother:

> **STAN.** Katie, your mother, Mary Halnan, was a wonderful woman. She was beautiful and all that. A crowd of them, long ago, were in love with her. I loved her; I could have knocked down the world for her. But – she said I was too young. (14)

This revelation immediately precedes his proposal. Katie, confused by this doubling of her own identity with the ghost of her dead mother, can only respond: 'Now is it ... or ... or then?' (15). She is not taken seriously in her desires and expressions by this older man not only because she is a woman and extremely young but because by doubling for her absent mother she is a substitute for a beautiful romantic icon.

Katie Roche, it might be argued, has her own romantic yearnings: to come from an aristocratic line, to enter a convent. She certainly has her illusions about what married life with Stanislaus will be like. But her romantic dreams must be seen in the context provided by Stan's *idée fixe* about her. His romantic obsession ('a long time ago I made up my mind that I'd marry Katie' (39), proceeds from the fact of his economic empowerment, as her employer and therefore a man able to be masterful; his desires may be enforced because they are underwritten by the society and his secure place within it:

> **STAN.** Now I don't suppose you know why I'm here – because how could you?
> **KATIE.** Sure I couldn't. Unless you were short of the money and to stop here till you'll make more.
> **STAN.** I was not short of money. I'm thinking of buying this place.
> **KATIE.** And what would become of me? (13)

Katie's romantic yearnings, by contrast, proceed from and are fuelled by her powerlessness. She announces early on that she intends to be a nun. The proposal is scoffed at and even the audience can see that this wildly impulsive young woman is not about to go quietly into a convent. The idea was formed early in life by her reading of the *Spiritual Maxims* and of the lives of women saints – almost the only female role models that would have been available to her in anything but romantic fiction. Katie's reservations about the convent as a means to sainthood derive from personal experience. For working at Miss Gregg's, as she says herself, is preferable to 'minding the kids at the convent beyond. [...] When you'd be working for nuns you'd never be finished. (*Moves about her work.*) In at half-eight every night. But they had a grand library' (12). Her experience of the nuns would derive from the long-prevalent practice in Ireland of farming out illegitimate young women to work as unpaid labour in convents. Katie has been rescued from this fate, first through adoption by the Mrs Roche who seems to have given her little but a distinguished name, then by working for the relatively benign Amelia. The stigma of illegitimacy can be erased in only a few instances: entering a convent she imagines to be one of them.

In the matter of forming relations in the secular world, Katie fears that her lack of a name will militate against her chance of a good match. In particular, she worries that her affair with the young Michael will founder on that rock of respectability. The Michael of *Katie Roche* is just like his namesake in the Synge play, proving as spineless before Stan Gregg as Nora's lover did before old Dan Burke. When Stan asks Michael if he has any intentions towards Katie, he denies those we have already heard him promise her with the man-to-man remark:

> What chance has she? Sure there's no one round here would think of her for want of a name.[...] My mother would die if I were to bring her in the door. (36-7)

In the face of a social reality which denies her any proper place, Katie instead is prone to romanticize her origins. She does so by imagining that she comes from an aristocratic background. When her father reveals himself to her, he does so with the avowed aim of beating such pride out of her. But his revelation confirms that behind the fictional persona of Reuben the Tramp lies Fitzsimon of Kylebeg, just as behind the letters to the actress Molly Allgood signed 'Your Old Tramp' lay John Millington Synge, a scion of the landed ascendancy class. Where Synge disguised his landed status in the guise of an unaccommodated Tramp, Reuben is revealed not as a Tramp but as an errant member of the ascendancy class. The notions of nobility that Katie asserts ('I'll be a great woman. I'll make my own goodness' (60), are less those of aspiration to a decaying social order than a Yeatsian aristocracy of the individual. Katie Roche's exercises in personal style and self-invention work against the shortcomings and fragmentations of the society in which she has been raised. The more general question that emerges for her is: what am I to do, what course of action should I pursue to lead a meaningful life? The feminist dimension of the question is expressed through the mirroring of Katie's plight in the subplot involving Amelia Gregg, herself the recipient of an unexpected marriage proposal from a long-time suitor. The degree of sisterly feeling that develops between Katie and Amelia leads the latter in Act 3 to a most uncharacteristic challenging of her brother's decision to punish Katie by taking her away:

> **AMELIA.** Stan, Katie is very good.
> **STAN.** Thank you, Amelia.
> **AMELIA.** No, – but I mean, she does her best. She's a brave little soul. I think you're not quite fair to her, Stan! I came back to say that. (*Puts her hands on* **STANISLAUS'** *shoulders. He does not move. She withdraws.*) (107-8)

The most romantic conception of herself that Katie Roche owns, which she brings with her into the marriage with Stan, is one that is intimately related to Teresa Deevy as a woman playwright working within the inherited patriarchal structures of Irish, as indeed of most, theatre. For this heroine conceives of her life as inherently theatrical and of her identity as a restless search for the role that will most fulfil her desires. What the experience of married life teaches Katie is that her view of what is acceptably dramatic does not accord with her husband's. This is confirmed by what Stan says in responding to one of Katie's gestures: 'Very romantic. You're not taking part in theatricals now' (63). What has prompted her to go ahead and marry Stan is the possibility he holds out that she might help him in his work. There is much in Deevy's approach that recalls the drama of Ibsen; I have already mentioned Nora's plight in *A Doll's House* in relation to both the Synge and Deevy plays. The ironic, tragic gap between the heightened expectations with which Katie approaches life and the banal, humdrum routine embraced by her husband recalls the marriage in *Hedda Gabler*. Both the Ibsen and the Deevy convey a sense of the heroine operating at one level of theatrical reality while the play in which she finds herself trapped insists on operating at another. The cramped theatrical environment in which Hedda Gabler and Katie Roche must live seems determined to frustrate their ever-altering desires, to allow them no adequate expression. The fact that Stanislaus Gregg is an architect, and in particular the scene at the opening of Act 2, argue that Deevy is also re-working Ibsen's *The Master Builder*. There, the ageing architect Solness is rescued from his soured marriage and his compromised artistic ideals by the arrival of a young woman who remembers him at his most inspired. This resembles the role Katie sees for herself in marrying her architect husband, that she will inspire him to create his romantic structures. In describing Stan's drawings to Amelia, Katie's account echoes *The Master Builder*: 'Can you see it all now like it was built there before you? The spire – can you see it? With maybe the sun shining on it?' (46-7). Stan does not respond to Katie as the Master Builder does to Hilde Wangel but rather as he does to his wife, regarding her as an encumbrance and a reproach. By combining the two figures of the wife and the young woman that Ibsen keeps apart and polarizes, Teresa Deevy shifts the focus away from the demanding sexual egotism of the male artist towards the denial of those women whose lives are subject to his every whim.

Katie's response to Stan's anal retentiveness, his withholding of any real exchange about his architectural designs from her, is to turn once more to the outside world, to assert her independence by going out the door. The consequences are more grave in Act 2 than they were in Act 1, since she is now a married woman. This move in turn brings us back to Synge and what he, rather than Ibsen, had represented on and for the Irish stage. As with *The Shadow of a Glen* and those early Abbey plays, the setting of *Katie Roche* is within a rural cottage, now extended across three acts rather than one. And Katie Roche is a more liminal character than Nora Burke, whose legitimacy is not in question. Katie is marginal to the Gregg household and to the society of the play because of the clouded, indeterminate nature of her origins. She has two father figures, a man of the roads who betrays an aristocratic background and a respectable bourgeois who signals the consolidation of the Catholic middle-classes in the professions. She has two mothers, her natural mother Mary Halnan whom she knows only by romantic report and the Mrs Roche who helped to raise her. She has two employers, ostensibly Amelia Gregg, actually Stanislaus. And there are two milieus in the play with which she is associated and to which she is attracted, the outside world of music, dancing and walks across the hills and the inside world of an economic comfort and social respectability she has all along been denied.

The conflict in Act 1 centres on Katie's desire to go to a dance, to celebrate the annual regatta. The time is August and the season connects the dance with the idea of a harvest festival. In the design at the Peacock, a cornfield was visible outside the door, recalling as it must the setting and action of Friel's *Dancing at Lughnasa* (1990). Friel's play is set in the same period as Deevy's and the lives of his woman bear on hers. The nineteen thirties was the period in Ireland when opposition to dancing of both the foreign ('jazz') and native ('crossroads') variety was mounting; by the time Eamon de Valera came to apotheosize those comely maidens dancing at the crossroads in 1943, they had ceased as a social reality and become entirely symbolic. Amelia opposes Katie going to the dance on the grounds that dancing is neither 'nice' nor respectable and that she would not wish it for herself. Despite Katie's plea to Stan that he intervene on her behalf, he backs up his sister in her disapproval, not wanting to see the young woman he is romanticizing make herself cheap, or move outside the strict control of his gaze. Katie's failure to go to the dance lingers over the Deevy play as that of the Mundy sisters does over Friel's.

Katie's behaviour as a married woman in asking Michael into the house and sharing a drink with him is bound to be misunderstood. From Stan's point of view he must read it as a betrayal of the absolute hold he thinks marriage has conferred upon him. But Michael is no less cocky on this score, seeing himself as the romantic male chosen by the disappointed wife. He reads a great deal into her asking him in while she bridles against the assumption that the choices implied by her behaviour amount to no more than a choice between men:

> **MICHAEL.** What a great fool you were, Katie.
> **KATIE.** (*Steps back from him*): Michael Maguire, do you think I regret the thing I done?
> **MICHAEL.** So what made you call me to come in an' I passing?
> [...]
> **KATIE.** I had ever a great love for your music. (54)

In reaction to this, Stan's first stratagem is to remove himself from the house and revert to the bachelor life he has enjoyed all his days. When he returns in Act 3 to tell Katie that he has decided to live with her again, his discovery that Michael has been in the house leads him to take her away for good. Throughout Act 3 Stan keeps entering when Reuben is expected or announced and vice-versa. The act of substitution or doubling between the older husband and the Tramp has never been more apparent. It is finally Stan who enters in Reuben's place and tells Katie that he is taking her away, not away to a better place but to a life that is the virtual extinction of her person. Deevy's ending resists the romantic allure of 'away' in the plays of Yeats and Synge. What Katie longs for instead is a life that could be lived in her own native place. There, the elements that have been at war within her, the forces to which she has been subjected by her liminality as a woman in Ireland of the nineteen thirties, might be integrated. Katie Roche's final cry before being led offstage is for a home – a place, a country, a dwelling – in which she could live and be herself:

> **STAN.** Go and get ready. We're going at once. We're not coming back ... Get all your things. [...]
> **KATIE.** Is it ... for always? (*Silence.* **STAN** *goes to the window, stands with his back to her.*) I'd like to come back. (*Pause.*) I'd like to

live my life here. *(Silence.)* I'd like the two of us to live here. [...] I
think we're meant for this place. (100-1)

In Marina Carr's *The Mai,* as with the two plays so far considered,
the troubled relationship between a married couple is central. The
greater equality that now exists between men and women is signalled by
no detail more forcefully than by the relative equality of their ages: the
Mai is forty, Robert is in his early forties. They have been married for
seventeen years and have four children, though the only one we get to
see is the eldest, their sixteen-year-old daughter, Millie. But what
persists so forcefully in the almost sixty-year transition from Deevy's
Katie Roche to 1994 is the pattern of withdrawals by which the husband
seeks to assert his relative independence and simultaneously to keep
the wife in her place at home. The first act of the play signals the Mai's
joyous reception of her errant husband's return after five years. Two of
the characters, speculating as to where he has been, suggest America,
like his father before him. In defending the male family line, Robert
asserts that his father went away to the USA to earn a living for his wife
and family back in Ireland. The Mai's grandmother retorts that he
should either have stayed at home or brought his family with him. In
the Deevy play Stan's return in Act 2 causes Katie no less delight but
turns out to be as provisional and qualified as Robert's. Both husbands
declare at one point that they need more time on their own, preferring
their own company or that of other people to the at-home demands of
the women they have married.

What is less overtly dramatic than the big entrances and exits by the
men every few months or years is the pattern of internal withdrawal
they practise while remaining physically present within the house.
Robert concentrates on playing his cello as he pursues his romantic
dream of being a great musician. The psychological transference was
expressed in Brian Brady's production of *The Mai* in a surreal moment
when Olwen Fouéré as the Mai was substituted for the cello. The idea
for this visual substitution is contained in a scene where the Mai plucks
at herself as if she *were* a cello. Robert is always buying her presents,
returning from another brief absence with chocolates and copies of
Cosmopolitan magazine as alibis. He pours himself drinks without
offering her one and sits reading his newspaper on Christmas Day.
Where the husband in the folktale of the Unfaithful Wife asserted his
authority with a stick, the twentieth century version does so by means
of silence and physical withdrawal. Synge has already developed this
more modern interpretation in *Shadow.* Dan Burke, while remaining
physically present and in a dominant position, has withdrawn to such

an extent that he appears dead and has given his wife an explicit injunction that his body is not to be touched. In *Katie Roche* 'Silence' is repeatedly inscribed as a stage direction as the ultimate sign of non-communication between husband and wife.

Nora Burke turns to the Tramp when her husband and lover reject her. Katie Roche has nowhere to turn: Amelia Gregg is too wedded to her brother to offer more than fleeting sympathy; Michael misunderstands her appeal; Reuben rejects her. To offset the Mai's isolation, Marina Carr has filled the stage of her drama with an ensemble, a support system of female energy: two sisters, two aunts, a daughter and a hundred-year-old grandmother. When Grandma Fraochlán makes her memorable entrance, she does so bearing a big colourful stick, not one with which to berate her granddaughter but an oar which she is determined to intrude and which is the flamboyant sign of her unorthodox and romantic life with her husband, the ninefingered fisherman. She even, one character remarks, takes the oar to bed with her. The grandmother bears in her first name an archetypal female status and in her second the name of the island on which she reared the Mai when the natural mother, her daughter Ellen, died young. What Grandma Fraochlain has to offer is stories, drawn from her 'ancient and fantastical memory'. As her great-granddaughter Millie recalls:

> The name alone evokes a thousand memories in me. She was known as the Spanish beauty though she was born and bred on lnis Fraochlán, north of Boffin. She was the result of a brief tryst between an ageing island spinster and a Spanish or Moroccan sailor – no one is quite sure – who was never heard of or seen since the night of her conception. [...]Whoever he was, he left Grandma Fraochlán his dark skin and a yearning for all that was exotic and unattainable.[5]

Grandma Fraochlán is the Tramp in the play, enlarging the scope of the environment with her exotic presence and her fund of storytelling, its connection to the world of myth and legend. The figure of the Tramp has changed gender and now offers a matrilineal line of support and continuity rather than a substitute patriarchy. Grandma Fraochlán's presence and the tales she tells do not induce a split in the consciousness of either Millie or the Mai. For she is the woman from whom they both claim their descent, the one whose stories can supply them with a personal history of Ellen and the other women in their past. She connects them more fully to a sense of their own identity, something they carry with them rather than something that is dependent on a particular place.

This legacy has borne fruit in Millie, who occupies a crucial dual role in Marina Carr's play. She is the daughter who bears the brunt of the tensions between Robert and the Mai. But as she talks, we gradually realize that Millie is not merely responding to what is occurring onstage but is narrating to the audience an entire drama that has occurred many years in the past. The first monologue to convey this is one which describes how, when she now meets her father, 'we shout and roar till we're exhausted or in tears or both, and then crawl away to lick our wounds already gathering venom for the next bout' (128). This speech not only establishes Millie as the play's storyteller but shows that, far from being aligned with the words and deeds of her father, the Mai's husband, she is battling him verbally for control of the mother's narrative.

Marina Carr is among those who have restored the storyteller's perspective to the drama. When Synge delegated the storytelling function to the figure of the Tramp in his plays, he made it the sole possession of only one character among many, even in as highly developed an examplar as Christy Mahon. The Tramp was no longer telling anyone's story but his own; and when the women in Synge's plays looked for ratification of their own life narratives, they rarely found it. (This is part of the loss that Pegeen Mike laments at the close of *The Playboy of the Western World*). The Tramp in *Katie Roche* seemed to offer the heroine greater access to her own personal history and identity when he revealed himself to be her father; but the paternity was one he was not able or willing to own in anything other than the strictest and most impersonal terms. When Katie cried out for acknowledgement by her father, she was met with harsh words of reproof and chastisement. Grandma Fraochlán strengthens the link with her granddaughter by acting as a living conduit to the dead. But Grandma Fraochlán can only do so much; and her other granddaughters argue that she may not have been the best of mothers, since her husband had all her love. She herself, however larger than life and dramatically energizing she may be, remains a character within the play.

The figure who takes responsibility for bringing the story of the Mai into the dramatic present is Millie, now aged thirty and with a five-year-old son of her own. Such a move is not without precedent in the recent history of contemporary Irish drama. In watching Derbhle Crotty as Millie in *The Mai,* one cannot help but recall the narrator Michael in Friel's *Dancing at Lughnasa* directly addressing the audience in order to conjure up his five aunts from the nineteen thirties. When Millie reveals before the play is half over that the Mai took her own life, the effect resembles that moment when Friel's Michael discloses the squalid death of one of the women we see so vibrantly alive before us. Although Carr's Millie and Friel's Michael occupy the sidelines of their respective plays, they are central to the construction of the drama, since they are the ones actively remembering all the other characters into existence. As I have argued elsewhere, Michael's ambivalent position could be read as Friel's acknowledgement that, for all of *Lughnasa's* emphasis on women, it is being authored by a man.[6] Similarly, the presence of a young woman narrator in *The Mai* is an acknowledgement that the play is being authored by a woman. Millie and Grandma Fraochlán reintroduce and reorientate the key roles of the storyteller and the Tramp that this chapter has examined, establishing less a line of continuity than a multiple embrace of the three women across chronological time in the recurring present of the play.

The final image is of the Mai, standing alone at the window of the house. This is the dream house she has constructed from her teacher's salary, from the cleaning jobs she has taken, and from getting the builder to let her have it for a song. It has been built according to her specifications, to house herself and her four children and to prepare a place for the long-desired return of her husband. Its central feature in terms of the staging and Kathy Strachan's design is a huge window centrestage which gives out on to Owl Lake, the pattern of the lake reflected around the stage. When characters appear up the steps, it would seem more natural for them to step through than to go round to the door. The Mai is most often to be found standing in that window, as much looking in as looking out, not fully contained by the house she has built. Millie the storyteller brings Act 1 and the first half of the play to a close by telling us the legend of Owl Lake:

> Owl Lake comes from the Irish, *loch cailleach oíche*, Lake of the Night Hag or Pool of the Dark Witch. The legend goes that Coillte, daughter of the Mountain God Bloom, fell in love with Bláth, Lord of all the flowers, so away she bounded like a young deer [...]over the dark witch's boglands till she came to Bláth's domain. There he lay, under an oak tree [...]. And so they lived freely through the spring and summer [...]. One evening approaching autumn Bláth told Coillte that soon he must go and live with the dark witch of the bog, that he would return in the spring, and the next morning he was gone. Coillte followed him and found him ensconced in the dark witch's lair. He would not speak to her, look at her, touch her, and heartbroken Coillte lay down outside the dark witch's lair and cried a lake of tears that stretched for miles around. One night, seizing a long-awaited opportunity, the dark witch pushed Coillte into her lake of tears. When spring came around again Bláth was released from the dark witch's

spell and he went in search of Coillte, only to be told that she had dissolved. Sam Brady told me that when the geese are restless or the swans suddenly take flight, it's because they hear Bláth's pipes among the reeds, still playing for Coillte. (147)

This mythic narrative is acoustically echoed at the play's close when *'sounds of geese and swans taking flight'* (186) accompany the image of the Mai at her window. We are never directly given the Mai's death; it would be unnecessary and untrue to the way in which her story is told. Her search is like that of the old woman in Beckett's *Rockaby,* looking 'for another / at her window / another like herself / a little like'.[7] In choosing to build her house at Owl Lake, the Mai has according to her daughter been 'looking for that magic thread that would stitch us together again' (111). It is not to be found there, as the play poignantly demonstrates. The magic thread stitching the women's lives together is the act of shared memory which is the play itself, the thread of affiliation which binds Grandma Fraochlán, the Mai and Millie together across time, space and the absence of death. Grandma Fraochlán is as old as the century and Synge's drama; she resembles his characters in the closeness of her speech to Irish, her Rabelaisian humour and her myth-making capacities. The Mai is caught in the same in-between space as Deevy's Katie Roche; both are poised on the threshold between an inner security never experienced and an outer freedom never fully within reach. Millie is of the present and the future, like Marina Carr herself, expressing uncertainty and openness in the telling of a story and the making of a play. Through the hundred year span covered by Synge's *The Shadow of the Glen,* Deevy's *Katie Roche* and Carr's *The Mai* there runs a magic thread which this chapter has sought to elucidate.

---

[1] See Appendix: Irish Women Playwrights for the full list, in Melissa Sihra (editor), *Women in Irish Drama: A Century of Authorship and Representation* (Houndmills: Palgrave Macmillan, 2007), pp. 221-230.

[2] Cited by Robert Hogan and James Kilroy, *Laying the Foundations 1902-1904: The Second Volume of The Modern Irish Drama* (Dublin: The Dolmen Press, 1976), p. 79.

[3] Cited in Hogan and Kilroy, *Laying the Foundations 1902-1904,* p., 78.

[4] Teresa Deevy, *Three Plays: Katie Roche, The King of Spain's Daughter, The Wild Goose* (London: Macmillan, 1939), p. 59. All subsequent quotations from *Katie Roche* are from this edition and will be incorporated in the text.

5 Marina Carr, *The Mai*, in *Plays One* (London: Faber and Faber, 1999), pp.115-6. All subsequent quotations from *The Mai* are from this edition and will be inorporated in the text.

6 See Anthony Roche, *Contemporary Irish Drama: Second Edition* (Houndmills: Palgrave Macmillan, 2009), p. 77.

7 Samuel Beckett, *Rockaby*, in *The Complete Dramatic Works* (London: Faber and Faber, 1990), p. 437.

7 | Marginal Zones and Liminality: Synge's *The Well of the Saints* and Samuel Beckett's *Waiting for Godot*

The Well of the Saints has always had something of a marginal status in relation to Synge's drama as a whole and to its position in the repertoire of the Abbey Theatre. It was not prejudged as too shocking to be staged in Dublin, as was the case with *The Tinker's Wedding*, which was not seen on the Abbey or Peacock stages until 1971, over sixty years after the playwright's death. It did not cause massive demonstrations and walkouts, as had been the case with *The Shadow of the Glen* in 1903 and was notoriously to attend the first week of *The Playboy of the Western World* in January 1907. It marked Synge's transition from the one-act play so favoured by Yeats, Gregory and (until then) himself. In *The Well of the Saints* he developed a three-act form very different from the late nineteenth-century well-made play and one which was proto-modernist in its implications.

The new Synge play was finished in time for the opening of the Irish National Theatre's doors on 27 December 1904, but had to wait for its premiere until February of 1905. Perhaps this was owing to his adoption of the three-act form and to Yeats and Gregory wanting to occupy the opening slots with their one-act plays. Or perhaps it was slowed by the determined opposition of one of the two Fay brothers, Frank, as Synge revealed to Lady Gregory in a letter of 11 September 1904 arising from a meeting to discuss the opening programme:

> The difficulty is that F.F. [Frank Fay] is dead set against my play or Cuchulain [Yeats's *On Baile's Strand*, which did in the event open the Abbey Theatre] so one does not know what to suggest. He says my work is only addressed to blasé town-dwelling theatre-goers, that as long as we play that sort of work we are only doing what [André] Antoine does in Paris [at the Théatre Libre] and doing it worse, that he

wants a National Theatre that will draw the people, etc., etc., etc. He's
got Brian Ború on the brain it seems. (CL I, 94)[1]

During rehearsals, director Willie Fay complained to Synge that all of
the characters in the play were bad-tempered and feared that this would
infect and prove off-putting to the audience. Fay asked that 'the Saint
anyway might be made into a good-natured easy-going man, or that
Molly Byrne might be made into a lovable young girl'.[2] On this
occasion, however, the playwright was not for turning. Fay reports the
response: 'But Synge would not budge. He said he wanted to write "like
a monochrome painting, all in shades of the one colour." [...] We had to
agree to differ.'[3] But Willie Fay has left an enduring imprint on *The
Well of the Saints*, if not for his direction, then for his performance as
the chief protagonist, Martin Doul. He was once memorably described,
in a comment by Declan Kiberd, as the Abbey Theatre's answer to
Woody Allen; and we get some sense of Willie Fay's diminutive stature
and vocal charisma when Molly Byrne gives Martin Doul a rare
compliment: 'It's queer talk you have if it's a little, old, shabby stump of
a man you are itself' (III, 115). *The Well of the Saints* was staged in
February 1905 at the Abbey to small houses and a mixture of
indifference and incomprehension – quite a contrast to the arrival of
The Playboy two years later. But the play has always had its admirers
and defenders, such as the contemporary Irish playwright Tom
Murphy, who directed a production at the Abbey in 1979 and prefaced it
with a curtain-raiser entitled *Epitaph Under Ether* compiled from
various of Synge's poems, prose and plays.[4] Its critical stock has risen
steadily over the years to the point where W.J. McCormack, in his 2000
biography of the dramatist, could assert in the last sentence of his two-
page Prologue: 'The great achievement is not *The Playboy of the
Western World* but *The Well of the Saints*.'[5]

It is *The Well of the Saints* among all of Synge's plays that stands
most free of its own time. As the stage directions indicate, it is set in
'some lonely mountainous district on the east [coast] of Ireland' (which
the place names identify as County Wicklow) 'one or more centuries
ago' (III, 69). This deliberate temporal imprecision lifts the play free of
any particular time, in the past or in the present, and gives it a great
deal of freedom in that respect (not least to its directors and costume
designers). By being set outside of its own time, *The Well of the Saints*
was never entirely assimilated into and by it. The play also points to the
future and the way the playwright might have developed, had he lived.
It can certainly be said to have prophesied and influenced some of the

most important of Synge's successors in the field of twentieth-century Irish drama.

Of these unquestionably the most important, and the one I wish to concentrate on in this chapter, is Samuel Beckett. When Beckett's first stage play *En Attendant Godot* was staged in Paris in 1953, it appeared to come from nowhere and to inhabit a vacuum. If any theatrical comparison was made, it was to a contemporary existentialist drama like Sartre's *Huis Clos* (1944) and in time to what Martin Esslin was to term 'the Theatre of the Absurd'.[6] But in a letter to Irish actor Cyril Cusack in the late 1950s, Beckett himself helped to establish an Irish genealogy for his play-writing career. Responding to Cusack's request that he contribute a critical note to a season of Shaw's plays, he wrote:

> I wouldn't suggest that G.B.S. is not a great playwright, whatever that is when it's at home.
> What I would do is give the whole unupsettable apple-cart [the title of a Shaw play] for a sup of the Hawk's Well, or the Saints', or a whiff of Juno, to go no further.[7]

In this letter, Beckett explicitly identifies three important dramatic precursors to his own work from the Irish Dramatic Revival: Yeats's *At the Hawk's Well*, the first of his 'Plays for Dancers' modeled on the Japanese Noh tradition and already explored earlier in this study in relation to the drama of Synge; *The Well of the Saints*, in which a blind couple are cured by a miracle which has ironic repercussions; and Sean O'Casey's *Juno and the Paycock* (1924), in which Captain Boyle and Joxer Daly anaesthetize themselves to the surrounding 'chassis' [chaos] through a regular flow of drink and talk. Over the years, as one might expect from a minimalist like Beckett, he refined and reduced rather than added to the list of Irish (or other) theatrical progenitors he was prepared to acknowledge. When asked by his official biographer James Knowlson in the last year of his life (1989) 'who he himself felt had influenced his theatre most of all, Beckett suggested only the name of Synge.'[8] The pre-eminence Synge had attained by the end of Beckett's life is evident earlier on, even among the three Irish playwrights he cites. The dialect term in which the praise is cast, the 'sup' to be taken from the two dramatic wells of Yeats and Synge, is taken directly from a remark in *The Well of the Saints*. The miraculous cure is going to be effected by water which has been taken from a well on the Aran Islands and carried overland to the east coast of Ireland.[9] The quote establishes just how rare and precious is the quantity of water remaining: '[MARTIN *shakes the can*.] There's a small sup only' (III, 85). What also establishes Synge's pre-eminence in the three cited is chronology.

The Well of the Saints was written twelve years before *At the Hawk's Well* and was the play of Synge's to have had the most profound and influential impact on Yeats, as we have seen. There is a striking metaphor of religious conversion used by Yeats to describe his reaction on first seeing the play staged:

> Perhaps I was Synge's convert. It was certainly a day of triumph when the first act of *The Well of the Saints* held its audience, though the two chief persons sat side by side under a stone cross from start to finish.[10]

The emphasis on a drama of inaction brings us back to Beckett.[11] The critical act of placing *Waiting For Godot* beside *The Well of the Saints* brings to the fore certain modernist features of this Synge play which the unhelpful category of 'peasant drama' serves only to obscure. The first of these is his debt to Synge for his two leading characters, Vladimir and Estragon, as liminal figures on the margins of society. For what Synge brought to prominence in the materials he adapted for his plays is the figure of the tramp. This process can best be seen in his reworking of the Story of the Unfaithful Wife into *The Shadow of the Glen* where as we have seen the subordinate narrator of the Aran narrative gives way to the dramatically independent creation of the Tramp, who brings a different perspective to bear on the claustrophobia of the cottage existence Nora has to suffer. Christy Mahon is a version of the Tramp figure, at least in the life he has led since he fled his father's murder. And at the close he beckons his father, not to a return to the family farm, but to a life of open-ended wandering he is not afraid to call 'romancing' (IV, 173). The tinker Sarah Casey in *The Tinker's Wedding* is temporarily seduced by the temptation of a bourgeois married life with her partner Michael Byrne; but that life is summarily and finally rejected by all three at play's end as they once more take to the open road. In all of his plays, Synge was attracted to figures living on the margins of society – tramps, wanderers, vagrants, tinkers. His own life was not as secure as it might have appeared, and certainly Yeats's description of him in 'The Municipal Gallery Revisited' as 'that rooted man'[12] seems singularly inappropriate. Synge spent almost a decade on the Continent after his graduation from Trinity, a period described by W.J. McCormack in his biography as 'The Wander Years'. And for a number of years he alternated between Ireland in the summers and Paris in the winters. Even after Synge gave up his flat in the rue d'Assas in 1903 and returned permanently to Ireland, the sense of coming home is an odd one. For one thing, he continued to live at home with his widowed mother, and failed to set up an independent household, even when he became engaged to Molly Allgood. The 'home' to which he returned was not the property in Wicklow which the Synge family had owned well into the nineteenth century. They were no longer landowners by the time Synge was born, and frequently found themselves renting property on their former estates. What Mrs. Synge and her family lived in was a series of rented properties. In the mass of correspondence which survives from Synge to his fiancée, which Chapter Nine will explore, the letters to Molly are almost always signed 'Your Old Tramp'.

   The Well of the Saints is centred not on one but on two tramps and so there is a marked shift away from the single romantic male outsider in *Shadow of the Glen* and *The Playboy of the Western World*. Unlike those two plays also, the setting is not inside the peasant cottage, but outside, on the open road, by a crossroads. The play is quite explicit about the liminal or in-between nature of the Douls' existence. They live at one remove and in an awkward relationship with the settled community, who are primarily represented in the play by Timmy the smith and who acts as go-between or mediator between the blind couple and that community. Martin and Mary Doul have come from an unspecified outside years before, and will be sent away at the end of the play. They spend their days at the crossroads, a significantly open and multiple location, stripping rushes for lights. It is not specified where they spend their nights, but likely to be the same as the one offered by Vladimir and Estragon in *Waiting For Godot*:

> **VLADIMIR.** May one inquire where His Highness spent the night?
> **ESTRAGON.** In a ditch.
> **VLADIMIR.** [*Admiringly.*] A ditch! Where?
> **ESTRAGON.** [*Without gesture.*] Over there. [13]

As has already been noted, there is a particularly loaded reference to 'ditches' in *The Well of the Saints* as the place where 'a drunken man [might be] [...] talking with a girl' (III, 106). The primary activity in which the blind old couple are engaged is talk, as the primary means by which their world is constituted. As Martin Doul remarks: 'If I didn't talk, I'd be destroyed in a short while' (III, 71). But the play makes an important distinction between talk as a solo activity (as in Martin's just-quoted remark) and talk as dialogue, and dialogue of a particular kind: the love-talk of a man in a ditch with a young woman. The love-talk which flourishes in Act One between Martin and Mary Doul is centred on the notion of their being beautiful to behold and their fixed conviction that if they could only see themselves, they could confirm the belief that they are 'the finest man, and the finest woman, of the east' (III, 73). *The Well of the Saints* is a play in which monologues usually proceed from and are fuelled by a sense of desperation, such as those spoken by Martin during his sundering from Mary in Act Two, which his physical isolation only underscores. In *Waiting For Godot*, Vladimir is the one pining to be the primary, authoritative talker; but his partner and the play will not have it so. His efforts to launch into a monologue do not proceed far until they are inevitably interrupted by Estragon, in the latter's role of refractory auditor:

> **VLADIMIR.** The two thieves. Do you remember the story?
> **ESTRAGON.** No.
> **VLADIMIR.** Shall I tell it to you?
> **ESTRAGON.** No.
> **VLADIMIR.** It'll pass the time. [*Pause.*] Two thieves, crucified at the same time as our Saviour. One –
> **ESTRAGON.** Our what?
> **VLADIMIR.** Our Saviour. [14]

The only occasion on which Vladimir gets to deliver an uninterrupted monologue is when Estragon is briefly asleep. Otherwise, their primary activity is making dialogue or 'blathering', as the play more than once characterizes it. As Estragon remarks when asked to describe their activities of the day before: 'Do? [...] Yes, now I remember, yesterday evening we spent blathering about nothing in particular. That's been going on now for half a century.' [15]

The emphasis in Synge's play on the two blind people and their talk undergoes a significant change when other people enter. Then they are obliged to beg and do so in an assumed, wheedling voice rather than the natural authority with which they usually speak:

> **MARTIN DOUL.** [*with a begging voice*]. Leave a bit of silver for blind Martin, your honour. Leave a bit of silver, or a penny copper itself, and we'll be praying the Lord to bless you and you going the way. (III, 75)

When he realizes it is Timmy the Smith he is addressing, Martin then speaks with his usual confidence and, as the stage directions indicate, '*with his natural voice*'. When Pozzo and Lucky enter the space of *Waiting For Godot*, the language of the two tramps undergoes a similar transformation, from robust independence to subservient imploration:

> **ESTRAGON.** Excuse me, Mister, the bones, you won't be wanting the bones? [16]

In the social vacuum which the tramps in both plays inhabit and fill with their talk, they establish an independent zone, at one crucial remove from the social world of class divisions. It is not just social hierarchy which is kept in abeyance in this liminal zone. In terms of dramatic as well as social hierarchy, the traditional theatrical emphasis on a leading man, a star performer, is no longer sustainable. Now the stage space has to be shared equally between two male actors, neither of whom can claim the lion's share of the verbal action. There is an incipient egalitarianism, a base democracy, in the co-equal presence of two people having to share the same stage. For the socialist in Bertolt Brecht, it was as much a necessity in the field of human relationships as in the theatre: 'For the smallest social unit is not the single person but two people.'[17]

The democratic equilibrium which the opening scenes of both plays establish, however much it may be threatened in the more aggressive exchanges between the two tramps, is always maintained as long as they are the sole occupiers of the space. But when someone else enters – in particular a person invested with the trappings of authority – the nature of that space and the language spoken in it undergo a profound change. The two tramps are displaced from the centre of their liminal zone to the margins by the newcomer confidently and ostentatiously taking centre-stage. Pozzo does so when he enters brandishing a whip. He makes what are self-consciously speeches – monologues, rather than dialogue – by asking if everybody is listening and by spraying his throat with a vaporizer so that his voice is suitably resonant. The Saint enters Synge's play towards the close of Acts One and Three, and after a great deal of preparation and anticipation of his arrival. He is surrounded by the crowd of villagers, dresses himself with his effects (heavy cloak, bell and can of holy water) and addresses the pair whose blindness he is going to cure. When he speaks of the wretchedness of their condition in a lengthy monologue, Martin is moved to contradict him but is rapidly silenced by Timmy:

> **SAINT.** [...] So it's to the like of yourselves I do be going, who are wrinkled and poor, a thing rich men would hardly look at at all, but would throw a coin to or a crust of bread.
> **MARTIN DOUL.** [*moving uneasily*]. When they look on herself who is a fine woman –
> **TIMMY.** [*shaking him*]. Whisht now, and be listening to the saint. (III, 89)

When the couple are cured and look on each other's appearances with disillusioned horror, the Saint emerges from the church and comes forward to the '*centre*' to blandly inquire: 'Are their minds troubled with joy?' (III, 99). The Saint arrives in the play to perform a miracle, an event which moves Synge's *The Well of the Saints* definitively away from realism and which is of a piece with the vague locale and the temporal imprecision. In Beckett's *Waiting For Godot*, there is someone endlessly anticipated who famously fails to appear, the eponymous Godot. When he does so, it is the expectation of the two tramps that the wretchedness of their conditions will be alleviated; even more, their hope is that they will be (and Vladimir finally employs the religious metaphor in the play's closing lines) 'saved'.[18] Beckett most likely drew on Synge for both the possibility of miracle in his play but also for the considerable irony with which the subject is treated. The miracle the Saint performs leaves Martin and Mary Doul much worse off than before, plunging them into a mire of disillusionment and leaving them physically separated from each other and forced to look elsewhere for the attempted restoration of their former state. There is likewise a greater level of despair in Act Two of Beckett's play when Pozzo, Lucky and the Boy have come and gone (the first two in a physically impaired condition) but Godot has still failed to appear.

The two 'central persons' of *The Well of the Saints*, as Yeats noted, are sole occupiers of the stage space well into Act One, and the same holds true for Beckett's play. The couple are thus free to work out the nature of their relationship to each other and to define the nature of their dramatic world. This process is supported by the open and minimalist nature of the setting. In both cases, it is (to quote from *Waiting For Godot*) 'a country road'.[19] The open setting of *The Well*, and of the as yet unstaged *Tinker's Wedding*, stands in marked contrast to the peasant cottage interiors of Synge's two plays so far produced and of *The Playboy*. The claustrophobic peasant cottage settings, maintained for the duration of the play, privilege the social world in which they are set. This was memorably described by Augustine Martin (drawing on a phrase of Pegeen Mike's father) as the 'household' people of Dan Burke and Michael James Flaherty as opposed to the romantic outsiders like the Tramp and Christy Mahon.[20] The peasant cottage foregrounds actuality over possibility. In such a setting, the tramp – however eloquent his speech and destabilizing his presence – can never pretend to be anything more than an interloper. So it proves with Christy Mahon: he comes from nowhere and returns to nowhere. What he promises to Pegeen remains reliant on his language, as does the promise offered by the Tramp at the end of *The Shadow of the Glen*. If Pegeen looks with skepticism at her disenthroned playboy, how can the audience of *The Well of the Saints* not do likewise with the verbal claims made by Martin and Mary Doul? They may claim to possess beauty and insist that Mary be called 'the beautiful dark woman' of Ballinatone (III, 73). But Synge's casting directions explicitly call for Martin Doul to be a *'weather-beaten, blind beggar'* (III, 69) and the same for his wife, with the additional specifications of ugliness and old age. This creates an oddly unsettling effect on the audience from the start. They can see with their own organs of perception that the physical appearance of the two tramps does not correspond to the ways in which they describe themselves, that there is a central contradiction between what we see and what we hear.

The net theatrical effect of both *Well* and *Godot* is to promote the audience to a special role, one in which they are forced to attend closely to what the two central characters are saying, not least because there is so little else to engage with. The natural alignment of the audience in *Well* would tend to be with the onstage members of the community who can see. But it is some time before we meet any such. And when we do their behaviour is not such as to encourage our identification. Timmy and the other villagers have over the years encouraged the two blind tramps in their illusions about themselves. Timmy's growing awareness of what they have done leads him to try and warn Martin and Mary of what is to come: 'you're after believing a power of things weren't as likely at all' (III, 79). Timmy and the others generally make the two beggars the butt of their jokes and, as the play develops, consolidate their status as a community around the scapegoating of its two most marginalized members. The community's violent reaction prompted by the play's final act, when Martin dashes the can of holy water out of the Saint's hands to prevent a second cure, is similar to the occasion in *Playboy* when the villagers turn on Christy and try to torture him. In *Godot*, the closest we come to a bourgeois community is Pozzo and Lucky, even if it no longer enjoys a settled status. Pozzo prides himself on being a landowner and charges Vladimir and Estragon with trespassing on his property. He observes all of the social niceties in his speech and behaviour while simultaneously acting in a brutal fashion. Both plays align themselves with the most marginalized members of the society, who dramatically occupy centre stage, while the socially powerful arrive to enforce their hegemony in an empty setting which lays bare their coercive strategies. The social order is not ratified by the resolution of the plays, despite the promise that weddings will take place and that Godot will arrive. Christy Mahon does not end up marrying Pegeen Mike, despite all the indications that he will and the breach in society remains unhealed at the end. The tinkers' wedding does not proceed. *The Well of the Saints* does end with a marriage – the only one in Synge – between Timmy the smith and Molly Byrne. But that festive ending is undercut and ironized by the act immediately preceding it, when the two beggars are driven from the stage by the wedding guests, sent on their way with the wish that they be drowned in a short while. In Patrick Mason's 1994 production at the Abbey Theatre, Derry Power (Martin) and a clearly arthritic Pat Leavy (Mary) had to descend painfully from the stage, walk up the aisles past the audience and go out the theatre doors. As contemporary Irish playwright Anne Devlin wrote to me when she saw and was enthralled by Mason's production, the two tramps go out from the theatre 'and straight into *Waiting For Godot*'.[21] Katharine Worth forged the same connection across the almost fifty years separating the two plays when she wrote: 'At the far end of the shadowy road the Douls go out on at the end of the play, one seems to see coming to meet them the pathetic and alarming figure of Lucky, his long white hair falling round him, leading the blind Pozzo.'[22] The world is tilted on its axis in these two plays, through their emphasis on the liminal; the normative members of society and their behaviour come to seem and be seen as surreal.

The removal to the outdoors and the dramatic concentration on the tramps move the audience away from any immediate identification with the settled community or the *status quo*. The removal of the peasant cottage may be construed as a process of stripping away the stage artifice, acknowledging that what we are watching is a piece of theatre and making us self-conscious of that fact. The open road can be represented by the bare boards of the stage, as it most certainly is in Beckett, where a number of self-conscious jokes draw attention to the fact that we are in a theatre. In both plays the two characters on stage present themselves directly to each other and to the audience: indeed, they are frequently looking directly at us. Martin and Mary Doul, being blind, cannot see us; the actors who play them can. As Vladimir says when looking at the sleeping Estragon: 'At me too someone is looking, of me too someone is saying, he is sleeping, he knows nothing, let him sleep on.'[23] This creates a mirroring effect not only between the two onstage characters but between their dramatic situation and that of the audience, who are also constrained to wait, watch and listen. As Randolph Parker has put it, 'the position of the audience is itself inherently liminal,'[24] caught as they are between the world of everyday reality they have left behind on entering the theatre and the onstage represented world they witness. But that in-betweenness is only increased when the enacted world is itself markedly liminal, as I have been arguing is the case in both the Synge and Beckett plays.

Contemporary Irish playwright Thomas Kilroy has written of the Anglo-Irish playwrights of the late nineteenth and twentieth centuries in ways which meaningfully connect Synge and Beckett. He does so by relating the concept of distance from the subject matter to that of deliberate theatrical artifice:

> All creative distancing involves some movement towards abstraction and the perfection of the idea, the radical reshaping of human action for particular effects. [...] In this respect Beckett's plays could be read as bringing to a conclusion the whole tradition of Anglo-Irish theatricality, a theatricality of disconnection, of lines which can never meet except in the perfect diagram of the stage action, a theatricality of imagined space between the mind of the playwright and the material on which he is working. [25]

Both Synge and Beckett have chosen the form of the dramatic parable for their plays, with its movement towards abstraction and the perfection of the idea. As Protestants writing within an increasingly dominant Catholic culture, they were removed from the central if uneasy position their class had traditionally occupied. This historic displacement is another source of the attraction they both displayed to figures with a marginal status – the vagrants, tramps and wanderers of their plays – who are not assimilated within the settled community and whose very existence can be taken as a standing rebuke to it.

For all that their impulses can be seen as proto-modernist, Synge's *The Well of the Saints* and Beckett's *Waiting For Godot* also mark a return to and a reworking of medieval theatre (already suggested by their characterization as miracle plays). Synge remarked more than once that he derived the idea for *Well* from a 'pre-Molière French farce' which Gertrude Schoepperle identified in 1921 (and which Synge's notebooks from his Sorbonne lectures subsequently confirmed) as Andrieu de la Vigne's medieval play, *Moralité de l'Aveugle et du Boiteux* (*Morality of the Blind Man and the Lame Man*). [26] In this one-act play, a blind man and a lame man join forces to compensate for each other's physical shortcomings and are cured without their asking. The blind man rejoices at his cure but the lame man is mindful of his lost occupation and resolves to feign a handicap in order to continue begging. The play was also to influence Yeats's 1925 comedy, *The Cat and the Moon*, which was compared to Synge's *The Well of the Saints* and to Beckett's *Waiting For Godot* in Chapter Three. It establishes the dramatic idea central to all three plays of the interdependence of the two central characters. In Martin and Mary, as with Pozzo and Lucky, the interdependence is physical, symbolized by the rope around Lucky's neck; and in Act II of *Godot* the resemblance is all the closer when it turns out that Pozzo has gone blind since last they met. (There is a similar physical interdependence between the blind master Hamm and his servant Clov in Beckett's 1956 *Endgame*.) There is a certain physical interdependence between Vladimir and Estragon in that the one supplies the other with radishes, carrots and turnips; but it is the psychic interdependence between the pair which is the more pronounced. Though they part for brief occasions, 'you always come crawling back', as one remarks to the other.[27] What the medieval stage offered most to Synge and Beckett was a redefinition of the minima of drama, a stripping away of all the theatrical effects which the stage accumulated from the Renaissance on in terms of scenery, sub-plots and exposition, an increase both in realism and ultimately in bourgeoisification. The legacy of the medieval stage can be seen most explicitly in the Synge play by the characterization of its people through a dominant trait: 'Doul' is not a sur-name but the Irish word for 'blind' ('dall'), hence Martin the Blind and Mary the Blind; the suggestion that they are a married couple may be just that. Or characters may be named after their profession or trade, hence Timmy the smith.[28]

Waiting For Godot has the skeletal remains of a medieval morality play in certain key moments of its stage action, especially when the two tramps raise the blinded Pozzo from the ground. Medieval drama's framework of divine judgement, an explicitly eschatological beginning and end, have been removed; but there remain traces of religious judgement and a recurrent concern with spiritual matters. The form of *Waiting For Godot* provides an appropriate context for Estragon to ask, when he is miming a crucifixion: 'Do you think God sees me?'[29] And there is a lengthy discussion in Beckett's play concerning the fate of the two thieves crucified along with Christ as to whether they were saved or damned. The thinness of Godot's fictional veneer, the archetypal mode of its characterization, encourages an audience to make the parallel between the two onstage tramps and the two thieves.[30] Both *The Well of the Saints* and *Waiting For Godot* are parables, deliberately abstracted from a specific time and setting, inherently liminal in the in-between space they delineate.

In writing of the marginal or liminal setting for Synge's play, W.J. McCormack remarks that 'the well of the saints remains permanently absent from the play it names'.[31] But he fails to note that there are three wells in the play, one for each act (just as there are three wishes to be fulfilled in this ironic fairy-tale). The first is the one from Synge's own source in *The Aran Islands*, whereby the water is taken from its source in Inishmaan and conveyed to the east coast of Ireland. This constitutes on at least one level Synge's own awareness of the cultural practices in which he was engaged (and for which he, Yeats and Lady Gregory were to receive so much criticism): going to the Irish-speaking west of

Ireland and appropriating its native materials as cultural propaganda for a Protestant elite. But *The Well of the Saints* is as concerned with deconstructing or at least laying bare that process as in mystifying it. For the legend that Synge found his true artistic vocation when, and only when, he went to the Aran Islands serves only to cut off his complex artistic development from the rest of the island of Ireland and indeed from the Continent on which he spent so much time. It remains a stubborn fact that only one of Synge's six plays – seven, if we include *When the Moon Has Set* – is located on the Aran Islands, whereas a full four of the seven take Wicklow as their setting, the county adjacent to Dublin from which his family derived and to which he frequently returned. Above all, the static Aran myth denies by overlooking Synge's profound interest in and awareness of cultural transmission. This play is stubbornly set in the east of Ireland, well within the Pale. This fact, combined with its movement outside of the representational bind of the peasant cottage setting, may help to explain why *The Well of the Saints* has remained so marginal within the canon of Irish theatre – and why it proved so attractive to Beckett. He certainly showed his awareness of the connotations of Martin Doul's remark that 'there's a small sup only' (III, 85) when he shakes the Saint's can of holy water. Beckett's application of the phrase to three plays from the Irish Dramatic Revival, and the foregrounding of Synge in the use of 'sup' itself, places himself in a line of transmission of the water from the well in Connemara (the repeatedly invoked 'Connemara' of Lucky's speech) through the Abbey Theatre in its heyday to the Paris in which Synge sojourned and to which Beckett moved.

While the Saint is engaged in curing Martin Doul, Molly Byrne questions the need for such a commodity as holy water to be imported from outside their own region. She wonders whether they could not find a way to be more self-empowering:

> It'd be a fine thing if some one in this place could pray the like of him [the Saint], for I'm thinking the water from our own blessed well would do rightly if a man knew the way to be saying prayers, and then there'd be no call to be bringing water from that wild place, where, I'm told, there are no decent houses, or fine-looking people at all. (III, 91)

However much they may betray a creeping middle-class respectability that Shaw would have recognized, Molly's remarks nevertheless articulate for the play an important impulse towards decolonization. Act Two calls in its opening stage directions for a well to be placed '*near [the] centre [of the stage], with board above it, and room to pass behind it*'. Appropriately enough, it is Molly Byrne who comes onstage midway through the act to make use of the well, a point underscored in Patrick Mason's production by her having to break the ice of the bleak mid-winter in order to draw on it for a literal supply of water. Act Two sees Martin and Mary living out and enduring the weight of the disillusionment they have experienced after their cure. They do so separately, with the emphasis on Martin Doul labouring in the sweat of his brow at Timmy the Smith's forge. This act is suffused with Biblical imagery, notably two key references to the Day of Judgement. Martin's attempted love-talk with Molly Byrne ends with an echo of 'Your young men shall see visions and your old men dream dreams' (Acts 2.7) as he pleads: 'Let you not put shame on me and I after saying fine words to you, and dreaming... dreams... in the night' (III, 119). The darkening of Martin's vision indicates that he is going blind again, but also serves to give a darker colouring to this Act in a play which as discussed earlier its author wanted to be 'like a monochrome painting, all in shades of the one colour.'[32] The flames of Timmy's forge, the pounding of the hammers and the presence of an authoritarian figure keeping the victim chained to his repetitive task all combine to sketch an emblematic tableau of Hell. Perhaps Purgatory might be the more accurate term and location, since Martin at one point refers to Timmy 'beating pot-hooks till the judgement day' (III, 121). Such apocalyptic phrases underwrite Yeats's belief that Synge was 'one of those unmoving souls in whom there is a perpetual "Last Day", a perpetual trumpeting and coming to judgement.'[33]

Although Martin and Mary find their way back to each other at the start of Act Three, the knowledge they have painfully acquired of 'the muck' (III, 105) of the seeing world and each other, stands between them and the restoration of their vision. This is where the third well comes into play. It is neither on or off the stage, in a literal sense, as the first two wells have been. Rather, it is conjured into being for the blind couple and for the audience by what they say. Martin, intending to be ironic, reminds Mary of how she now appears to him: 'You'll be bearing in mind, I'm thinking, what you seen a while back when you looked down into a well, or a clear pool, maybe' (III, 129). Mary responds in a disconcertingly positive key: 'I seen a thing in them pools put joy and blessing in my heart.' The term 'joy' is at the heart of Synge's dramatic credo; in the Preface to The Playboy of the Western World, he asserted that on 'the stage one must have reality, and one must have joy' (IV, 54). And Mary Doul expands on her assertion to detail how this third well mirrors, not just what she and Martin are in the literal present, but projects what they might become, as she prophesies:

For when I seen myself in them pools, I seen my hair would be grey or
white maybe in a short while, and I seen with it that I'd a face would
be a great wonder when it'll have soft white hair around it, the way
when I'm an old woman there won't be the like of me surely in the
seven counties of the east. (III, 129)

Martin's response is one of real admiration – 'You're a cute thinking
woman, Mary Doul, and it's no lie' – and suggests the couple are once
more opening a space of possibility in which they can survive and
thrive.

The term for that liminal space of possibility in Synge's dramatic
world is the 'gap'. In *The Well of the Saints*, the opening stage
directions call for '*a low loose wall at [the] back with [a] gap near [the]
centre*' (III, 71). The opening of Act Three specifies the same '*scene as in
[the] first Act, but gap in centre has been filled with briars, or
branches of some sort*' (III, 125). Martin discovers the obstruction when
they try to hide in the gap from the villagers and the Saint:

> [*They grope about gap.*] There's a tree pulled into the gap, or a
> strange thing happened since I was passing it before.
> **MARY DOUL.** Would we have a right to be crawling in below under
> the sticks? (III, 133)

To which question Martin can only reply: 'It's hard set I am to know
what would be right.' Heaven/hell; blind/seeing: the linguistic markers
have been so confused and inverted for the tramps that they may really
be said to have lost their way. With the gap blocked, they scramble
inside a bush which they hope will provide sufficient cover. Instead,
they are exposed in plain sight when the Saint and the villagers enter:
'*They all look over and see* MARTIN DOUL' (III, 137). This scene is
visually and verbally replicated in Act Two of *Waiting For Godot* when
Estragon seeks to escape the returning Pozzo and Lucky:

> **VLADIMIR.** [*He reflects.*] Your only hope left is to disappear.
> **ESTRAGON.** Where?
> **VLADIMIR.** Behind the tree. [**ESTRAGON** *hesitates.*] Quick!
> Behind the tree. [**ESTRAGON** *goes and crouches behind the tree,
> realizes he is not hidden, comes out from behind the tree.*] Decidedly
> this tree will not have been of the slightest use to us. [34]

By the end of Act Three, when the second attempt at a cure has been
definitively rejected, Martin is clear, articulate and impassioned about
knowing and asserting what is right for them:

> I'm thinking it's a good right ourselves have to be sitting blind, hearing
> a soft wind [...] and feeling the sun, and we not tormenting our souls
> with the sight of the grey days, and the holy men, and the dirty feet is
> trampling the world. (III, 149)

In Beckett's play at one point, Estragon inquires whether 'we've lost our rights' to which Vladimir trenchantly replies: 'We got rid of them.'35

It is striking in the denouement of *The Well of the Saints* how the Saint stands idly (and mutely) by while the blind people are driven from the stage. Although at one level he maintains throughout the play his role as solitary, wandering ascetic, the Saint's position undergoes a subtle change in relation to the settled community. On his first visit, before he appears on stage, the villagers play with his saintly props and make fun of his sexual naiveté. They put the Saint's clothes temporarily on Martin. This symbolic investiture suggests that the plural in the play's title comprehends Martin and Mary Doul as well as the Saint — who is as McCormack remarks 'a tramp himself'.36 And there is a clear overlap between the visionary speeches of the three characters and the 'wonders' of nature to which they attest. But in his second appearance the Saint has come not to effect cures and remedies but primarily to perform the marriage of Timmy the smith and Molly Byrne and therefore to preside over and sanction the consolidation of this developing society. His co-option by that society is represented by the extent to which in Act Two the Saint is sidelined from the central position he earlier occupied by the bullying tactics of the crowd. In *Waiting For Godot* the changes Pozzo and Lucky have undergone between the play's two Acts are much more marked: Pozzo has gone blind, Lucky can no longer speak. This has the effect of socially marginalizing them: Pozzo can no longer command the attention of the tramps with his socially intimidating airs and lengthy self-centred monologues; Lucky cannot perform. But the change does not move them closer to the status quo, as with Synge's Saint. Since this is already what Pozzo and Lucky's master-and-slave double act represents, the change in their condition instead moves them closer to the world of the marginalized tramps, as the moment in Act Two when all four are helpless on the ground signifies. Pozzo, in going blind, has given up his incessant time-keeping for an insight into eternity: 'They give birth astride of a grave, the light gleams an instant, then it's night once more.'37

Synge's play ends by going with the two old blind people as they are banished from the stage, on their progress into inner exile. *Waiting For Godot* ends with the famous disjunction between verbal and visual sign:

> **VLADIMIR.** Well? Shall we go?
> **ESTRAGON.** Yes, let's go.
> [*They do not move.*]
> CURTAIN. 38

The effect is the same: the stage follows the departing tramps, whose presence and perspective are its animating principle. To put it another way: we the audience depart, they remain.

---

[1] In the production, Frank Fay played the part of the Saint, under his brother Willie and Synge's co-direction.

[2] William G. Fay, '*The Well of the Saints*', in E.H. Mikhail (editor), *J.M. Synge: Interviews and Recollections* (London and Basingstoke: Macmillan, 1977), p. 31. The piece is extracted from William G. Fay and Catherine Carswell, *The Fays of the Abbey Theatre* (London: Rich and Cowan, 1935).

[3] William G. Fay, '*The Well of the Saints*', p. 31.

[4] For an account of Tom Murphy's 1979 production of *The Well of the Saints*, see Anthony Roche, 'Synge and contemporary Irish drama', in P.J. Mathews (editor), *The Cambridge Companion to J.M Synge* (Cambridge: Cambridge University Press, 2009), p. 177.

[5] W.J. McCormack, *Fool of the Family: A Life of J.M. Synge* (London: Weidenfeld and Nicolson, 2000), p. xii.

[6] See Martin Esslin, *The Theatre of the Absurd* (Harmondsworth: Penguin Books, Third Edition, 1980), *passim*. Beckett occupies much of the Introduction and the whole of a lengthy first chapter.

[7] Cited in Vivian Mercier, *Beckett/Beckett* (New York: Oxford University Press, 1977), p. 23.

[8] James Knowlson, *Damned To Fame: The Life of Samuel Beckett* (London: Bloomsbury, 1996), pp. 56-57.

[9] For a fascinating interpretation of the implications of this move eastwards in *The Well of the Saints*, see W.J. McCormack, *From Burke to Beckett: Ascendancy, Tradition and Betrayal in Literary History* (Cork: Cork University Press, 1994), pp. 242-247.

[10] W.B. Yeats, 'An Introduction for my Plays' (1937), *Essays and Introductions* (London and Basingstoke: Macmillan, 1961), p. 528.

[11] See Katharine Worth, *The Irish Drama of Europe from Yeats to Beckett* (London: The Athlone Press, 1978), p. 134.

[12] W.B. Yeats, 'The Municipal Gallery Revisited', *The Variorum Edition of the Poems of W.B. Yeats*, edited by Peter Allt and Russell K. Alspach (New York: Macmillan, 1957), p. 603.

[13] Samuel Beckett, *Waiting For Godot, The Complete Dramatic Works* (London and Boston: Faber and Faber, 1990), p. 11. Nicholas Grene has pointed out to me that Martin's reference in Act One to 'the bit of money we have hid in the thatch' implies that the beggars are not homeless but live in some sort of thatched house.

[14] Samuel Beckett, *Waiting For Godot*, p. 14.

[15] Samuel Beckett, *Waiting For Godot*, p. 61.

[16] Samuel Beckett, *Waiting For Godot*, p. 28.

[17] Bertolt Brecht, 'A Short Organum for the Theatre', *Brecht on Theatre*, edited and translated by John Willett (New York: Hill and Wang; London: Methuen, 1964), p. 197.

[18] Samuel Beckett, *Waiting For Godot*, p. 88.

[19] Samuel Beckett, *Waiting For Godot*, p. 11.

[20] Augustine Martin, 'Christy Mahon and the Apotheosis of Loneliness,' in Anthony Roche (editor), *Bearing Witness: Essays on Anglo-Irish Literature* (Dublin: University College Dublin Press, 1996), pp. 32-43.

[21] Anne Devlin, private correspondence, September 1994.

[22] Katharine Worth, *The Irish Drama of Europe from Yeats to Beckett*, p. 134.

[23] Samuel Beckett, *Waiting For Godot*, pp. 84-5.

[24] Randolph Parker, '"Gaming in the Gap": Language and Liminality in *The Playboy of the Western World*,' *Theatre Journal* 37:1 (March 1985), p. 78.

[25] Thomas Kilroy, 'The Anglo-Irish Theatrical Imagination', *Bullán: An Irish Studies Journal* 3:2 (Winter 1997/Spring 1998), pp. 5-12.

[26] See Gertrude Schoepperle, 'John Synge and His Old French Farce,' *North American Review* CCXIV (October 1921), pp. 503-513.

[27] Samuel Beckett, *Waiting For Godot*, p.55.

[28] See Toni O'Brien Johnson, *Synge: The Medieval and the Grotesque* (Gerrards Cross: Colin Smythe; Totowa, New Jersey: Barnes and Noble, 1982). She draws Beckett into her chapter on *The Well of the Saints*, pp. 29-53.

[29] Samuel Beckett, *Waiting For Godot*, p. 71.

[30] See Bert O. States, *The Shape of Paradox: An Essay on 'Waiting For Godot'* (Berkeley: University of California Press, 1979), *passim*.

[31] W.J. McCormack, *From Burke to Beckett*, p. 242.

[32] William G. Fay, *'The Well of the Saints'*, p. 31. Many of Beckett's later plays work to create the same theatrical and visual effect through subtle gradations of lighting.

[33] W.B. Yeats, 'Journal', *Memoirs*, edited by Denis Donoghue (London: Macmillan, 1972), p. 205.

[34] Samuel Beckett, *Waiting For Godot*, p. 69.

[35] Samuel Beckett, *Waiting For Godot*, p. 20.

[36] W.J. McCormack, *From Burke to Beckett*, p. 242.

[37] Samuel Beckett, *Waiting For Godot*, p. 83.

[38] Samuel Beckett, *Waiting For Godot*, p. 88.

8 | Postmodern *Playboy* : Synge in the Twenty-First Century

If 'postmodernism' is interpreted as a term of periodization succeeding 'modernism', then the earliest it might be located historically is in the 1950s, with the emergence of Samuel Beckett's *Waiting For Godot*. Synge's *The Playboy of the Western World* would accordingly be located as a modernist work, part of the movement incorporating Yeats and Joyce, dramatizing the process by which the title character, Christy Mahon, emerges as an individual from a successful struggle with tradition and in which there is a self-consciousness about the style and construction of the work.[1]

There is no doubt, since there is such ample record of the reactions, of the potential of Synge's play to shock when it was first staged at the Abbey Theatre on 26 January 1907. His earlier *The Shadow of the Glen* had caused controversy and so there was a good turnout for the new play's premiere. The audience appeared to accept without demur the Mayo villagers' tolerance of a declared father-slayer in their midst; but they became increasingly restive as the play went on and, as Lady Gregory's notorious telegram to an absent Yeats recorded, 'broke up in disorder at the word "shift"',[2] a reference to Christy's speech at the climax of Act III: 'It's Pegeen I'm seeking only, and what'd I care if you brought me a drift of chosen females, standing in their shifts itself maybe, from this place to the Eastern World' (IV, 167). A week of further disturbances concluded in a formal debate conducted in the theatre between supporters and opponents of the play, although there were frequent interjections from the audience. Yeats mounted the defence that Synge had the right to claim the 'freedom of the artist' to interpret his subject as he saw fit. The most frequent counter-charge, 'That's not the West', raised the serious charge of misrepresentation, that a theatre which claimed to be Irish and national had a responsibility in the way it sought to address important themes. The charge was that the countrymen and women of 1907 Ireland did not resemble those represented in the Mayo of Synge's imaginings.

I do not propose to go into all of the details and intricacies of the argument: they are widely available.3 For a long time the critical consensus, in more formal academic criticism, was that Yeats won the argument, or at least that he was right where the rioters were wrong. More recent criticism has accorded more legitimacy to the views of the rioters, and even questioned the use of the term 'riot' as what a character in an O'Casey play might term 'derogatory'. The history of the theatre has long been subject to debate about what constitutes appropriate as opposed to offensive or improper material and treatment. An act of violence is central to Synge's play and the issue remains a contentious one. What I would stress is how the audience reaction to The Playboy in a curious way mirrors the progress of the play itself, where an onstage audience is first perfectly willing to accept and indeed to applaud Christy's storytelling, but turns increasingly hostile and ultimately violent in its final act.4 And the debate over whether Synge's drama is an authentic or imagined representation of the Irish people has its basis in the debate within the play as to whether Christy is a stuttering lout or the only playboy of the western world.

In the process by which they become classics, works of art and literature lose their power to shock. The initial strangeness with which a play like The Playboy or Beckett's Godot makes its appearance in the world becomes depleted as its familiarity increases and it becomes known by and for the very qualities which first set it apart. Most audiences now approaching The Playboy of the Western World are aware from the start that Christy Mahon's father is not dead but returns many times in the course of the play to be killed and that those who first acclaim Christy turn on and try to destroy him. Another way of saying this is that the work acquires the patina of a classic and, if it is a play, there is increasing pressure to reproduce the mode of production and burden of interpretation with which the work was first presented. This has notably been the case with the 'Dublin trilogy' of Sean O'Casey, where the emphasis in Irish productions has traditionally been on the plays' comedy more than their tragedy, where the women characters have been privileged as the playwrights' true heroes while the men are characteristically weak and vacillating. Efforts to introduce new styles of playing O'Casey were tried in Dublin in the 1990s. In Garry Hynes's neo-Brechtian production of The Plough and the Stars (1926) at the Abbey in 1991 the characters had shaved heads and directly addressed the audience; when the actor Stephen Rea directed it at Dublin's Gaiety Theatre in 1999, the setting appeared to have shifted to Belfast in the 1970s. But these efforts have met with a mixed response.

The case with Synge's play is rather anomalous. Where it is generally accepted as a masterpiece, both in Ireland and abroad, *The Playboy of the Western World* rarely receives an English-language production outside Ireland. And this despite the fact that two of Synge's plays, *The Playboy* and *Riders to the Sea*, are on the Oxford syllabus as acknowledged masterpieces of twentieth-century world or English language drama. The same holds true for the United States, where Synge's *Playboy* is a frequently taught text on American campuses, and yet the play is rarely produced professionally. The situation is somewhat different in Ireland, where the play's classic status assures a certain regularity of production, although less than O'Casey and very much within the subsidized rather than the commercial sector. Why is this? It might well be that the play has dated and while retaining a literary and historic interest, which means it will continue to be read and studied, is no longer amenable to a modern production. This is certainly the case, a century later, with many of the plays of the Literary Revival and the intervening decades: they are entrapped within a set of conventions that have lost their immediacy and within which the work has stultified. But *The Playboy* has received enough regular productions on the Irish stage for an assessment of its current playability at least to be attempted.

What has always struck me about productions of *The Playboy* is that I have never seen an entirely successful one or, to put it another way, one in which all of its primary elements achieved successful theatrical articulation. And this is not just the case of period or author. The first two productions of Synge's 1904 play *The Well of the Saints* which I attended, both at the Abbey Theatre – one by Hugh Hunt in 1969, the other by Patrick Mason in 1994 – were extremely effective theatrically, in part because (as Nicholas Grene has remarked) with the example of Beckett we are more accustomed to 'a drama of inaction' and waiting.[5] But *The Well* is attempting a great deal less than *The Playboy*. Synge himself gives a typically understated and reticent hint about this in a remark he makes in his letter to *The Irish Times* in the week of the play's first production:

> As a rule the less a writer says about his own work the better, but as my views have been rather misunderstood in an interview which appeared in one of the evening papers [the *Dublin Evening Mail*, 29 January 1907] and was alluded to in your leader to-day, I would like to say a word or two to put myself right. [...] 'The Playboy of the Western

World' is not a play with 'a purpose' in the modern sense of the word, but although parts of it are, or are meant to be, extravagant comedy, still a great deal that is in it, and a great deal more that is behind it, is perfectly serious, when looked at in a certain light. That is often the case, I think, with comedy, and no one is quite sure today whether 'Shylock' and 'Alceste' should be played seriously or not. There are, it may be hinted, several sides to 'The Playboy'. 'Pat', I am glad to notice, has seen some of them in his own way. [P.D. Kenny in his *Irish Times* review called the play 'more a psychological revelation than a dramatic process, but it is both']. There may be still others if anyone cares to look for them. (CL I, 286)

This is a remarkable artistic statement, and much more useful for our purposes than the 'official' interpretation of the play Synge provided in his Preface to the published version. There, he was keen to stress (one senses at Yeats's urging) his claims, and the play's, to be an authentic representation of the Irish country people and their habits of speech. What the letter to *The Irish Times* addresses is the play's mimetic status and how its meanings may be realized over time (the two examples he chose being a number of centuries old). 'There are, it may be hinted, several sides to "The Playboy".' There are, it may confidently be asserted, many sides to 'The Playboy', only several of which can expect to be realized in any one production, then or now. At least one of them is explicitly adverted to in Synge's letter, the central issue of how to get the balance right between *The Playboy*'s tragedy and comedy. And this is not something that can be decided in advance. It will depend on how other key issues of the play are addressed, as we shall see.

It could be argued that every dramatic script is only a cue for performance and contains manifold potential meanings which can only be realized through multiple productions over time. This is not quite what I am claiming for *The Playboy*. For one thing, I think Synge's letter and the play's own text collectively suggest a manifold meaning for *The Playboy* which not every text can either claim or support. But also we live not in 1907 but the twenty-first century and bring to the act of interpretation, as readers and audience, our own sets of cultural assumptions and experiences. Again, one could argue that any audience will bring a degree and kind of interpretation to a work which will exceed or subvert any conscious or stated intention of the dramatist's. This openness to interpretation has been particularly claimed with regard to a great deal of contemporary work which might be labelled 'postmodern'.

In *Postmodern/Drama: Reading the Contemporary Stage*, Stephen Watt sees the difficulty I have just outlined as that of discriminating between 'undecideability', the 'myriad responses the audience is capable of recognizing as the potential of the work', and 'indeterminacy', a 'function of the work itself, its internal contradictions and ambiguities.'[6] Watt's own response would appear to shift the onus of postmodernism away from the work itself in the direction of the audience. This may be because of the problematic he defines at the outset of his study when, by bringing together the two terms 'postmodern' and 'drama', he suggests they combine in a potentially divisive way: 'a form [drama] whose cultural work ostensibly includes the establishment of a "civilization" and an adjective [postmodern] that connotes, to a great extent, deconstructive and subversive impulses.'[7] But this binary opposition breaks down if the play itself could be said simultaneously to work towards the establishment of an independent Irish drama and also to contain 'deconstructive and subversive impulses', as critics of *The Playboy* pro and con have always recognized it does.

Whether or not J.M. Synge was a postmodernist *avant la lettre*, what has advanced his claims as such is a phenomonon which has been increasingly remarked upon: the extent to which the generation of Irish playwrights who emerged during the 1990s – Conor McPherson, Marina Carr, Martin McDonagh – has frequently, recognizably and multiply drawn upon Synge's plays. That they have not always done so piously has also been noted. Frequently, the resort to J.M. Synge as an established classic has been more in the manner of a smash-and-grab raid than a polite literary reference. Indeed, the freeplaying references to Synge in such work, with no clear index as to the grounds of their appropriation, has been a crucial factor in contributing to the emergence of a postmodern Synge. At the very least, the work of the playwrights of the 1990s causes us to look anew at features of Synge's work which may well have been tamed by familiarity or assimilated into a critical consensus, where their strangeness has been glossed into normality. The effect has been to reawaken the controversy which originally attended Synge's appearance and to stimulate fresh interest in his drama.

The figure who most epitomizes the Irish playwrights of the 1990s, and the one to whom most of my comparative remarks in this chapter will be addressed, is Martin McDonagh, author of three plays which have been dubbed 'The Leenane Trilogy'.[8] His name evokes an eerie resonance for any student of Synge because Máirtín Mac Donncha was the name of the islander who taught Synge Irish on Inishmaan. There would appear to be little in common between the Mac Donncha Synge describes in *The Aran Islands* as 'the youngest son of my boatman, a

boy of about seventeen, who is to be my teacher and guide' on
Inishmaan (II, 58) and the McDonagh who wrote the Leenane trilogy, a
young urbanized Londoner with an accent to match. But exile and
emigration were not a one-way and permanent condition in either late
nineteenth or twentieth century Ireland. Rather, the repeated patterns
of departure and return which have marked Irish experience for over a
century introduce a web of affiliation between the two McDonaghs. For
the contemporary London playwright is the son of Irish parents who
emigrated to England, a Sligo mother and a Galway father. He spent
many of his summer holidays in the parental West of Ireland, a factor
that came into play as he struggled to create a credible speech for his
fledgeling dramas. McDonagh had tried writing plays set in London or
America but without success. It was when he recalled the setting and
conversations from his summer visits as a child to the West of Ireland
that he found his dramatic idiom, 'close to home, but distant', as he
himself put it in a 1998 RTÉ documentary on his work. Although not
named as such, the Irish diaspora existed at the turn of the last century
also. When Synge returned to the Aran Islands for a second year in
1900, he encountered his island teacher Máirtín Mac Donncha on the
mainland to which the young man had emigrated in order to find work.
Synge describes Máirtín as now 'dressed in the heavy brown flannels of
the Connaught labourer' (II, 105) rather than in the woollens of the
native Aran Islander. Synge is keen to stress how much of the fineness
of the islander Martin yet retains in this urbanized work environment;
but given his hostility to the onset of modernity on the islands, this has
to be read carefully. The cultural complexity of the process Synge is
witnessing is best attested to by the occasion on which Máirtín writes
back to his family on the islands, while Synge is staying with them. As
W.J. McCormack puts it:

> emigration took sons and sent back remittances; languages played
> leapfrog with each other so that Máirtín Mac Donncha was obliged to
> write home in English, being the only one among them who could read
> and write in Gaelic. Synge, who came to learn, found himself
> translating his tutor's letter for the household.[9]

The two McDonaghs are best seen in a historic continuum where the
first emigrates to find work and the latter returns to find plays.

The parallel that most needs asserting is a comparison between John
Millington Synge and Martin McDonagh. In interviews, McDonagh has
always claimed to be influenced by English dramatists like Pinter rather
than the more traditional playwrights of the Irish Literary Revival.
Further, his interest lies more with the movies than with theatre, as

critics were quick to pick up on when they compared the casual cruelty of McDonagh's plays to the films of Quentin Tarantino.[10] But the evidence of the plays themselves belies McDonagh's claims, in particular in relation to Synge and his writings. For the title of the third play of The Leenane Trilogy, *The Lonesome West*, is itself a direct quotation from *The Playboy of the Western World*: when the villagers are taunting Shaun Keogh for his fear of Father Reilly, Pegeen's father holds up Shaun's coat and proclaims: 'Well, there's the coat of a Christian man. Oh, there's sainted glory this day in the lonesome west' (III, 65). And the key moment in the middle play, *A Skull in Connemara* (its title deriving from Lucky's speech in Beckett's *Waiting for Godot*), is provided by the young gravedigger crawling back on stage after he has apparently been killed with a spade driven into his skull. The diversity and kind of McDonagh's borrowings, its eclectic mix, has itself been seen as postmodern; but there is no doubt that Synge is central to the enterprise.[11] The connections between the two playwrights were noted by the reviewers of the trilogy in 1997, where the Syngean debt was more apparent than it had been in the premiere of *The Beauty Queen of Leenane* the year before. For example, *The Guardian*'s Michael Billington wrote:

> McDonagh's purpose over the long haul becomes clear – to explode the myth of rural Ireland as a place of whimsical gaiety and folksy charm. The reality, he suggests, is murder, self-slaughter, spite, ignorance and familial hatred. McDonagh is not the first writer to tell us that the travel-poster Ireland conceals dark impulses: Synge, to whom he remains deeply indebted, made the point back in 1907. But McDonagh's great strength is that he combines a love of traditional storytelling with the savage ironic humour of the modern generation.[12]

For those critics, then, who take a positive view of both Synge and McDonagh, the close kinship between the two writers is clear.

But for those who take a negative view of McDonagh's dramatic project, the criticisms sound remarkably like those made concerning Synge almost a hundred years ago. For many theatre critics and academics from outside the country, Synge is an unproblematically 'Irish' writer who chose, as a contributor to Yeats and Lady Gregory's noble plan for an Irish National Theatre, to take Irish character, place and theme for his plays rather than setting them in London with English characters as previous Irish playwrights up to and including Wilde and Shaw had done. But within Ireland the situation was not so clear cut. For, in a view most fully articulated by writer Daniel Corkery in his 1931 study, *Synge and Anglo-Irish Literature*, J.M. Synge was not native Irish but Anglo-Irish, descended from English settlers who had taken part in the plantation of Ireland under Queen Elizabeth I. Synge, like almost all of those involved in the Irish Literary Revival, was not a Catholic of the majority but a Protestant of the oppressive colonial minority, and so as a writer unable to identify with the three great themes of Land, Religion (by which Corkery meant Catholicism) and Nationalism which constituted an authentic Irish literature. Corkery's study is a subtle and sympathetic one; he exonerates Synge from many of the charges brought against Yeats and others, deeming that he went as far as he could to identify with the people about whom he wrote. But the traces still remain of the usual charge against Synge, that he exploited and misrepresented the people about whom he wrote, separated from them as he was by uncrossable chasms of class, social and cultural formation, religion and language – and that the end product is a Syngesong of his own devising rather than any authentic and realistic representation of Ireland at the turn of the last century.

This is very close to the critique of McDonagh that has emerged in the wake of the trilogy, where the playwright appears to have sacrificed the empathy of the mother-daughter conflict in *The Beauty Queen of Leenane* in favour of the unrelieved cartoon violence of the other two plays. What McDonagh's plays are emphatic about is their naming of real places – Leenane, Connemara, Inishmaan (in *The Cripple of Inishmaan* [1997]) – in the West of Ireland which this foreigner, this outsider, this Englishman who has been palmed off as an Irishman, has chosen as his locale for the scenarios of his psychotic characters. In *The Beauty Queen*, the rain pours relentlessly down on the stylized peasant cottage, dominated by an enormous crucifix. In *Skull*, two characters excavate the local graveyard and indulge in an orgy of infantile skull-bashing. In *The Lonesome West*, two brothers, having killed off their father, strive to do each other in with ever more grotesque inventiveness. Offence has been caused by the perpetration of such stereotypes of the Irish, representing them as a people with an innate propensity to violence, a somewhat dim intelligence and the inability to take anything seriously.[13]

The issues of representation that arise from the question of racial stereotype have bedevilled Irish drama from the start, or rather from any of its self-conscious 'beginnings'. For like any group which has first and hitherto been represented by a dominant Other – whether it is women by men, or blacks by whites – those terms in which the group is represented can come to seem demeaning and hence unusable (because tainted) when that group assumes responsibility for its own representation. Put an Irishman on the stage and, arguably, you have a

Stage Irishman. When Yeats and Lady Gregory wrote their manifesto for the Irish Literary Theatre in 1897 they claimed that their theatre movement would 'show that Ireland is not the home of buffoonery and of easy sentiment, as it has been represented, but the home of an ancient idealism.'[14] As Nicholas Grene argues in *The Politics of Irish Drama*, 'every dramatic movement claims that they can deliver the true Ireland which has previously been misrepresented, travestied, rendered in sentimental cliché or political caricature'.[15] Yeats and Gregory's emphasis on 'an ancient idealism' raises as many questions and issues in its turn as the stage buffoonery and sentiment it seeks to supplant. But my more immediate concern is with the first part of their manifesto, an attack on the Stage Irishman which had so far been put forward as the national image on (implicitly foreign and English) stages and which the Irish Literary Theatre, and subsequently the Abbey Theatre, would seek to redress. The more specific target is the popular nineteenth-century actor-manager-playwright Dion Boucicault, author of melodramas set in various countries and settings but whose latter productions – notably *The Colleen Bawn* (1860), *Arrah-na-Pogue* (1864) and *The Shaughraun* (1874) – had introduced Irish characters and settings. Boucicault himself had usually taken the role of the Stage Irishman figure, the tricky servant ostensibly subordinate to the 'master' whose romantic and political intrigues he helped to resolve but who was actually the stage manager of much of what we witness. Synge was far less opposed to the Stage Irishman figure than Yeats and Lady Gregory – for one thing, the theatre he envisaged and practised was much more of a hybrid, a mix of high and low elements, than the resolutely high art favoured by Yeats. In a review of Boucicault's *The Shaughraun* at the popular Queen's Theatre in Dublin, Synge lamented that 'at the present time few are perhaps aware what good acting comedy some of his work contains' and that the turn against Boucicault's drama had lost for the modern stage a great deal of 'personal humour'. Indeed, he observes, as if anticipating objections to *The Playboy*, 'the Irish National Theatre Society is sometimes accused of degrading Ireland's vision of herself by throwing a shadow of the typical Stage Irishman upon her mirror' (II, 398).

This unsigned review of 1904 was identified as being Synge's by the French critic Maurice Bourgeois, whose important 1913 study of the playwright characterized the Stage Irishman as follows:

> The stage Irishman habitually bears the generic name of Pat, Paddy or Teague. He has an atrocious Irish brogue, makes perpetual jokes, blunders and bulls in speaking, and never fails to utter [...] some wild screech or oath of Gaelic origin at every third word; he has an un-

surpassable gift of 'blarney' and cadges for tips and free drinks. [...] He is rosy-cheeked, massive and whisky-loving. His face is one of simian bestiality [....] In his right hand he brandishes a stout blackthorn [...] and threatens to belabour therewith the daring person who will 'tread on the tails of his coat'. For his main characteristics (if there is any such thing as psychology in the stage Irishman) are his swagger, his boisterousness and his pugnacity. He is always ready with a challenge, always anxious to pick a quarrel.[16]

Although Bourgeois does not proceed to do so in his analysis of the play, his pathology of the Stage Irishman is helpful in identifying the one true example of the type in Synge's *The Playboy of the Western World*. Christy Mahon does not conform to the Stage Irishman stereotype, however much he may be striving to do so through the story he relates of his violent deed. When he first enters the Mayo shebeen, he sits down and drinks a quiet pint, but shows no propensity to drunkenness; and his storytelling seems involuntary rather than practised. But his father is a different matter. All of Old Mahon's entrances into the play are as violent as they are unexpected. Christy's father is always on the lookout for drink, and is much given to the swearing of mighty oaths:

> Then the blight of the sacred drought upon myself and him, for I never went mad to this day, and I not three weeks with the Limerick girls drinking myself silly and parlatic from the dusk to dawn. (III, 143)

But the entrance of this Stage Irishman occurs late in Synge's play. And a careful dramatic context has been created so that it can be critically assessed rather than just indulged.

There are many ways in which Synge's *Playboy*, for all of its exaggeration and heightening, can be seen as a realistic play, careful to source its more elaborate stretches of mythmaking in the conditions and lives of the people it represents. The exception to this is the father-slaying, which Synge consciously heightens and exaggerates to stress credulity and to allow for an allegorical or symbolic reading. The overthrow of a tyrannical father by a young, oppressed son can invite a political reading, and the trope had been employed in the journalism of the period 'as a symbol of national rebellion'.[17] In terms of representation, what I would suggest is that the 'shadow' of the Stage Irishman, as Synge identifies it in his review of the Boucicault melodrama, is not as readily or as easily thrown off as all that. Indeed, he suggests that (whether acknowledged or denied) it will continue to 'shadow' efforts at authentic Irish representation and has to be confronted in order to see what of value – of genuine humour, for one thing – can be reclaimed.

Against the charge of using stereotypes that has been levelled at Martin McDonagh, Fintan O'Toole – whose critical writing was enormously influential in the initial favourable reception accorded the playwright and in establishing the high claims made on his behalf – has this to say:

> Of course he's dealing with stereotypes, of course he's dealing in a stage Irish mode, but it seems to me that he's the first writer of a generation where those stereotypes can be played with in an almost innocent way. This is a culture in which those stereotypes have lost their power and in which they can be played with, they can be altered. That in itself is quite an important cultural moment because it's a moment of liberation, we're no longer enthralled to those stage-Irish stereotypes, or to the need to get out of them.[18]

Synge called for such a moment of self- and cultural liberation when he wrote of those Irish who, 'with their eyes glued on John Bull's navel, [...] dare not be Europeans for fear the huckster across the street might call them English' (II, 400).

The appeal in O'Toole's defence to 'a culture in which those stereotypes have lost their power' refers presumably to the culture of Ireland in the present moment, suggesting that the country has achieved the decolonization which Synge gestures towards. But theatre works in performance have different audiences. An Irish audience secure in its own cultural identity and free to enjoy a play on its own merits is one thing, a non-Irish audience laughing at an onstage play of Irish stereotypes on a London stage may well be another. This is where McDonagh's London origins come into question and, even more, the fact that the Leenane trilogy, though premiered at Galway's Druid Theatre by the artistic director Garry Hynes, was always destined (before the Irish reaction to the plays had been gauged) for a London run at the Royal Court Theatre, where Hynes was an associate director. A *TLS* reviewer of a subsequent Irish play directed by Hynes which underwent this journey ended his review by querying: 'It makes me wonder what kind of postcolonial transaction is going on as I sit on the Royal Court's magnificent new upholstery, watching those wild Irish Yahoos, again.'[19]

Where the emotional reality of the middle-aged daughter oppressed by the old mother has been seen to lend weight and credibility to McDonagh's *The Beauty Queen of Leenane*, the chief charge of the Stage Irishman stereotype – the spectacle of 'those wild Irish Yahoos' – has been levelled at the male-centred violence of the other two plays. It is instructive to watch McDonagh attempt to get to grips with this dilemma – of being open to the charge of Stage Irishness – in *The*

Lonesome West. The chief dramatic emphasis in the play is on the life-long feud between two brothers, Valene and Coleman, primarily carried out at the level of verbal hostility but always with the possibility of physical violence. Usually, the supporting male characters in a McDonagh play are young male teenagers who come by to waste some time and annoy the protagonists. But here the main supporting male character is a priest who has come to the neighbourhood hoping to do good, Father Welsh or Walsh (nobody can agree on his name – a rather lame and tirelessly repeated gag, but a clear sign that he has failed in his worthy ambition). The priest finally decides to commit suicide but before he does he pens the brothers a letter in which he says it would all have been worthwhile 'if only I could restore to ye the love for each other as brothers ye do so woefully lack, that must have been there some day.'[20] When the brothers receive and read out the letter after the priest's drowning, it does cause a flicker of remorse and moral recognition in Coleman and Valene. But moments later the hostility resumes when it turns out that Coleman has spent rather than invested the insurance money. Valene shoots a gun after him and then sets fire to the priest's letter, saying as he does:

> And you, you whiny fecking priest. Do I need your soul hovering o'er me the rest of me fecking life? How could anybody be getting on with that feck?
> *He strikes a match and lights the letter* [...] *After a couple of seconds, the letter barely singed,* **VALENE** *blows the flames out and looks at it on the table, sighing.*
> (*Quietly.*) I'm too fecking kind-hearted is my fecking trouble.
> *He returns to the cross and pins the chain and letter back on to it, smoothing the letter out* [....] [21]

Valene makes his final exit and the stage is left with the light lingering on the singed remains of Father Walsh/Welsh's letter pinned to the crucifix.

For a critic like Fintan O'Toole, both Synge and McDonagh are to be praised for their theatrical audacity and their liberating play with stereotypes. But others have insisted on a categorical distinction between the two playwrights, despite superficial resemblances. In an influential article entitled 'Decolonization Postponed: The Theatre of Tiger Trash', Vic Merriman posited an absolute difference in their two dramatic projects for an Ireland undergoing decolonization:

> McDonagh's plays are often greeted as parodies of the works of John Millington Synge. This needs to be challenged. In staging peasant life, Synge unambiguously confronted the ideological project to which it had been co-opted: a travesty serving the need felt by a resurgent nationalist bourgeoisie for a foundational myth.[...] Far from being an

early, naïve version of McDonagh, *The Playboy of the Western World* and *The Well of the Saints* embody a cultural project which could hardly be more different. Such plays vigorously assert the dignity and spirit of people whose image, emptied of their life experiences, would be mobilised in the service of bourgeois neocolonialism.[...] McDonagh's work [...] parades the emptied shell of peasant life for smug dismissal by a metropolitan audience. The journey from Synge to McDonagh takes us all the way from images which challenge the submerged ideological positions of an emergent neocolonial class to those which collude in reinforcing them.[22]

Has as much distance been travelled between Synge and McDonagh as Merriman states? Are the images offered of the peasant people in both dramas, and the cultural projects they underwrite, as absolutely different as is claimed? What most challenges this argument, the area where Synge and McDonagh most disturbingly replicate and resemble each other, is in the proliferation and foregrounding of violence, both verbal and physical. I am not here thinking primarily of the contest between father and son. As I argued earlier, its extreme verbal stylization in Christy's telling and the repeated physical enactments whenever Old Mahon appears both work to move their conflict away from realism to a level of allegorical abstraction. When the emphasis is shifted to the milieu in which *The Playboy of the Western World* is located for the duration of its three acts, Michael James Flaherty's shebeen and its customers in County Mayo, what is most striking – certainly when one revisits the play after an encounter with McDonagh – is the pervasiveness of violence in the normative, everyday lives of these characters. The McDonagh 'effect' on Synge's drama is to foreground the number and kind of violent incidents with which the Mayo villagers' speech is filled, and the readiness with which they resort to it. They do so not only or primarily to defend themselves but often for sheer amusement's sake or to relieve their boredom.

One of the most gratuitously shocking exchanges between the brothers in *The Lonesome West* takes place when Coleman reveals that he was the one who snipped the ears off Valene's dog:

> To the brookeen I dragged him, me scissors in hand, and him whimpering his fat gob off 'til the deed was done and he dropped down dead with not a fecking peep out of that whining fecking dog.[23]

When read intertextually with Synge's play, does this speech not work to defamiliarize and put some of the harm back into Pegeen Mike's gratuitous reference to Jimmy Farrell's exchange with the authorities over a dog licence:

> You never hanged him [Christy's father], the way Jimmy Farrell hanged his dog from the licence and had it screeching and wriggling

three hours at the butt of a string, and himself swearing it was a dead
dog, and the peelers swearing it had life? (III, 73)

This speech occurs only a few lines after Pegeen has jeeringly said to
Christy: 'A soft lad the like of you wouldn't slit the wind-pipe of a
screeching sow' (III, 71).

Nicholas Grene has epitomized the violence of Synge's play as
follows:

> The language of *The Playboy* is pervaded by a sportive violence no less
> unsettling for its casualness. Images of hanging, of madness, of
> grotesque cruelty, are the mere subject of amused anecdote. [...] The
> Widow Quin [...] warns Old Mahon, whom she has convinced of his
> insanity, that he should disappear unobtrusively from the scene, 'for
> them lads caught a maniac one time and pelted the poor creature till
> he ran out raving and foaming and was drowned in the sea'. This is no
> realistic picture of Irish country life as it is lived; the high colour of
> violence throughout is a feature of the grotesquely fantastic version of
> reality which the play presents.[24]

Grene's concluding statement here directly contradicts the claims made
by Synge in his Preface about the linguistic verisimilitude of his play to
establish its realism and authenticity: 'I have used one or two words
only, that I have not heard among the country people of Ireland [...]. A
certain number of the phrases I employ I have heard also from herds
and fishermen along the coast from Kerry to Mayo, or from beggar-
women and ballad-singers nearer Dublin' (III, 54). The terms favoured
in Grene's critical assessment of Synge's masterpiece – highly coloured
violence, grotesque unrealistic fantasy – might seem to be preparing the
ground for a close comparison, and a positive one, with McDonagh's
Leenane Trilogy. But no such detailed comparison emerges in *The
Politics of Irish Drama*, despite the book's concern with younger
contemporary playwrights like Frank McGuinness and Sebastian Barry.
The plays of Martin McDonagh are accorded only one sentence in the
closing pages of Grene's book, where McDonagh is described as a
playwright of 'doubtful originality' who has managed to achieve his
success solely by 'manipulating the formulae of the Irish play'.[25] Clearly,
there is no room in such an argument for the critical concept of
postmodern pastiche. Elsewhere Nicholas Grene has stated that 'I don't
think these plays have a secure place in the canon. I think that
McDonagh will be seen as a kind of fashion. It seems to me that there is
a good deal of writing skill, particularly in *The Beauty Queen of
Leenane*, but I think it's fairly downhill from there. The same kind of
basic comic jokes are re-worked in the other plays and it's just a case of
further outraging, further pushing certain limits.'[26] Despite Grene's

stringently trying to downplay McDonagh's influence and importance, his efforts are undercut by the very terms in which he analyses Synge's *Playboy* in his 1999 study. His analysis of Synge, an author about whom Grene has been thinking and writing for over thirty years, now shows the unmistakeable imprint of what one might term 'the McDonagh phenomenon'. What appears more striking than hitherto, and receives the emphasis, in his most recent analysis is not the lyricism but the sportive, casual violence and the 'grotesquely fantastic version of reality' presented by Synge's play. I would use this critical example to argue that it is now impossible to consider the plays of J.M. Synge without reference to those of Martin McDonagh (and vice-versa). The phenomenal and pervasive impact of the latter will influence the reading of the former, whether the individual critic cares for McDonagh's work or not. The unsettling nature of the violence in Synge's play was an unusual and innovative component of Garry Hynes's production for her Druid Theatre Company in Galway of Synge's *Playboy* in the 1980s; and Garry Hynes and her company directly shaped the theatrical presentation of McDonagh's Leenane Trilogy in the 1990s. When the same theatrical features are being highlighted in two different bodies of work, how can one author be read as unambiguously positive and the other unremittingly negative (as Vic Merriman has also sought to do)? I very much doubt that postmodernism will have it so. As Shaun Richards has argued:

> It is then difficult to determine some absolute difference between the staged worlds of the two playwrights: violence, deprivation and longing are the lot of all the characters. But while Synge is accorded a social seriousness beyond the comedy of his plot and extravagance of his language this is denied to McDonagh.[27]

Part of the disequilibrium which attends *The Playboy of the Western World* which I discussed at the outset, its too-muchness and contending qualities, has to do with how much emphasis is accorded to the struggle between Christy and his father. If the emphasis shifts to the characters and milieu of the play's actual setting, then the emphasis on a certain kind of violence is increased, as I have just argued. But the shift also has important consequences for the gender politics of the play, something that has come to prominence since the rise of feminism in the 1970s. In a discussion at that time with the actress Sinéad Cusack, daughter of the famed actor Cyril Cusack who had become so associated with the part of Christy Mahon, she remarked to me: 'Remember, it's also a play about Pegeen Mike.' Sinéad Cusack had just (in 1975) played the part of Pegeen in a BBC-TV version along with John Hurt as the playboy and had brought a fine contemporary edge to the part, suggesting a woman of resource and independence as well as a sharp-tongued heroine. The emphasis on Pegeen shifts the interpretation of *The Playboy* from a more fantastic setting, whether to do with the father-slaying or the violent grotesquerie of much of the imagery, to a detailed observation of everyday life. The play begins and ends by concentrating on the figure of Pegeen Mike, opening with her letter ordering goods for her wedding day to her closing tragic cry of grief over lost possibilities. These scenes establish the detail of her life, and in particular the social conditions of her existence, as the ground of the drama. As Declan Kiberd argues in *Inventing Ireland*: 'Synge put the debate about rural womanhood back on the agenda in the persons of Nora Burke and Pegeen Mike. After all, *The Playboy* starts and ends with Pegeen's plight as a trapped rural woman in a landscape virtually bereft of enterprising men.'[28] Accordingly, when an enterprising man shows up, it looks increasingly likely that Pegeen will depart with him. But Synge had already developed that romantic possibility in his earlier *The Shadow of the Glen*. This time, he refuses the easy option of having the woman leave and instead reinserts her altered consciousness back into the settled community. Where the male hegemony at the end of *Shadow* could reassert itself by sitting down and taking a quiet drink, with its order restored and indeed secured after purging its most disruptive elements, the attempt to replicate this procedure at the end of *The Playboy of the Western World* between Michael James Flaherty and Shawn Keogh is disrupted by a piercing protest:

> **PEGEEN.** [*hitting him a box on the ear*]. Quit my sight. [*Putting her shawl over her head and breaking out into wild lamentations.*] Oh my grief, I've lost him surely. I've lost the only playboy of the western world. (III, 173)

This development throws the emphasis, as I have said, on the conditions in which Pegeen lives and suggests the need for a more thoroughgoing revolution than the personal one effected between Christy Mahon and his reformed father. The most developed feminist analysis of Synge's *Playboy* has been advanced in Gail Finney's 1989 study, *Women in Modern Drama: Freud, Feminism and European Theater at the Turn of the Century*. Finney stresses the similarities between Pegeen Mike and Christy Mahon: both lacking mothers, both with dominant fathers, both poised at various stages of rebellion. She also emphasizes the extent to which the transformed Christy is Pegeen's creation by arguing how much he is the vehicle of her frustrated creativity: as penny potboy, as ladies' man, as poet, as well as father-slayer. This is, after all, a woman who encounters no internal obstacle to (re-)imagining herself as the Pope of Rome, a latter-day Pope Joan, when she remarks: 'It's a wonder, Shaneen, the Holy Father'd be taking notice of the likes of you, for if I was him, I wouldn't bother with this place' (III, 59). Finney's interpretation occurs late enough in the development of feminist theory to allow for a more nuanced reading of gender roles. As she observes, it is entirely appropriate in a play concerned with role-playing that the women should take on some of the more traditionally 'masculine' aspects of behaviour – forceful, competitive, vigorous, unsentimental and occasionally violent – while Christy's behaviour shows much that is traditionally associated with women, not least when he hides the mirror in which he has been admiring himself and is accused of vanity by the young women.[29] As Declan Kiberd points out:

> what mesmerizes *all* of the women is [Christy's] femininity. Pegeen praises his small aristocratic feet [...]; the village women enjoy his nuances of delicate phrasing [...]; and the Widow Quin has fantasies of putting him into a woman's dress by way of securing his liberation from persecution.[30]

Finney goes so far as to see 'the blurring of gender distinctions' which is so much a feature of the play and which culminates 'in Pegeen's hypermasculine show of violence' when she burns Christy's leg 'as responsible as Christy's notorious mention of 'a drift of chosen females standing in their shifts' for the bewilderment of the play's audiences and the opening night riots.[31] If hypermasculinity finally wins out in Pegeen Mike over her subtler intuitions of gender interplay, it was a hypermasculinity which was not only pervasive in the environment of the play created by Michael James Flaherty and his drinking cronies but in the ideals promoted by turn-of-the-century nationalists. Whatever final judgement Christy Mahon may come to about the people of Mayo, he is not obliged to live among them. He comes and goes in the course of the play, an abstract cipher onto which the villagers have projected their fantasies, none more so than Pegeen Mike.

The play for Christy, potentially tragic, turns out to be a comedy. Indeed, it has been argued that Synge's *Playboy* is a version of Sophocles' tragedy *Oedipus the King*, with its father-slaying and the threat to marry Christy to a widow who has suckled him.[32] What provides the ground for comparison between the two plays is the prominence accorded to father-slaying. The greatest ambivalence attaches to Oedipus as public figure in this respect. On the one hand, he is the man who appeared at a providential moment some years earlier to rescue Thebes from the plague by solving the riddle of the Sphinx. He is asked to repeat this therapeutic function in the play's present by seeking out the murderer of King Laius. On the other, when the murder is brought both to public consciousness and to full recollection by Oedipus, he paradoxically emerges as the source of the plague. Christy Mahon comes on virtually from the beginning as a man who slew his father and who is acclaimed rather than reviled for his deed. But the terms of that father-slaying undergo complex and frequent renegotiation in the course of Synge's play. And when Christy's father makes his unexpected entrance and is identified in the flesh, the mood of the onstage audience shifts into a much more negative key. In both plays, the parricide is in the past and can only be approached through a verbal re-enactment; each work dramatizes a making present of that event and a consequent disruption of the present order by that act of parricide.

Synge's play offers a proliferation of fathers. Before Old Mahon makes his belated and unexpected entrance, Pegeen Mike has had much to say on the score of *her* father, Michael James Flaherty, and his desire to be a *pater absconditus* who makes off to Kate Cassidy's wake. In relation to Christy's father-slaying, Pegeen remarks, 'I never killed my father. I'd be afeard to do that' (III, 81); she does not say she would not want to. But there is also a third father in the play, much invoked by Pegeen's threatened fiancé, Shawn Keogh, and that is the local priest. Father Reilly, though repeatedly invoked verbally, never appears directly onstage. But his looming offstage presence is felt throughout as he monitors the sexual behaviour of Christy and Pegeen through his surrogates, Shawn and the Widow Quin.

The most striking difference between Sophocles' *Oedipus* and Synge's *Playboy* is that the former is a tragedy while the latter is predominantly a comedy. Synge could write pure tragedy when he wanted to; his *Riders to the Sea* has often been discussed in direct correlation with Greek tragedy.33 In seeking for a theoretical frame to evaluate the shift from tragedy to comedy, and one that is avowedly postmodern, I would refer to the work of Gilles Deleuze and Felix Guattari. Quoting Kafka, they write of what they call a comic or 'exaggerated Oedipus' in the following terms: 'Dramas and tragedies are written about [the revolt of the son against the father], yet in reality it is material for comedy.'34 Working from a postFreudian and postmodernist perspective, Deleuze and Guattari seek to find a way out of the Oedipal impasse, which simply has the effect of returning the subject to the position where the father is 'hated, accused and declared to be guilty'.[35] This is the position which Christy Mahon still occupies at the close of Act Two where he wishes 'that the Lord God would send a high wave to wash him [his father] from the world' (III, 125). But a substantive reconfiguring of the father-son relationship occurs in Act Three when Christy and Old Mahon square off, first against each other, then against the Mayo villagers. As a result of this process, Christy as son is brought to admit a measure of sympathy and degree of understanding for his father Old Mahon who, in Deleuze and Guattari's terms, 'demands only that the son submit because he [the father] himself is in submission to a dominant order'.[36] In order to work out a mode of escape for both father and son from this shared impasse, *Oedipus* has to be enlarged to the point of absurdity, a comic extreme, something Synge accomplishes through his play's increasingly more elaborate and frequent mood swings. The son and father's joint compact as they depart is to be 'hav[ing] great times from this out telling stories of the villainy of Mayo' (III, 173) and the forces they saw ranged against them there, exposed by their repeated dramatic enactment of the slaying.

There is a residue of tragedy in Synge's *Playboy* and it associates itself with the figure and fate of woman in the play. In part, this has to do with the suppression of the other half of the Oedipal equation – the sleeping with the mother. Because if this dramatic world is overburdened with fathers, it seems remarkably bereft of mothers. Neither Christy Mahon nor Pegeen Mike has or refers to a mother. The sole verbal trace of the incest taboo surfaces in one of the multiple reasons adduced by Christy for killing his father, who he claims has sought to marry him to the Widow Casey: '"I won't wed her," says I, "when all know she did suckle me for six weeks when I came into the world"' (III, 103). Listening to his story is the Widow Quin, who has not only killed her husband but buried her children. The association of widowhood links her with the Widow Casey as a potential mother-figure against whom the incest taboo operates, even as or especially as she seeks to represent herself as a fit mate for Christy.[37] Maternity is threatening throughout the play and frequently generates some of its most grotesque images, such as Pegeen's description of the Widow Quin 'rear[ing] a black ram at [her] own breast' (III, 89). And verbal slippage in the Widow's repeated self-identification as someone who 'has buried her children and destroyed her man' (III, 89) blurs the sexual and the deadly in equal measure between her mate and her offspring.

But this account leaves Pegeen out of the equation. For if the play turns from a tragedy to a comedy for Christy, it takes the alternative route for Pegeen. For much of its duration, it would have been Pegeen's as much as the audience's expectation that she is operating within the conventions of a romantic comedy.[38] Her very first speech announces the imminence of her wedding and creates an aura of heightened, sexualized expectation. Shaun Keogh, her intended, is soon revealed as an unworthy suitor, craven and abject. But into his place and shoes steps the figure of Christy Mahon, whom the Widow Quin and the play increasingly endorse, and with diminishing irony, as the only playboy of the western world. Until late in the third act, it still seems likely that – according to the conventions of romantic comedy – parental opposition will be converted into support and the couple will wed. In Act Three, upon his return from Kate Cassidy's wake, Michael James switches his consent from Shaun Keogh to Christy Mahon, averring that in the union of his daughter with Christy he'd prefer to see 'a score of grandsons growing up little gallant swearers by the name of God, than go peopling my bedside with puny weeds the like of what you'd breed, I'm thinking, out of Shaneen Keogh' (III, 157). But Old Mahon remains unconverted in his opposition to the union and the exchange of father and son develops in the ultimate direction of the 'Comic Oedipus' resolution adumbrated by Deleuze and Guattari. The failure of the play to end with the marriage of Christy and Pegeen means that the social order remains untransformed; indeed, the refusal of the traditional marriage at the end is the climax to the play's simmering critique of the *status quo*.

I would like to return to Synge's statement, with which I began this chapter, that 'although parts of *The Playboy* are, or are meant to be, extravagant comedy, still a great deal that is in it, and a great deal more that is behind it, is perfectly serious, when looked at in a certain light'. In relation to this authorial assertion, Gail Finney remarks:

> One 'serious' aspect is surely Pegeen's fate, which verges on tragedy – not death, as in the cases of more traditional late nineteenth-century heroines, but the failure of self-realization, symbolized by a union with Christy. In Synge's play Pegeen's liberating identification with Christy is directed, in terms of her development, toward a comic resolution. Yet the play's final emphasis on the failure of this resolution, highlighting not Christy's triumph but Pegeen's tragic lamentations at losing him, produces a stylistic rupture that points ahead formally to postmodern drama while calling attention thematically to the entrapment of Irish women in the conventions of their time.[39]

Finlay's last sentence in the above strives to align postmodernism and feminism within the same statement but does so with some degree of uneasiness. It might therefore be said to replicate the uneasiness or instability with which the play confronts its audience and readers in its third act. Striking a balance between the emphasis on Christy and Pegeen has been a challenge for any production from 1907 on. As Synge's own comments attest, *The Playboy of the Western World* contains both 'extravagant comedy' and more serious elements. Its author was aware that the proportions and relations between these two could alter over historical time, as Shakespeare's *The Merchant of Venice* and Molière's *Le Misanthrope* had done. In Finney's statement the feminist dimension would appear to address the historical moment of the play's composition and first performance, relating the plight of Pegeen (and by extension the other female characters like the Widow Quin and the village girls) to 'the entrapment of Irish women in the conventions of their time'. But that analysis is only made possible by the historical progress of feminism from the agitation on behalf of suffrage at the turn of the previous century to the widespread emergence of feminism in the 1970s as an academic discipline and as a major force for social transformation in Western society. For all of its theoretical dimension, feminism is a political ideology closely related to historical process and change, to advocating an emancipatory politics. The more a production of Synge's *Playboy* adopts a realistic approach, the more the entrapping conditions of the society the women occupy are potentially illuminated. Pegeen's tragedy is such, not because of a predestined or predetermined fate, but because of an insufficiently elaborated project of feminist revolution.

Christy Mahon comes from nowhere and returns to nowhere, entering briefly into the lived social community of Mayo in the early twentieth century. As has been argued, Pegeen lives in that community, from start to finish, and is bound by its people, its mores and its customs. They are predominantly patriarchal, as the overdetermination of fathers in the play demonstrates, and by the fact that one of the fathers – the Catholic priest – is not biological but hegemonic. Pegeen is moved by Christy's example to defy *her* father, standing up to him and demanding that her own desires be ratified. Her entrapment by the social attitudes of the time proves in the end to be the more powerful, influenced as she is by how she will be regarded in the community's eyes for linking herself to an acclaimed hero who has done nothing. But those desires are not extinguished by the close of the play, despite appearances. They flare up in the final moments, in the wake of Christy's departure, and suggest that he has left an 'unmanageable revolutionary' behind him.[40]

What has sidelined the progress of Pegeen's emancipation in Synge's play is the return of Christy's father and the violent resumption of the

Oedipal struggle. That development dominates the remainder of the play, not only upstaging Pegeen's developmental trajectory but arguably leaving her with no theatrical or symbolic space to articulate a position from other than a fierce return to the *status quo*. This seems a prescient articulation on Synge's part of how Ireland's political and cultural nationalism would develop in the twentieth century, with the repeated co-opting and erasure of the contribution made by women to the nationalist struggle. The one position available was the symbolic role of Cathleen ní Houlihan, as represented by Maud Gonne. Synge had close relations with a number of advanced feminists on the Continent.[41] There is the distinct possibility that his withdrawal from Maud Gonne's revolutionary organization, Irlande Libre, occurred because it was hypermasculine in the incendiary violence it favoured and insufficiently feminist in its ideals. In April 1897 he tendered his letter of resignation to Gonne, saying: 'You already know how widely my theory of regeneration for Ireland differs from yours and most of the other members of the Jeune Irlande' (CL I, 47). Synge's letter presages the subsequent break of both Maud Gonne and Arthur Griffith from the nascent national theatre movement over the sympathetic and revolutionary portrayal of Nora in *The Shadow of the Glen*.

The predominantly masculinist ethos of Irish nationalism has been discussed explicitly in terms of the Oedipal crisis by Moynagh Sullivan: 'Within [Irish] cultural nationalism the view of the child was repeated until it achieved the status of a historical orthodoxy.'[42] The Oedipal triangle allots a space to the woman, but only by insisting on reading her as mother. The mother's selflessness confirms the son's (and hence the nation's) subjectivity, as in Patrick Pearse's poem 'The Mother'. And while father and son engage in the admittedly difficult and problematic task of reconstituting their relations along the lines adumbrated by Deleuze and Guattarri, the woman is not only consigned to an isolated space but one that functions effectively as a space of exclusion, of absence, rather than of presence and individuation. The loss of the mother is required so that 'the child subject can be seen to come into existence in the symbolic through the Oedipal crisis'.[43] *The Playboy* implies that Christy Mahon's mother died in childbirth, from which point on he was tended to by his father. Pegeen also has no mother but her gender precludes her from occupying or participating fully in the role of 'son' in the Oedipal model (her masculinization and attraction to violence show how far she has travelled in that direction). Instead, she must occupy the place of wife/mother as the only space available to her, and must compete with the other women for the privilege of occupying that space.

Because the Oedipal model is so dominant in the development of Irish political and cultural nationalism, and in the development of Synge's *The Playboy of the Western World*, women's full subjectivity cannot emerge. Rather, they are forced to compete with each other, as all of the women do in the play's first two acts. The critical narrative of Irish nationalism, in order to sustain its momentum and development, is forced to reinvest repeatedly in the Oedipal model and the consequence, in Sullivan's formulation, is 'a constitutional insistence on the muting of the woman'.44 This narrative has become familiar, through the feminist scholarship of Margaret Ward and others, in the history of Irish nationalism, documenting the ways in which the entry of the Republican party into constitutional politics in 1930s Ireland (as Fianna Fáil) saw not a less repressive regime than its predecessor but arguably a greater restriction of freedom. This was certainly the case as far as women were concerned, with their dismissal from the Civil Service upon marriage and their symbolic and actual restriction to the 'home' in the 1937 Constitution. *The Playboy*'s reinvestment in the Oedipal struggle in its latter stages leads to a no less shocking 'muting' of the hitherto vocal and expressive Pegeen Mike. From the point at which old Mahon's aggressive re-entry takes centre stage, Pegeen either says nothing or voices a language of denial. When she is directly asked by Christy to speak – 'And what is it you'll say to me?' – Pegeen can only reply:

> I'll say a strange man is a marvel with his mighty talk; but what's a squabble in your back-yard and the blow of a loy, have taught me that there's a great gap between a gallous story and a dirty deed. (III,169)

Pegeen is here making an absolute distinction between word and deed, between the ostentatious romance of the one and the brute realism of the other. In so doing, she is reinstating the hierarchical value system she displayed when Christy first entered the shebeen and she reiterated that he was only talking and had 'done nothing so' (III, 71). There would have been very little Irish drama in the twentieth century if language had not operated as a form of action. The development of Synge's influential play, increasingly evident as the playwright gains ever more confidence through the many drafts, is to demonstrate that language has a constitutive, creative power and that as in the Old Testament the act of creation begins with the word. Christy's act of self-fashioning, in which he becomes 'a likely gaffer in the end of all' (III, 173), can happen because a space of possibility is opened up in the play's developments. His metamorphosis occurs precisely because the absolute distinction between word and deed is not maintained. The operative term, a favourite in Synge's lexicon, is 'gap'.[45] Where Pegeen ends by referring to 'a great gap between a gallous story and a dirty deed', the high point in the love-talk between them in Act III is marked by Christy's sexual and lyrical evocation of the two lovers 'gaming in a gap of sunshine' (III, 149). The remark is inspired, ironically, by Pegeen's praise of his eloquence. Where she finally reifies word and deed into conflicting opposites, Christy has instead chosen to interpret the 'gap' as a space where word and deed interact and intersect, an interstitial zone of potential freedom made possible through the medium of play.

'Gaming in the gap' may be taken as a metatheatrical reflexive comment on the play's dramatic strategies. As Randolph Parker puts it: '*The Playboy of the Western World* leaves us in the inevitable gap between gallous stories and dirty deeds, a liminal zone in which the joy of language and the lure of fantasy are in a continually unresolved dialectic with the need to perceive life realistically.'[46] What poses a problem for any production is that it must situate itself somewhere in the gap between romance and realism, and that it cannot definitively be seen as either. Synge's drama is never a wholly realistic account of the near-contemporary lives of impoverished peasants in a shebeen in the west of Ireland; but that dimension of the play has to be respected and realized to some degree. Neither is it wholly a self-conscious exercise in myth-making enacted through the mutual attraction of two young lovers and a supporting cast with fertile imaginations. Any production must steer a hazardous path between the Scylla and Charybdis of romance and realism. Any director approaching Synge's play must do so with an awareness that, to the extent that s/he decides on interpreting the play in one mode, it forecloses possibilities in the other.

Gail Finney's remarks quoted earlier pointed forward to both the feminist and postmodern possibilities encouraged by the 'stylistic rupture' of the play's ending. But these two theoretical possibilities can prove difficult to marry in the event of actual production. It can equally seem that there is a 'great gap' between feminism and postmodernism as theoretical positions. Both came to the forefront in close historic proximity, from the 1970s on. But just at the point where women were claiming autonomy and independence for their subjectivity, postmodernism proclaimed that subjecthood was problematic, if not a fiction. Further, because postmodernism shares 'an understanding of the feminine and woman as coterminous', the result is potentially to 'foreclose the possibility of dialogue with feminist theory'.[47] Feminism's emancipatory politics is grounded in the social and political contexts in which women must operate and follows a historical trajectory; postmodernism prefers the ahistorical free play of pastiche.

In productions of *The Playboy of the Western World*, the impact of feminism can be measured best not only in the foregrounding of Pegeen but also in how the Widow Quin is represented. For decades, the tradition was to play the Widow as a woman in her fifties, with the result that the sexual setting of her cap at Christy as a potential new husband could only register as grotesque. The prospect of a (much) older woman pursuing a man young enough to be her son deepened and aligned itself with the Oedipus scenario. But in Garry Hynes's groundbreaking 1982 production the Widow Quin was played by Marie Mullen, an actress then in her late twenties. Since Synge had indicated in his notes to *The Playboy* that the Widow Quin was 'thirty' (III, 86), this radical reenvisioning of her role could be seen as part of the production's claim to be more authentic. By making Synge so much a feature of their development, Galway's Druid Theatre not only lent cultural weight to their enterprise but made a decisive claim in favour of the playwright's much-disputed authenticity, as argued in the Introduction to this book. Their productions of Synge brought the speech closer in rhythm and delivery to the Irish language, and stressed a realistic immediacy in the production style. As was discussed earlier, they did not shy away from but underlined the violence in *The Playboy*, taking advantage of their small, intimate theatre to make the audience draw back when the bloody-pated Old Mahon attacked his son. But it was in the presentation of the women characters that the Druid production most revealed a contemporary edge, showing not just Pegeen but the Widow and the village girls as confident in their sexuality and their speech. The representation of a young, sexually alluring Widow Quin restores the currency to Christy's delighted response at the close of Act 1 to having 'two fine women fighting for the likes of me' (III, 93). But the increasing practice of casting the Widow as a woman of 'thirty' has introduced the problem of her stealing, if not Christy, then the theatrical high ground ('the show') from Pegeen Mike. In Garry Hynes' 2004 return to *The Playboy* Ann-Marie Duff's pale, nervous, virginal Pegeen was hard-pressed to compete with Aisling O'Sullivan's sexually experienced, witty and confident Widow Quin.[48] Pegeen was for once costumed as a bourgeois, a middle-class woman keeping her distance from the young peasant girls with their slovenly dress and uncouth ways. But if this provided a strong link to Ibsen, it also raised the question – in its portrayal of an entrapped Pegeen – of whether the realistic portrayal of a young woman oppressed by the social conditions of 1907 has not run its course a hundred years later, when feminism has achieved many of its declared goals and when the traditional social landscape of Ireland has been altered beyond recognition by the impact of the 'Celtic Tiger' economy of the 1990s. Has the representation of Pegeen as entrapped not itself become a straitjacket for productions of Synge's *Playboy*?

The 1990s also saw the impact of postmodernism on Irish productions of Synge. In the vanguard of such interpreters was director Niall Henry and the Blue Raincoat Theatre Company of Sligo.[49] Although that area is primarily associated with Yeats, here (as with Druid) was another notable instance of a theatre company originating from the site of representation of many Revival cultural artefacts who put on strikingly innovative productions of those works. Blue Raincoat's hallmark was a noted emphasis on physical movement and corporeal mime (Henry had trained at the Jacques Lecoq School in Paris), part of a move in the 1980s and 1990s away from the text- and word-centred emphasis of most Irish theatre. Henry directed two productions of Synge's *Playboy* in the decade between 1992 and 2002, the first for Blue Raincoat, the second for the National Theatre at the Peacock. The first placed more emphasis on physical movement than the text, with Synge's words sometimes no more than a mumble. The 2001 Peacock production, perhaps at the National Theatre's insistence, gave a forceful reading of Synge's language but matched it with a no less physically expressive reading of the script. Christy was played by Mikel Murfi, co-founder of the clowning theatrical troupe Barabbas the Company, who spent much of the first act in a foetal posture, signifying the extent to which Christy has not yet been born into a full sense of his own potential. Most of the race on the strand occurred off-stage, as usual, with the exception of a magnificent flying leap across the stage of the Peacock by Murfi in his white-and-green jockey's outfit, looking like one of the Jack B. Yeats illustrations come to hyperactive life. And in a dazzling metatheatrical touch the girls did not actually appear at the opening of Act Two but were conjured up by Murfi/Christy in his play with the mirror. Henry made significant changes in the ages of some of the cast. Jimmy and Philly, the two aged bachelors, were transformed into young punks and ranged the stage menacingly with Michael James Flaherty in a pose remininscent of Quentin Tarantino's *Reservoir Dogs*. Given that Martin McDonagh has been likened to a cross between Synge and Tarantino, here was a postmodern acknowledgement of those lines of cultural cross-reference. Cathy Belton's Widow Quin was, as has become the norm, young and sexy. But what was so surprising was that she was considerably younger than Pegeen.

In both of his productions, Niall Henry cast an older actress as the eighteen-year-old Pegeen: a thirty-eight-year old woman in the first, a forty-something actress in the second. Olwen Fouéré's Pegeen paced the dimensions of the Peacock stage like a character out of Beckett's *Footfalls*. This was not the first older actress to play Pegeen. Siobhán McKenna was still acting the part, and committed it to celluloid in 1962, at an age considerably in advance of eighteen. But hers was a classical performance, availing of the unspoken assumption that a great role could be assayed by an actor associated with the part long after they had passed an age at which it was credible.[50] Henry's decision was deliberate, a means of moving the dilemma in *The Playboy* away from the romantic complication and towards an exercise in postmodern aesthetics. But although he deepens the theatrical representation of Pegeen, and places her existential dilemma at the core of the play, he does not extend to her any of the imaginative and expressive freedoms lavishly bestowed on Murfi's Christy.

The dialogue between a postmodern and a feminist version of Synge's *Playboy* needs to be pursued further in production. This is, after all, a woman who can briefly consider herself in the role of Pope, has been 'tempted often to go sailing the seas' (III, 151), and has demonstrated the frustrated creativity of a Pygmalion in the ways she, more than any other of the Mayo villagers, has fashioned an undistinguished lump of an Irish lad into the 'only playboy of the western world' (III, 173). At the play's denouement, Pegeen has sought to destroy what she has created. Her final cry testifies not only to what she has lost, but the degree to which her exercise in creativity has been successful. A production of *The Playboy of the Western World* which can find inventive means to represent the range of Pegeen's desires will contribute much to the necessary dialogue between feminism and postmodernism.

---

[1] Thomas Kilroy has discussed the ways in which Synge may, and may not, be considered a Modernist writer. Identifying the Anglo-Irish Literary Revival as a 'late phase of European Romanticism', he argues that Synge was the first to bring the Revival within the ambit of Modernism and that he did so by acting upon 'traditional forms' in a 'radical fashion'. See Thomas Kilroy, 'Synge and Modernism', in *J.M. Synge Centenary Papers: 1971*, edited by Maurice Harmon (Dublin: The Dolmen Press, 1972), p. 172.

2 David H. Greene and Edward M. Stephens, *J.M. Synge 1871-1909* (New York and London: New York University Press, 1989; revised edition), p. 256.

3 For the most detailed documentary account, see James Kilroy, *The 'Playboy' Riots* (Dublin: The Dolmen Press, 1971); Robert Hogan and James Kilroy, *The Abbey Theatre: The Years of Synge 1905-1909* (Dublin: The Dolmen Press; New Jersey: The Humanities Press, 1978), pp. 123-162. Christopher Morash provides a cultural and historic analysis of the audience's various contending forces in 'All Playboys Now: The Audience and the Riot', in *Interpreting Synge*, ed. Nicholas Grene (Dublin: The Lilliput Press, 2000), pp. 135-150; a shorter version is reprinted as 'A night at the theatre 4', in Christopher Morash, *A History of Irish Theatre 1601-2000* (Cambridge: Cambridge University Press, 2002), pp. 130-138.

4 On a more nuanced construction of the Abbey audience's response, see Paige Reynolds, *'The First Playboy'*, in *Playboys of the Western World: Production Histories*, edited by Adrian Frazier (Dublin: Carysfort Press, 2004), pp. 13-28.

5 See Introduction to J.M. Synge, *The Well of the Saints*, edited by Nicholas Grene (Washington, D.C.: The Catholic University of America Press; Gerrards Cross, Bucks.: Colin Smythe, 1982), p. 25.

6 Stephen Watt, *Postmodern/Drama: Reading the Contemporary Stage* (Ann Arbor: The University of Michigan Press, 1998), p. 27.

7 Stephen Watt, *Postmodern/Drama*, p. 13.

8 The individual plays comprising McDonagh's 'Leenane Trilogy' are: *The Beauty Queen of Leenane* (1996); *A Skull in Connemara* (1997); and *The Lonesome West* (1997).

9 W.J. McCormack, *Fool of the Family: A Life of J.M. Synge* (London: Weidenfeld and Nicolson, 2000), p. 210.

10 Claiming that 'I always thought theatre was the least interesting of the art forms', McDonagh also asserted that at the time of writing the Trilogy, he had not read Synge's *Playboy of the Western World*. See Fintan O'Toole, 'Nowhere Man', *The Irish Times*, 26 April 1997.

11 See Shaun Richards, '"The Outpouring of a Morbid, Unhealthy Mind": The Critical Condition of Synge and McDonagh,' *Irish University Review* 33.1 (2003), p. 210. Richards describes Synge as providing the 'depth-effect' to McDonagh's Leenane trilogy.

12 Michael Billington, *The Guardian*, July 28, 1997.

13 The negative reaction to McDonagh's plays in Ireland is outlined in Ian Kilroy, 'The One-Trick-Pony of Connemara?', *Magill* (January 2000), pp. 54-57. Part of the problem, according to Kilroy, is that the praise comes from Fintan O'Toole in the official paper of record, *The Irish Times*, while much of the Irish critical dissent is vocal, rather than published, and hence off the record. An exception is

Susan Conley's review of a production of *The Beauty Queen of Leenane* in *Irish Theatre Magazine* 2.5 (2000), pp. 63-64

14 Cited in Lady Gregory, *Our Irish Theatre* (Gerrards Cross: Colin Smythe, 1972), p. 20.

15 Nicholas Grene, *The Politics of Irish Drama: Plays in Context from Boucicault to Friel* (Cambridge: Cambridge University Press, 1999), p. 6.

16 Maurice Bourgeois, *John Millington Synge and the Irish Theatre* (London: Constable, 1913), pp. 109-110.

17 Ben Levitas, *The Theatre of Nation: Irish Drama and Cultural Nationalism 1890-1916* (Oxford: Clarendon Press, 2002), p. 117. Levitas adds: 'The audience would have been alert to the allegorical possibilities of the situation Synge was in the process of engineering.'

18 Fintan O'Toole, as quoted in Ian Kilroy, 'The One-Trick Pony of Connemara?', p. 57.

19 Stephen Brown, review of Marina Carr's *On Raftery's Hill* at the Royal Court Theatre, *TLS*, 21 July 2000.

20 Martin McDonagh, *Plays: One [The Beauty Queen of Leenane, A Skull in Connemara, The Lonesome West]* (London: Methuen, 1999), p. 169.

21 Martin McDonagh, *Plays:One*, p. 196.

22 Vic Merriman, 'Decolonisation Postponed: The Theatre of Tiger Trash,' *Irish University Review* 29:2 (Autumn/Winter 1999), p. 316.

23 Martin McDonagh, *Plays: One*, p. 189.

24 Nicholas Grene, *The Politics of Irish Drama*, pp. 94-95.

25 Nicholas Grene, *The Politics of Irish Drama*, p. 262.

26 Nicholas Grene, quoted in Ian Kilroy, 'The One-Trick Pony of Connemara?', p. 54.

27 Shaun Richards, 'Lost Playboys of the Western World: Martin McDonagh's Leenane Trilogy,' paper delivered at ESSE 5 Conference, Helsinki, August 2000, p. 3. These remarks are not in the revised version of the talk published as '"The Outpouring of a Morbid, Unhealthy Mind": The Critical Condition of Synge and McDonagh', *Irish University Review* 33:1 (Spring/Summer 2003).

28 Declan Kiberd, *Inventing Ireland* (London: Jonathan Cape, 1995), p. 179.

29 Gail Finney, *Women in Modern Drama: Freud, Feminism and European Theatre at the Turn of the Century* (Ithaca and London: Cornell University Press, 1989), pp. 113-114.

30 Declan Kiberd, *Inventing Ireland*, p. 176.

31 Gail Finney, *Women in Modern Drama*, p. 119.

32 For a detailed comparison of Sophocles and Synge, see Mary Rose Sullivan, 'Synge, Sophocles and the Un-Making of Myth', *Modern*

Drama 12:3 (1969), pp. 242-253, and D.J. Conacher, 'Some Profane Variations on a Tragic Theme', *Phoenix* 23:1 (1969), pp. 33-38.

33 See Fiona Macintosh, *Dying Acts: Death in Ancient Greek and Modern Irish Tragic Drama* (Cork: Cork University Press, 1994)

34 Gilles Deleuze and Felix Guattari, *Kafka: Towards a Minor Literature*, translated by Dana Polan (Minneapolis: University of Minneapolis Press, 1986), pp. 10-11.

35 Gilles Deleuze and Felix Guattari, *Kafka*, p. 9.

36 Gilles Deleuze and Felix Guattari, *Kafka*, p. 10.

37 D.J. Conacher describes the Widow Quin as 'a Jocasta-figure, maternally erotic in the first half of the play [...] and maternally protective in the second half'. 'Some Profane Variations on a Tragic Theme', p. 35.

38 For a discussion of how Synge uses 'the form of traditional Romantic Comedy' in the play, see Thomas Kilroy, 'Synge and Modernism', pp. 172-173.

39 Gail Finney, *Women in Modern Irish Drama*, pp. 121-122.

40 The phrase 'unmanageable revolutionaries' was Eamon De Valera's, used to describe the women involved in the republican movement. See Margaret Ward, *Unmanageable Revolutionaries* (London: Pluto Press, 1983).

41 Prominent among these was Synge's close friend, Thérèse Beydon, a teacher of drawing at a girls' school in Paris. Edward Stephens describes her as follows: 'Besides art, with which her occupation was concerned, she was interested in politics. She sympathized generally with the feminist movement which was then taking shape and, in particular, with the efforts that were being made to organize the nursing profession'. See *My Uncle John: Edward Stephens's Life of J.M. Synge*, edited by Andrew Carpenter (London: Oxford University Press, 1974), p. 92.

42 Moynagh Sullivan, 'I am, therefore I'm not (Woman)', *International Journal of English Studies* 2:2 (2002), pp. 124-125.

43 Moynagh Sullivan, 'I am, therefore I'm not (Woman)', p. 126.

44 Moynagh Sullivan, 'I am, therefore I'm not (Woman)', p. 127.

45 The term 'gap' was also crucial in *The Well of the Saints*, as discussed in the previous chapter.

46 Randolph Parker, '"Gaming in the Gap": Language and Liminality in *The Playboy of the Western World*,' *Theatre Journal* 37:1 (March 1985), p. 84.

47 See Moynagh Sullivan, 'Feminism, Postmodernism and the Subjects of Irish and Women's Studies,' in *New Voices in Irish Criticism*, edited by P.J. Mathews (Dublin: Four Courts Press, 2000), p. 243.

48 The following year, in the 2005 DruidSynge production of *The Playboy*, Marie Mullen returned to the part of the Widow Quin

twenty-three years after she had first introduced the notion of a
younger Widow.

49Another postmodern 'take' on Synge's play should be noted in the
production *Play-boy* by a performance group, desperate optimists,
who toured Ireland and the UK between 1992 and 1999. As Cathy
Leeney recounts: 'the desperates made video footage of people
talking about Synge's *Playboy*, about being lonely and about what
our lives would be like if we had made a different set of decisions.
These talking heads interrupt and disrupt the live performances of
Christine Molloy and Joe Lawlor, who narrate a fantasy account of
an encounter between Synge and Trotsky, against a soundtrack of
Latin dance music. Each person on video, in turn, unnerves the
audience by taking a loaded gun and firing it at us.' See Cathy
Leeney, 'Hard wired/tender bodies', *Performing Ireland,* special
issue of *Australasian Drama Studies* guest-edited by Brian
Singleton and Anna McMullan, 43 (October 2003), p. 81.

50 See Adrian Frazier, '"Quaint Pastoral Numbskulls": Siobhán
McKenna's *Playboy* Film,' in *Playboys of the Western World:
Production Histories*, pp. 59-74.

9 | J.M. Synge and Molly Allgood: The Woman and the Tramp

Synge wrote in his Preface to *The Playboy of the Western World* that '[a]ll art is a collaboration' (IV, 53). The most significant collaboration between the playwright and an Abbey Theatre actor, and the one which this chapter wishes to explore, was that with the actress Molly Allgood.[1] It was she for whom he wrote his two final, and arguably greatest, female roles, Pegeen Mike in *The Playboy* and the eponymous heroine of *Deirdre of the Sorrows*. But J.M. Synge and Molly Allgood were also intimately involved offstage, their romance leading to a formal engagement and a deferred plan to marry. This close relationship between a Protestant and a Catholic, between a director of the Irish National Theatre and one of the employees, sent shock waves through his strict evangelical family and his fellow directors. The inner drama is laid bare in the almost daily letters they exchanged across a period of several years. As one might expect from a couple who both seek their profession in the theatre, there is a strong degree of role-playing, most manifestly evidenced by the personae they chose to adopt in their correspondence. Synge's letters to Molly were addressed to his 'changeling' and were signed 'Your old Tramp'; hers have not survived. These key terms were also deployed in his plays and suggest that the letters may be read as further textual evidence of the complex interchange in Synge between life and art, with both clearly undergoing a substantial degree of self-fashioning.

Synge's identification with the figure of the tramp was deep-rooted and of long standing. It preceded his first meeting with Molly Allgood. In his essay, 'The Vagrants of Wicklow', which the editor of his *Prose* surmises was probably written in 1901-2, Synge in an oft-quoted passage makes a parallel between 'the gifted son of a family' and 'a tramp on the roadside':

> In the middle classes the gifted son of a family is always the poorest –
> usually a writer or artist with no sense for speculation – and in a
> family of peasants, where the average comfort is just over penury, the
> gifted son sinks also, and is soon a tramp on the roadside. (II, 202)

What interests me in this passage is the elision, the sleight of hand, by
which the self-identification of Synge as a writer/artist from a middle-
class family and the sense of alienation which this has bred in him finds
its way to the desired objective of a tramp on the roadside. This
transformation is achieved not by means of anything resembling
rational argument – none is offered, only its appearance – but through
verbal parallelism and the introduction of a middle term, a peasant
family. The passage does not literally claim that a son of the middle-
classes is ineluctably or indeed ever going to end up as a tramp on the
roadside; that is felt to be the natural prospect of a son from a peasant
family. But the careful verbal orchestration enables that end to be
arrived at syntactically by its parallel and by a consequent blurring into
near oneness of the two gifted sons. The passage, for all of its
romanticism, also exudes a sense of financial insecurity, of a downward
mobility which has obscured the first term, the landowning classes to
which the Synges had belonged a generation or two earlier.

A less often quoted passage occurs later in 'The Vagrants of Wicklow'
where Synge writes that 'some incident of tramp life gives a local
human intensity to the shadow of one's own mood' (II, 204). This
passage has a direct bearing on his one-act play, *The Shadow of the
Glen*, in which the figure of the Tramp makes a memorable appearance.
As was discussed earlier, the story which was to form the basis for the
play was first told to Synge on the Aran Islands. But that story was not
set on the islands, as so many he heard were. Rather, it had a mainland
setting, with the narrator 'travelling on foot from Galway to Dublin' (II,
70). When he came to write the play based on the folk tale, its setting
was to be carefully translated by Synge into the detailed Wicklow
landscape he knew so well. The other two aspects he developed in his
play were the role of the wife, considerably expanded from the original
in terms of what she says and does, as was examined in Chapter Six,
and the replacement of the anonymous narration of the storyteller by
the figure of the Tramp.

In the light of Synge's comment, what is so striking is the extent to
which the presence and dramatic deployment of the Tramp in the
scenario greatly increases the 'human intensity' of the piece, deflecting
it away from farce or melodrama. In part, this is achieved through the
Tramp's sympathy towards the plight of the young wife Nora as she
unfolds her tale of loneliness in a barren married relationship. The

sympathy is made manifest in his crucial decision to intervene when
Nora's husband threatens to throw her out: 'It's a hard thing you're
saying, for an old man, master of the house, and what would the like of
her do if you put her out on the roads?' (III, 53). The Tramp and Nora
have found common ground in their mutual admiration for the recently
deceased Patch Darcy, a social renegade from the 'back hills'. When
Dan Burke revives, he specifically rebukes the 'blathering' between his
wife and the Tramp about 'Darcy [*bitterly*] – the devil choke him' (III,
43) as indicating the growing bond he detects between them. The play
maintains a deliberate oscillation between the romance and realism of
life on the roads. On the negative side, there is the fate of Patch Darcy,
his decomposing body eaten by the crows; and the woman whom Nora
has identified as a negative emblem of her possible fate: 'Peggy
Cavanagh, who had the lightest hand at milking a cow that wouldn't be
easy, or turning a cake, and there she is now walking round on the
roads, [...] with no teeth in her mouth, and no sense' (III, 51). When
Dan banishes his wife from the household to a life on the roadside, he
again evokes the figure of Peggy Cavanagh as his wife's negative fate:
'Let her walk round the like of Peggy Cavanagh below, and be begging
money at the cross roads, or selling song to the men' (III, 53). Nora is
quick to point out that there is no escape from dying or decay in any
locale, and that her husband's masquerade is only a rehearsal for the
death he will one day undergo. It is the Tramp who verbally undertakes
to transform the material conditions of the natural environment into a
fine imaginative prospect, as Nora was only the first of many critics to
recognize.

But this final reworking of the play's material conditions does not
come from nowhere, as may appear. For the dramatic function of the
Tramp in part resides in his activity throughout the play, subjecting
everything he sees and hears to enquiry. Rather than neutrally entering
his environment and receiving his shelter and drink, the Tramp
comments repeatedly on the oddity of what he sees: of the elaborate
preparations for a wake which no one is attending; of the 'queer' look
on the face of a man who is reputedly dead. In so doing, he isolates and
renders self-conscious the folkoric elements so seamlessly presented in
the folktale Synge originally heard, facilitating the process by which his
creator will manipulate them and send them in a different direction
from the original. The Tramp's most brazen efforts in this regard *vis-à-vis* Nora Burke occur when he comments on his own strangeness, and
notes how she has not flinched from admitting a strange man into her
house. The Tramp is more than the vehicle by which the psychological

and social truths underlying the folktale are laid bare; he plays an active part in their deconstruction.

Although Molly Allgood did not originate the part of Nora Burke in *The Shadow of the Glen*, Synge cast her in the play when he conducted rehearsals himself for an English tour in early 1906. As he reminds her in a later letter: 'Don't you remember how clear I was when I was teaching you Nora B[urke]?' (CL I, 217) The nineteen-year-old actress had followed her older sister, Sara Allgood, into the Abbey Theatre in late 1905.[2] Her first stage role was a walk-on part in Synge's *The Well of the Saints*. But it was her being cast as Nora some months later that brought her acting to wider attention and inaugurated her romance with the playwright. As Ann Saddlemyer puts it in her edition of the Letters: 'through the speeches of the Tramp, [Synge] courted her [...] [and] when [he] accompanied the players to Wexford on 26 February [1906], his relationship with Molly was apparent to all'. (*CL*1, 146)[3] Undoubtedly, there is a strong vein in the letters which Synge and Molly soon exchanged which recalls in its romantic mood and natural imagery the final lengthy speech by the Tramp in Synge's play: 'Remember in three little weeks there'll be another new moon, and then with the help of God, we'll have great walking and talking at the fall of night' (CL I, 200). But the letters reveal a great deal else besides and frequently adopt a querulous, carping tone that less resembles the romantic outsider than it does the aged, possessive, jealous husband, as Synge himself appears to half-recognize when he signs an early letter to Molly 'Your old Tramp alias Dan Burke!' (CL I,178)

The letter in question has to do with the prospect of Molly stepping out into the natural world, not with the playwright, but with her fellow Abbey Theatre actors, and with one in particular: 'I heard accidentally of your walking arm in arm with Wright [Udolphus 'Dossie' Wright, also nineteen] at Longford. Is that true?'(CL I, 176). It is in this context, and on this occasion, that Synge changes the way he addresses her in the letters, switching from 'Molly' to 'Changeling'. The latter term comes freighted with fairy associations. Its use underlines the extent to which the relationship with Molly has transported Synge from everyday cares and a lonely existence into the heightened possibility of otherness with which all romantic affairs in his plays and poems are infused. It is also a tribute to her art, to her ability as an actress which he consistently praises, not least when she is performing in his plays. As he writes to her at the height of the row over *The Playboy of the Western World*: 'You don't know how much I admire the way you are playing P[egeen] Mike in spite of all the row' (CL I, 288). But Synge's attitude towards

Molly's acting only remains consistent, and consistently positive, so long as she is on the stage. When she is off it, other realities intrude, social, sexual and cultural. His letters on their backstage meetings at the Abbey Theatre register degrees of distance, in particular an inhibition on the talk which is so much cherished and sought after in the letters. In their social relations at the theatre one is more aware of the Synge who is on the Board of Directors and the Molly who is a paid employee:

> You must not mind if I seem a little distant at the Theatre, every one is watching us, and even when we are publicly engaged I do not care to let outsiders see anything. [...] Last spring we had to do our talking in the Theatre as we did not see each other elsewhere but now, thank God, we can have our talk on green hills, that are better than all the green rooms in the world. (CL I, 211)

The uneasiness Synge expresses in the letters with regard to Molly's temperament and behaviour most often locates itself in the term 'actress'. When he speaks of their imagined future and of 'the sort of life you'll have with me', he frames and expresses it in terms of nature and art: 'the life I mean that we have out on the hills, and by the sea on Bray head and in the art we both live for'. And yet what threatens to 'ruin' that happiness forever is that Molly is 'so young and so quick and an actress' (CL I, 208-9). Part of the paradox involved here is that acting is something which requires his beloved to remain true to herself and to her instincts – 'I think you may turn out a very fine actress – if you can only preserve your sincerity' (CL I, 249) – and yet also to change, to undergo conscious training and development: 'you will never reach the very top [...] unless you read plenty of what is best and train your natural instincts. There is a sermon!!' (CL I, 303). Synge's letters to Molly are full of advice on what to read if she is to 'improve' herself, and it is often hard to determine whether he means professionally or socially. The strain of the 'actress' paradox continues to exercise itself through repeated statements that he loves her just as she is mingled with complaints that she is not other than she is.

The couple cemented their relations when they were on tour in Scotland in early 1906; fellow actors spoke of their surprise when they saw the normally reserved Synge with his arm around her; and Annie Horniman was appalled at their visible intimacy. It was not unheard of, in the theatre or elsewhere, for male members of a wealthier class or in a more privileged position to take sexual short-term advantage of beautiful young women. As Vivian Mercier remarks:

Synge was consciously a gentleman by birth and upbringing. At 35,
when he first met Miss Mary Allgood, he might have allowed himself
liberties with a woman of his own age and class who happened to love
him, but with a girl still in her teens he had too much integrity to play
the role of 'seducer'.[4]

Other men might not show the same restraint and, as Synge's illness
increased the physical separation between them, he frequently thinks of
Molly in the company of 'men who dangle after actresses', those for
whom the lady is a tramp, and warns her accordingly to 'keep clear' of
them: 'I know too well how medicals and their like think and speak of
the women they run after in Theatres, and it wrings my heart when I
think what that man may be saying and thinking of my little changling,
who is so sweet and so innocent and whom I love so utterly' (CL I, 249).
When he thinks of her in this light, the term 'actress' takes on the
sexually ambiguous connotations it would have had for members of his
own class, the same puritanical dread that kept his immediate family
from ever entering a theatre.

The opposition in this letter strives to hold separate and to contrast
the urban world of theatres as the world of (fallen) experience with the
rural world of the Wicklow hills, with its magical associations of
innocence. But the term 'changeling' with which Synge interpellated
Molly in his letters is the most slippery and uncertain of those in the
fairy lexicon. Angela Bourke has written of a case where an Irish woman
Bridget Cleary was burned to death by her husband in 1895 because, it
was claimed, she was a changeling. The term 'changeling', according to
Burke, gives ambivalence 'a stage on which to perform'.[5] Where most of
those who are taken by the fairies can be deemed absent, in the case of a
changeling the young woman has, and has not, gone away to fairyland,
since her place has been taken by one of the 'others' (the fairy people)
magicked into her likeness: 'she did not wholly disappear into fairyland,
therefore what was left in her place was a changeling'.[6] The changeling
is not fully absent, because visually present, while appearing curiously
removed. The term also can be used to 'explain' behaviour that is
aberrant, intolerable or somehow threatening to the social order. Synge
longs to be with his changeling in the hills of Wicklow, the location
where she can be most fully herself; but more often they find
themselves in the daylight urban world where Molly both is and is not
herself.

The different strains that the letters between Synge and Molly
reveal, the conflicting moods or character that they may be seen to
possess, can be mapped symbolically on a geographic continuum.
Between the refuge of the Wicklow hills and the ambivalent space of the

Abbey Theatre falls the suburbs, that zone in which Synge lived, from which he forayed but to which he always returned. Vivian Mercier has written of Synge as a suburban writer as follows: 'The flight to the suburbs in the second half of the nineteenth century, with its concomitant building of Evangelical Protestant churches, [...] was principally a Protestant one. Hence the middle-class constrictions of suburban life, notoriously galling to the artistic temperament, were intensified by the rigours of a voluntary ghetto.'[7] Mercier views Synge's suburban status as informing the 'cult' of tramps, tinkers and beggars in his plays: the temporary refuge from his real environment which the summer sojourns with his mother in various Wicklow houses also provided. But it is in the first year of Synge's relationship with Molly that it becomes clear how 'his suburban roots went much deeper than he had imagined.'[8] These suburbs, as Mercier points out, were made possible by new developments in technology – of railways, trams, etc. The different psychic strata of Synge's identity which I have outlined above had a peculiar reliance on the railway. The meetings with Molly were invariably arranged as follows: she would take the train from the centre of Dublin, southwards towards Bray; Synge would board the train at either Glenageary or Sandycove, and both would get off at Bray.[9] If he did not spy her on the platform, he would assume she had not come and would return home. From Bray the couple had unfettered access to Wicklow. (Synge's biographer, W.J. McCormack, has noted, however, that their walks never went so far into Wicklow as to trespass on the lands of the former Synge estate.)[10]

But the clandestine, anonymous cover (or 'privacy') given to burgeoning sexual relationships by the railway system could not last forever. As the relationship between Synge and Molly continued, it became natural that she should wish to come and visit him at his 'home' – the house in Glenageary where he and his mother most often resided, with its name ('Glendalough House') transported from County Wicklow to the Dublin suburbs. Synge agonizes and frets over Molly's appearing at the house, postponing it until he can do so no longer. The inhibitions which clearly prevailed at Molly's first entrance across the Synge family threshold are described in the letter he wrote to her immediately after that visit: 'It is curious what a little thing checks the flow of the emotions. Last evening because there was a sort of vague difficulty or uncertainty about our positions in this house we were as stiff as strangers.' The paralysis only eases when Molly has departed and Synge is free to imagine: 'As soon as you were gone I began imagining that you would get into the wrong train and be carried off to Bray and then have no money to take you home. I saw you as plainly as possible standing in your long coat on the platform in Bray explaining your case to the station master and porters! It looked very funny. Dear heart I wish I had you here every day what a difference it would make' (CL I, 239-40). The final wish is poignant but unconvincing; one cannot imagine any suburban dwelling comfortably housing the pair of them. Synge only sees his fiancée plain when he is free to imagine her in scenarios which she has inspired.

When it comes to assessing Molly Allgood's side of the relationship, and her contribution to the collaboration, it is to the dramatic scenarios of *The Playboy of the Western World* and *Deirdre of the Sorrows* that one must turn. We do not have Molly's side of the correspondence: Synge appears to have destroyed her letters just before he entered the Elpis Nursing Home for the last time early in 1909. But there are a few surviving indications of her side of the exchange, notably the one word comments she has written over several over his letters: 'idiotic', 'appalling', 'peculiar' and 'reconcile' give the flavour. Her one surviving handwritten letter, scribbled across the top of one of his, suggests that she may have given as good as she got:

> you may stop your letters if you like, I dont care if I never heard from you or saw you again so there! & please dont let thoughts of me come into you your head when you are writing your play. It would be dreadful if your speeches were upset. I don't care a 'rap' for the theatre or anyone in it the pantomime season is coming on & I can easily get a shop; in fact I shall go out this afternoon & apply for one. (CL I, 218)

The context of the letter from Synge which provoked this angry response is revealing. He was in the toils of writing *The Playboy of the Western World* and used his absorption in the act of composition as the reason for not going to see Mrs. Allgood (presumably to win her around to the idea of marrying her younger daughter) and for putting off a walk with Molly herself:

> I am very bothered with my play again now, the Second Act has got out of joint in some way, and now its all in a mess. Dont be uneasy changling, everything is going on all right I think, I will go and see your mother soon, I dont much like the job so I keep putting it off. [...] I half thought of going in to town to take you for a walk but I thought it better to stick to my work. (CL I, 217; letter of 16 October 1906)

The conflict between life and art evident here also has the personal dimension of a spirited exchange between two argumentative individuals with strong personalities. This quality is no less apparent in many of the speeches between Christy Mahon and Pegeen Mike in the play on which Synge was working. The verbal snap of the fingers which

Molly delivers in her line 'I don't care a "rap" for the theatre or anyone in it' is reproduced in the speech with which Pegeen concludes her longest and bitterest row with Christy: 'if you vexed me a while since with your leaguing with the girls, I wouldn't give a thraneen for a lad hadn't a mighty spirit in him and a gamey heart' (IV, 113).

In the letter from Synge which Molly objected to, part of the conflict centres around the single greatest recurring motif in their letters: the deferral of their plans to marry. External reasons are not far to seek: the opposition of both families; the straitened financial circumstances the couple would inherit (both were living at home); the uncertainty surrounding Synge's health. But throughout the letters there is, even before the operation in Easter 1908 when it became fatally clear how ill he was, the sense of their marriage as an ever-receding goal. Synge finally gets around to telling his mother of their intention of marrying – doing so from England, since he fears his own violence in the face of her reaction – only to have Molly ask him to hold off from telling Lady Gregory. On the surface, his letters during the composition of *The Playboy of the Western World* never break with a positive and forward-looking view of their marriage; it is only in the composition of *Deirdre of the Sorrows* from September 1907 on that they take a more pessimistic turn. However, in the numerous drafts which Synge wrote for *The Playboy* and all of the different options he tried out in relation to the scenario – including in the earliest draft directly representing the argument between father and son – the one possibility that was never considered was that the play should conclude with the marriage of Christy and Pegeen. There was always to be a sundering.

I wish to consider this artistic decision never to have Christy and Pegeen marry in the light of *The Playboy*'s development of the woman and the tramp scenario. Henrik Ibsen followed *A Doll's House* with the even more shocking *Ghosts*, where Mrs. Alving had been prevailed upon as a younger woman to reverse her decision to leave her husband; the latter play dramatizes the tragic consequences of the life of hypocrisy she is then required to lead. Similarly, I would argue that *The Playboy of the Western World* is among other things a return upon the material and core situation of his 1902 play *The Shadow of the Glen* to test the hypothesis of what happens when the Irish woman behaves as Arthur Griffith would have her do and does *not* go away with the Tramp. The adulterous side of both the two Ibsen plays and of Synge's *Shadow* has been lost, since Pegeen is still single, though in many ways bound to her widowed father in the role of carer. The removal of the woman from a situation carrying with it a good deal of internal colonization and thwarted opportunities is no longer advanced as an uncomplicated possibility and cannot be realized through the figure of the play's Tramp character, Christy Mahon. In the light of what I have so far considered elsewhere in this book and earlier in this chapter, the promise that the wanderer holds out of a refuge through an imaginative interaction with nature can no longer be so readily sustained. When Christy indulges in descriptions of his earlier solitary forays into the natural world, where 'I'd be as happy as the sunshine of St. Martin's Day, watching the light passing the north or the patches of fog' (IV, 83), Pegeen in Act III advances the possibility that 'If I was your wife, I'd be along with you those nights, Christy Mahon', not taking her death but 'shelter[ing] easy in a narrow bush' (IV, 149). But the romantic vision cannot embrace the shared possibility of marriage. Scarcely are the words out of Pegeen's mouth than she immediately withdraws and cancels her marital hypothesis with the qualification that 'we're only talking maybe, for this would be a poor thatched place to hold a fine lad is the like of you'. Their shared existence in the natural world is denied because, paradoxically, they cannot continue to cohabit in their present environment. The prospect Christy holds out is only verbal, and cannot be translated fully or successfully into their present material conditions. The woman in this dramatic instance will *not* go away with the Tramp because, in a reversal of the earlier play, all he has to offer is a fine bit of talk.

It would be wrong, of course, too absolutely to identify Synge and Molly with Christy Mahon and Pegeen Mike. For one thing, Synge has given his own rarely used 'Christian' name, John, to the most craven character in the play, Shawneen Keogh (little John or Johnny). For another, Pegeen has to share space with the Widow Quin, who makes a determined set for Christy, despite the Oedipal implications explored in the eighth chapter of a woman who has not only killed her husband but buried her children. Is there a shadow here of the closeness between 'Johnnie' Synge and his widowed mother which persisted up until her death, less than six months before his own? Certain it is that, in Synge's last two plays, the natural world no longer offers the positive and uncomplicated alternative to the household community it did in his earlier work and that this alteration has profound bearings on relations between hero and heroine and the life they seek to lead together.

What a study of the relationship between J.M. Synge and Molly Allgood as textually represented in his letters suggests strongly is the extent to which he wrote his last play as a vehicle for his actress-fiancée. Here was a title role for her at last, one that would crown her rising through the ranks of the Abbey Theatre. The kind of play and choice of part could be seen as of a piece with Synge's efforts to 'improve' Molly, urging her away from trashy romantic novels and towards the world of poetry and art. It would also impress Yeats, a concern that emerges in the letters when Synge reports back to Molly on any positive remarks made about her acting by the great man, who was initially unimpressed by her performance as Nora Burke. Yeats had also denied that any one in the present Abbey company (i.e. an Irish Catholic actress who lacked the necessary 'passion') was up to the demands of playing the tragic queen. Accordingly, when he came to cast his own version of *Deirdre* some years earlier, Yeats had gone to great lengths (and expense) to import a Miss Darragh from England to play the tragic heroine. Synge was also responding to and rebutting Yeats's conception of the role by writing in an earthier, more vigorous style and by trying to imagine how these 'Saga' people lived, moved, thought and managed their day-to-day existence. These were qualities that he thought Molly would bring out in the role.

The parallel between the letters exchanged by Synge and Molly and the writing of the scenario of *Deirdre of the Sorrows* is much more exact than was the case with *The Playboy*. In one of those letters, he chides her that she must not be 'jealous' of the time and energy he is devoting to *Deirdre* because he is writing 'a part for YOU' (CL 2, 75). The same conflict between writing the play and advancing the marriage with Molly reemerges; but now the writing of the play is represented in explicitly sexual terms which indicate the degree of displacement at work: 'I am squirming and thrilling and quivering with the excitement of writing Deirdre and I *daren't* break the thread of composition by going out to look for digs and moving into them at this moment. [...] Let me get Deirdre out of danger – she may be safe in a week – then Marriage in God's name. Would you mind a *registry office* if that saves time?' (CL 2, 92; letter of 29 November 1907). But the composition of *Deirdre of the Sorrows* was not completed in a week; it continued through the sixteen months of life remaining and was left unfinished, though he continued to work on it to the very end. Nor were Synge and Molly ever to be married. In the play itself, Synge found a means of articulating the great divide – divisions of class, of age, of sensibility – which lay between himself and Molly, differences which he could not admit in the letters. The parallel between his life and his art rather leads him to distort the scenario's development, stressing the role of King Conchubor at the expense of the young lover, Naisi; the latter lacks all dramatic conviction, and is admitted by Synge to be the weakest part, while the former is full of passionate intensity. Naisi is the wanderer who enters Deirdre's cottage from the woods and who brings her away to an enchanted sojourn in Scotland/Alba. But Synge in striking contrast with his earlier plays can now find little identification with this figure from the outdoors, and the promise of nature is an empty one; the two lovers are soon on their way back to Ireland for Deirdre's final encounter with the aged High King.

In the play, the old woman Lavarcham points out to the King the inappropriateness of his proposal to marry Deirdre: 'it's a poor thing, Conchubor, to see a High King the way you are this day, prying after her needles and numbering her lines of thread' (IV, 189). Lavarcham has already spoken of the King's jealousy and of the quarrels that repeatedly blow up between Deirdre and himself. But what emerges most strikingly in the play of *Deirdre* is a factor never explicitly mentioned in the letters between Synge and Molly: the great age difference between the two lovers. The High King admits her youth as a major source of his attraction to Deirdre; and in their final scene together Deirdre declares that away from the councils of state, face to face with her, 'in this place you are an old man and a fool only' (IV, 265). The most painful letter in the Synge-Molly correspondence is one of the last, just before Christmas 1908. Synge had spoken to her earlier, when she was meeting Annie Horniman, of the importance of wearing masks. But one feels in the following that there are no more masks as he tells her how serious his condition is:

> I feel humiliated that I showed you so much of my weakness and emotion yesterday. I will not [be] trouble you any more with complaints about my health – you have taught me that I should not – but I think I owe it to myself to let you know that if I am so 'self-Pitiful' I have some reason to be so [and] as Dr. Parsons' report of my health, though uncertain, was much more unsatisfactory than I thought it well to tell you. I only tell you now because I am unable to bare the thought that you should think of me with the contempt I saw in your face yesterday. (CL 2, 236-7)

In Synge's next letter to Molly on the following day (25 December), the mask is back in place: he concentrates on the writing of *Deirdre of the Sorrows* and on the new parts he has added, principally a character, Owen, who is driven crazy for the love of Deirdre. But it is in the direction of the grave that both the letters and the play are moving, and Deirdre's reply may also speak for Molly Allgood: 'I'll say so near that grave we seem three lonesome people, and by a new made grave there's no man will keep brooding on a woman's lips' (IV, 253).

The last collaborative exchange between Synge and Molly was a poem he completed in October 1908. As he wrote to her:

> 'I did one new poem – that is partly your work – that he [Yeats] says is
> *Magnificent*
> I asked if I got sick and died would you
> With my black funeral go walking too,
> If you'd stand close to hear them talk and pray
> While I'm let down in that steep bank of clay.
> And No, you said, for if you saw a crew
> Of living idiots, pressing round that new
> Oak-Coffin – they alive, I dead beneath
> That board – you'd rave and rend them with your teeth.
> (CL 2, 204-5) (I, 64)

Synge's poem has added violence to Molly's original reply: 'No, for I could not bear you dead and others living on' (CL 2, 205). But the same sentiment she uttered remains at the core of the poem, emerging from this dialogue between the two lovers, with the frank admission that one of them is not going to survive. *Deirdre of the Sorrows* was staged at the Abbey Theatre on 13 January 1910; Synge's death had provoked a most extensive and unusual collaboration. The play had been assembled and edited by Yeats, Lady Gregory and Molly Allgood; the production was co-directed by the two women; and, as Synge had always intended, Molly played Deirdre. In the play's final moments, it is the woman who has the last word in some of the greatest lines the playwright had ever written, the two speeches beginning 'Draw a little back with the squabbling of fools when I am broken up with misery' and 'I have put away sorrow like a shoe that is worn out and muddy' (IV, 267). The Tramp and his swaggering speeches give way to the enfeebled, aged figure of Conchubar, who is 'hard set to see the way before' him (IV, 269) and is led off stage by Lavarcham.

No letters were needed for Synge's final five weeks in the Elpis Nursing Home. Molly attended him every day except for a week's touring in Edinburgh. This enabled a degree of intimacy and access which they had never formerly enjoyed; and made her an invaluable oral resource for Yeats as he began the mythologizing of Synge who 'dying chose the living world for text'.[11] The most important difference between the two writers had emerged in a letter written by Synge to Molly on the death of his mother which gave what may well be his most considered view on the life-art debate which this chapter has considered:

> As you are not here I feel as if I ought to keep writting [sic] to you all
> the time though tonight I cannot write all that I am feeling. People like
> Yeats who sneer at old fashioned goodness and steadiness in women

seem to want to rob the world of what is most sacred in it. [...] I am afraid to think how terrible my loneliness would be tonight if I had not found you. It makes me rage when I think of the people who go on as if art and literature and writing were the first thing in the world. There is nothing so great and sacred as what is most simple in life. (CL, 221; letter of 9 November 1908)

---

1 Molly Allgood acted under the stage name of Máire O'Neill, to avoid confusion with her older sister Sara Allgood, who also acted at the Abbey Theatre.

2 For a biographical account of Molly and Sara Allgood, see Elizabeth Coxhead, *Daughters of Erin: Five Women of the Irish Renascence* (Gerrards Cross: Colin Smythe, 1965), pp. 167-224.

3 All biographical details are drawn from Ann Saddlemyer's annotations to the two-volume *Collected Letters*, unless otherwise indicated.

4 Vivian Mercier, *Modern Irish Literature: Sources and Founders*, ed Eilis Dillon (Oxford: Clarendon Press, 1994), p. 203.

5 Angela Bourke, *The Burning of Bridget Cleary: A True Story* (London: Pimlico, 1999), p. 107.

6 Angela Bourke, *The Burning of Bridget Cleary*, p. 177.

7 Vivian Mercier, *Modern Irish Literature*, p. 209.

8 Vivian Mercier, *Modern Irish Literature*, p. 211.

9 These scenes are memorably dramatized in the novel by Joseph O'Connor about the relationship between J.M. Synge and Molly Allgood, *Ghost Light* (London: Michael Joseph, 2011).

10 W.J. McCormack, *Fool of the Family: A Life of J.M. Synge* (London: Weidenfeld and Nicolson, 2000), p. 291. McCormack's biography provides a valuable and detailed account of the relationship between Synge and Molly.

11 'In Memory of Major Robert Gregory', *The Variorum Edition of the Plays of W.B. Yeats*, edited by Peter Allt and Russell K. Alspach (New York: Macmillan, 1940), p. 324.

10 | Friel and Synge: Towards a Theatrical Language

One of the most valuable features of Richard Pine's 1990 study of Brian Friel is the access its author gained to this (along with Beckett) most reticent of latter-day twentieth-century Irish playwrights. The statements from Friel featured in the text, credited in the footnotes as deriving from 'conversation with the author', have clearly been elicited in response to questions from Pine. One of these concerns John Millington Synge and presumably derives from a question concerning Friel's views of his illustrious dramatic predecessor. Friel responded by saying that 'we have not yet discovered a language appropriate to the theatre in this country – as singularly appropriate as Synge's invention'.[1] The statement is complex and double-edged. On the one hand, it pays Synge a high compliment and chimes with Friel's other claim (also cited by Pine) that 'apart from Synge, all our dramatists have pitched their voice for English acceptance and recognition'.[2] On the other hand, it somehow manages to place Synge to one side – or in the past – and deny him a relevant role in any ongoing quest for a contemporary theatrical language.

If language is considered purely and exclusively at the level of speech, this may well be true. A direct imitation of Synge's speech, for purposes other than those of parody (as in Stewart Parker's *Northern Star*), is clearly out of the question. Any contemporary playwright adopting a dramatic speech in English closely modelled on the syntax and speech patterns of Irish cannot help but sound Syngean. In the main, throughout his plays, Friel has opted for a syntactically restrained, relatively neutral speech in which Irishisms are consciously introduced as an element within the overall dramatic and linguistic framework. An important instance would be the careful handling of the placenames to dramatize the erosion and loss of the Irish language in

Translations (1980); or the introduction of a more obviously 'Irish' dramatic language in Friel's plays when the tone is self-consciously parodic, as it is in so many of Gar Private's remarks to his alter-ego in *Philadelphia, Here I Come!* (1964):

> By God, Gar, aul sod, it was a sore hoke on the aul prestige,
> eh? Between ourselves, aul son, [...] between you and me and the wall,
> as the fella says, has it left a deep scar on the aul
> skitter of a soul, eh?[3]

The question of an appropriate language in relation to a major precursor like Synge is first raised by Friel not in one of his plays but in a short story, 'Mr. Sing My Heart's Delight'. Synge's name resounds throughout Friel text and, while the spelling may be different, the pronunciation is the same. For as Synge wrote to his German translator, Max Meyerfeld, about the origins of his name: 'My Christian names are John Millington, my family were originally called Millington, and Queen Elisabeth is said to have changed their name to "Synge" they sang so finely. Synge is, of course, pronounced "sing"' (CL I, 129). In Friel's short story the title character is a 'packman' or travelling salesman from the Punjab marooned in Donegal. His name emerges when the child narrator's grandmother questions him as follows:

> 'Tell me, Packman,' she called to him from her work, 'What do they call you, what?' 'Singh,' he said. 'What?' 'Singh,' he repeated. 'Man, but that's a strange name. Sing. Sing,' she said, feeling the sound on her tongue. 'I'll tell you what I'll call you, Packman,' she went on, 'I'll call you Mr. Sing My Heart's Delight! That's what I'll call you – a good, big mouthful. Mr. Sing My Heart's Delight!'[4]

The linguistic evidence of the above makes the identification between Mr. Sing and Mr. Synge more likely, with the Granny's translation of the Indian outsider's evocative name into a speech which is 'as fully flavoured as a nut or apple' (IV, 54). But the cultural contours of the story also bring it into a recognizably Syngean landscape. For as the narrator tells us early on: 'A constant source of fun was Granny's English. Gaelic was her first tongue and she never felt at ease in English which she shouted and spat out as if it were getting in her way.' In the ensuing exchange, the Granny turns to the narrator to translate – 'What is he saying, son, what? Tell me what it is he's saying' – since, as she puts it to the Indian, 'Mister, I don't speak English too good, Mister'.[5] But then again neither does he. What the Grandmother does speak is an English closely modelled on the syntactic, and in particular the verbal structures, of the Irish language ('let the sleep come over you for an hour'[6]) – a speech resembling most of all the music of Mr. Synge. And in this encounter between a male tinker coming to a rural house and the female insider longing for escape and a more exotic locale, there are clear echoes of Synge's plays.

For the first ten years or so of his career, Brian Friel alternated between writing plays and short stories. His eventual decision in the nineteen sixties to give up the short story and concentrate solely on the theatre has generally been sensed to derive from the recognition that he might equal but would never outdo Frank O'Connor and Sean O'Faolain in the former genre; whereas in the drama, with the ground-breaking precedent of *Philadelphia, Here I Come!*, there was evidence to suggest that he might do much to advance the possibilities of Irish theatre. In the decades since, Brian Friel has both kept faith with the medium of theatre as a form and has been a major figure in reinterpreting the terms in which we think about that theatre. In doing so, he has I think drawn upon Synge. I do not mean this solely or primarily as an influence. Indeed, the evidence and dangers of the influence are only too apparent in 'Mr. Sing My Heart's Delight', especially in the lines spoken by the Granny. The irony is that this short story, even as he abandons the form for the drama, evidences the risk Friel runs by becoming exclusively a playwright – that Synge will prove too overwhelming an influence. Friel puts himself on his guard, however, as he develops his dramatic practice, and never more so than on the score of speech, as I mentioned at the outset. But if his dramatic career can be seen as a rejection of Synge as the source of the language his people speak, I believe that he continues to draw on Synge as a profound theatrical resource in ways I would like to pursue in this chapter.

Where Friel and Synge are at one, I believe, is in their determination to devise 'a language appropriate to the theatre in this country'. They seek to achieve this through the degree and kind of theatrical self-consciousness they bring to bear on the subject-matter and situations of their plays. Neither dramatist works with pre-existing models or forms, realizing as they both do the colonial implications of imposing a foreign sense of order on native subjects. Each seeks to elicit a formal procedure from the material on which they are working, one which will best serve to articulate what lies hidden within while seeking no further justification. In the short story already discussed, there is much that anticipates Friel's later work as a playwright: the exotic outsider arriving in Donegal; the child-narrator; the two-way difficulties of communication for two non-native speakers of English. But there is also much that recalls Synge and suggests shared common ground: the stranger who arrives at a country cottage and offers the woman living within a sense of other possibilities; the acute sense of distance and alienation conveyed by these lonely lives. What both playwrights are seeking is a theatrical syntax in which these obsessions can be explored. That Synge was concerned in each of his plays to initiate such a procedure has much to do with his ongoing interest and relevance to contemporary Irish playwrights; that Friel regards the project of developing such a language of Irish theatre as far from complete is evidenced by his remarks quoted at the start and by his continuing restlessness and experimentation as a dramatist. I intend looking at the father-son relationship in *Philadelphia, Here I Come!*; the interface between truth and fiction in 1979's *Faith Healer*; and some aspects of two more recent Friel plays where Synge's presence has been widely recognized, *Dancing at Lughnasa* (1990) and *Molly Sweeney* (1994).

The father-son relationship is as absolutely central to Friel's *Philadelphia* as it is to Synge's *The Playboy of the Western World*. And yet is the father-son theme not equally to be found in other Irish genres, notably the fiction of Joyce, as an abiding concern in a society where questions of authority and legitimacy remain problematic? What brings the father-son relationship into acute connection in Synge and Friel is the way in which both authors have chosen to address the subject through an exploration of the medium of drama itself. Specifically, what *Philadelphia* and *Playboy* share is the dramatic situation in which the son undergoes a negative transformation in the presence of the father. In Friel's opening scene with the housekeeper Madge, the twenty-five-year old Gar O'Donnell is relatively easygoing, bantering with her and doing a brief song and dance. This as yet gives no indication of the deep divisions within his psyche. But the contrast with his behaviour when his father S.B. O'Donnell enters a little later could not be more acute: the hitherto loquacious Gar at once becomes surly, monosyllabic, stammering, unable to answer his father's question. We begin to divine why the play requires not one but two Gareth O'Donnells to represent this dilemma: 'The two Gars, PUBLIC GAR and PRIVATE GAR, are two views of the one man. PUBLIC GAR is the Gar that people see, talk to, talk about. PRIVATE GAR is the unseen man, the man within, the conscience, the *alter ego*, the secret thoughts, the id' (27). Another way of putting this is to say that, in theatrical terms, Private Gar has been conjured up in an effort to fill the vacuum, the pervasive silence between father and son.

In the use of this brilliant dramatic device, Friel has built on Synge's representation of relations between Christy Mahon and *his* father. The Christy who enters the Mayo shebeen is a relatively neutral character, quiet and diffident. But by the middle of Act Two, encouraged by the local villagers to expand and develop the tale of his father-slaying, Christy is in full confident flight:

> From this out I'll have no want of company when all sorts is bringing me their food and clothing [*he swaggers to the door, tightening his belt*], the way they'd set their eyes upon a gallant orphan cleft his father with one blow to the breeches belt. [*He opens the door, then staggers back.*] [...] It's the walking spirit of my murdered da! [...] Where'll I hide my poor body from that ghost of hell? (IV,119)

Such is the degree of instability induced by Old Mahon's appearance that Christy comes to seem virtually two different people, though it is in the interests of Widow Quin to exaggerate the differences: the stuttering, squinting loony of Mahon's or the only Playboy of the Western World. Christy's description to Pegeen of his earlier life with his father is the one area of his narrative activities which he refuses to romanticize: he has led a life of unimaginative, unvarying drudgery, 'toiling, moiling, digging, dodging from the dawn till dusk' (83). Having escaped to the relative freedom of the Mayo shebeen, he has not only developed his expressive powers until he begs comparison with 'Owen Roe O'Sullivan or the poets of the Dingle Bay' (81) but goes on to outdo all others in the mule-race on the strand and sports of all sorts. Gar O'Donnell's life with his father is also characterized by unremitting drudgery, minimal exchanges about gutting fish and rearranging sacks of flour, punctuated by long silences. In the relative freedom of Gar's imagination, there is a much greater degree of verbal and physical expressiveness; the flow of talk between Private and Public is more rapid, colourful and heightened; and Gar accomplishes a number of heroic feats in the imaginary zone of his bedroom, not only scoring the winning goal for the Ballybeg team but simultaneously conducting and playing in an orchestra.

Gar O'Donnell's fantasies are projected into a place of exile: the USA to which he emigrates the following day. But they are enacted simultaneously on the stage for us as an act of pure theatre. Christy Mahon's freedom is developed in explicitly theatrical terms, with the other characters responding as an audience to his histrionic skills: 'That's a grand story./ He tells it lovely' (103). The problem within the fiction of both plays is one of fusion, of reintegration or reconciliation of the protagonists' contradictory personae. In the face of Gar Public's last-ditch effort to address his father on the memory of a childhood outing, to see if S.B. can recall and hence validate the experience, Gar Private recedes and almost disappears; but when his father refuses to confirm the details of Gar's narrative and so condemns him to solipsism, the alter-ego returns with a vengeance. The delight with which he does so, crowing over the defeat of Gar's hopes as illusory, suggests the less than benign aspects of this relentless joker; and the two personae remain stubbornly unreconciled in the play's closing moments. When old Mahon returns from the dead for a second time, Christy insists on taking the upper hand and they exit together to 'go romancing through a romping lifetime' (173). But Christy loses Pegeen Mike and leaves without her, as Gar O'Donnell loses his beloved Kate Doogan. Accordingly, the conditions which prevailed at the outset of each play, in Michael James Flaherty's Mayo shebeen and S.B. O'Donnell's Donegal shop, remain untransformed.

The chapter on *The Playboy of the Western World* highlighted the proliferation of fathers and the absence of mothers. The same holds true for the dramatic landscape of *Philadelphia, Here I Come!* The relationship between Gar and his father stands at the centre of Friel's play. But it is ramified by the presence of other father-figures. Two such enter from the surrounding community: the schoolteacher Boyle and the Canon. The fact that Gar's mother had gone out with Master Boyle before she married S.B. makes clear the extent to which Gar regards him as a surrogate father – a man whose encouragement of literature and self-expression makes him something of a mentor to his former pupil. But Master Boyle is a failure who drinks too much and his clumsy effort at embracing Gar is resisted by the young man. Canon Mick O'Boyle is another patriarchal, 'moulder of the mind' (52), whose primary activity seems to be making asinine conversation and who is accused by Gar's alter-ego of having failed in what should have been his vocation: 'you could translate all this loneliness, this groping, this dreadful bloody buffoonery into Christian terms that will make this life bearable for us all. And yet you don't say a word. Why, Canon? [...] Isn't this your job? – to translate? Why don't you speak, then?' (88). And there is Senator Doogan, father of the woman Gar intends to marry. In a crucial flashback scene, we witness Gar meeting and being daunted by his future father-in-law at the latter's comfortable bourgeois home. Gar comes to speak of Kate and himself and their hopes of marrying but, in the face of the social aspirations which Senator Doogan voices on behalf of his family and daughter, Gar's tongue fails him and he flees. When compared to these surrogates, S.B. O'Donnell may finally reassert his claims to paternity for, as Private puts it to Public, 'when you think of a bugger like that, you want to get down on your knees and thank God for aul Screwballs' (45).

If both dramatic environments are overrun with fathers, Synge's and Friel's plays are equally bereft of mothers. No reference is made to any mother for Pegeen Mike; she has clearly taken on that role within the Flaherty household herself, domestically caring for Michael James. Likewise, we hear virtually nothing about a mother for Christy Mahon, except a passing reference by old Mahon which suggests she died in childbirth: 'it was I did tend him from his hour of birth' (IV, 137). So, too, has Gar's beautiful young mother, three days after her son's birth; the sequence of events suggests consequence, and is a huge source of guilt on Gar's part. The housekeeper Madge is clearly the closest thing Gar has to a source of maternal affection, and she is the one who most prompts a sense of regret about his leaving. But a more complicated maternal figure emerges in the flashback through the figure of Aunt Lizzie, the sole survivor of his mother and her four sisters, with Gar as the only child of the five. This situation is to be reworked more positively in Friel's *Dancing at Lughnasa*; but in *Philadelphia, Here I Come!* Gar's agreement to emigrate to his relatives in the USA concludes with his succumbing to the embrace of his Aunt Lizzie, a scene with clear Oedipal overtones.

One half of the Oedipus scenario is foregrounded in Synge's play about father-slaying, as Chapter Eight examined. But mothers, actual or surrogate, are hard to find. The one suggestion of the mother complex is adduced by Christy as a further motive for killing a father who would insist on marrying him to a physically grotesque widow: '"I won't wed her," says I, "when all know she did suckle me for six weeks when I came into the world"' (IV, 103). This line sets up an association in the body of the play itself with the Widow Quin, a better-looking widow, to be sure, but one who is identified not only with slaying her man but with burying her children. The whiff of incest which attaches itself to the marrying of first cousins, and which requires a special dispensation from the Courts of Rome, is even stronger in the sexual pursuit of Christy Mahon by the Widow Quin and stands as the single most potent if unstated reason why the play will never permit them to marry; this is an important dimension to the Oedipal argument pursued in Chapter Eight. But the Widow Quin's associations with maternity, once identified, show it as pervasive and threatening throughout the play. Christy and Pegeen hope to marry and, in the words of Michael James, '[produce] a score of grandsons' (IV, 157). Gar O'Donnell, in his love talk with Kate Doogan, imagines himself 'the father of fourteen children' (43). But both weddings are baulked as the plays deviate from the traditional endings of romantic comedy: the marriage of the young generation by which the older society undergoes criticism and renewal. In their withholding of marriage from their respective male protagonists, Synge and Friel throw us back on their criticisms of the society itself.

By this early stage in his playwriting career, Brian Friel had not produced in Kate Doogan a character to equal Pegeen Mike, in the way that the complex double character of Gar O'Donnell genuinely invites comparison with Christy Mahon. There would, of course, be the foregrounding of female energies in *Dancing at Lughnasa*. But the superb characterizations of Madge the housekeeper and Aunt Lizzie in the early play show that the question of Friel's success or failure in characterization cannot be divided up crudely along gender lines. There is also a tendency throughout Friel's career for him to go back and reexplore some facet of an earlier play whose expression he thinks he can better. With regard to the characterization of a young woman from a settled household who is wooed by a wandering male figure with little or no money but a good line in talk, Friel was to produce one of his most powerful female characters in *Faith Healer*'s Grace Hardy. In associating the figure of Grace with that of Synge's Pegeen Mike, I am responding to the fruitful suggestion by Richard Kearney that Friel's *Faith Healer* can be seen as a kind of sequel to *The Playboy of the Western World*, showing 'how Synge's Pegeen Mike might have mused to herself had she left her homeland of Mayo and taken to the roads with her story-telling playboy'.[7] There is, I think, a deliberate echo of the most famous closing line in the Anglo-Irish dramatic canon – 'Oh my grief, I've lost him surely. I've lost the only playboy of the western world' (IV, 173) – in the closing lines of Grace's monologue: "O my God I'm in such a mess – how I want that door to open – how I want that man to come across that floor and put his white hands on my face and still this tumult inside me – [...] O my God I don't know if I can go on without his sustenance.'[8] Pegeen's brief closing self-lament is amplified by Friel into Grace's twelve-page monologue, looking back in the wake of her husband's death into the memory of their shared life on the roads. Most of it has been anything but romantic. The play's third character recalls 'the bitterness and the fighting and the wettings and the bloody van and the smell of the primus stove and the bills and the booze and the dirty halls and that hassle that we never seemed to be able to rise above' (367). Much of Frank and Grace's life reads like an extended gloss on the young wife Nora's realistic response in Synge's *The Shadow of the Glen* to the Tramp's romantic evocation of their shared life on the roads: 'I'm thinking it's myself will be wheezing that time with lying down under the Heavens when the night is cold, but you've a fine bit of talk, stranger, and it's with yourself I'll go' (III, 57).

The promise held out by the self-delighting artifice of the stranger's 'talk' is matched in *Faith Healer* by those rare moments of transcendence in which Frank Hardy is able to make good on his promise of a cure. Teddy the manager cites one such, the night in Wales when ten people came looking for a miracle: 'There's two kids, I know; one of them has this great lump on his cheek. And there's a woman with crutches.[...] And there's a young [blind] man [...] and an old man, a farmer – he's lame – he's helped in by his daughter' (358). In Synge's play Christy Mahon works his own brand of faith-healing amidst the physically and psychically maimed community of County Mayo. As Pegeen scornfully remarks:

> I wouldn't bother with this place where you'll meet none but Red
> Linahan, has a squint in his eye, and Patcheen is lame in his heel, or
> the mad Mulrannies were driven from California and they lost in their
> wits. (IV, 59)

Christy Mahon manages to cure his own squint and to give Pegeen Mike a sense of hope; Frank Hardy's great gift was not only to take 'away whatever it was was wrong with them, but [to give] them some great content in themselves as well' (359). This is no less true for his wife Grace and his manager Teddy than the physically debilitated people on whom Frank more directly works.

But that need is two-fold. For Frank Hardy's faith-healing, like Christy Mahon's story-telling, is 'a craft without an apprenticeship, a ministry without responsibility, a vocation without a ministry' (333) and, one might add, a religion in need of believers, a theatre in search of an audience. Both plays find their origins in a primary, and primal, act of story-telling and do not develop as drama without keeping faith with those origins. The story Christy tells is initially bare and unpromising: 'I just riz the loy and let fall the edge of it on the ridge of his skull' (IV, 73). But that monosyllabic line undergoes a considerable degree of artifice and expansion, primarily at the promptings of Pegeen Mike. She is the one Christy seeks to claim, the ultimate guarantor of the truth of his storytelling, and the one most sceptical of the claims of language. As she remarks as early as Act One: 'You're only saying it. You did nothing at all (IV, 71). When Teddy opens their doors on the night of Frank's miraculous performance in Wales, he has first to admit a sceptical Grace, who spits scorn in the face of the Celtic 'genius' (358).

The question of authority is one that haunts both plays. Synge and Friel's characters are far from the metropolitan centres and display an ambivalence towards the forms of written authentication those imperial centres can offer. Synge's characters are free in their speech but gesture at the permission to sell drink inscribed in white letters above the shebeen door and the written dispensation to marry from the Courts of Rome. Friel's faith healer at one point takes from his pocket a newspaper account of the 'truly remarkable event' (370) and ostentatiously tears it up; Grace describes her husband to the doctor as an 'artist' but only finally believes it when she sees him writing it down. It is primarily in the presence of Pegeen Mike that Christy for most of the play can believe in his transformed possibilities; and Frank needs Grace to be present even as he looks beyond her. Christy stakes his authority on an act of violent murder which turns out to be fictive; Frank and his two partners' narratives converge on an act of violent murder in which he is dismembered. Richard Kearney accordingly reads *Faith Healer*

> as a cautionary tale in response to the romantic optimism of Synge's *Playboy*. For if the belief in the power of a lie made Christy into a likely gaffer in the end of all, it makes Frank into a mutilated corpse.[9]

The greatest gap of all in both plays, the most unsettling for an audience to react and adjust to, is the radical disjunction between Frank and Christy as liars or charlatans and as quasi-religious truth-tellers. This nagging question is bound up with the intense and self-conscious theatricality of *Playboy* and *Faith Healer*. The fiction of the stage space repeatedly gives way before the actuality of performance. As Frank, Grace and Teddy directly confront the audience in the theatre with their stories and ask in turn to be believed, they recreate the conditions of performance in which the faith-healing occurred, in all those small Welsh and Scottish village halls, with Teddy's record-player turning out 'The Way You Look Tonight', Grace at her table with the takings, and Frank shifting from private to public persona in the hope that the act will work. Synge's *Playboy* makes of its cast of characters an on-stage audience who listen to Christy's narrative claims with increasing credulity, until those claims are tested in succeeding acts. The volatility of the onstage characters would appear to have transmitted itself to the offstage audience in the Abbey Theatre in its first performances. The most open question in both plays is: how much faith do we repose in the truth of theatrical storytelling? As Richard Pine has put it: 'The "power of a lie" is, in Friel's terms, a pretence, a fiction of theatre, which persuades his audience of a certain truth which they themselves can act out in their lives.'[10]

In two of Friel's plays of the nineteen nineties, *Dancing at Lughnasa* and *Molly Sweeney*, the themes announce themselves as more overtly Syngean. With *Lughnasa* the depiction of a traditional Irish society in which Catholicism or Christianity is only the most recent layer covering over a profound paganism has long been associated with Synge's representations in his plays and prose writings, as the first chapter of this book demonstrated. In *Molly Sweeney* the restoring of sight to a blind person in a miraculous cure which leaves them arguably worse off than before cannot but recall Synge's treatment of the theme in *The Well of the Saints*. Again, this is not merely or even a question of influence. By this late stage of his career, Friel's own dramatic landscape is firmly established and is best evoked by the recurrent place name 'Ballybeg'. Friel's confidence in his own dramatic terrain is at least one reason for the more explicit appropriation and treatment of Syngean landmarks.

It is often the case in Friel's preparation for writing a play that he draws on several prose works from anthropological, linguistic or historic areas of study. The most well-known case is *Translations*, where much analysis has been carried out of the dramatic use he made of George Steiner on translation, J.H. Andrews on the Ordnance Survey, etc.[11] In the case of *Dancing at Lughnasa* an obvious and frequently cited pretext is Maire O'Neill's classic study, *The Festival of Lughnasa* (1961); but while that scholarly volume may have contributed some details to the account of the Lughnasa rituals in the play, the debt is slight. Of greater account, I would contend, is Synge's prose study, *The Aran Islands*, which gives a fuller representation than any of his plays of the stubborn hold pagan practices had on the Irish imagination. Over and over again in his encounters with the Aran Islanders, Synge's interest gravitates towards the body of imaginative beliefs dating from preChristian times, 'the wild mythology that is accepted on the islands' (II, 54). As discussed in the first chapter, this discernible bias led to charges that Synge wilfully ignored the deeply held Catholicism of the islanders, downplaying its central role in their lives in favour of exaggerating the remnants of a few prior superstitions. This was the charge levelled by Daniel Corkery in *Synge and Anglo-Irish Literature*, published in the same decade as that in which Friel *Dancing at Lughnasa* is set. The same charge could be levelled at Friel's play where Kate, alone of the five Mundy sisters, advocates an orthodox Catholicism that would be seen as the 1930s norm. Corkery made 'The Religious Consciousness of the People' one of the three distinguishing factors of the Irish people, but went on to interpret this exclusively as

Catholicism.[12] Synge's counter-evidence would be his account of the keening which attended the burial of one of the islanders with 'each old woman [...] seem[ing] possessed for the moment with a wild ecstasy of grief' (II, 74). This is the same wild ecstasy that is released in the Mundy sisters during their celebrated dance. When the dance ceases, Kate urges them to act and think with 'propriety'; during the dance itself, she has finally succumbed by 'suddenly leap[ing] to her feet, fling[ing] her head back, and emit[ting] a loud 'Yaaaah'[13].

A further irony is that Synge was not the first of his family to visit the islands. As discussed in Chapter One, he had been preceded there in 1851 by his uncle, the Reverend Alexander Synge, the first Protestant missionary to the Aran Islands, who wrote: 'I get on with the people so far very well, but how it will be when we begin to attack their bad ways & religion etc. I don't know.'[14] If the Reverend Alexander Synge came to the Aran Islands to convert, as I remarked earlier, his nephew John travelled there fifty years later to be converted. This reversal is not unlike what has happened to the missionary Father Jack in Friel's play; and young Johnny caused no less grief to his loving evangelical mother for going over to the Irish nationalists, as she saw it, than her brother Jack does to sister Kate by his admiring talk of the Ryangans. The parallel is the more exact because we have only Jack's word and reenactments for those pagan practices rather than the testimony of the natives themselves. Likewise, Synge's prose work now foregrounds and presents the pagan rituals and folktales of the native Aran Islanders which proved to him the most compelling.

There is, however, a significant detail within one of Synge's plays, *The Shadow of the Glen*, that matches up with an important feature of *Dancing at Lughnasa* in its treatment of Catholicism and paganism. It leads me to a consideration of the setting of the play. The cottage kitchen to which the women in Friel's play are most confined is too realistic and dominant a feature of Irish social life to be particularly associated with Synge. The parallel begins to emerge when the inside and the outside are contrasted – the world of order and security which Kate is struggling to maintain contrasted with all those outside forces which threaten social and sexual anarchy. The locale which comes to represent these forces in *Dancing at Lughnasa* is inscribed in the phrase, 'the back hills'. It is to the 'back hills' that, the young and simple Rose tells her sisters, the sexually predatory Danny Bradley proposes taking her; it is also in the 'back hills' that the Lughnasa ritual is celebrated:

> That young Sweeney boy from the back hills – the boy who was anointed – his trousers didn't catch fire, as Rose said. They were doing some devilish thing with a goat – some sort of sacrifice for the Lughnasa Festival. (56)

The phrase 'the back hills' resounds throughout Synge's *The Shadow of the Glen* and with precisely the same connotations of socially and sexually aberrant behaviour. The Tramp first introduces the term in association with the irrational and insanity: 'If myself was easily afeard, I'm telling you, it's long ago I'd have been locked into the Richmond Asylum, or maybe have run up into the back hills with nothing on me but an old shirt, and been eaten with crows the like of Patch Darcy – the Lord have mercy on him – in the year that's gone' (III, 37). The verbal emergence of the 'back hills' in Synge's play always occurs in relation to the enigmatic figure of Patch Darcy, as it does in *Lughnasa* in relation to Danny Bradley and the Sweeney boy. A ground of sympathy is established between Nora and the Tramp by their attitude towards the renegade Darcy. His name provokes sexual jealousy in Nora's lover Michael, since she herself admits that Darcy would 'always look in here and he passing up or passing down' (III, 39). Nora's husband and lover both condemn Nora's 'queer talk', 'the like of that talk you do hear from men, and they after being a great while on the back hills' (III, 49). The suggestion is that the 'talk' and the association are barred to Nora on the grounds both of class and gender. Patch Darcy is a ghost in a play where the husband pretends to be dead but proves all too real; his suggestive presence troubles and disturbs the complacent pieties of the Burke household as the naming of Danny Bradley and the Sweeney boy does that of the Mundys.

The symbolic landscape of *Dancing at Lughnasa* also briefly adverts to a well. When Chris Mundy and Gerry Evans think of making love, he proposes that they go to the well; when Rose goes missing, it is one of the places to be searched. Clearly, there is more than water to be got from it. The well in Irish society is one of those nodal points where symbolic force accumulated and which persisted in the conversion from a pagan to a Christian society. As this book has examined, the well has also served as something of an imaginative touchstone and resource in the Irish theatre of the last century, not only in Synge's *The Well of the Saints* but also Yeats's *At the Hawk's Well,* as Samuel Beckett was only too aware. In his play *Translations* Friel considers what kind of knowledge it is best to preserve and communicate by bringing the fraught act of translation to bear on an empty well called Tobair Vree (the well of Brian).[15] When Friel decided to write a play about a miraculous cure of blindness, the most relevant precursor proved to be Synge's play.

Synge's *The Well of the Saints* and Friel's *Molly Sweeney* both follow the progress of a blind person or persons whose sight is restored to them and who undergo a process of disillusionment and disorientation before their sight departs for good and they fiercely embrace their newfound condition. That linear development is not only followed in the plays but intensified and dwelt upon: the state in which they first exist, the world that they inhabit and the sights they see in their blindness, the hopes and excitement that attend the prospect of a cure, the pain that accompanies the restoration of their sight, the disorientation that follows, and the (for the audience) disturbing arbitrariness and wilfulness that attends their final state. But the intensity in part derives from our knowledge that the progress will not be a straightforward one; it proceeds from the double vision with which the audience views the miraculous cure. In Friel's play the event is narrated in retrospect through the monologues of all three characters, as it was in *Faith Healer*. Molly, her husband Frank and surgeon Mr. Rice view the proceedings not only from their own perspective, but from an isolated and alienated position very much at odds with the prospect of unified celebration held out by the cure itself. In Synge's play what the blind couple believe about their own physical appearance is so much at odds with the visible reality and the stories they are fed by the community that we realize the play will dramatize the gap between the two perceptions.

The characters in the two plays match up fairly exactly.[16] Molly Sweeney is in the position of Martin and Mary Doul, the blind person who has occupied a position since childhood in which she comes to trust. As the surgeon Mr. Rice notes, she is marked by her assurance and independence: 'I liked her. I liked her calm and her independence.'[17] As Timmy the smith likewise notes, Martin and Mary, though blind, are 'not mournful at all, but talking out straight with a full voice, and making game with them that likes it' (III, 89). There is a close parallel between Mr. Rice and the Saint; both bring the possibility of a cure and are self-interested on the score of its results. The Saint has drawn his water from a pagan well, but is anxious to underscore the debt owed to a Christian God for 'the gift of sight'. Mr. Rice operates as a surgeon but has been cast out from the high-flying circle of globetrotting professionals and is looking for a 'miraculous' cure to restore him to professional esteem, to redeem his sense of failure: 'if, oh my God, if by some miracle [I could] pull it off perhaps...' (460). Molly's husband Frank has only recently married her. In his blundering and limited good will, that ultimately turns self-interested and abandons Molly, he seems at one with the seeing community and characters like Timmy the smith in the Synge play with regard to Martin and Mary Doul.

Neither couple has any children. This fact is made much of in the mutual recriminations exchanged between Martin and Mary when they first see each other: 'I wouldn't rear a crumpled whelp the like of you. It's many a woman is married with finer than yourself should be praising God if she's no child' (III, 99). In his disillusionment, Martin compares their earlier condition to that of deluded children, speaking of that 'bad black day when I was roused up and found I was the like of the little children do be listening to the stories of an old woman' (III, 113). Molly's condition, in her opening speech, is linked to her childhood and to the lessons in interpreting her experience linguistically which she derived from her father. The cured blind people undergo an enforced maturation when they confront the actual and find it degraded and sullied. The flowers called 'Baby Blue Eyes' in which Molly has delighted, although she names and identifies them correctly, turn out to be not 'nearly as pretty as buttercups. Weren't pretty at all' (497). When the blind couple wake from their dream, it's to a perception of 'the cold, and the thatch dripping maybe, and the starved ass braying in the yard' (III, 113).

The blind characters refuse in Synge's play to be cured a second time and are castigated by Timmy the smith as 'choosing a wilful blindness'(143). But Martin claims that they possess 'finer sight than the lot of you' as they look up 'in our own minds into a grand sky, and seeing lakes, and broadening rivers' (III, 141). Where their earlier state can be described as innocence, in that they believed in the literal truth of their visions, what they are describing now is a way of seeing, one which he defends at the end of the play: 'I'm thinking it's a good right ourselves have to be sitting blind, hearing a soft wind turning round the little leaves of the spring and feeling the sun' (III, 149). Molly Sweeney, in her last monologue, confirms that she physically sees nothing at all now, whereas earlier she could at least discriminate between light and shade. She now describes herself as living in her 'borderline country' (509), an imagined place she has described earlier as 'a borderline between fantasy and reality' (500). But the distinction is one that no longer concerns her, 'that what I think I see may be fantasy or indeed what I take to be imagined may very well be real– what's Frank's term? – external reality. Real – imagined – fact – fiction – fantasy – reality –

there it seems to be' (509). As in the Synge play, the final vision in Friel's *Molly Sweeney* is radically subjective and disturbing in its assertion of the truth of fable against the lies of the everyday. In the contemporary Irish context, the term 'borders' cannot but have a political dimension. As Fintan O'Toole has noted of Friel in this regard, 'he comes from Northern Ireland but lives across the border in the Republic. Borders and boundaries, exile, shifting between states – these are consistent keynotes in his work, and they recur in *Molly Sweeney*.'[18] The play was written and performed in 1994, the year of the first Northern Ireland ceasefire. In Molly's final stance, it echoes the words of Martin about ways of seeing and individual rights or, as O'Toole puts it, 'the folly of believing that the way you see the world is the only valid way'.[19]

As the twentieth century came to a close, Synge's presence seems to re-emerge in the diverse writings of Martin McDonagh, Marina Carr and others. But he has also been a marked feature, as I have sought to show, in the theatrical landscape of the plays Friel has written in that same decade of the 1990s. Where *Dancing at Lughnasa* and Friel's plays of the 1980s like *Translations* and *Making History* are set in the historic past and work to subvert received notions of Irishness, *Molly Sweeney* is set in the present and in the area of uncertainty which the present moment represents. Like Synge's *The Well of the Saints*, it too chooses the form of parable and, while addressing the immediacies of the 1994 Northern Irish ceasefire and Good Friday agreement, also leaves itself open to the future and what may (or may not) develop. Synge remains a relevant and necessary presence in the field of contemporary Irish drama and I have no doubt will continue to be so well into the twenty-first century.

---

[1] Richard Pine, *Brian Friel and Ireland's Drama* (London: Routledge, 1990), p. 166.

[2] Richard Pine, *Brian Friel and Ireland's Drama*, p. 46.

[3] Brian Friel, *Philadelphia, Here I Come!*, *Plays:One* (London and Boston: Faber and Faber, 1996), p. 44. All further references to the play are to this edition and will be incorporated in the text.

[4] Brian Friel, *The Saucer of Larks: Stories of Ireland* (London: Arrow Books, 1969), pp. 66-67.

[5] Brian Friel, *The Saucer of Larks*, p. 64.

[6] Brian Friel, *The Saucer of Larks*, p. 67.

[7] Richard Kearney, 'The Language Plays of Brian Friel', in *Transitions: Narratives in Modern Irish Culture* (Dublin: Wolfhound Press,

1988), p. 129. Kearney's essay is reprinted in *Brian Friel: A Casebook*, edited by William Kerwin (New York and London: Garland Press, 1997).

8 Brian Friel, *Faith Healer, Plays:One*, p. 353. All future references to the play are to this edition and will be incorporated in the text.

9 Richard Kearney, 'The Language Plays of Brian Friel', p. 194.

10 Richard Pine, *Brian Friel and Ireland's Drama*, p. 194.

11 See Richard Kearney, 'The Language Plays of Brian Friel', and Richard Pine, *Brian Friel and Ireland's Drama, passim*.

12 Daniel Corkery, *Synge and Anglo-Irish Literature: A Study* (Cork University Press, 1931), p. 19.

13 Brian Friel, *Dancing at Lughnasa, Plays:Two* (London: Faber and Faber, 1999), p. 36. All future references to the play are to this edition and will be incorporated in the text.

14 Letter of 26 June 1851 from the Reverend Alexander Synge to his brother John, in *The Aran Reader*, edited by Breandán and Ruairí O hÉithir (Dublin: The Lilliput Press, 1991), pp. 30-31.

15 See Richard Pine, 'Yeats, Friel and the Politics of Failure', in *Yeats: An Annual of Critical and Textual Studies*, guest-edited by James W. Flannery (Ann Arbor: University of Michigan Press, 1992), p. 166, where Pine connects the well in Yeats's play with Tobair Vree in Friel's *Translations*.

16 For a detailed comparison of the two plays, see Carole-Ann Upton, 'Visions of the Sightless in Friel's *Molly Sweeney* and Synge's *The Well of the Saints*', *Modern Drama* 40:3 (1997), pp. 347-358.

17 Brian Friel, *Molly Sweeney, Plays:Two*, p. 458. All future references to the play are to this edition and will be incorporated in the text.

18 Fintan O'Toole, 'The End of the World'; programme note for the British premiere of Friel's *Molly Sweeney* at London's Almeida Theatre, October 1994.

19 Fintan O'Toole, 'The End of the World'.

Conclusion

I am aware, as I come to the conclusion of this book on John Millington Synge and his writing, of how much remains to be said on the subject. In these chapters, I have concentrated on four of the six canonical plays – *Riders to the Sea*, *The Shadow of the Glen*, *The Well of the Saints* and *The Playboy of the Western World*, finding that they yield further insights whenever a new approach or topic is considered. That is and will remain the case, I feel, both for myself and other critics who write about Synge. It is striking how few single authored critical monographs there have been on his work since Mary King's *The Drama of J.M. Synge* in 1985.[1] On the other hand, there have been at least five collections of critical essays on Synge published since 2000. An important development was the publication of a *Cambridge Companion* on his work in 2009, edited by P.J. Mathews. (*The Cambridge Companion to Yeats* had only appeared in 2006.) Patrick Lonergan's edited collection, *Synge and His Influences*, gathered from three years of lectures delivered at the Synge Summer School in Rathdrum, County Wicklow, shows the diversity of topics Synge's work attracts and is capable of sustaining: evolutionary theory, material culture, Irish folklore, anarchism and the European avant-garde, translation.[2] The fact that there have been multi-authored volumes in ever-growing number seems to me appropriate for a writer whose work evokes such a wide range of contexts (dramatic, philosophic, linguistic, political, ethnographic, etc.) and whose influence has not only been pervasive in the past hundred plus years but has spread in so many directions: forward into contemporary Irish drama, outward into other languages and cultures. Because of the complexity of Synge's life and the diversity of his interests, a straightforward chronological approach no longer seems feasible or desirable. W.J. McCormack recognized this in his biography of a man he described as 'a contradiction, a provoking enigma'.3 Even in a single-authored monograph such as this, the diversity of Synge demands that a roughly chronological exposition of the plays is cut across by later developments in his life and career and by important subsequent developments in Irish drama and theatre.

The four plays analysed in detail here were the four that were first produced in Synge's lifetime. They made a rapid transition from the writing of an ever-increasing number of drafts to full productions on stage and in a theatre which had a group of actors primed to put them on, actors who had contributed to the creation of those characters. These four plays also involved the author in their direction: the loaded exchange between Synge and Willie Fay about whether the characters in *The Well of the Saints* could be made more 'lovable' is a particularly illuminating case in point.4 They have remained in fairly continuous production in Ireland ever since. Seeing various productions over the years has been influential and inspirational in term of my writing about Synge, from the moment I had the good fortune to attend Hugh Hunt's visionary staging of *The Well of the Saints* at the Abbey in the summer of 1969. In particular, there has been the opportunity to view the profound involvement of director Garry Hynes and the Druid Theatre Company in the staging of Synge's plays across a span of almost three decades, culminating in the DruidSynge project.

If Hynes and Druid offered a series of memorable interpretations of the four Synge plays I have foregrounded, the DruidSynge staging of the six offered two rare opportunities: to see productions of *The Tinker's Wedding* and *Deirdre of the Sorrows*. I had never seen a production of Synge's final play until Druid staged it in 2005 and I remain grateful that I will not go to my grave unsatisfied in that regard. The play itself is inherently problematic, given that it was never finished to Synge's satisfaction in his lifetime and that it is in the Irish mythological style which has gone so much out of theatrical fashion. And the DruidSynge required a more experienced actor than the one who played Deirdre. But it had huge satisfactions. I have already mentioned the pleasure of watching Druid co-founders Mick Lally and Marie Mullen in their lively exchanges as King Conchubar and Deirdre's nurse, Lavarcham. Marie Mullen's performance throughout the DruidSynge event, in which she played Maurya in *Riders to the Sea*, Mary Byrne in *The Tinker's Wedding*, Mary Doul in *The Well of the Saints* and Lavarcham in *Deirdre of the Sorrows*, was one of the most memorable, versatile and moving I have ever witnessed. Hynes also let some moments of more contemporary violence from Northern Ireland colour her interpretation of *Deirdre of the Sorrows*. And in Aaron Monaghan (the DruidSynge's other tour-de-force performer) she found someone with the protean skills to embody the fool Owen, deranged for the love of Deirdre, who erupts into the play before exiting suicidally. But the surrounding scenes between the young lovers seemed theatrically staid by comparison. A more completely contemporary staging might have been interesting to see, given how well it worked for Hynes' approach to *The Tinker's Wedding*. This decision served to underscore how persistent a presence in Irish life travelling people are, and how consistently marginalized. The play has come to increased critical attention through such works as Mary Burke's *'Tinkers': Synge and the Cultural History of the Irish Traveller*, where she writes that Synge's interest in the figure arises from 'his desire to stress Ireland's genetic and cultural diversity during an era in which ultra nationalism' came to prevail.[5] Less has been written of *Deirdre of the Sorrows*, though Declan Kiberd and Anne Fogarty have both suggested the play's modernity by linking its treatment of exile to the writing of James Joyce and Brian Friel.[6] And there is the fascinating case of *When the Moon has Set*, Synge's first play, in both one-act and two-act versions, about which both W.J. McCormack and Mary King have written illuminatingly and which this study has sought to restore to its important place in Synge's development as a playwright.

There remains, therefore, a good deal more to explore and discuss in Synge's dramatic work. A feminist emphasis in relation to *The Tinker's Wedding* would shed light on the extent to which the older and younger women in the play set the terms both linguistic and dramatic, and the men on both sides of the social divide are reduced to mulish resentment. Another important production of *The Tinker's Wedding* was the Irish-language version, *Pósadh an Tincéara*, produced and toured by the Amharclann de hÍde company in the 1990s.[7] This was a radical revisiting of the play, not just because it was in Irish but because it restored elements from earlier drafts that Synge had deleted, most notably the two children which the unmarried couple had raised.[8] In thereby representing an alternative community on stage speaking in Irish, the Amharclann de hÍde production disclosed new possibilities in what is still one of Synge's most critically neglected plays. And there has been insufficient building on the excellent foundation to Synge and the Irish language provided by Declan Kiberd.[9] In the midst of a row with Yeats and Gregory, Synge is reputed to have said that he would give it all up (his involvement in the Abbey Theatre) and go and found an Irish language theatre on the Blasket Islands. While *The Aran Islands* provided stories and phrases from Irish that Synge was to build upon in the plays he later wrote, the attitude towards the Irish language embedded in his seminal prose work is a conservative one, seeking to preserve the older language and protect it from modern contamination. But if Synge was in a distinguished train of writers who visited and made cultural capital of the Aran Islands, he was the very first to go to the Blaskets as a site of literary pilgrimage. The less-discussed essays about west Kerry which resulted (written almost a decade later and after Synge had become established as a playwright) highlight a different and more radical approach in the attitude expressed towards the people and their use of the Irish language. Synge is now coming to the Irish hinterland with the eye of a practiced playwright, but one who has grown increasingly frustrated by aspects of that practice, as his outburst to his fellow Abbey Theatre directors suggests. If he visited the Aran Islands as a man who was (almost unknown to himself) looking for the means to create an Irish theatre in English, he visits Kerry and the Blasket Islands with the idea of developing an Irish language theatre that would be far less urban in its orientation. Many of the incidents and events which draw Synge's interest in his Kerry sojourn (such as the Rabelaisian ceremony at Puck Fair) contain proto-dramatic elements intimating a new kind of theatre.

The field of contemporary Irish drama continues to reveal Synge's profound influence – indeed, it is unimaginable without him. In *Synge and His Contexts*, there are essays relating Synge's work to the plays of Tom Murphy and Marina Carr. The two great contemporary Irish playwrights, Friel and Murphy, began their careers in the 1950s by needing to distance themselves from the anxiety of Synge's still culturally proximate influence. Chapter Ten examined how that operated in Friel's career, from the distancing of the short story 'Mr. Sing, My Heart's Delight' to the full-on engagement in the later plays *Dancing at Lughnasa* and *Molly Sweeney*. Tom Murphy has always claimed that he was uninterested as a young man in Irish drama, finding anything Irish 'a pain in the arse [including] O'Casey and Synge', preferring American playwrights like Eugene O'Neill, Arthur Miller and (in particular) Tennessee Williams.[10] But a photograph in the programme for the 2001 season of Murphy plays at the Abbey Theatre shows an extremely youthful Tom Murphy clad in a jockey's outfit and hoisted aloft by a cheering crowd in an amateur production of Synge's *Playboy of the Western World* in his home town of Tuam, Co. Galway. If he sought to flee the influence of Synge at the outset of his career in 1958, Tom Murphy was willing to re-engage by 1979 when he agreed to direct a production of Synge's *The Well of the Saints* at the

Abbey. He went further by providing a curtain-raiser in a piece he devised from the writings of Synge entitled *Under Ether*. The title refers to a prose work by Synge, 'Under Ether: Personal Experiences During an Operation', a Poe-like phantasmagoria of the visions he experienced while anaesthetized during one of his operations. Murphy used this dramatically to frame the various other writings he drew on, with Synge re-experiencing his life as if it were a dream. The Murphy play which bears the greatest imprint of *The Well of the Saints* is *The Morning After Optimism*, premiered at the Abbey in 1971 and directed by Hugh Hunt, who had directed Synge's play there two years earlier. A thoroughly modern play, it yet has direct links to the theatre of Synge and Yeats, which Hunt's production made clear. Murphy viewed Synge's play as a fairy story. The same could be said of the fairy tale forest of *Optimism* into which Murphy's odd couple, James and Rosie, have fled, pursued by unnamed but threatening forces. Both of them are old and their worldly experience is signified by their occupations: he is a pimp; she is an (ageing) whore. In the forest they encounter idealized representations of their younger selves, who disconcert them with the contrast of what they have become, to the point that each kills his other. Rosie is as concerned by James's obsessive talk about 'young girls' as Synge's Mary is about Martin Doul, and in time James makes as determined an effort to seduce the young, beautiful Anastasia as Martin Doul does with Molly Byrne, though with no greater success. In their speech, James and Rosie move between a slangy idiom – especially when they deliberately 'talk dirty' – and a more lyrical vein, exhibiting the same verbal range and contrast as in Synge's play.[11]

Synge has proved no less an influence on the younger generation of contemporary Irish playwrights. They quote more explicitly from his work, in a postmodern and inter-textual way. To this newer generation of playwrights Synge is a cultural resource available to be appropriated – along with a proliferating range of references in other media (notably television and cinema) – rather than an intimidating historical presence to be faced up to. This phenomenon has been examined in this book in relation to Martin McDonagh's Leenane trilogy, Stewart Parker's *Pentecost* and Marina Carr's *The Mai*. It could have been extended to Carr's other plays[12] and to those of Conor McPherson, whose breakthrough play *The Weir* (1997) is predicated on four characters in a rural pub telling stories of ghostly visitations. The three older men, natives of the place, are at one level trying to impress if not scare Valerie, the pretty young urban newcomer who has recently moved into this desolate and windswept area, with its dark nights and isolation.

The men's stories all tell of a rural way of life which is passing away and enact the trauma of displacement, of the psychic disturbance caused by the inroads of social progress on traditional custom. Valerie responds with her own story, set in an urban environment but even more disturbing, about the recent death by drowning of her young daughter and a communication from beyond the grave – it may be modernized, but the grieving of a mother for a drowned child in a dramatic context cannot but suggest Synge. The question raised by the impact of Valerie's story on the male listeners – is it true? – radiates outward to everything that has been said in the course of the evening's talk in the pub. There is nothing, finally, but the words as spoken on stage, not even the degree of verification afforded by Synge's *Playboy of the Western World*.

Another way to come at Synge and his enigma is the creative route, that of the prose novelist rather than of the biographer or academic interpreter. In *Ghost Light*, his magnificent novel of 2011, Joseph O'Connor uses the spaces in the story of J.M. Synge and Molly Allgood to imagine their relationship through to a consummation in a Wicklow cottage in the summer of 1907. He draws on Synge's letters, as I did in Chapter Nine, but also supplies Molly's half of the correspondence, giving her the novel's last word in an unsent letter she writes him back in Dublin when she visits his beloved West of Ireland with the Abbey players. But the novel is not set in the first decade of the twentieth century. It keeps an air of fantastication and romance about the relationship by being cast in the prism of the memories of a sixty-six-year old Molly Allgood, living in London, a prematurely aged figure and given to the drink. So even in the novel Synge is a ghost who has to be conjured. The present-day reality is Molly's desolate but spirited trudge through snow-strewn London streets to perform a brief part in a BBC Radio broadcast of a Sean O'Casey play.[13] The novel reconstructs the scene in Glenageary in which Molly is presented by a deeply repressed son to his severe mother but also imagines the awkward occasion of Synge sitting down at table with the Allgoods in inner city Dublin. The wonder is that these two people ever managed to overcome the huge differences in class, religion and the conventions of gender which separated them and to come together in the ways and degrees they did. What O'Connor suggests is that their relationship only became possible in the space of the Abbey Theatre, that zone of play where the rigidities enforced by Irish society became more flexible and enabled a freer intercourse between men and women of differing classes. The key is in the title: 'Ghost light. An ancient superstition among people of the stage. One lamp must always be left burning when the theatre is dark, so the ghosts can perform their own works.'[14] What Joseph O'Connor's *Ghost Light* demonstrates is what animates *Synge and the Making of Modern Irish Drama*: that the ghost of Synge still lights Irish theatre and sees it forward into the future.

---

[1] Nelson O'Ceallaigh Ritschel's *Synge and Irish Nationalism: The Precursor to Revolution* (Westport, Ct.: Greenwood Press, 2002) is the only one I am aware of.

[2] *Synge and His Influences: Centenary Essays from the Synge Summer School*, edited by Patrick Lonergan (Dublin: Carysfort Press, 2011). The essays were drawn from lectures delivered at the School from 2009, the final year I was Director, through 2011, the first two years of Patrick Lonergan's Directorship.

[3] W.J. McCormack, *Fool of the Family: A Life of J.M. Synge* (London: Weidenfeld and Nicolson, 2000), p, 3.

[4] William G. Fay, '*The Well of the Saints*', in *J.M. Synge: Interviews and Recollections*, edited by E.H. Mikhail (London and Basingstoke: Macmillan, 1977), p. 31.

[5] Mary Burke, '*Tinkers*': *Synge and the Cultural History of the Irish Traveller* (Oxford and New York: Oxford University Press, 2009), p. 112.

[6] See Declan Kiberd, '*Faith Healer*' in *Brian Friel: A Casebook*, edited by William Kerwin (New York and London: Garland Press, 1997), pp. 211-225; and Anne Fogarty, 'Ghostly Intertexts: James Joyce and the Legacy of Synge', in *Synge and Edwardian Ireland*, edited by Brian Cliff and Nicholas Grene (Oxford and New York: Oxford University Press, 2012), pp. 235-236.

[7] The translation of *The Tinker's Wedding* into Irish is by Tom Sailí O Flaithearta.

[8] There remains only one fleeting verbal residue in the finished text, when Michael chides Sarah at the start of the play for her foolish talk: 'You to be going beside me a great while, and rearing a lot of them, and then to be setting off with your talk of getting married.' (IV, 7).

[9] Declan Kiberd, *Synge and the Irish Language* (1979; revised second edition, Dublin: Gill and Macmillan , 1993).

[10] See *Talking About Tom Murphy*, edited by Nicholas Grene (Dublin: Carysfort Press, 2002), p. 94.

[11] See Anthony Roche, 'Synge and contemporary Irish drama', in *The Cambridge Companion to J.M. Synge*, edited by P.J. Mathews (Cambridge: Cambridge University Press, 2009), pp. 177-179; and Alexandra Poulain, 'Synge and Tom Murphy: Beyond Naturalism', in *Synge and His Influences*, pp. 199-214.

[12] See Emilie Pine, 'Living With Ghosts: Synge and Marina Carr', in *Synge and His Influences*, pp. 215-224.

[13] Joseph O'Connor has told me that Molly died the day before the broadcast was to take place, not the day after.

[14] Joseph O'Connor, *Ghost Light* (London: Harvill Secker, 2010), p, 206.

Select Bibliography

Works by John Millington Synge

J.M. Synge, *Collected Works* (4 volumes), general editor Robin Skelton.
---- Volume I: *Poems*, edited by Robin Skelton (London: Oxford University Press, 1962; reprinted Gerrards Cross, Colin Smythe, 1982).
---- Volume II: *Prose*, edited by Alan Price (London: Oxford University Press, 1966; reprinted Gerrards Cross: Colin Smythe, 1982).
---- Volume III: *Plays* Book I, edited by Ann Saddlemyer (London: Oxford University Press, 1968; reprinted Gerrards Cross: Colin Smythe, 1982).
---- Volume IV: *Plays* Book II, edited by Ann Saddlemyer (London: Oxford University Press, 1968; reprinted Gerrards Cross: Colin Smythe, 1982).
The Collected Letters of John Millington Synge, Volume One: 1871-1907, edited by Ann Saddlemyer (Oxford: Clarendon Press, 1983).
The Collected Letters of John Millington Synge, Volume Two: 1907-1909, edited by Ann Saddlemyer (Oxford: Clarendon Press, 1984).
Theatre Business: The Correspondence of the first Abbey Theatre Directors: William Butler Yeats, Lady Gregory and J.M. Synge, edited by Ann Saddlemyer (Gerrards Cross: Colin Smythe, 1982).
'The Dramatic Movement in Ireland,' in *The Abbey Theatre: Interviews and Recollections*, edited by E.H. Mikhail (London: Macmillan, 1988).
The Well of the Saints by J.M. Synge, edited by Nicholas Grene. Irish Dramatic Texts (Washington, D.C.: The Catholic University of America Press; Gerrards Cross: Colin Smythe, 1982).
When the Moon Has Set, with an introduction by Mary C. King, in *The Long Room* 24 and 25 (Spring/Autumn 1982), published by the Friends of the Library, Trinity College, Dublin.

The Aran Islands, edited with an introduction by Tim Robinson (London: Penguin, 1992).

Shadows: A Trinity of Plays by J.M. Synge and W.B. Yeats (London: Oberon Books, 1998).

Manuscripts

The Synge Manuscripts are held in the Library of Trinity College, Dublin.

The Synge Manuscripts in the Library of Trinity College, Dublin: A Catalogue Prepared on the Occasion of the Synge Centenary Exhibition 1971, compiled by Nicholas Grene (Dublin: Dolmen Press, 1971).

The script of *The Playboy of the Western World* submitted to the Lord Chamberlain in 1907 is held in the file for that year in the Lord Chamberlain's Collection, Manuscript Division, British Library, London.

Books on J.M. Synge

Bourgeois, Maurice, *John Millington Synge and the Irish Theatre* (London: Constable, 1913).

Carpenter, Andrew (editor), *My Uncle John: Edward Stephens's Life of J.M. Synge* (London: Oxford University Press, 1974).

Corkery, Daniel, *Synge and Anglo-Irish Literature: A Study* (Dublin and Cork: Cork University Press; London: Longmans, Green, 1931).

Greene, David H., and Edward M. Stephens, *J.M. Synge 1871-1909* (New York: Macmillan, 1959; revised edition New York and London: New York University Press, 1989).

Grene, Nicholas, *Synge; A Critical Study of the Plays* (London: Macmillan, 1975).

Johnston, Denis, *John Millington Synge* (New York and London: Columbia University Press, 1965).

Kiberd, Declan, *Synge and the Irish Language* (London: Macmillan, 1979; revised edition Dublin: Gill and Macmillan, 1993).

King, Mary C., *The Drama of J.M. Synge* (Syracuse: Syracuse University Press, 1985).

McCormack, W.J., *Fool of the Family: A Life of J.M. Synge* (London: Weidenfeld and Nicolson, 2000).

O'Brien Johnson, Toni, *Synge: The Medieval and the Grotesque* (Gerrards Cross: Colin Smythe; Totowa, N.J.: Barnes and Noble, 1982).

O'Ceallaigh Ristschel, Nelson, *Synge and Irish Nationalism: The Precursor to Revolution* (Westport, Ct.: Greenwood Press, 2002).

Skelton, Robin, *The Writings of J.M. Synge* (Indianapolis and New York: Bobbs-Merrill, 1971).

---- *J.M. Synge*. The Irish Writers Series (Lewisburg, Pa.: Bucknell University Press, 1972).

Thornton, Weldon, *J.M. Synge and the Western Mind* (Gerrards Cross: Colin Smythe, 1979).

Edited Collections of Essays on J.M. Synge

Bushrui, Suheil Badi (editor), *A Centenary Tribute to John Millington Synge, 1871-1909: Sunshine and the Moon's Delight* (Gerrards Cross: Colin Smythe; New York: Barnes and Noble, 1972).

Casey, Daniel J. (editor), *Critical Essays on John Millington Synge* (New York: G.K. Hall and Co., 1994).

Clark, David R. (editor), *John Millington Synge: Riders to the Sea*. The Merrill Literary Casebook Series (Columbus: Charles R. Merrill, 1970).

Cliff, Brian, and Nicholas Grene (editors), *Synge and Edwardian Ireland* (Oxford and New York: Oxford University Press, 2012).

Frazier, Adrian (editor), *Playboys of the Western World: Production Histories* (Dublin: Carysfort Press, 2004).

Grene, Nicholas (editor), *Interpreting Synge: Essays from the Synge Summer School 1991-2000* (Dublin: The Lilliput Press, 2000).

Harmon, Maurice (editor), *J.M. Synge Centenary Papers 1971* (Dublin: Dolmen Press, 1972).

Kopper, Edward A., Jr. (editor), *A J.M. Synge Literary Companion* (New York, Wesport, Ct., and London: Greenwood Press, 1988).

Lonergan, Patrick (editor), *Synge and His Influences: Centenary Essays from the Synge Summer School* (Dublin: Carysfort Press, 2011).

Mathews, P.J. (editor), *The Cambridge Companion to J.M. Synge* (Cambridge: Cambridge University Press, 2009).

Mikhail, E.H. (editor), *J.M. Synge: Interviews and Recollections* (London and Basingstoke: Macmillan, 1977).

Whitaker, Thomas R. (editor), *The Playboy of the Western World: A Collection of Critical Essays*. Twentieth Century Interpretations (Englewood Cliffs, N.J.: Prentice-Hall, 1969).

Books with Material on Synge

Burke, Mary, *'Tinkers': Synge and the Cultural History of the Irish Traveller* (Oxford: Oxford University Press, 2009).

Castle, Gregory, *Modernism and the Celtic Revival* (Cambridge: Cambridge University Press, 2001).

Connolly, Peter (editor), *Literature and the Changing Ireland* (Gerrards Cross: Colin Smythe; New York: Barnes and Noble, 1982).

Coxhead, Elizabeth, *Daughters of Erin: Five Women of the Irish Renascence* (Gerrards Cross: Colin Smythe, 1965).

Fay, William G., and Catherine Carswell, *The Fays of the Abbey Theatre: An Autobiographical Record* (New York: Harcourt Brace; London: Rich and Cowan, 1935).

Finney, Gail, *Women in Modern Drama: Freud, Feminism and European Theatre at the Turn of the Century* (Ithaca and London: Cornell University Press, 1989).

Grene, Nicholas, *The Politics of Irish Drama: Plays in Context from Boucicault to Friel* (Cambridge: Cambridge University Press, 1999).

Hogan, Robert, and James Kilroy, *Laying the Foundations 1902-1904: The Second Volume of the Modern Irish Drama* (Dublin: The Dolmen Press, 1976).

Hogan, Robert, and James Kilroy, *The Abbey Theatre: The Years of Synge 1905-1909: The Third Volume of the Modern Irish Drama* (Dublin: The Dolmen Press, 1978).

Kiberd, Declan, *Inventing Ireland* (London: Jonathan Cape, 1995).

Kilroy, James, *The 'Playboy' Riots* (Dublin: The Dolmen Press, 1971).

Levitas, Ben, *The Theatre of Nation: Irish Drama and Cultural Nationalism 1890-1916* (Oxford: Clarendon Press, 2002).

Macintosh, Fiona, *Dying Acts: Death in Ancient Greek and Modern Irish Tragic Drama* (Cork: Cork University Press, 1994).

Mattar, Sinead Garrigan, *Primitivism, Science and the Irish Revival* (Oxford and New York: Clarendon Press, 2004).

Martin, Augustine, *Bearing Witness: Essays on Anglo-Irish Literature*, edited by Anthony Roche (Dublin: University College Dublin Press, 1996).

McCormack, W.J., *From Burke to Beckett: Ascendancy, Tradition and Betrayal in Literary History* (Cork: Cork University Press, 1994).

Mercier, Vivian, *Modern Irish Literature: Sources and Founders*, edited by Eilis Dillon (Oxford: Clarendon Press, 1994).

Morash, Christopher, *A History of Irish Theatre 1601-2000* (Cambridge: Cambridge University Press, 2002).

Selected Essays on J.M. Synge

Conacher, D.J., 'Some Profane Variations on a Tragic Theme,' *Phoenix* 23:1 (1969).

Foster, R.F., 'Good Behaviour: Yeats, Synge and Anglo-Irish Etiquette,' in *Paddy and Mr. Punch: Connections in Irish and English History* (London: Allen Lane/The Penguin Press, 1993).

Grene, Nicholas, 'Yeats and the Re-making of Synge,' in *Tradition and Influence in Anglo-Irish Poetry*, edited by Terence Brown and Nicholas Grene (Houndmills: Macmillan, 1989).

Kiberd, Declan, 'The Frenzy of Christy: Synge and *Buile Shuibhne*,' *Éire-Ireland* 14:2 (1979).

Krause, David, '"The Rageous Ossean": Patron-Hero of Synge and O'Casey,' *Modern Drama* 4:3 (1961).

Leeney, Cathy, 'Hard wired/tender bodies,' *Performing Ireland*, special issue of *Australasian Drama Studies*, guest-edited by Brian Singleton and Anna McMullan, 43 (October 2003).

Merriman, Vic, 'Decolonisation Postponed: The Theatre of Tiger Trash', *Irish University Review* 29:2 (Autumn/Winter 1999).

Parker, Randolph, '"Gaming in the Gap": Language and Liminality in *The Playboy of the Western World*,' *Theatre Journal* 37:1 (March 1985).

Richards, Shaun, '"The Outpourings of a Morbid, Unhealthy mind": The Critical Condition of Synge and McDonagh,' *Irish University Review* 33:1 (Spring/Summer 2003).

Roche, Anthony, 'The Two Worlds of Synge's *The Well of the Saints*,' *Genre* 12 (1979); reprinted in book form as Ronald Schliefer (editor), *The Genres of the Irish Literary Revival* (Norman, Ok.: Pilgrim Books; Dublin: Wolfhound Press, 1980). Reprinted in Daniel J. Casey (editor), *Critical Essays on John Millington Synge* (New York: G.K. Hall and Co., 1994).

Schoepperle, Gertrude, 'John Synge and His Old French Farce,' *North American Review* CCXIV (October 1921).

Sullivan, Mary Rose, 'Synge, Sophocles and the Un-Making of Myth,' *Modern Drama* 12:3 (1969).

Upton, Carole-Ann, 'Visions of the Sightless in Friel's *Molly Sweeney* and Synge's *The Well of the Saints*,' *Modern Drama* 40:3 (1997).

Other Works Cited

Aristotle, *The Poetics*, translated by Preston H. Epps (Chapel Hill: The University of North Carolina Press, 1970).

Beckett, Samuel, *The Complete Dramatic Works* (London: Faber and Faber, 1990).

Benjamin, Walter, *Illuminations*, translated by Harry Zohn, edited by Hannah Arendt (New York: Schocken, 1969).

Bloom, Harold, *The Anxiety of Influence: A Theory of Poetry*, Second Edition (New York and Oxford: Oxford University Press, 1997; 1973).

Bourke, Angela, *The Burning of Bridget Cleary: A True Story* (London: Pimlico, 1999).

Brecht, Bertolt, *Brecht on Theatre*, translated by John Willett (New York: Hill and Wang; London: Methuen, 1964).

---- *Diaries 1920-1922*, edited by Herta Rumthun, translated by John Willett (London: Eyre Methuen, 1979).

---- *Life of Galileo*, translated by John Willett, in Bertolt Brecht, *Collected Plays* 5, edited by John Willett and Ralph Manheim (London: Methuen, 1995).

---- *Senora Carrar's Rifles*, translated by Wolfgang Sauerlander, in Bertolt Brecht, *Collected Plays* 4, edited by Tom Kuhn and John Willett (London: Methuen, 2001).

---- *Stücke* 4, edited by Werner Hecht, Jan Knopf, Werner Mittenzwei and Klaus-Detlef Muller (Frankfurt am Main: Suhrkamp Verlag, 1988).

Carr, Marina, *Plays:One* (London: Faber and Faber, 1999).

Deevy, Teresa, *Three Plays* (London: Macmillan, 1939).

Deleuze, Gilles, and Felix Guattari, *Kafka: Towards a Minor Literature*, translated by Dana Polan (Minneapolis: The University of Minneapolis Press, 1986).

Duffy, Enda, *The Subaltern Ulysses* (Minneapolis and London: University of Minnesota Press, 1995).

Ellmann, Richard, *James Joyce*, new and revised edition (New York: Oxford University Press, 1982; 1959).

Esslin, Martin, *The Theatre of the Absurd* (Harmondsworth: Penguin Books, Third Edition, 1980; 1963).

Foster, R.F., *W.B. Yeats, A Life, 1, The Apprentice Mage* (Oxford: Oxford University Press, 1997).

Friel, Brian, *The Saucer of Larks: Stories of Ireland* (London: Arrow Books, 1969).

---- *Plays:One* (London and Boston: Faber and Faber, 1996).

---- *Plays: Two* (London: Faber and Faber, 1999).

Gogarty, Oliver St. John, *As I Was Going Down Sackville Street* (New York: Reynall and Hitchcock, 1937; reprinted Dublin: The O'Brien Press, 1994).

Gorman, Herbert, *James Joyce: a definitive biography* (London: John Lane, The Bodley Head, 1941).

Gregory, Augusta Lady, *Cuchulain of Muirhemne* (Gerrards Cross: Colin Smythe, 1970).

---- *Our Irish Theatre: A Chapter of Autobiography* (Gerrards Cross: Colin Smythe, 1972).

Grene, Nicholas (editor), *Talking About Tom Murphy* (Dublin: Carysfort Press, 2002).

Hillgarth, J.N. (editor), *Christianity and Paganism 350-700: The Conversion of Western Europe* (Philadelphia: University of Pennsylvania Press, 1969).

Hyde, Douglas, *A Literary History of Ireland* (London: Unwin, 1899).

Ibsen, Henrik, *Ghosts and Other Plays*, translated by Peter Watts (Harmondsworth: Penguin, 1964).

Joyce, James, *The Critical Writings of James Joyce*, edited by Ellsworth Mason and Richard Ellmann (New York: The Viking Press, 1959).

---- *Dubliners*, edited by Terence Brown (Harmondsworth: Penguin, 1992).

---- *Occasional, Political and Critical Writing*, edited by Kevin Barry (Oxford: Oxford University Press, 2000).

---- *Poems and Exiles*, edited by J.C.C. Mays (Harmondsworth: Penguin, 1992).

---- *A Portrait of the Artist as a Young Man* (Harmondsworth: Penguin, 1976).

---- *Ulysses*, introduced by Declan Kiberd (Harmondsworth: Penguin, 1992).

Joyce, Stanislaus, *My Brother's Keeper*, edited by Richard Ellmann (London: Faber and Faber, 1958).

The Letters of James Joyce, Volume II, edited by Richard Ellmann (New York: The Viking Press, 1966).

Kenner, Hugh, *A Colder Eye: The Modern Irish Writers* (New York: Alfred A. Knopf, 1983).

Kerwin, William (editor), *Brian Friel: A Casebook* (New York and London: Garland Press, 1997).

Kilroy, Thomas, 'The Anglo-Irish Theatrical Imagination,' *Bullán: An Irish Studies Journal* 3:2 (Winter 1997/Spring 1998).

Knowlson, James, *Damned to Fame: The Life of Samuel Beckett* (London: Bloomsbury, 1996).

MacCana, Prionsias, *Celtic Mythology* (London: Newnes, 1983).

Maddox, Brenda, *Nora: A Biography of Nora Joyce* (London: Hamish Hamilton, 1988).

McDonagh, Martin, *Plays: One* (London: Methuen, 1999).

Mercier, Vivian, *Beckett/Beckett* (New York: Oxford University Press, 1977).

Meyer, Kuno (editor and translator), *The Voyage of Bran Son of Febal*, 2 volumes (London: David Nutt, 1895).

Miller, Liam, *The Noble Drama of W.B. Yeats* (Dublin: The Dolmen Press, 1977).

Nolan, Emer, *James Joyce and Nationalism* (London: Routledge, 1995).

O'Connor, Joseph, *Ghost Light* (London: Michael Joseph, 2011).

O hÉithir, Breandán and Ruairí (editors), *The Aran Reader* (Dublin: The Lilliput Press, 1991).

O'Malley, Aidan, *Field Day and the Translation of Irish Identities* (Houndmills: Palgrave Macmillan, 2011).

Parker, Stewart, *Plays: 2* (London: Methuen Drama, 2000).

Pearce, Donald R., 'Hours with the Domestic Sibyl: Remembering George Yeats,' *The Southern Review* 28:3 (Summer 1992).

Pine, Richard, *Brian Friel and Ireland's Drama* (London: Routledge, 1990).

---- 'Yeats, Friel and the Politics of Failure,' in *Yeats: An Annual of Critical and Textual Studies*, guest-edited by James W. Flannery (Ann Arbor: University of Michigan Press, 1992).

Roche, Anthony, '"The Strange Light of Some New World": Stephen's Vision in *A Portrait,*' *James Joyce Quarterly* 25.3 (Spring 1988).

---- *Contemporary Irish Drama: Second Edition* (Houndmills: Palgrave Macmillan, 2009).

Sihra, Melissa (editor), *Women in Irish Drama: A Century of Authorship and Representation* (Houndmills: Palgrave Macmillan, 2007).

States, Bert O., *The Shape of Paradox: An Essay on 'Waiting For Godot'* (Berkeley: University of California Press, 1979).

Sullivan, Moynagh, 'Feminism, Postmodernism and the Subjects of Irish and Women's Studies,' in *New Voices in Irish Criticism*, edited by P.J. Mathews (Dublin: Four Courts Press, 2000).

---- 'I am, therefore I'm not (Woman),' *International Journal of Women's Studies* 2:2 (2002).

Taylor, Richard, *The Drama of W.B. Yeats: Irish Myth and the Japanese Noh* (New Haven: Yale University Press, 1976).

Ward, Margaret, *Unmanageable Revolutionaries* (London: Pluto Press, 1983).

Watt, Stephen, *Postmodern/Drama: Reading the Contemporary Stage* (Ann Arbor: The University of Michigan Press, 1998).

Worth, Katharine, *The Irish Drama of Europe from Yeats to Beckett* (London: The Athlone Press, 1978).

---- 'Ibsen and the Irish Theatre,' *Theatre Research International* 15 (1990).

Yeats, W.B., *Autobiographies* (London: Macmillan, 1955).

---- *A Critical Edition of Yeats's 'A Vision'*, edited by George Mills Harper and Walter Kelly Hood (London: Macmillan, 1978).

---- *Essays and Introductions* (London: Macmillan, 1961).

---- *Explorations* (New York: Macmillan, 1962).

---- *Memoirs: Autobiography: First Draft/Journal*, edited by Denis Donoghue (London: Macmillan, 1972).

---- *Mythologies* (New York: Macmillan, 1959)

---- *The Letters of W.B. Yeats*, edited by Allan Wade (New York: Macmillan, 1955).

---- *The Speckled Bird*, 2 volumes, edited by William H. O'Donnell (Dublin: The Cuala Press, 1974).

---- *Uncollected Prose of W.B. Yeats*, Volume One, edited by John P. Frayne (London: Macmillan, 1970).

---- *The Variorum Edition of the Plays of W.B. Yeats*, edited by Russell K. Alspach (London: Macmillan, 1966).

---- *The Variorum Edition of the Poems of W.B. Yeats*, edited by Peter Allt and Russell K. Alspach (New York: Macmillan, 1957).

Film

DruidSynge: The Plays of John Millington Synge, directed by Garry Hynes (RTÉ, Wildfire Films and Druid Theatre, 2007).

Synge agus an Domhain Thiar [*Synge and the Western World*], directed by Macdara O Curraidhín (TG Cathair, 1999).

Index

Carysfort Press was formed in the summer of 1998. It receives annual funding from the Arts Council.

The directors believe that drama is playing an ever-increasing role in today's society and that enjoyment of the theatre, both professional and amateur, currently plays a central part in Irish culture.

The Press aims to produce high quality publications which, though written and/or edited by academics, will be made accessible to a general readership. The organisation would also like to provide a forum for critical thinking in the Arts in Ireland, again keeping the needs and interests of the general public in view.

The company publishes contemporary Irish writing for and about the theatre.

Editorial and publishing inquiries to:
Carysfort Press Ltd.,
58 Woodfield,
Scholarstown Road,
Rathfarnham,
Dublin 16,
Republic of Ireland.

T (353 1) 493 7383
F (353 1) 406 9815
E: info@carysfortpress.com
www.carysfortpress.com

HOW TO ORDER

TRADE ORDERS DIRECTLY TO:
Irish Book Distribution
Unit 12, North Park, North Road,
Finglas, Dublin 11.

T: (353 1) 8239580
F: (353 1) 8239599
E: mary@argosybooks.ie
www.argosybooks.ie

INDIVIDUAL ORDERS DIRECTLY TO:
eprint Ltd.
35 Coolmine Industrial Estate,
Blanchardstown, Dublin 15.
T: (353 1) 827 8860
F: (353 1) 827 8804 Order online @
E: books@eprint.ie
www.eprint.ie

FOR SALES IN NORTH AMERICA AND CANADA:
Dufour Editions Inc.,
124 Byers Road,
PO Box 7,
Chester Springs,
PA 19425,
USA

T: 1-610-458-5005
F: 1-610-458-7103

The Art Of Billy Roche: Wexford As The World

Edited by Kevin Kerrane

Billy Roche – musician, actor, novelist, dramatist, screenwriter – is one of Ireland's most versatile talents. This anthology, the first comprehensive survey of Roche's work, focuses on his portrayal of one Irish town as a microcosm of human life itself, elemental and timeless. Among the contributors are fellow artists (Colm Tóibín, Conor McPherson, Belinda McKeon), theatre professionals (Benedict Nightingale, Dominic Dromgoole, Ingrid Craigie), and scholars on both sides of the Atlantic.

ISBN: 978-1-904505-60-0   €20

The Theatre of Conor McPherson: 'Right beside the Beyond'

Edited by Lilian Chambers and Eamonn Jordan

Multiple productions and the international successes of plays like *The Weir* have led to Conor McPherson being regarded by many as one of the finest writers of his generation. McPherson has also been hugely prolific as a theatre director, as a screenwriter and film director, garnering many awards in these different roles. In this collection of essays, commentators from around the world address the substantial range of McPherson's output to date in theatre and film, a body of work written primarily during and in the aftermath of Ireland's Celtic Tiger period. These critics approach the work in challenging and dynamic ways, considering the crucial issues of morality, the rupturing of the real, storytelling, and the significance of space, violence and gender. Explicit considerations are given to comedy and humour, and to theatrical form, especially that of the monologue and to the ways that the otherworldly, the unconscious and supernatural are accommodated dramaturgically, with frequent emphasis placed on the specific aspects of performance in both theatre and film.

ISBN: 978 1 904505 61 7   €20

The Story of Barabbas, The Company

Carmen Szabo

Acclaimed by audiences and critics alike for their highly innovative, adventurous and entertaining theatre, Barabbas The Company have created playful, intelligent and dynamic productions for over 17 years. Breaking the mould of Irish theatrical tradition and moving away from a text dominated theatre, Barabbas The Company's productions have established an instantly recognizable performance style influenced by the theatre of clown, circus, mime, puppetry, object manipulation and commedia dell'arte. This is the story of a unique company within the framework of Irish theatre, discussing the influences that shape their performances and establish their position within the history and development of contemporary Irish theatre. This book addresses the overwhelming necessity to reconsider Irish theatre history and to explore, in a language accessible to a wide range of readers, the issues of physicality and movement based theatre in Ireland.

ISBN: 978-1-904505-59-4   €25

Irish Drama: Local and Global Perspectives

Edited by Nicholas Grene and Patrick Lonergan

Since the late 1970s there has been a marked internationalization of Irish drama, with individual plays, playwrights, and theatrical companies establishing newly global reputations. This book reflects upon these developments, drawing together leading scholars and playwrights to consider the consequences that arise when Irish theatre travels abroad.

Contributors: Chris Morash, Martine Pelletier, José Lanters, Richard Cave, James Moran, Werner Huber, Rhona Trench, Christopher Murray, Ursula Rani Sarma, Jesse Weaver, Enda Walsh, Elizabeth Kuti

ISBN: 978-1-904505-63-1   €20

What Shakespeare Stole From Rome

Brian Arkins

What Shakespeare Stole From Rome analyses the multiple ways Shakespeare used material from Roman history and Latin poetry in his plays and poems. From the history of the Roman Republic to the tragedies of Seneca; from the Comedies of Platus to Ovid's poetry; this enlightening book examines the important influence of Rome and Greece on Shakespeare's work.

ISBN: 978-1-904505-58-7   €20

Polite Forms

Harry White

Polite Forms is a sequence of poems that meditates on family life. These poems remember and reimagine scenes from childhood and adolescence through the formal composure of the sonnet, so that the uniformity of this framing device promotes a tension as between a neatly arranged album of photographs and the chaos and flow of experience itself. Throughout the collection there is a constant preoccupation with the difference between actual remembrance and the illumination or meaning which poetry can afford. Some of the poems 'rewind the tapes of childhood' across two or three generations, and all of them are akin to pictures at an exhibition which survey individual impressions of childhood and parenthood in a thematically continuous series of portraits drawn from life.

Harry White was born in Dublin in 1958. He is Professor of Music at University College Dublin and widely known for his work in musicology and cultural history. His publications include "Music and the Irish Literary Imagination" (Oxford, 2008), which was awarded the Michael J. Durkan prize of the American Conference for Irish Studies in 2009. "Polite Forms" is his first collection of poems

ISBN: 978-1-904505-55-6   €10

Ibsen and Chekhov on the Irish Stage

Edited by Ros Dixon and Irina Ruppo Malone

Ibsen and Chekhov on the Irish Stage presents articles on the theories of translation and adaptation, new insights on the work of Brian Friel, Frank McGuinness, Thomas Kilroy, and Tom Murphy, historical analyses of theatrical productions during the Irish Revival, interviews with contemporary theatre directors, and a round-table discussion with the playwrights, Michael West and Thomas Kilroy.

Ibsen and Chekhov on the Irish Stage challenges the notion that a country's dramatic tradition develops in cultural isolation. It uncovers connections between past productions of plays by Ibsen and Chekhov and contemporary literary adaptations of their works by Irish playwrights, demonstrating the significance of international influence for the formation of national canon.

Conceived in the spirit of a round-table discussion, *Ibsen and Chekhov on the Irish Stage* is a collective study of the intricacies of trans-cultural migration of dramatic works and a re-examination of Irish theatre history from 1890 to the present day.

ISBN: 978-1-904505-57-0   €20

Tom Swift Selected Plays

With an introduction by Peter Crawley.

The inaugural production of Performance Corporation in 2002 matched Voltaire's withering assault against the doctrine of optimism with a playful aesthetic and endlessly inventive stagecraft.

Each play in this collection was originally staged by the Performance Corporation and though Swift has explored different avenues ever since, such playfulness is a constant. The writing is precise, but leaves room for the discoveries of rehearsals, the flesh of the theatre. All plays are blueprints for performance, but several of these scripts – many of which are site-specific and all of them slyly topical – are documents for something unrepeatable.

ISBN: 978-1-904505-56-3   €20

Synge and His Influences: Centenary Essays from the Synge Summer School

Edited by Patrick Lonergan

The year 2009 was the centenary of the death of John Millington Synge, one of the world's great dramatists. To mark the occasion, this book gathers essays by leading scholars of Irish drama, aiming to explore the writers and movements that shaped Synge, and to consider his enduring legacies. Essays discuss Synge's work in its Irish, European and world contexts – showing his engagement not just with the Irish literary revival but with European politics and culture too. The book also explores Synge's influence on later writers: Irish dramatists such as Brian Friel, Tom Murphy and Marina Carr, as well as international writers like Mustapha Matura and Erisa Kironde. It also considers Synge's place in Ireland today, revealing how *The Playboy of the Western World* has helped to shape Ireland's responses to globalisation and multiculturalism, in celebrated productions by the Abbey Theatre, Druid Theatre, and Pan Pan Theatre Company.

Contributors include Ann Saddlemyer, Ben Levitas, Mary Burke, Paige Reynolds, Eilís Ní Dhuibhne, Mark Phelan, Shaun Richards, Ondřej Pilný, Richard Pine, Alexandra Poulain, Emilie Pine, Melissa Sihra, Sara Keating, Bisi Adigun, Adrian Frazier and Anthony Roche.

ISBN: 978-1-904505-50-1   €20.00

Constellations - The Life and Music of John Buckley

Benjamin Dwyer

Benjamin Dwyer provides a long overdue assessment of one of Ireland's most prolific composers of the last decades. He looks at John Buckley's music in the context of his biography and Irish cultural life. This is no hagiography but a critical assessment of Buckley's work, his roots and aesthetics. While looking closely at several of Buckley's compositions, the book is written in a comprehensible style that makes it easily accessible to anybody interested in Irish musical and cultural history.   *Wolfgang Marx*

As well as providing a very readable and comprehensive study of the life and music of John Buckley, Constellations also offers an up-to-date and informative catalogue of compositions, a complete discography, translations of set texts and the full libretto of his chamber opera, making this book an essential guide for both students and professional scholars alike.

ISBN: 978-1-904505-52-5   €20.00

'Because We Are Poor': Irish Theatre in the 1990s

Victor Merriman

"Victor Merriman's work on Irish theatre is in the vanguard of a whole new paradigm in Irish theatre scholarship, one that is not content to contemplate monuments of past or present achievement, but for which the theatre is a lens that makes visible the hidden malaises in Irish society. That he has been able to do so by focusing on a period when so much else in Irish culture conspired to hide those problems is only testimony to the considerable power of his critical scrutiny." Chris Morash, NUI Maynooth.

ISBN: 978-1-904505-51-8   €20.00

'Buffoonery and Easy Sentiment':
Popular Irish Plays in the Decade Prior to the Opening of The Abbey Theatre

Christopher Fitz-Simon

In this fascinating reappraisal of the non-literary drama of the late 19th - early 20th century, Christopher Fitz-Simon discloses a unique world of plays, players and producers in metropolitan theatres in Ireland and other countries where Ireland was viewed as a source of extraordinary topics at once contemporary and comfortably remote: revolution, eviction, famine, agrarian agitation, political assassination.

The form was the fashionable one of melodrama, yet Irish melodrama was of a particular kind replete with hidden messages, and the language was far more allusive, colourful and entertaining than that of its English equivalent.

ISBN: 978-1-9045505-49-5   €20.00

The Fourth Seamus Heaney Lectures, 'Mirror up to Nature':

Ed. Patrick Burke

What, in particular, is the contemporary usefulness for the building of societies of one of our oldest and culturally valued ideals, that of drama? The Fourth Seamus Heaney Lectures, 'Mirror up to Nature': Drama and Theatre in the Modern World, given at St Patrick's College, Drumcondra, between October 2006 and April 2007, addressed these and related questions. Patrick Mason spoke on the essence of theatre, Thomas Kilroy on Ireland's contribution to the art of theatre, Cecily O'Neill and Jonothan Neelands on the rich potential of drama in the classroom. Brenna Katz Clarke examined the relationship between drama and film, and John Buckley spoke on opera and its history and gave an illuminating account of his own *Words Upon The Window-Pane.*

ISBN 978-1-9045505-48-8   €12

The Theatre of Tom Mac Intyre: 'Strays from the ether'

Eds. Bernadette Sweeney and Marie Kelly

This long overdue anthology captures the soul of Mac Intyre's dramatic canon – its ethereal qualities, its extraordinary diversity, its emphasis on the poetic and on performance – in an extensive range of visual, journalistic and scholarly contributions from writers, theatre practitioners.

ISBN 978-1-904505-46-4 €25

Irish Appropriation Of Greek Tragedy

Brian Arkins

This book presents an analysis of more than 30 plays written by Irish dramatists and poets that are based on the tragedies of Sophocles, Euripides and Aeschylus. These plays proceed from the time of Yeats and Synge through MacNeice and the Longfords on to many of today's leading writers.

ISBN 978-1-904505-47-1 €20

Alive in Time: The Enduring Drama of Tom Murphy

Ed. Christopher Murray

Almost 50 years after he first hit the headlines as Ireland's most challenging playwright, the 'angry young man' of those times Tom Murphy still commands his place at the pinnacle of Irish theatre. Here 17 new essays by prominent critics and academics, with an introduction by Christopher Murray, survey Murphy's dramatic oeuvre in a concerted attempt to define his greatness and enduring appeal, making this book a significant study of a unique genius.

ISBN 978-1-904505-45-7 €25

Performing Violence in Contemporary Ireland

Ed. Lisa Fitzpatrick

This interdisciplinary collection of fifteen new essays by scholars of theatre, Irish studies, music, design and politics explores aspects of the performance of violence in contemporary Ireland. With chapters on the work of playwrights Martin McDonagh, Martin Lynch, Conor McPherson and Gary Mitchell, on Republican commemorations and the 90th anniversary ceremonies for the Battle of the Somme and the Easter Rising, this book aims to contribute to the ongoing international debate on the performance of violence in contemporary societies.

ISBN 978-1-904505-44-0 (2009) €20

Ireland's Economic Crisis - Time to Act. Essays from over 40 leading Irish thinkers at the MacGill Summer School 2009

Eds. Joe Mulholland and Finbarr Bradley

Ireland's economic crisis requires a radical transformation in policymaking. In this volume, political, industrial, academic, trade union and business leaders and commentators tell the story of the Irish economy and its rise and fall. Contributions at Glenties range from policy, vision and context to practical suggestions on how the country can emerge from its crisis.

ISBN 978-1-904505-43-3 (2009) €20

Deviant Acts: Essays on Queer Performance

Ed. David Cregan

This book contains an exciting collection of essays focusing on a variety of alternative performances happening in contemporary Ireland. While it highlights the particular representations of gay and lesbian identity it also brings to light how diversity has always been a part of Irish culture and is, in fact, shaping what it means to be Irish today.

ISBN 978-1-904505-42-6 (2009) €20

Seán Keating in Context: Responses to Culture and Politics in Post-Civil War Ireland

Compiled, edited and introduced by Éimear O'Connor

Irish artist Seán Keating has been judged by his critics as the personification of old-fashioned traditionalist values. This book presents a different view. The story reveals Keating's early determination to attain government support for the visual arts. It also illustrates his socialist leanings, his disappointment with capitalism, and his attitude to cultural snobbery, to art critics, and to the Academy. Given the national and global circumstances nowadays, Keating's critical and wry observations are prophetic – and highly amusing.

ISBN 978-1-904505-41-9 €25

Dialogue of the Ancients of Ireland: A new translation of Acallam na Senorach

Translated with introduction and notes by Maurice Harmon

One of Ireland's greatest collections of stories and poems, The Dialogue of the Ancients of Ireland is a new translation by Maurice Harmon of the 12th century *Acallam na Senorach*. Retold in a refreshing modern idiom, the *Dialogue* is an extraordinary account of journeys to the four provinces by St. Patrick and the pagan Cailte, one of the surviving Fian. Within the frame story are over 200 other stories reflecting many genres – wonder tales, sea journeys, romances, stories of revenge, tales of monsters and magic. The poems are equally varied – lyrics, nature poems, eulogies, prophecies, laments, genealogical poems. After the *Tain Bo Cuailnge*, the *Acallam* is the largest surviving prose work in Old and Middle Irish.

ISBN: 978-1-904505-39-6 (2009)   €20

Literary and Cultural Relations between Ireland and Hungary and Central and Eastern Europe

Ed. Maria Kurdi

This lively, informative and incisive collection of essays sheds fascinating new light on the literary interrelations between Ireland, Hungary, Poland, Romania and the Czech Republic. It charts a hitherto under-explored history of the reception of modern Irish culture in Central and Eastern Europe and also investigates how key authors have been translated, performed and adapted. The revealing explorations undertaken in this volume of a wide array of Irish dramatic and literary texts, ranging from *Gulliver's Travels* to *Translations* and *The Pillowman*, tease out the subtly altered nuances that they acquire in a Central European context.

ISBN: 978-1-904505-40-2 (2009)   €20

Plays and Controversies: Abbey Theatre Diaries 2000-2005

Ben Barnes

In diaries covering the period of his artistic directorship of the Abbey, Ben Barnes offers a frank, honest, and probing account of a much commented upon and controversial period in the history of the national theatre. These diaries also provide fascinating personal insights into the day-to- day pressures, joys, and frustrations of running one of Ireland's most iconic institutions.

ISBN: 978-1-904505-38-9 (2008)   €20

Interactions: Dublin Theatre Festival 1957-2007. Irish Theatrical Diaspora Series: 3

Eds. Nicholas Grene and Patrick Lonergan with Lilian Chambers

For over 50 years the Dublin Theatre Festival has been one of Ireland's most important cultural events, bringing countless new Irish plays to the world stage, while introducing Irish audiences to the most important international theatre companies and artists. Interactions explores and celebrates the achievements of the renowned Festival since 1957 and includes specially commissioned memoirs from past organizers, offering a unique perspective on the controversies and successes that have marked the event's history. An especially valuable feature of the volume, also, is a complete listing of the shows that have appeared at the Festival from 1957 to 2008.

ISBN: 978-1-904505-36-5 €20

The Informer: A play by Tom Murphy based on the novel by Liam O'Flaherty

The Informer, Tom Murphy's stage adaptation of Liam O'Flaherty's novel, was produced in the 1981 Dublin Theatre Festival, directed by the playwright himself, with Liam Neeson in the leading role. The central subject of the play is the quest of a character at the point of emotional and moral breakdown for some source of meaning or identity. In the case of Gypo Nolan, the informer of the title, this involves a nightmarish progress through a Dublin underworld in which he changes from a Judas figure to a scapegoat surrogate for Jesus, taking upon himself the sins of the world. A cinematic style, with flash-back and intercut scenes, is used rather than a conventional theatrical structure to catch the fevered and phantasmagoric progression of Gypo's mind. The language, characteristically for Murphy, mixes graphically colloquial Dublin slang with the haunted intricacies of the central character groping for the meaning of his own actions. The dynamic rhythm of the action builds towards an inevitable but theatrically satisfying tragic catastrophe. ' [The Informer] is, in many ways closer to being an original Murphy play than it is to O'Flaherty...' Fintan O'Toole.

ISBN: 978-1-904505-37-2 (2008) €10

Shifting Scenes: Irish theatre-going 1955-1985

Eds. Nicholas Grene and Chris Morash

Transcript of conversations with John Devitt, academic and reviewer, about his lifelong passion for the theatre. A fascinating and entertaining insight into Dublin theatre over the course of thirty years provided by Devitt's vivid reminiscences and astute observations.

ISBN: 978-1-904505-33-4 (2008) €10

Irish Literature: Feminist Perspectives

Eds. Patricia Coughlan and Tina O'Toole

The collection discusses texts from the early 18th century to the present. A central theme of the book is the need to renegotiate the relations of feminism with nationalism and to transact the potential contest of these two important narratives, each possessing powerful emancipatory force. Irish Literature: Feminist Perspectives contributes incisively to contemporary debates about Irish culture, gender and ideology.

ISBN: 978-1-904505-35-8 (2008) €20

Silenced Voices: Hungarian Plays from Transylvania

Selected and translated by Csilla Bertha and Donald E. Morse

The five plays are wonderfully theatrical, moving fluidly from absurdism to tragedy, and from satire to the darkly comic. Donald Morse and Csilla Bertha's translations capture these qualities perfectly, giving voice to the 'forgotten playwrights of Central Europe'. They also deeply enrich our understanding of the relationship between art, ethics, and politics in Europe.

ISBN: 978-1-904505-34-1 (2008) €20

A Hazardous Melody of Being:
Seóirse Bodley's Song Cycles on the poems of Micheal O'Siadhail

Ed. Lorraine Byrne Bodley

This apograph is the first publication of Bodley's O'Siadhail song cycles and is the first book to explore the composer's lyrical modernity from a number of perspectives. Lorraine Byrne Bodley's insightful introduction describes in detail the development and essence of Bodley's musical thinking, the European influences he absorbed which linger in these cycles, and the importance of his work as a composer of the Irish art song.

ISBN: 978-1-904505-31-0 (2008) €25

Irish Theatre in England: Irish Theatrical Diaspora Series: 2

Eds. Richard Cave and Ben Levitas

Irish theatre in England has frequently illustrated the complex relations between two distinct cultures. How English reviewers and audiences interpret Irish plays is often decidedly different from how the plays were read in performance in Ireland. How certain Irish performers have chosen to be understood in Dublin is not necessarily how audiences in London have perceived their constructed stage personae. Though a collection by diverse authors, the twelve essays in this volume investigate these issues from a variety of perspectives that together chart the trajectory of Irish performance in England from the mid-nineteenth century till today.

ISBN: 978-1-904505-26-6 (2007) €20

Goethe and Anna Amalia: A Forbidden Love?

Ettore Ghibellino, Trans. Dan Farrelly

In this study Ghibellino sets out to show that the platonic relationship between Goethe and Charlotte von Stein – lady-in-waiting to Anna Amalia, the Dowager Duchess of Weimar – was used as part of a cover-up for Goethe's intense and prolonged love relationship with the Duchess Anna Amalia herself. The book attempts to uncover a hitherto closely-kept state secret. Readers convinced by the evidence supporting Ghibellino's hypothesis will see in it one of the very great love stories in European history – to rank with that of Dante and Beatrice, and Petrarch and Laura.

ISBN: 978-1-904505-24-2 €20

Ireland on Stage: Beckett and After

Eds. Hiroko Mikami, Minako Okamuro, Naoko Yagi

The collection focuses primarily on Irish playwrights and their work, both in text and on the stage during the latter half of the twentieth century. The central figure is Samuel Beckett, but the contributors freely draw on Beckett and his work provides a springboard to discuss contemporary playwrights such as Brian Friel, Frank McGuinness, Marina Carr and Conor McPherson amongst others. Contributors include: Anthony Roche, Hiroko Mikami, Naoko Yagi, Cathy Leeney, Joseph Long, Noreem Doody, Minako Okamuro, Christopher Murray, Futoshi Sakauchi and Declan Kiberd

ISBN: 978-1-904505-23-5 (2007) €20

'Echoes Down the Corridor': Irish Theatre - Past, Present and Future

Eds. Patrick Lonergan and Riana O'Dwyer

This collection of fourteen new essays explores Irish theatre from exciting new perspectives. How has Irish theatre been received internationally - and, as the country becomes more multicultural, how will international theatre influence the development of drama in Ireland? These and many other important questions.

ISBN: 978-1-904505-25-9 (2007) €20

Musics of Belonging: The Poetry of Micheal O'Siadhail

Eds. Marc Caball & David F. Ford

An overall account is given of O'Siadhail's life, his work and the reception of his poetry so far. There are close readings of some poems, analyses of his artistry in matching diverse content with both classical and innovative forms, and studies of recurrent themes such as love, death, language, music, and the shifts of modern life.

ISBN: 978-1-904505-22-8 (2007) €25 (Paperback)
ISBN: 978-1-904505-21-1 (2007) €50 (Casebound)

Modern Death: The End of Civilization

Carl-Henning Wijkmark. Trans: Dan Farrelly

Modern Death is written in the form of a symposium, in which a government agency brings together a group of experts to discuss a strategy for dealing with an ageing population.

The speakers take up the thread of the ongoing debates about care for the aged and about euthanasia. In dark satirical mode the author shows what grim developments are possible. The theme of a 'final solution' is mentioned, though the connection with Hitler is explicitly denied. The most inhuman crimes against human dignity are discussed in the symposium as if they were a necessary condition of future progress.

The fiercely ironical treatment of the material tears off the thin veil that disguises the specious arguments and insidious expressions of concern for the well-being of the younger generation. Though the text was written nearly thirty years ago, the play has a terrifyingly modern relevance.

ISBN: 978 1 904505 28 0 (2007) €8

Brian Friel's Dramatic Artistry: 'The Work has Value'

Eds. Donald E. Morse, Csilla Bertha and Maria Kurdi

Brian Friel's Dramatic Artistry presents a refreshingly broad range of voices: new work from some of the leading English-speaking authorities on Friel, and fascinating essays from scholars in Germany, Italy, Portugal, and Hungary. This book will deepen our knowledge and enjoyment of Friel's work.

ISBN: 978-1-904505-17-4 (2006) €25

The Theatre of Martin McDonagh: 'A World of Savage Stories'

Eds. Lilian Chambers and Eamonn Jordan

The book is a vital response to the many challenges set by McDonagh for those involved in the production and reception of his work. Critics and commentators from around the world offer a diverse range of often provocative approaches. What is not surprising is the focus and commitment of the engagement, given the controversial and stimulating nature of the work.

ISBN: 978-1-904505-19-8 (2006) €30

Edna O'Brien: New Critical Perspectives

Eds. Kathryn Laing, Sinead Mooney and Maureen O'Connor

The essays collected here illustrate some of the range, complexity, and interest of Edna O'Brien as a fiction writer and dramatist. They will contribute to a broader appreciation of her work and to an evolution of new critical approaches, as well as igniting more interest in the many unexplored areas of her considerable oeuvre.

ISBN: 978-1-904505-20-4 (2006) €20

Irish Theatre on Tour

Eds. Nicholas Grene and Chris Morash

'Touring has been at the strategic heart of Druid's artistic policy since the early eighties. Everyone has the right to see professional theatre in their own communities. Irish theatre on tour is a crucial part of Irish theatre as a whole'. Garry Hynes

ISBN 978-1-904505-13-6 (2005) €20

Poems 2000-2005 by Hugh Maxton

Poems 2000-2005 is a transitional collection written while the author – also known to be W.J. Mc Cormack, literary historian – was in the process of moving back from London to settle in rural Ireland.

ISBN 978-1-904505-12-9 (2005) €10

Synge: A Celebration

Ed. Colm Tóibín

A collection of essays by some of Ireland's most creative writers on the work of John Millington Synge, featuring Sebastian Barry, Marina Carr, Anthony Cronin, Roddy Doyle, Anne Enright, Hugo Hamilton, Joseph O'Connor, Mary O'Malley, Fintan O'Toole, Colm Toibin, Vincent Woods.

ISBN 978-1-904505-14-3 (2005) €15

East of Eden: New Romanian Plays

Ed. Andrei Marinescu

Four of the most promising Romanian playwrights, young and very young, are in this collection, each one with a specific way of seeing the Romanian reality, each one with a style of communicating an articulated artistic vision of the society we are living in. Ion Caramitru, General Director Romanian National Theatre Bucharest.
ISBN 978-1-904505-15-0 (2005) €10

George Fitzmaurice: 'Wild in His Own Way', Biography of an Irish Playwright

Fiona Brennan

'Fiona Brennan's introduction to his considerable output allows us a much greater appreciation and understanding of Fitzmaurice, the one remaining under-celebrated genius of twentieth-century Irish drama'. Conall Morrison

ISBN 978-1-904505-16-7 (2005) €20

Out of History: Essays on the Writings of Sebastian Barry

Ed. Christina Hunt Mahony

The essays address Barry's engagement with the contemporary cultural debate in Ireland and also with issues that inform postcolonial critical theory. The range and selection of contributors has ensured a high level of critical expression and an insightful assessment of Barry and his works.

ISBN: 978-1-904505-18-1 (2005) €20

Three Congregational Masses

Seoirse Bodley

'From the simpler congregational settings in the Mass of Peace and the Mass of Joy to the richer textures of the Mass of Glory, they are immediately attractive and accessible, and with a distinctively Irish melodic quality.' Barra Boydell

ISBN: 978-1-904505-11-2 (2005) €15

Georg Büchner's Woyzeck,

A new translation by Dan Farrelly

The most up-to-date German scholarship of Thomas Michael Mayer and Burghard Dedner has finally made it possible to establish an authentic sequence of scenes. The wide-spread view that this play is a prime example of loose, open theatre is no longer sustainable. Directors and teachers are challenged to "read it again".

ISBN: 978-1-904505-02-0 (2004) €10

Playboys of the Western World: Production Histories

Ed. Adrian Frazier

'The book is remarkably well-focused: half is a series of production histories of Playboy performances through the twentieth century in the UK, Northern Ireland, the USA, and Ireland. The remainder focuses on one contemporary performance, that of Druid Theatre, as directed by Garry Hynes. The various contemporary social issues that are addressed in relation to Synge's play and this performance of it give the volume an additional interest: it shows how the arts matter.' Kevin Barry

ISBN: 978-1-904505-06-8 (2004) €20

The Power of Laughter: Comedy and Contemporary Irish Theatre

Ed. Eric Weitz

The collection draws on a wide range of perspectives and voices including critics, playwrights, directors and performers. The result is a series of fascinating and provocative debates about the myriad functions of comedy in contemporary Irish theatre. Anna McMullan

As Stan Laurel said, 'it takes only an onion to cry. Peel it and weep. Comedy is harder'. 'These essays listen to the power of laughter. They hear the tough heart of Irish theatre – hard and wicked and funny'. Frank McGuinness

ISBN: 978-1-904505-05-1 (2004)   €20

Sacred Play: Soul-Journeys in contemporary Irish Theatre

Anne F. O'Reilly

'Theatre as a space or container for sacred play allows audiences to glimpse mystery and to experience transformation. This book charts how Irish playwrights negotiate the labyrinth of the Irish soul and shows how their plays contribute to a poetics of Irish culture that enables a new imagining. Playwrights discussed are: McGuinness, Murphy, Friel, Le Marquand Hartigan, Burke Brogan, Harding, Meehan, Carr, Parker, Devlin, and Barry.'

ISBN: 978-1-904505-07-5 (2004) €20

The Irish Harp Book

Sheila Larchet Cuthbert

This is a facsimile of the edition originally published by Mercier Press in 1993. There is a new preface by Sheila Larchet Cuthbert, and the biographical material has been updated. It is a collection of studies and exercises for the use of teachers and pupils of the Irish harp.

ISBN: 978-1-904505-08-2 (2004)   €35

The Drunkard

Tom Murphy

'The Drunkard is a wonderfully eloquent play. Murphy's ear is finely attuned to the glories and absurdities of melodramatic exclamation, and even while he is wringing out its ludicrous overstatement, he is also making it sing.' The Irish Times

ISBN: 978-1-90 05-09-9 (2004)   €10

Goethe: Musical Poet, Musical Catalyst

Ed. Lorraine Byrne

'Goethe was interested in, and acutely aware of, the place of music in human experience generally - and of its particular role in modern culture. Moreover, his own literary work - especially the poetry and Faust - inspired some of the major composers of the European tradition to produce some of their finest works.' Martin Swales

ISBN: 978-1-9045-10-5 (2004) €25

The Theatre of Marina Carr: "Before rules was made"

Eds. Anna McMullan & Cathy Leeney

As the first published collection of articles on the theatre of Marina Carr, this volume explores the world of Carr's theatrical imagination, the place of her plays in contemporary theatre in Ireland and abroad and the significance of her highly individual voice.

ISBN: 978-0-9534257-7-8 (2003) €20

Critical Moments: Fintan O'Toole on Modern Irish Theatre

Eds. Julia Furay & Redmond O'Hanlon

This new book on the work of Fintan O'Toole, the internationally acclaimed theatre critic and cultural commentator, offers percussive analyses and assessments of the major plays and playwrights in the canon of modern Irish theatre. Fearless and provocative in his judgements, O'Toole is essential reading for anyone interested in criticism or in the current state of Irish theatre.

ISBN: 978-1-904505-03-7 (2003) €20

Goethe and Schubert: Across the Divide

Eds. Lorraine Byrne & Dan Farrelly

Proceedings of the International Conference, 'Goethe and Schubert in Perspective and Performance', Trinity College Dublin, 2003. This volume includes essays by leading scholars – Barkhoff, Boyle, Byrne, Canisius, Dürr, Fischer, Hill, Kramer, Lamport, Lund, Meikle, Newbould, Norman McKay, White, Whitton, Wright, Youens – on Goethe's musicality and his relationship to Schubert; Schubert's contribution to sacred music and the Lied and his setting of Goethe's Singspiel, Claudine. A companion volume of this Singspiel (with piano reduction and English translation) is also available.

ISBN: 978-1-904505-04-4 (2003) €25

Goethe's Singspiel, 'Claudine von Villa Bella'

Set by Franz Schubert

Goethe's Singspiel in three acts was set to music by Schubert in 1815. Only Act One of Schuberts's Claudine score is extant. The present volume makes Act One available for performance in English and German. It comprises both a piano reduction by Lorraine Byrne of the original Schubert orchestral score and a bilingual text translated for the modern stage by Dan Farrelly. This is a tale, wittily told, of lovers and vagabonds, romance, reconciliation, and resolution of family conflict.

ISBN: 978-0-9544290-0-3 (2002) €14

Theatre of Sound, Radio and the Dramatic Imagination

Dermot Rattigan

An innovative study of the challenges that radio drama poses to the creative imagination of the writer, the production team, and the listener.
"A remarkably fine study of radio drama – everywhere informed by the writer's professional experience of such drama in the making…A new theoretical and analytical approach – informative, illuminating and at all times readable." Richard Allen Cave

ISBN: 978- 0-9534-257-5-4 (2002) €20

Talking about Tom Murphy

Ed. Nicholas Grene

Talking About Tom Murphy is shaped around the six plays in the landmark Abbey Theatre Murphy Season of 2001, assembling some of the best-known commentators on his work: Fintan O'Toole, Chris Morash, Lionel Pilkington, Alexandra Poulain, Shaun Richards, Nicholas Grene and Declan Kiberd.

ISBN: 978-0-9534-257-9-2 (2002) €12

Hamlet: The Shakespearean Director

Mike Wilcock

"This study of the Shakespearean director as viewed through various interpretations of HAMLET is a welcome addition to our understanding of how essential it is for a director to have a clear vision of a great play. It is an important study from which all of us who love Shakespeare and who understand the importance of continuing contemporary exploration may gain new insights." From the Foreword, by Joe Dowling, Artistic Director, The Guthrie Theater, Minneapolis, MN

ISBN: 978-1-904505-00-6 (2002) €20

The Theatre of Frank Mc Guinness: Stages of Mutability

Ed. Helen Lojek

The first edited collection of essays about internationally renowned Irish playwright Frank McGuinness focuses on both performance and text. Interpreters come to diverse conclusions, creating a vigorous dialogue that enriches understanding and reflects a strong consensus about the value of McGuinness's complex work.

ISBN: 978-1904505-01-3. (2002) €20

Theatre Talk: Voices of Irish Theatre Practitioners

Eds Lilian Chambers, Ger Fitzgibbon and Eamonn Jordan

"This book is the right approach - asking practitioners what they feel." Sebastian Barry, Playwright "... an invaluable and informative collection of interviews with those who make and shape the landscape of Irish Theatre." Ben Barnes, Artistic Director of the Abbey Theatre

ISBN: 978-0-9534-257-6-1 (2001) €20

In Search of the South African Iphigenie

Erika von Wietersheim and Dan Farrelly

Discussions of Goethe's "Iphigenie auf Tauris" (Under the Curse) as relevant to women's issues in modern South Africa: women in family and public life; the force of women's spirituality; experience of personal relationships; attitudes to parents and ancestors; involvement with religion.

ISBN: 978-0-9534257-8-5 (2001) €10

'The Starving' and 'October Song':

Two contemporary Irish plays by Andrew Hinds

The Starving, set during and after the siege of Derry in 1689, is a moving and engrossing drama of the emotional journey of two men.

October Song, a superbly written family drama set in real time in pre-ceasefire Derry.

ISBN: 978-0-9534-257-4-7 (2001) €10

Seen and Heard: Six new plays by Irish women

Ed. Cathy Leeney

A rich and funny, moving and theatrically exciting collection of plays by Mary Elizabeth Burke-Kennedy, Síofra Campbell, Emma Donoghue, Anne Le Marquand Hartigan, Michelle Read and Dolores Walshe.

ISBN: 978-0-9534-257-3-0 (2001) €20

Theatre Stuff: Critical essays on contemporary Irish theatre

Ed. Eamonn Jordan

Best selling essays on the successes and debates of contemporary Irish theatre at home and abroad. Contributors include: Thomas Kilroy, Declan Hughes, Anna McMullan, Declan Kiberd, Deirdre Mulrooney, Fintan O'Toole, Christopher Murray, Caoimhe McAvinchey and Terry Eagleton.

ISBN: 978-0-9534-2571-1-6 (2000) €20

Under the Curse. Goethe's "Iphigenie Auf Tauris", A New Version

Dan Farrelly

The Greek myth of Iphigenie grappling with the curse on the house of Atreus is brought vividly to life. This version is currently being used in Johannesburg to explore problems of ancestry, religion, and Black African women's spirituality.

ISBN: 978-09534-257-8-5 (2000) €10

Urfaust, A New Version of Goethe's early "Faust" in Brechtian Mode

Dan Farrelly

This version is based on Brecht's irreverent and daring re-interpretation of the German classic. "Urfaust is a kind of well-spring for German theatre… The love-story is the most daring and the most profound in German dramatic literature." Brecht

ISBN: 978-0-9534-257-0-9 (1998) €10